Gone with the Windsors

Wallis and the Empire

Gone with the Windsors

BY ILES BRODY

ILLUSTRATED

THE JOHN C. WINSTON COMPANY

Philadelphia • Toronto

Made in the United States of America

L. C. Card #53-7341   M-953

To my wife, Sanna

CONTENTS

1

The Other Side of the Medal

J'ai mon métier du roi.
— KING EDWARD THE SEVENTH

*Where the press is free and every man able to read,
all is safe.*
— THOMAS JEFFERSON

THE TRUE STORY of the Duke and Duchess of Windsor cannot be told without clarifying one point right at the beginning: there was only one man who forced Edward VIII off the throne—himself. Yet millions have been led to believe and still cling to the impression that Prime Minister and Primate got together with the peers, and, with the help of the press, they compelled the King to abandon his trust.

Winston Churchill, directly after the abdication, expressed quite a different view:

> I accept wholeheartedly what the Prime Minister (*the late Stanley Baldwin*) has proved, namely, that the decision (*to abdicate*) has been taken by his Majesty freely, voluntarily and spontaneously in his own time and in his own way. (Author's italics.)

And so today there is a young anointed Queen on the throne of England. A Queen who knows that the Sovereign *is* England, Britain, the Commonwealth; that a resolute Monarch adds a sense of security to the subjects and thus protects and cherishes and defends them; that there is only one course the Supreme Magistrate can follow: the path of duty.

When Edward VIII chose the wrong course, monarchy in England was in great danger of coming to an abrupt end—it was almost gone with the Windsors. The "royal throne of kings" was tottering when the King abandoned it to marry the twice-divorced Mrs. Simpson. Nowadays the press does not hesitate to report on the Duchess of

Windsor's activities and her fondness for male escorts. It is not for one moment to be imagined that the Duchess would want still another divorce. Or that she would ever allow herself to become seriously interested in another man. How could she do that? It would be tantamount to abdication . . .

With his abdication, the former Edward VIII undermined the concept of kingship as the English had known it for centuries.

The foundation of English kingship (and also of English Government) was laid down by William the Conqueror, the bastard Norman. According to the ancient dictum, in law the King can do no wrong; he is bound by no limit of time; and his office is not broken at his death, but continues in his successor. He is remote from criticism, emulation or envy. He is above all political strife. He is supposed to be sacrosanct. The King consecrates his life to the good of his subjects.

Nearly 888 years have passed since William the Conqueror's accession. Forty kings and queens reigned over England during this near-millennium. These sovereigns came from five dynasties, all of them foreign—Norman, French, Welsh, Scottish and German.

Norman, Plantagenet, Tudor, Stuart, Guelph are not really the concern of this book. What this book tries to establish is that the story of the only English Sovereign who abdicated "freely, voluntarily and spontaneously" is not a private one. It is a vitally important sociological problem.

The King who abdicates and thus turns his back on his people cannot be remote from criticism. It is to be hoped that no one envies Edward; and it is unlikely that future British monarchs will try to emulate his melancholy example.

Nevertheless, to a large number of Americans, the Duke still represents a hero and the Duchess a heroine—a romantic couple, mistreated and misunderstood in his native, cold and old England. Many of these Americans still believe that he had to pay the price for falling in love with an American woman! Nothing could be further from the truth. When, as Prince of Wales, he visited America for the first time, his parents, King George V and Queen Mary, said that "they would be delighted if he found a suitable wife in America."

For the objection was not, of course, that Mrs. Simpson was an American and a commoner; the main trouble was that she had already divorced two husbands, which is not exactly a recommendation in the case of a Queen of England.

Other objections could have been raised even after the abdication—

there was the Royal Marriages Act of 1772 (12 Geo. III C.11). According to this Act, no descendant of his late Majesty, George II, shall be capable of contracting matrimony without the previous consent of the Sovereign, signified under the Great Seal. If, however, the royal person proposing to contract the marriage without the Sovereign's consent is over twenty-five years of age, he may do so, providing that he gives a twelve months' notice to the Privy Council, and if this notice is duly entered in the books of the Privy Council. During this twelve months' notice, both Houses of Parliament may expressly declare their disapprobation of the intended marriage. Any person who is present at, or assists, or solemnizes a marriage which does not take place according to this law, shall be duly convicted, provided for by the Statute of Provisions and Praemunire (made in the 16th of Richard II).

When Edward VIII abdicated, he became a subject of the new King, his brother, George VI, who declared him in letters patent a royal prince, and gave him the title Duke of Windsor. Therefore, the Royal Marriages Act was fully applicable in his case.

Did he ask for the Sovereign's consent to marry Mrs. Simpson? Did the King give his consent? Was this consent—if ever given—enacted according to law and signified under the Great Seal?

If the consent was not given, did the Duke of Windsor give a twelve months' notice to the Privy Council? Was the notice duly entered in the books of the Privy Council? Could the Houses of Parliament express disapprobation of the intended marriage (which was "solemnized" *before* the expiration of the twelve months' notice provided for by the Act) they officially knew nothing about? Was any member of the Royal Family present at the ceremony? Many questions obtrude themselves when it comes to the Windsor saga.

True, there are more important problems today. The world is staggering. The stage is set for much tragedy and a bit of comedy. Communism menaces Christendom; dictators plan the ruin of democracy; disaster threatens decency. While the aging couple presents a grotesque spectacle and utter amusing statements. For example, years ago the Windsors let it be known that their lives had been dedicated. They said that they were "anxious to help some of the vital problems that beset the world." (New York *Times*, May 28, 1938.) One wonders what were the causes the Windsors have helped since this declaration was made—could it be that they had in mind the business worries of couturiers and jewelers? As to the Duke's interest in the vital problems of his native country, when he arrived in New York after one of his visits to England, he gave an exclusive interview to Elsa Maxwell, the society columnist. Among other things, Miss Maxwell asked the Duke whether he was glad to go home. "Why, Elsa," the Duke replied, "home to me is where the Duchess is."

Though the suffering of others is apparently of deep concern to the Duchess—in January 1953, in the name of charity, she opened the "Duchess of Windsor Ball" at the Waldorf-Astoria. However, malicious people intimated that the affair served the purpose of publicity as far as the Duchess of Windsor was concerned. She merely lent her name; she was abroad while it was being prepared; and her four gowns for the evening were paid for by as many sponsors. Whether in the name of charity or publicity, sixty-six photographers were at hand to take pictures of the glamorous Duchess.

But she is not the only photogenic member of the family: her husband, too, receives from the cameramen as much attention as a Hollywood movie star; it is surely an unedifying sight to see the former Emperor in such inconsequential, humiliating pictures. There is not a single photo that shows the Duke of Windsor or his Duchess exerting themselves on behalf of their fellowmen, not a single account of their efforts to help a civilization in peril, not a word spoken on behalf of a world in jeopardy of dissolution. Theirs is a life devoted to purely personal pleasures. Their friends, anxious to explain away their mode of living, are ready with excuses:

"It's nobody's business how the Windsors spend their money."

In the case of less important and more private figures, this would be true. People make money and naturally they spend it the way they want to.

However, the Windsors never had to work hard for their money. As Prince of Wales, King, and Duke of Windsor, he has cost more to his country, formerly rich, today poor, than any other figure in history. Mr. Churchill's first move after he regained the premiership, was to cut his own and his fellow-Ministers' salaries. Did the Duke of Windsor accordingly adjust his own pension? Although his coffers were full when Mr. Churchill made his gesture, for at that time the Duke of Windsor's *A King's Story* was published.

And probably this present book, which *had* to be written, would not have been published had it not been for the appearance of the Duke of Windsor's best-selling memoirs.

Until the present writer read the Duke's naive, opinionated self-revelations, this royal apologia without precedent, he had, like millions of others, esteem and even a certain affection for the Windsors.

All the world loves a lover. But after reading the story in a large-circulation weekly, where it came out in serial form, and then later the book version, this writer's feelings changed. Tactfully, he waited for one of America's half-million amateur or 5,000 professional authors to reply, but when no one did so, he took it upon himself to answer, also in serial form, in the pages of a small magazine, for slightly lower rates than the Duke's reported one million dollars.

His answer could hardly be called a panegyric, and pandemonium promptly broke out.

Fearfully, this writer felt his neck. However, on further reflection, he figured that his head would not be chopped off. After all, the United States is one of the last strongholds of free speech; in any event, *lèse majesté* is outmoded.

Honi soit qui mal y pense—he hadn't in mind to hurt the Duke either. The Duke has done a good job on that score himself. In the matter of self-imposed suffering and difficulty, the sky is the limit. One can mess up one's own life, and the lives of others, on a colossal scale.

When Edward VIII gave up his throne, people were mainly concerned with the damage that might befall the world as a result of his act. Yet openly or secretly, millions shed a tear for him. Together with the greater part of mankind, this writer, too, was stunned as he listened to Edward Windsor broadcasting after his abdication for "the woman I love."

One hated to see him go because one feared that a new and dreadful era would come with his going. But at that time people tried their best to explain away the event, so tragic for Great Britain, and the whole Empire—an event which was perhaps partly responsible for the present plight of the world—and blame all on the caprices of love.

Like many another man, the present writer, too, has sinned in the name of love, that sacred but treacherous passion. And as so often happens, in his youth he encountered a particularly beautiful and difficult woman. A *femme fatale*, to use a banal but expressive phrase. But this writer is, and always has been, a private individual, not the "father" of a half-billion people who looked to him as a symbol of hope.

After Edward VIII met his *femme fatale*, both symbol and hope quickly vanished. The King of England became the Duke of Windsor, more or less a private person. "I now quit altogether public affairs," he promised in his famous radio speech on December 11, 1936.

In the case of monarchs, publication of the facts has usually been delayed until after their deaths. The death of Edward VIII took place on December 11, 1936; for abdication is the despotic demise of the Sovereign even in a limited monarchy, where consent of Parliament is *pro forma* required. By divesting himself of all regalities, the former Edward VIII forfeited the consideration which customarily protects monarchs.

Still, until 1950, people all over the world either wished him well or had forgotten about him. But the moment he began to write, saying, "It was my duty to history to put down the facts" concerning his princeship, short reign, and abdication, his status immediately and drastically changed.

The instant *A King's Story* appeared in print, the Duke of Windsor, who gave up everything and let down everyone for the sake of his own happiness, became once more as private as a goldfish in a bowl. By the publication of his memoirs, he exposed himself to comment on the same footing as any other author.

No one would have wished to disturb this "anchorite" were it not for the memoirs; and for the fact that the memoirs are one-sided. Among other persons well qualified to judge, Alan Pitt Robbins, Editor of the London *Times*, branded them by saying that they gave an untruthful picture.

The simple trick in memoir writing is to tell the truth, omitting nothing, adding nothing, and writing about oneself objectively. In relating one's life story one must not be biased or self-seeking, misleading millions of readers. Unhappy events—most people have a closetful of skeletons—may be told with disarming candor. Openness is always an advantage. But these fundamental principles in the writing of autobiography were disregarded by the Duke of Windsor.

Everyone has a flatterer hidden in him, but most people also employ a judge. It seems that the Duke fired the latter. Why deny it? We are all guilty. Except the Duke, according to himself.

He whitewashed the facts. Sincerity and courage, honor and conscience, are among the many virtues usually attributed to princes. These virtues are also necessary to authors. Yet the ex-Sovereign recorded significant historical events incorrectly.

The Duke of Windsor should have remembered that there are millions with keen memories. He should not have ignored the fact that people are unwilling to be shown one side of the medal only.

2

The Royal Author

Truth is the best guide to make a man write forcibly, naturally, and delicately.

—JEAN DE LA BRUYÈRE

A writer's job is to tell the truth. His standard of fidelity to the truth should be so high that his invention, out of his experience, should produce a truer account than anything factual can be. For facts can be observed badly; but when a good writer is creating something, he has time and scope to make it of an absolute truth.

—ERNEST HEMINGWAY: in *Men at War*

BETWEEN the Proclamation and the Coronation of Queen Elizabeth II, the big question in international café society was: Would the Windsors go to the coronation?

A member of the Windsors' entourage sharply remarked, "He didn't go to his own, why should he go to his niece's?"

When it was pointed out to this lady that her explanation only covered the Duke, she simply replied that the Duchess still had no place in the Order of Precedence, "and of course the Duke will not go alone."

Finally café society received an official answer:

> The Duke of Windsor said today he and his American-born Duchess will stay away from the June 2 coronation of Queen Elizabeth II of Britain. . . . The Duke made a solo visit to London last month, reportedly in the hope of dispelling the royal family's coldness toward his wife.
>
> (The New York *Journal-American*, December 16, 1952)

Thus the coronation of Elizabeth II had taken place as arranged—without the Windsors' disquieting presence.

If there had ever been a possibility of recognition for Wallis Windsor, it was destroyed by the publication of *A King's Story*. When the Duke at last achieved his literary ambition, other ambitions had to be given up.

For in his youth, the Duke of Windsor toyed with the idea of writing a novel. Later, when he started his wanderings, he promised the world—and his host, a Rothschild—a book in defense of persecuted Israel. Nothing came of these literary plans, however; and it wasn't until 1949 that the Duke became a practicing author.

The great chance to display his literary ability presented itself in the Land of Opportunity: American friends of the Duke urged him to write his memoirs—naturally with special emphasis on his love story, undoubtedly the most curious in all history.

The author usually redeems the man. If he writes from his heart the man's former apparent weaknesses disappear; his blunderings are forgotten; and laurel leaves are in order. A great writer's fame is even more enduring than that of an emperor.

However, the Duke of Windsor missed his opportunity. His book will hardly make a page in history. As a matter of fact, *A King's Story* bobbed up on the shores of America, and later, on those of England, like a bottle enclosing the message of a shipwrecked sailor. But the Duke marked the latitude and longitude of the disaster wrongly.

Recently he was corrected by Beaverbrook, the Canadian-born press lord who was one of the people most intimately involved in the drama of the abdication. It was he who muzzled Fleet Street for as long as it could be muzzled.

But since the publication of the Windsor memoirs, Beaverbrook seems to have felt that he himself was no longer bound to silence on the events of 1936—perhaps he was annoyed by the Duke's reference to the "Conspiracy" (That Failed), to induce Mrs. Simpson to renounce the idea of marriage. Whatever the explanation, "the Beaver" decided to break the silence of sixteen years. Having been invited to broadcast on the history of the London *Times*, just before the Duke visited England in May 1952, Beaverbrook elected to refer to the abdication. Whatever might be thought of the tact of his remarks, there could be no question as to their general interest.

Obviously, he said, it had been the intention of Edward VIII to confront the Government with a threat of abdication in order to compel acceptance of a morganatic marriage; but the threat had been unavailing against the combined forces of the *Times* and Mr. Baldwin.

When Beaverbrook met the ex-King again in Paris not long after the abdication, Windsor said to him: "I always thought I could get away with a morganatic marriage." The Duke of Windsor kept silent about this broadcast, but the press, excepting, naturally, the *Daily Express*, did not. They condemned Beaverbrook's attack on the *Times* and its former editor, the late Geoffrey Dawson, and pointed out that the *Times* had not written anything about the crisis before the other papers.

True, Edward VIII was the first King of England to abdicate of his own free will; but he was not the first to threaten abdication. Both George III and George IV had used this weapon on several occasions, only to find it break in their hands. And to do these monarchs justice, their threats sometimes concerned matters of greater moment than a morganatic marriage. For example, George III had tried to rule as an absolute monarch; and, when in 1782 and again in 1783, he found that his policies were not agreeable to the Government of the day, he drew up forms of abdication remarkable for the dignity of their language.

George IV once acted in a very undignified manner (when called upon to assent to Catholic emancipation in 1828) as he threatened abdication. Eventually he signed the Bill, burst into tears, and—stayed.

As George III was a madman, and his son a hysterical weakling; as the one was opposed by the younger Pitt, a genius, and the other by Wellington, the Iron Duke, it is not surprising that neither monarch had his own way. But as their threats helped to establish that policy must be decided by the Government and not by the Sovereign, they were of great importance in the development of the British Constitution—as historians are careful to point out.

Since the almost forgotten ex-King decided to become his own historian he can blame no one but himself if others comment on his annals. There is always an isolated critic ready to wield the sling of David against the Goliath of a royal author. Princes shouldn't try to write, anyway. The mediocrity of most royal compositions is truly remarkable despite the great material advantages enjoyed by the authors. The Roman Emperors are exceptions to this rule—of the first twenty, ten had talent, some even genius.

There were other exceptions, even in England. Henry VI managed to jot down these touching lines during his long imprisonment in the Tower:

> Kingdoms are but cares;
> State is devoid of stay;
> Riches are ready snares,
> And hasten to decay.

James I also wrote poetry; but of his fourteen books and pamphlets, not one, not even the once-famous and politically important *Basilicon Doron*, qualifies for inclusion in a list of "The Hundred Best Books."

A little earlier, Henry VIII employed the quill as well as the ax. He wrote a book, *The Glass of Truth*, and another one, *The Seven Sacraments*, which took Luther apart. Both dealt with theology—the King had originally been trained for the Church—and even if they were not best-sellers, their author was rewarded by the Pope, who conferred on him the title once sported by Windsor, Defender of the Faith.

But one of Henry's wives, that poor Anne Boleyn, had the real talent in the family! Only two of her works remain, both as brief as her life, but they are enough to establish her as a first-rate writer. Here is her farewell message to the world, written just before her execution:

> Oh, death! Rock me asleep,
> Bring on my quiet rest,
> Let pass my very guiltless ghost
> Out of my careful breast.
> Ring out the doleful knell;
> Let its sound my death tell—
> For I must die,
> There is no remedy,
> For now I die.
> My pains who can express?
> Alas! They are so strong,
> My dolour will not suffer strength
> My life for to prolong!
> Alone in prison strange,
> I wail my destiny;
> Woe worth this cruel hap, that I
> Should taste this misery!
> Farewell my pleasures past,
> Welcome my present pain,
> I feel my torments so increase
> That life cannot remain . . .

Henry's daughter Elizabeth, who like all three of his children, inherited much of his intellectual ability, wrote some charmingly pathetic verses on the departure of her favored suitor, the Duc d'Alençon (son of Catherine de Medici):

> I am, and am not—freeze, and yet I burn;
> Since from myself my other self I turn

she complained.

Elizabeth also translated from the French a 120-page book, entitled *The Lamentation of a Sinner*, with the subtitle, "The Utter Vanity of all Earthly Grandeur and Distinction"—recommended reading to the Duchess of Windsor.

The Duke of Windsor, on the other hand, ought to read Charles II's account of his adventures; and compare the crystal-clear simplicity and fun of this journal with the testiness of his own narrative in the latter part of the memoirs. Here is a sample of Charles II's style:

> As I was holding my horse's foot, I asked the smith what news? He told me that there was no news that he knew of, since the good news of the beating of the rogues the Scots. I asked him whether there was none of the English taken that joined the Scots? He answered that he did not hear that that rogue Charles Stuart was taken, but some of the others, he said, were taken, but not Charles Stuart. I told him that if that rogue were taken, he deserved to be hanged more than all the rest for bringing in the Scots, upon which he said that I spoke like an honest man, and so we parted.

Charles II, a profligate if ever there was one, knew instinctively that the best way to write memoirs is to laugh at oneself. But the former Edward VIII has but little of the light and talented Stuart strain in him. The heavy Teutonic strain and the long medical history of his family may help to explain his superiority and show-off complexes.

How then can one account for the fact that the Duke's great-grandmother, Queen Victoria, with German blood even thicker than his, wrote a "Journal" quite lacking any *duchesse*-lace embroidery? The answer is plain—her life needed no mantle of fancy needlework. The great Queen presented to Lord Tennyson, her poet laureate, a copy of the "Journal" inscribed by her with the following words: "Written by a very humble and unpretending author, the only merits of whose writing are simplicity and truth." Dedicated to her loyal Highlanders, "and especially to the memory of my devoted personal attendant and faithful friend, John Brown," the "Journal" was just that—simple and truthful.

The Duchess of Windsor too has published a book. (The writer has seen in a friend's library a copy of this work, autographed by the author.) The Duchess' book concerns cookery. It is a compilation of recipes.

As everyone knows, recipe books are like phoenixes—the young nestlings are born out of the ashes of the parent bird. And a new dish is almost as difficult to discover as a sure cure for baldness. However, because the Duchess' favorite recipes have been put between covers, she may be included in the list of royal authors. Bookmaking seems to be contagious; the Duke caught the malady.

The ex-King—is there a more melancholy prefix than this "ex," this two-letter stigma of has-beens, a mournful word that can be erased so seldom in life?—the ex-King says in his memoirs that when he was twenty-five years old he had only the vaguest idea of his duties or what was expected of him!

A sixteenth-century English ruler, Edward VI (recorded the Bishop of Ely) "at the age of seven was conscious of his future high mission and read Solomon's Proverbs at rising; and when he was thirteen he translated Cicero's *De Philosophia* from Latin into elegant Greek."

But even the earliest kings, like Hardicanute, Harold Harefoot, Henry III, had some notion of what their subjects expected of the King of England long before they reached maturity or the throne. And stupid and obdurate as they might have been, they were willing to listen to counsel.

The former Edward VIII, too, was willing to listen—to this sort of counsel concerning princeship:

> Perhaps one of the only positive pieces of advice that I was ever given was that supplied by an old courtier who observed, "Only two rules really count. Never miss an opportunity to relieve yourself; never miss a chance to sit down."

The "never miss a chance to sit down" phrase of the magazine version was augmented in the book with ". . . and rest your feet." Do the four additional words make a great deal of difference? Hardly. Yet some of the critics of *A King's Story* acclaimed this and similar passages as superb witticism. One is puzzled to know what humor they discerned in this supposed *bon mot*.

But let it be granted that it is a clever saying with a double meaning, fabricated by a cynical peer in order to amuse the young Prince of

Wales. According to *A King's Story* it constituted the sole equipment of the extremely popular, handsome little man with the straw-colored hair. The future head of the great Empire apparently took the nobleman's epigram to heart.

This piffle was readily accepted by the successor of Alfred the Great, and of that Black Prince who fought so valiantly at Crécy and Poitiers! This advice was eagerly embraced by the heir of that medieval hero, Henry V of Agincourt! These words were remembered and written down for future generations by the inheritor of the throne of that Edward the Confessor who refounded Westminster Abbey, the sacred spot where every Sovereign was crowned since William the Conqueror—except those unfortunate children, Edward V and Edward VIII. Edward V, aged 13, was imprisoned in the Tower the day his coronation was scheduled to take place. And Edward VIII, aged 42, kept another, to him much more important, date . . .

The Duke of Windsor was a mature 54 when he decided to make public his total recall. Certain inescapable conclusions result from the reading of these memoirs: (1) They ought never to have been written; (2) they are not factual; (3) to repeat, they are whitewash; (4) the book is not history.

It has been put together for the justification of two, with the help of thirty-seven (the present author put this work together with the assistance of a part-time secretary), to lead astray that most important personage, the reader.

The first part—until the Duke meets his *femme fatale*—has the fairy-tale atmosphere and charm of any very wealthy child's life. But even in this portion of the book, the careful reader already becomes aware that the Duke is given to rationalization. He is beginning at an early stage to put the blame on fate and father, tutor and alma mater, war and peace.

Of course, the Duke's book received an enthusiastic press in the States. The leading flatterer—writing an extraordinarily warm appreciation in the Sunday book section of what is probably the most serious and authoritative newspaper in the United States—is a curious fellow. Born an Englishman, he used to be a Bloomsbury semipoet of a deep pink hue. Then, during the Spanish Civil War, he went to Spain on behalf of the London *Daily Worker*. Later he visited the United States. The Duke and the poet met in New York. It was easy for the ex-King to win him over. So no one would have expected anything but saccharine criticism from this writer.

And this is perhaps the proper place to mention that on May 27, 1937, *Cavalcade*, the British news weekly, counterpart of *Time*, had an item that the Royal Family was willing to sacrifice and make a financial settlement on the Windsors, providing "they would refrain from writing memoirs, appearing on the radio or in the movies."

This curtailment of free speech—such an unjust request!—has never been denied by the Duke.

It would be interesting to know if the reported stipulation in the settlement was recently erased with consent of the Royal Family. Or whether the Duke just went ahead and published *A King's Story* anyhow. Talent will out—nothing, and no one can stop a writer from writing. Not even golden sovereigns.

However, among the thirty-seven people whom the Duke of Windsor thanks in his foreword for helping him, no member of the Royal Family is mentioned. So it seems probable that the manuscript of *A King's Story* was not submitted to Buckingham Palace for approval.

Pondering over such matters, the thoughtful reader may well be vexed; or he may be tempted to a cynical smile. But whatever his feeling of merriment, it must desert him when he considers the passage relating the courtier's advice. When he reflects that the frivolous words of a decadent earl served as a beacon to the youngest Knight of the Most Noble Order of the Garter, the highest honor an English gentleman and patriot can hope to receive . . .

And what prevents the Duke from suing himself for his next piece of gaucherie—a quite indiscreet question—in his memoirs?

For he actually asks himself in his story: "Who exactly was I?"

Not, you will notice, "*What* was I!" but "*Who* was I!"

The man musing over this momentous question was already twenty-five years of age.

The youngest page in the palace could have told him what he was, the Prince of Wales.

He was also the Duke of Cornwall, Earl of Chester, Lord Carrick, Baron Renfrew, Baron Rothesay, Lord of the Isles, Great Steward of Scotland, Lord High Steward of Plymouth, High Steward of Windsor, etc., midshipman (later Admiral of the Fleet), corporal (later Field Marshal), honorary colonel in the Guards, the Welsh Guards, the Household Cavalry, the Queen's Own Hussars, Colonel of the Prince of Wales' Royal Lancers, the Prince of Wales' Own Hussars, Colonel of the 35th, 36th and 92nd Punjabi Horse, 51st Sikhs, 37th Gurkhas,

Personal Aide-de-Camp to the King, his father, staff major in the Canadian Army, even a general in the Japanese Imperial Army and an admiral in the Danish Navy. The initials at the end of all his titles, K.G., P.C., K.T., K.P., G.O.B., G.O.S.I., G.O.M.G., G.O.I.E., G.O.V.O., G.B.E., M.C., stood for very high honors. In his raw youth the Prince had a yearly income of around $350,000, the revenue of the Duchy of Cornwall, the customary pocket money of the Princes of Wales.

When he was born, the family name was not yet Windsor: it was Saxe-Coburg-Gotha. The beautiful baby was baptized with seven names: Edward Albert Christian George Andrew Patrick David. In this multitude of given names the inclusion of all four patron saints of the United Kingdom (England, Scotland, Wales and Ireland) must be noted. This was duly recorded in the Duke's book, but it should be repeated here because at the time of the christening the venerable *Punch* commented that this was a happy selection, "that ought to help him to dodge ill luck in after years." His wife later simply called him "Davey," or "Little Man." She still does.

"Little Man" was the son and heir of George V. He was a fortunate infant: he was born with the lamp of Aladdin in his hand. Just the tiniest, gentlest rub on that mythical lamp, and all the genii would spring to gratify his most outlandish wishes.

Naturally there were certain obligations. A little work later, when he grew up. A bit of staying power. A marriage designed to ensure his own and his people's good.

The Prince was the next in line for the supreme magistracy, both spiritual and temporal, of a great Empire. This meant responsibilities, sometimes grave; authority, and therefore taking trouble for others. The Prince didn't quite like such thoughts—he hated to have authority, he said. But as wise Cicero pointed out, all authority has its end *outside* of *itself*.

Meaning, that a superior is never chosen for his own purposes but for the benefit of the inferior. Justice is done not for him who administers it, but for those for whom it is administered. A physician is there for the sake of the patient: we need the doctor to help us in suffering.

The Prince of Wales was born a doctor, holding his diploma even in the cradle. But he always considered himself his only patient, never facing the fact that Providence supplies a prince in monarchies to heal the wounds of his subjects.

King Alfred the Great says:

> But I hold, as do all Christian men, that a Divine Providence rules,
> and not fate . . .

Prince Edward was born to live *not* solely for his own ends and amusements, but also to lead his people and to guide them, when at a later time they should have lost their way amid the turns and changes of history. The Prince, and later King, would have had ample opportunity to enjoy all the personal pleasures he wanted in his private life.

For he was slated to be a modern king of a constitutional country, a sort of figurehead only.

Not a demigod like the kings of Thrace, who had a religion all their own, including a private god, Mercury, whom only the king was allowed to worship, while his serfs prayed to inferior gods like Bacchus, Mars and Diana.

The kingship the ancient Sumerian clerks described as having descended from heaven, was fortunately outmoded when the Prince grew to manhood.

Looking back to the time when he was twenty-five and the Prince of Wales, the Duke answers his own questions. He did not think it right that simply by reason of his birth he should be above other people. In fact, he is hinting that he wanted to be merely "one of the boys." Just an ordinary man. The Duke in his memoirs appears anxious to flatter egalitarian feeling both in the United States and in England.

But a king is not quite an ordinary man. He is above other people not only because of his high birth, but because he is called upon to exercise certain high qualities to a greater degree than is expected of others.

Gun salutes, equerries, fine palaces, pocketsful of money, curtsies, kneelings, and flattery don't add up to character. In a basic sense the Prince was the same as every man on the face of the earth, for in that sense all men are the same. But he had a calling. He was the Empire's hope. His subjects and the rest of the troubled world thought of him as the savior, and dreamed of him as:

> The man, who
> Can at all times himself subdue;
> Whom neither want, nor death, nor chains
> Appal. Who manfully restrains

His appetites. Nor cares to win
Titles or honors. And, within
Himself, self-centered and complete,
Life's chance and change can frankly meet.
Fronting the heaviest blows of fate
With courage, constant and sedate.
                                        (Horace)

"You must remember your position!" the Duke says his father, George V, once told him. Perhaps not once but many times. The young Prince, however, remembered his position only in rare instances, and then like a rookie cop, who is dizzy with his newly acquired authority. Once, when the Prince as a young student, whether at Osborne or at Oxford is immaterial, entered class, the boys stood up respectfully. "Oh, don't stand up," said the Prince engagingly. So the next day the students did not stand up when he came to class. The Prince was furious. "You ought to stand up!" he said. "After all, I'm the heir to the throne!"

It doesn't quite sound like Osborne or Oxford, does it? That solid British Navy or Magdalen training doesn't make people petty or capricious like that. The martial or the Latin education is supposed to make a real man, a good and strong man, of you. But had the Prince really all that classical education?

It is common knowledge, it is on record, that the Duke, when he was Prince of Wales, dreaded serious and instructive literature. That instead of Plutarch, Aristotle, Cicero, Shakespeare, Montaigne, Hume, Tolstoy and the like, he read the cheap kind of fiction. This perhaps accounts for the fact that he disregarded the dictum that the foremost duty of princes is self-sacrifice. That they are at the helm and if they leave their crucial post for selfish reasons, their country may become ". . . a ship without pilot in a mighty storm, no longer queen of provinces, but a brothel," as Dante so aptly put it in his *Purgatorio*.

This fate has not befallen England, because there was another Prince, possessing the necessary spirit of self-sacrifice, to take over. However, the shock of King Edward's action in abdicating was felt throughout Europe and the world; and could have destroyed the Commonwealth. Indeed, the idea that this wonderful political construct might disappear had once (by his own account) occurred to the Empire Salesman. "The thought occurred to me," writes the husband of the Duchess of Windsor, "that I was the last King of England to see the Empire intact." His thought led to many other bitter thoughts.

Edward's people did not have to ask what exactly he was—they *knew*.

He was their Prince. Their beloved Prince, who was to be their guardian, sentinel, protector through many years to come. He was their own handsome, darling Prince of Wales, about whom the women of a whole Empire dreamed, and at the thought of whom the men smiled happily, because he was the guarantee of their own and their families' future. He was a great Prince.

The Duke of Windsor says in his memoirs that he did not know exactly who he was!

He seemed to be the answer to the prayer of a sick world, desperately in need of an ideal. As Prince of Wales he embodied that ideal.

He wasn't yet the "Little Man."

3

The Grand Appearance

We are as good as they are, and a damned sight better!

—American saying, noted by
H. L. MENCKEN

IT IS both sad and amusing to see a former King of mighty England reduced by the woman he loved to "Little Man," to the rank of a meek husband.

What should one do, laugh or cry, when one looks at the man who was Edward VIII? The ex-Caesar in the role of a handbag-carrying *cavaliere servente*, a sort of ornament, a woman's background, is a melancholy sight.

One should neither laugh nor cry. One should look at the woman, the gracious Duchess whose profession seems to be what is called "Putting in the Grand Appearance."

For, according to society columnist Cholly Knickerbocker (Igor Cassini), the Duchess of Windsor is Number One in the list of the world's ten best-dressed women.

Cholly's opinion is supported by that of the press agent of the New York Dress Institute.

The Duchess, who seems to have a very alert conscience, realizes that her principal duty is to live up to her double Nobel Prize of Fashion.

Therefore, several times a week during her long sojourns in New York, she shows herself to the populace. Or rather, to the upper crust of the 152-million souls in the United States. This includes valiant armies of sycophants, snobs, and title-worshipers.

But back to the busy Duchess, and the manners and the morals of a make-believe world.

The Windsors have three favorite places in New York, Le Pavillon, The Colony, and El Morocco. All three of these are restaurants, of

course. The best in town. However, since it is impossible to be at
several spots at the same time, one may take The Colony as the *mise
en scene* of the Royal Entry.

This Royal Entry is quite a spectacle.

Gene Cavallero, the owner of the restaurant, is a genius. He knows
how to produce atmosphere. When he is expecting the Windsors, he
stands majestically in the small lobby, surrounded by his principal
aides. This welcoming committee looks very much like contemporary
oil paintings depicting the top brass before a decisive battle—for
instance, Pershing about to order the Meuse-Argonne attack, or
Napoleon and his marshals pondering over Borodino.

A hungry stranger coming to The Colony for the simple business
of eating might be taken aback by the sight of the elaborate stage
setting. The eager flow of his gastric juices could even be arrested for
a brief moment. He might well imagine that, by some mistake, he
has stumbled into a sacristy.

But there are no golden chalices or liturgical garments in the lobby
of The Colony. Merely some very good-looking food on buffet-
carriages. And baroque-style sofas, upholstered armchairs, low tables,
a Van Cleef and Arpels showcase displaying the latest in baubles, and
some paintings on the walls.

As if in an old-fashioned play about society, the lobby is teeming
with the elite. It is an open secret that the Windsors are coming, and
the lady members of the glamorous smart set are looking impatiently
toward the door. There is a feeling of excitement in the air.

Ah! At last! The Windsors are here!

Naturally the Duchess comes in first. The moment she steps into
the lobby, her face lights up. Her smile is a judicious blend of intimacy
and reserve, uniting the mesmeric charm of an earthly woman with
the aloof radiancy of a goddess.

Her smile seems to say, "Hello, I haven't seen you for a long time!
How very nice to see you again! Thank you, thank you, thank you!
Thank you from the bottom of my heart for your admiration and
homage."

Of course there is no applause. Such vulgar demonstrations would
be out of place at The Colony. In fact, you can hear a pin drop.

The women who have met the Duchess are waiting with bated
breath for a glance of recognition. When that supreme moment
arrives, they execute the neatest curtsies on this side of the Atlantic.

This strange idolatry, this pirouetting mania of well-bred or less well-bred American women is the most curious phenomenon in the history of a country based on social equality. It may be but a small component of the whole Windsor legend. But it is significant. And disturbing. It is clear proof that many people, here in America, refuse to face realities and insist on living in a fictional world. That the elite loves royalty and if there is no such specimen of earthly deity readily available, they will create one.

The social snobs are doing a great disservice to the people of this great republic, who are fighting to preserve the only decent way of life—democracy. Never before has the United States been in so much need of mature and sober judgment as now, and here are its notables playing like children.

The fact that only a princess of royal blood is entitled to this kind of ceremonial greeting, considered today as silly and outmoded even in England, is utterly disregarded by the elite, some of whose forefathers signed the Declaration of Independence.

As a matter of fact, the Duke of Windsor's wife is not even allowed the royal title of her husband. The faulty or convenient memory of the curtsying set may be corrected by quoting from an announcement made in the official *London Gazette* soon after the abdication of Edward VIII:

> The King [George VI] has been pleased by Letters Patent under the Great Seal of the Realm bearing date the 27th of May 1937, to declare that the Duke of Windsor shall, notwithstanding his Instrument of Abdication be entitled to hold and enjoy *for himself only* the title style and attribute of Royal Highness so however that his wife and descendants if any shall not hold the same title style or attribute.
>
> [Debrett's emphasis]

For the sake of contrast, consider an eighteenth-century duchess, *Her Royal Highness* the Duchess of Gloucester, who was supposed to be the most beautiful woman in England, even if not the best-dressed. Sir Joshua Reynolds painted her portrait six times.

She was born a Miss Clements, illegitimate daughter of Mary Clements, a seamstress, and Edward Walpole. Through her first marriage she became known as Lady Waldegrave; and when her husband died, she secretly married the Duke of Gloucester, who was the brother of King George III. This insane king had a family of fifteen children.

As you know, George III wanted to be a "father" in faraway

America too, but he ran into a little trouble. This tyrant "plundered our seas, ravaged our Coasts, burnt our towns, and destroyed the lives of our people"—such are the charges brought against him in the Declaration of Independence.

At any rate, when that beautiful eighteenth-century duchess became pregnant by the Duke of Gloucester, she wrote a letter to her father, Edward Walpole, which must be inserted here as the best letter any genuine duchess ever wrote:

St. Leonards, 19 May, 1772.

My Dear and Ever Honoured Sir.

You cannot easily imagine how much every past affliction has been increased to me by not being at liberty to make you quite easy. The duty to a husband being superior to that we owe a father I hope will plead my pardon, and that instead of blaming my past reserve, you will think it commendable. When the Duke of Gloucester married me (which was in September 1766) I promised him, upon no consideration in the world to own it, *even to you*, without his permission, which permission I never had till yesterday . . .

To secure my character, without injuring his, is the utmost of my wishes, and I dare say that you and all my relations will agree with me that *I shall be* much happier to be called *Lady Waldegrave* and respected as the Duchess of Gloucester than *to be called your royal highness.* I am prepared for the sort of abuse the newspapers will be full of. Very few will believe that a woman will refuse to be called princess if it is in her power.

To have the power is my pride, *and not using it in some measure pays the debt I owe the Duke for the honour he has done me.* All that I wish of my relations is that they will show the world that they are satisfied with my conduct . . . *If ever I am unfortunate enough to be called Duchess of Gloucester* there is an end of almost all the comforts which I now enjoy, which if things go on as they are, are many.

To this great lady all Americans would gladly render homage, realizing that nobility is in the soul.

As to the twentieth-century Duchess no picture ever did justice to her. She is more attractive in real life than in photographs. Somehow the camera caricatures her nose and chin, that jut out in pictures like promontories. Her mouth, too, is exaggerated and becomes an elongated thin slit when not smiling, and full of teeth when smiling. In reality her mouth is a marvel of perfection, a toothpaste ad dream, and it is fully open to inspection by the public when illuminated by the table candlestick at El Morocco's Champagne Room.

One of the wisdom teeth of the Duchess was removed years ago in

Miami. This minor operation started rumors at the time that she underwent a face lifting under the cloak of dental surgery, and that the intricate business was performed by a face-lifting wizard who did not possess a diploma.

Weigh this gossip carefully. Why would the Duchess of Windsor go under the scalpel of a quack when she could engage the best, the most prominent plastic surgeon to fix her face? She had her appendix removed by the most skilful surgeon in New York. Early in 1951, when a slight operation was to be performed on her person, a noted Edinburgh specialist was invited to fly to New York for consultation with nine other physicians. Would she then allow bootleg hands to tinker with the face which has proved to be her fortune? It simply isn't consistent.

Yet for years drawing-room conversation had it that not only her own, but the Duke's face, too, had been lifted. Second-rate plastic surgeons around would then flash an all-revealing smile, a wink of affirmation, befitting a medical man who has taken the Hippocratic oath of secrecy. And there was one physician, who, recognizing the immense publicity value of the thing, not only winked but talked. He managed to make the columns. Doc was promptly summoned by an ethical-minded medical society, and censored and fined for his canard.

But the Duchess and her Duke must not be made to linger in the lobby of The Colony. It isn't fair. Only the late Adolf Hitler permitted himself such shyster methods, when he made the Windsors cool their heels for a solid hour at Berchtesgaden before admitting the pilgrims into the Presence Chamber. That was long ago. Once upon a time . . .

The Duchess is not beautiful, but she certainly is a fascinating apparition. Almost always she is dressed in blue, Wallis blue, which is as universal an expression today as Dubonnet red or Chartreuse green. You will very seldom see her in the same dress twice; having served as a bedazzling prop in the Grand Entry, it is usually sold by the Duchess to intimate friends.

The jewels of the Duchess of Windsor are among the most fabulous in the world. But nowadays, in this troubled era, she exhibits her sympathy by being satisfied with wearing just a few of her enormous sapphires and diamonds in the evening, and merely a simple brooch or two and modest earrings in the daytime. Invariably she hides her hands—not so pretty—in gloves. For daytime wear she is addicted

to the short, white doeskin sort, infuriating designers, who regard
these gloves as passé. But who could alter a feminine fancy, which
through the years has become an obsession? Almost fifty years ago
she started to wear them and the world of fashion just has to accept
her with this single, but according to experts, serious breach of fashion.

Concerning another fetish, her feet, when she was married to a
comparatively poor man and her private income was only $55 per
month, she used to order eighteen pairs of shoes at a time. Don't let
your imagination run wild, though, when you think of her considerably increased income— it's still eighteen pairs at a clip. As to hats,
she holds the hat-buying record: she once bought forty-five of them
in one visit to a New York shop.

The Duke trails behind his Duchess at The Colony. His erstwhile
Majesty Edward VIII, by Grace of God, of Great Britain, Ireland,
and the British Dominions Beyond the Seas, King, Defender of the
Faith, Emperor of India, Sovereign of the Most Noble Order of the
Garter, is a short, frail, and vacant-faced man. He looks a bit bewildered and somewhat bored; and despite a youthful appearance
gives the impression of a very distinguished mummy. By some odd
travesty of fate that singles out certain physiognomies to play practical
jokes on, Windsor resembles the late John D. Rockefeller, Sr., minus
the shiny dimes that Croesus used to pass around. The Duke of
Windsor passes nothing around.

Except melancholy. One can't help pitying this hapless mortal who
by chance was born to such high station, who, at one time, held one
great lever to the equilibrium of the whole world in his hand, and
who now reappears as a middle-aged spouse, reverent and filled with
domestic fear like any husband after fifteen years of submissive
marriage. Looking at him, Shakespearean characters come to mind.
For instance, another King who resigned his crown, Richard II, and
that unhappy Monarch's miserable words to his subjects:

> . . . Throw away respect,
> Tradition, form, and ceremonious duty,
> For you have but mistook me all this while:
> I live with bread like you, feel want,
> Taste grief, need friends. . . .

Such declarations from a King of England, a valiant nation's common father and exalted leader, must feel to his people like the iciest
wind sweeping down from the desolate Orkneys. Come to think of it,

Eines Königs Geschichte—which, though sounding like a sneeze, means only *A King's Story*. Windsor looks at a German edition of his opus.

Keystone Pictures, Inc.

Playing the drum

Pix—Jean Howard

Loyal friends. The Duke of Windsor
and Miss Elsa Maxwell.

International News Photo

The Windsors and Mr. and Mrs. Charles Bedeaux, at a rented castle in
Borsódivánka, Hungary, planning their trip to the United States.

the British always regarded their ruler as a natural element; like the
sun or rain; shining one day, pouring the next, but there to stay.
And, of course, this feeling does not only apply to England. It is universal in monarchies. Vaguely, one remembers a passage about kings
in Montaigne's "Essays," making a mental note to look it up at home:

> We owe submission and allegiance to all Kings alike, for that con-
> cerns their office; but they should not command our esteem, anymore
> than our affection, unless they be worthy.
> And, when our relations are ended, there is no reason why, in the
> name of justice and our freedom, we should not express our true
> feelings.
> Those who wrongly espouse the memory of a prince undeserving of
> praise, do so at the expense of public justice. Livy says truly "That the
> language of men bred under royalty is always full of vain ostentation
> and false testimony."

Such is the Grand Appearance of "the greatest Romeo and Juliet
team in the world." This is what a radio executive called the Windsors
recently, offering them $100,000 for thirteen husband-and-wife
appearances.

The radio man's simile is not altogether happy; Romeo, a Montague, and a very private youth, fell in love with Juliet, nee Capulet.
Owing to a tragic accident the young lovers died before their marriage
could be acknowledged to their families, who were at variance with
each other. The only resemblance between those Shakespearean
figures and the Windsors is that the Duchess of Windsor's mother's
maiden name happened to be Montague. If such twisted coincidence
can be counted as a similarity.

As to the $100,000 offer, this is what Walter Winchell had to say
about it in his syndicated column on December 31, 1950:

> The Dook and Dookess received a radio offer of $100,000. Why the
> Big Money? The act wasn't good enough to play The Palace.

If you are not among the 25-million habitual readers of Mr. Winchell's fast and expressive column, this mention might need an
explanation. Here a double-entendre is brought into play, and "The
Palace" may mean London's Buckingham, or New York's famous
Palace Theater devoted to vaudeville shows, or both.

The Windsors meet their acquaintances in the restaurant's lobby.
They have many acquaintances. Chiefly among social climbers.

Most of them are ostentatious, vainglorious, yet nice and harmlessly stupid people, filled with false ideas of hero worship, whose greatest kick in life is to invite a runaway emperor and his wife for a historical meal at a well-frequented public place.

One wonders if these hosts ever think of some of the Windsors' former hosts—the ghosts of Hitler and Ribbentrop and Dr. Ley. And Bedaux, the renegade in whose castle the Windsors were united. And Metaxas, the Greek dictator; and Kemal Atatürk, the Turkish autocrat. There were other ghosts of a like kind, including that of Litvinoff, the arch-Communist.

"*Ma'am est servie*," says the headwaiter of The Colony with courtly ceremony. With these three little French words he announces that a royal lady's dinner is starting.

4

Voice of the Columnists

A good woman is a hidden treasure; he who discovers
her will do well not to boast about it.
—Duc de la Rochefucauld: *Maxims*

Sometime ago the Windsors began to receive an alarmingly
bad press. The world was more disturbed than ever, and the columnists in America did not like show-offs in the shadow of a possible
showdown.

The Duke and the Duchess had had their share of hostile publicity,
but never had it been as steady or spicy as it had now become. In the
past the wrath of the press had broken out in concentrated barrages;
very hard to withstand, but not long-lasting. While the press raged
there were luxurious foxholes, a villa on the Riviera or a mansion in
Paris, and the fire soon abated.

Now there was no booming and roaring of formidable armament.
But the rapiers of columnists, the Petronius Arbiters of our time, came
swishing out of their sheaths, as though these chroniclers had made
a pledge at a secret meeting to harass the Windsors with continual,
rapid thrusts. However, some deadly machetes and razor-sharp
tomahawks still remained in the corner, by order of friendly publishers.

The romance that had been thought of as one of the greatest and
most enduring in history seemed to be disintegrating almost as it had
started—suddenly and before the eyes of the whole world.

Walter Winchell was the first to remark in his column that the
marriage was now "only a front."

Cholly Knickerbocker reported in October 1950, in the New
York *Journal-American:*

> The newest aide-de-camp of the Duke and Duchess of Windsor in
> Paris is Woolworth heir Jimmy Donahue. Jimmy escorts the D. and D.
> everywhere and stays up playing cards with the Duchess even after
> His Royal Highness has retired.

27

A score of other columnists had similar information.

While the newspapers hissed and scoffed, the Duchess arrived in the United States alone; and instead of keeping out of the limelight she furnished the press with racy items. The royal flush with Mr. Donahue continued in New York.

The Duke in the meantime had gone to England to visit his mother, the only person in the world whose basic affection for him had never changed. Wallis was not afraid that her husband's rare visits to Queen Mary would lead to the disruption of their marriage—her name was never on royal lips. Miss Marion Crawford, governess of Princess Elizabeth (the present Queen) and Princess Margaret Rose, writes:

> . . . Uncle David was not dead, yet they (*the little princesses*) never saw him any more . . . In the palace and the castle, his name was never mentioned. (*The Little Princesses*, by Marion Crawford, Harcourt, Brace and Co.)

When eventually the Duke arrived in New York, the Duchess was at the pier early in the morning, spic and span as usual. There were kisses. The press counted exactly seven, and corroborated their story with pictures. One news photographer shouted during a royal embrace: "Hold it!" The Windsors obliged. There was laughter. And the Windsors, anxious to quiet rumors, carried on the familiar fun while the cameras clicked away.

But how long can that all-consuming passion, love, last? The sort Edward VIII felt for Wallis Simpson at the time he abandoned his throne for her.

Not too long. Chateaubriand said that the soul of man becomes weary and never loves the same object long and fully. Richard Whitford spoke of hot love soon cooling. John Heywood said: "Love me little, love me long." Byron wrote that sooner or later love is its own avenger.

There are many wise sayings on these foolish things. Shakespeare, who knew all about it, wrote:

> There lives within the very flame of love
> A kind of wick or snuff that will abate it.

Love is beautiful. But like measles, it runs its natural course. The most wonderful of all maladies also begins by the victim's contracting the disease; then there is fever, moving to a crisis; then he either dies or recovers.

Today people as a rule don't die from love or measles—they get well. Love has a sure cure: continual close association with the person who caused it. Of course one has in mind that certain burning, blazing, flaming passion. Once that terrible fever subsides, the patient awakes to find that like a lucky somnambulist he has fallen off the roof-top and has escaped cheaply, with a broken arm or leg. Or he finds himself married.

The Duke of Windsor is very much married.

The ever-glamorous Duchess of Windsor has never deviated from the smart feminine strategy that won the Prince of Wales the moment the two first met.

Later in this book will be described how the then Mrs. Simpson, sizing up the situation and the man, spoke to the Prince as no one had ever spoken to him before—in a challenging, provocative manner.

She still does. Sarcastic phrases like: "Are you out of your mind?" and "Don't be silly!" and "I'm not castle-bred as you are!" are not at all infrequent. Apart from this verbal flagellation, the Duke also receives other kinds of discipline.

Some time ago the Windsors were dinner guests of an American who maintains a home in Paris. Upon arrival, the Duchess, after the usual greetings, inquired: "Is —— here?" When the host replied that their good friend, who is *the* link between certain social groups, had not yet arrived, Wallis burst out: "Extremely rude! She was fifteen minutes late for dinner last night at my house!"

When at last her friend appeared, the Duchess upbraided her. The lady apologized. She then pointed out that the Duchess, observing the night before that her friend's hair looked "like nothing on earth," had arranged for her own hairdresser to fix it; this artist had come late, thus delaying her. She was awfully sorry.

She then turned to the Duke with a confident smile and asked: "Sir, do you also think that I have committed such a grave sin?"

Before answering, the Duke glanced at his wife. Then, frowning, he looked back at the culprit, and nodding his head vigorously said: "Yes, you oughtn't to arrive after Wallis. Extremely rude!" He then questioned his wife with his eyes, much as a small boy looks at his mother to learn if he has satisfied her or not.

Once the small boy, at a gala dinner for twenty-four, was sitting at the lower end of the table, far away from his wife, who sat at the head.

The Duke talked with his neighbor in a highly animated fashion on the topic most dear to him, aviation. Perhaps he was too ebullient. At any rate, the Duchess sent him a glance, and the Duke stopped talking and did not open his mouth for the rest of the evening.

For the Duchess treats the Duke as though he is still a little boy— a method highly successful in the case of a man who has forsaken all other affection and who has "freed" himself of all other ties. Most men are nothing but small boys and some women know it.

And some women are nothing but small girls—the Duchess always wishes to maintain the correct order of precedence. A Paris newspaper reported in 1950 that Wallis was quite perturbed when ex-King Umberto of Italy appeared at a party long after the Windsors had arrived.

Poor Umberto—some former monarchs are poor, down to their last million—explained that he had missed a few overcrowded buses. The Duchess is reported to have said: "He ought to have arrived before us. After all, Umberto was kicked off his throne, but David renounced his of his own free will."

The Windsors had been unusually free and friendly with New Yorkers since 1950. About this time a peculiar change came over the Duchess. She abandoned her former practice of seeking to move only among those who stand on the highest rung of the American social ladder. Instead, she suddenly turned her attention to the arts and to artists. She graciously accepted an invitation for dinner at the house of Clifton Webb, the comedian, and just as graciously received homage from the other guests—all the ladies present, bohemian or bourgeois, were requested to curtsy to the Duchess.

Newsweek magazine in its January 29, 1951 issue mentioned that the Windsors were present at the American National Theater and Academy Ball, where the Duke stayed only ten minutes in order to be photographed. Then he went home to bed while the Duchess danced till the end. Around six in the morning.

Alongside the brief *Newsweek* account there was an arrestingly candid camera shot. It showed the Duchess adjusting her strapless evening gown. Her head tossed back, she exhibited to an agonizing world a defiance surely born of her inferiority complex; and also a necklace of three clusters, the price of one of them enough to maintain an ordinary family for a lifetime (or purchase a jet fighter).

The Duchess' cavalier in the picture was Cecil Beaton, English photographer of royalty, who in his Photobiography has an incisive account of the Duchess. One of the striking comments made on Wallis by this sober expert of woman's beauty is as follows: "Her hands are extremely utilitarian-looking."

But for the general public Mr. Beaton figured in the scheme of things merely as a one-night dancing companion. The newspapers were still concentrating on Jimmy Donahue. The Duchess and Mr. Donahue did not always have a domestic evening with the cards; they were seen together at restaurants and night spots, and even if the Duke started out with them he seldom stayed later than midnight.

The sophisticated Duchess and the retiring Jimmy explored the town, enjoying innocent fun at the Stork Club; at El Morocco; and at Gogi's Larue. They gourmandized at Le Pavillon and at Maud Chez Elle, and one evening the Duchess and Jimmy surprised The Colony by bringing with them two violinists and a harmonica-player. This was perhaps the first time that diners in that temple of gastronomy had been serenaded. Mr. Angier Biddle Duke and a Canadian gentleman made up the rest of the party. The Duke was not listed in the press communiqués as being also present.

They made a trio, though, at the Midnight Mass on Christmas Eve, 1950 (as again they did in 1952), at St. Patrick's Cathedral. The Duchess suggested the idea of their attending the ceremony; the Duke readily embraced it; and Mr. Donahue, scion of prominent Catholics, respectfully opposed it. But two minds were made up as resolutely as ever, and Mr. Donahue led the former head of the Anglican Church and his wife, who were never noted churchgoers, to a pew near the altar. The midnight flock went on with its devotions until voices above a whisper were heard; a few heads—among them the billiard-ball-like one of Mr. James Farley, the former Postmaster General—were raised, and the Windsors and their friend were recognized.

However, the open and aboveboard friendship between the gracious Duchess and the young man of leisure did not stir the imagination of the populace so much as did another, at first known only to café society's privy council.

Walter Winchell began his January 29, 1951 column entitled *Man About Town* in a startling fashion. This was the initial sentence of his lead paragraph: "Ethel Merman's Big Scoop is the Big Talk among her Inner Circle . . ." and he ends this paragraph: ". . . The Duke and Duchess Set is Aghast and Agog."

Now there is no apparent direct connection between these two sentences separated by a dozen other hot items, but the dean of columnists is a wizard at making his point indirectly. For there had been plenty of talk among Miss Merman's "Inner Circle," by which Mr. Winchell meant the players of the successful musical, "Call Me Madam." Green Room gossip had it that the Duchess of Windsor was very friendly with Mr. Russell Nype, one of the talented actors in the show. She had been phoning the young man nightly, and sometimes called for him in her car. It seems that this friendship displeased the more austere acquaintances of the Windsors, and Mr. Winchell saw fit to say that their set was "aghast and agog."

People whispered that the Duchess gave her expert advice on interior decoration when in January 1951 Mr. Nype moved to a new apartment in New York's elegant East Seventies. And in the New York *Daily Mirror* of February 19, 1951, Walter Winchell's syndicated column *Man About Town* carried the following story:

> The Duchess of Windsor and Mrs. Vincent Astor clashed in a furious scene . . . Jimmy Donahue made a reservation at the Maisonette (in the St. Regis), and when they didn't arrive by 12:30 showtime the table was peddled . . . A few moments later James ankled in with Her Grace . . . A table was offered on the floor ringside, but it was spurned . . . She stalked out in a swivet . . . A few nights later (at a Plaza charity affair) Mrs. Astor danced by Mrs. Windsor's table . . . The latter got up, grabbed Minnie's best arm and said: "Minnie, you owe me an apology, and I feel it should be a public one" . . . Minnie said she didn't know what she was talking about . . . To which the Duchess responded: "I was insulted in that basement saloon your husband runs" . . . The diatribe continued with another demand for an apology . . . Minnie looked at her coldly and meow'd "My dear woman, why don't you act your age?" and then floated away . . . The noblewoman started after Minnie, but Russell Nype (of "Call Me Duchess") pleaded with the husbandless woman to sit down. To which, in her most regal tone, she barked: "Shaddup!"

In Louella Parsons' sweeter syndicated column of January 24, 1951 appeared this paragraph:

> From New York comes word that Russell Nype, Manhattan's new rave—he's with Ethel Merman in "Call Me Madam"—is the Duchess of Windsor's favorite dancing partner. She and the Duke, who are admirers of his, are reported giving a big party at the St. Regis, where he's booked for a midnight stint after the show.

Mr. Nype is said to possess a great deal of charm, a vast capacity for friendship, and "refined culture."

It is worthy of note that the Duchess' favorite escorts, like Mr. Donahue, Mr. Beaton, and Mr. Clifton Webb, have certain similarities in make-up, like that disarming charm, and ready and caustic wit; also they are good mixers.

They share another characteristic which has never failed to appeal to Wallis in a man—they are somewhat shy. At any rate, they are far from acting like cave men. All four of them possess polished manners, and what could be more pleasing to a great lady? Besides, they have a certain exclusiveness which puts them somewhat above other men. Their outstanding qualities were neatly summed up by a café society wit, who once referred to them as "the crêpes suzette set." Crêpes suzette, as you know, are those superlative, paper-thin, wonderful French pancakes.

The columnists did not forget, either, to touch the shoulder of Gayelord Hauser, the nutritionist, with their poniards, making him a knight, even if not Sir Loin, at least Sir Yogurt—he, too, belongs to the entourage of the Duchess. And to the crêpes suzette set.

But the "Duchess Set" was resentful of the new favorites. For instance, in 1951 the Duchess was not—as she used to be—among the guests of Mrs. William Randolph Hearst, who every January gives an important party. On the other hand, the Windsors have been the guests of honor at the stupendous New Year's Eve affair of Mr. and Mrs. Gilbert Miller.

The advent of 1953 was marked by rivalry in New York society. Besides the now traditional Miller New Year's Eve party, the Byron Foys had also arranged one. So the Windsors, friendly with both the Millers and the Foys, were obliged to shuttle between the two parties; and they seem to have preferred that of the Foys.

Both Mrs. Miller and Mrs. Foy inherited millions: the former's father was the late Jules Bache, the international banker, and the latter's father was Walter Chrysler, the automobile magnate. The beautiful Thelma Foy, a level-headed lady, with a delightful sense of humor, is not given to worshiping abdicated monarchs or royalty in general. However, with Mrs. Miller things stand on a different footing. To begin with, ever so slightly she resembles the Duchess of Windsor, dresses like her, and when she is mistaken for the Duchess by a cunning maître d'hôtel, she expresses genuine though forgivable joy. It is simply this: Mrs. Miller likes royalty. About fifteen years ago, when she summered in England, she made the acquaintance of the late Duke of Kent. Her husband, in New York, related this momentous event to friends: "Do you know what the Duke of Kent calls Kitty?" The friends replied that they had no idea. "Why, he calls her Kitty!" said Mr. Miller jubilantly.

At any rate, the usually careful Millers even engaged a uniformed gypsy band for the New Year's Eve party, and it is reported that, on this memorable occasion, the champagne was French and not American. Of course no matter how lavish the Millers' entertainment, it did not compare with the sedate elegance of that of the late Mrs. Cornelius Vanderbilt. This old lady sometimes invited the Windsors. Years ago she aired her thoughts—so rarely bestowed on the general public—on a momentous social problem. Somewhat influenced by the late Terence Philip, a mutual friend, she said that she had known the Duke of Windsor in his heyday, when he was Prince of Wales, and that she was not going to slight him now that he was married and his station had changed. Wallis soon repaid Mrs. Vanderbilt's kindness; in an article which was published in *Vogue* under the Duchess' by-line, she threw her royal scepter to Mrs. Vanderbilt, declaring that this great lady was still the undisputed ruler in the Western Hemisphere.

As has been said, the Duchess lately has mixed but little with American high society. The exact reason for this change is unknown: a year or two before she was still choosing her friends with great care.

The New York *Daily News* ran a feature story in its July 23, 1949 issue, containing various speculative opinions on the Windsors.

> An Englishman who is close to the Windsors had this to say: "Wallis is an ambitious woman. Her whole life reveals that she has constantly sought the friendship of important and powerful people; what could be more understandable than her present let-down after becoming engaged to a king and finding herself married to an exile?"

This *Daily News* article figured that the Windsors may be unhappy because the Duke had been unable to obtain a government post even before the Churchill Government of 1951 came into power. It failed to point out that he had tried his best to get a job. There was in the New York *Times* a rather pathetic account of how he sought from Mr. Attlee "a suitable colonial governorship," entering through the back door of No. 10 Downing Street, the Prime Minister's official residence. His failure to get that "suitable" appointment with its social standing, dignity and privilege, led to rumors of a rift between the Windsors.

An awkward situation had arisen: peace had broken out, and protocol was reinstated. During the war the Duke of Windsor could become head of a colony—the Bahamas—for wartimes are extraordinary times; more important still, Mr. Churchill, the mountain-mover, was then Premier, and all was arranged with Winnie's famous casual touch. When bombs were falling on England it was not, could not be, obligatory for a representative of the King to appear in the presence and "kiss hands." After the war, however, when things returned to normal, the Duke on receiving an appointment would have to go to London to be officially received in audience. This audience might have been accompanied by a howl from Parliamentary benches. Moreover, the Duchess could quite certainly have insisted on her prerogative—the right of an appointee's wife to go with her husband to Buckingham Palace. This would have been a *fait accompli*, leading the world to believe that Wallis was now on visiting terms with the Royal Family.

It has been suggested that this vain attempt to secure a governmental post, and the conclusion obviously to be drawn from this fiasco—that the Royal Family remained adamant in its refusal to receive the still-hopeful Wallis—pushed the Windsors to the writing of his memoirs, and the Duchess, in particular, to her final attitude of defiance.

Sometimes columnists try to better the poor public relations of the Windsors. This is not an easy task—as the popular saying goes, they are their own worst enemies.

But columnists are only human and although Cholly Knickerbocker often criticized the Windsors up to 1952, from that year on he adopted a kindlier tone toward them. This was natural, for Cholly married the very pretty daughter of Mr. Charles Wrightsman, who is a great friend of the Windsors. The *rapprochement* showed itself in various ways, the most important being that Cholly elected the Duchess to be honorary chairman of his Knickerbocker Ball at the Waldorf of January 5, 1953. This charity affair is given for the Foundling Hospital and the Sister Kenny Fund. Among co-chairmen were Jimmy Donahue and Milton "Doc" Holden. Mr. Holden used to be the Scotland Yard bodyguard of the Duke of Windsor when he first went into exile. After the Duke resigned his Bahamas post, Holden also retired into private life.

But the Windsors' mode of life calls for a peep through their keyhole.

5

America Under Edward VIII, Called Landless

High society is for those who have stopped working and no longer have anything to do.
—WOODROW WILSON:
Speech in Washington, Feb. 24, 1915

W<small>HEN</small> the Windsors are in New York, their keyhole is in the Waldorf-Astoria Tower. This is remarkable, for the bustling Waldorf affords about as much privacy as does Grand Central Station. Those members of café society who live in a perpetual agonized striving after "the correct thing" wonder why the Duke and Duchess do not seek a quieter hotel or an apartment for their New York home. Of course the Tower is the quieter portion of the Waldorf, containing ornate suites, some of them occupied permanently by people in the public eye—generals, politicians, millionaires, promoters, publishers, and even the owner of the Greatest Show on Earth. The Windsors are transients; they have an understanding whereby they notify the management of their intended visit about two months before their arrival, in order to make sure of finding their usual apartment, 28A, vacant.

The thirst of the traveler in Arabian deserts is as nothing compared to the thirst of hotels for the right sort of publicity. Those who bring business in their wake may be sure of finding their bill lightened, if only their visits are frequent enough, long enough, and accompanied by fanfare.

The publicity value of certain guests is so great that they sometimes receive a reduction of even fifty per cent, so that they pay some such ridiculously small sum as $39.79 per day. Or stay there free.

Now the publicity value of the Windsors is enormous. Politicians interest most Americans, generals interest many; but the Windsors interest every American. Particularly the Duchess. She magnetizes American women, for she embodies the American girl's dream, that wonderful Cinderella story, raised to the *n*th degree. Multiplied a millionfold, the sigh: "So romantic—he gave up a crown for her sake!" becomes in the popular press the following:

> The greatest reception hall in the world—New York Harbor—will soon be agog in greeting an uncrowned king and queen. And that queen is one of us! Let us make her proud by giving them the royal honors which his own homeland has denied.
>
> The Duke of Windsor is a man who knew what he wanted and had the courage to take it, paying the price without whining, and the Duchess is an American woman who had the self-respect to realize that a man's woman is worth more to him than his crown.

The operative words in this passage are "self-respect" and "courage." What interests the American woman must interest the American man; and it infallibly interests the American little girl, who will presently be the American woman in her turn. The Duchess of Windsor is sure of her public for at least another generation.

And a roof over her head as long as she lives—probably at a cut rate. A royal author cannot descend to plugging; but when the Duke in his memoirs compares the comforts of life aboard the *Nahlin* to those of the Waldorf-Astoria Tower, he shows his appreciation of the luxury and attention lavished on its clientele by this famous caravanserai.

The Windsor suite consists of a large living room, three bedrooms, three bathrooms, a dining room, and a kitchen. Though the Duchess has spoken of her interest in housekeeping, and has permitted herself to be photographed with a prize-winning pie, she is rarely next to the oven; not even to prepare her husband's breakfast. Reportedly the Duke enjoys doing this chore himself, having only tea, toast, and marmalade. And though he was once seen looking into a bookshop, as befits an author, his great field of interest is in the hardware stores. He is actually willing to walk miles in quest of a kitchen gadget such as a different egg-slicer, a cream-whipper or an orange-juicer.

The ducal entourage in New York consists simply of two secretaries (one male, one female, one English, one French), a butler, a valet, a chauffeur and one French maid. One of the secretaries sleeps in the apartment, and the other members of the staff have their own rooms in the hotel.

There is also the canine following. There were formerly five Companions of the Leash, bearing the humorous names of Pookie, Gremlin, Preezie, Bundles and Yackie. The Windsor dogs are mostly

Cairn terriers, famous as one-man dogs; and there is no doubt that the ex-King's canine friends are more loyal than was the greyhound of Richard II, which licked the hand of Henry IV the moment after he had deposed his cousin.

Some time ago a two-year-old terrier with the commonplace name of Thomas was added to the roll call; by way of contrast another newcomer, a pug, was named Disraeli. Her famed Prime Minister was not more devoted to Queen Victoria than is his namesake to the Duchess. No one can be surprised by Wallis' feeling for history ever since she helped to shape it; besides, she is known to enjoy reading biographies as well as culinary literature, and of course four daily papers (apart from her fashion magazines). Her friend, Miss Elsa Maxwell, recently also acquired a dog and named it Bismarck. Needless to say the pets have been nicknamed Dizzy and Bizzy.

Park Avenue and Worth Avenue strollers know the Windsors' dogs: as a rule the valet walks them, but sometimes the Duke does this, in New York or in Florida. Indeed, on Palm Beach's Worth Avenue the outing is quite a procession—the Duchess (equipped with a pink parasol not unlike that of Queen Victoria) walks ahead, stopping to gaze in shop windows; then comes the Duke, wearing a polo shirt which would arrest attention even in Cambodia, where men like their shirts to look like rainbows; and finally the ever-present obedient dogs.

It is not difficult to learn about the personal habits of the famous pair: their tastes in food, for instance. They are fond of lamb chops, steaks, game—especially partridges and Scotch grouse; puréed vegetables; but are cautious when they reach the dessert. For they regard *embonpoint* as a sort of disgrace; and living in constant fear of ungainly fat, are given to dieting. At such a period the Duchess' breakfast consists only of lemon juice in hot water and yogurt, prescribed by her "doctor," Gayelord Hauser.

Here is one of the Windsors' typical meals, according to café spies. On this particular night they had a frugal dinner, consisting of oysters Rockefeller, pressed wild duck with wild rice and vegetables, soufflé, and a bottle of Romanée Conti 1935, a heavenly Burgundy, at $14.50 per bottle. After coffee the Duke had a spot of brandy; but as he seldom addresses the personnel in a restaurant directly, the Duchess called for it.

The spot of brandy always follows the evening meal, and with it comes the peak moment in the daily life of the former King-Emperor:

he produces from one pocket a six and a half-inch cigar, and from another his own matches.

This book of matches looks like the Duke's real autobiography. The cover shows the rampant lion and the unicorn supporting a shield bearing an outsize "E" framed in the Ribbon of the Garter. The ribbon is inscribed with the famous Order's familiar motto: "*Honi soit qui mal y pense.*" Such a mock coat of arms could never be registered at the Heralds' College; but it throws a light on the Duke's secret state of mind—he is clinging to symbols of the glory he abandoned. It is nearly as significant as the tuft of horsehair burned before a newly elected Pope, horsehair being the only substance which is consumed in flame without leaving ashes; a rite which illustrates the truth that at the last nothing remains of all this world's glory, that all here on earth is passing, even the mightiest office. Only fame, good or ill, remains.

That book of matches reveals a definite trend of thought: a harking back to the past, a yearning for the native land which the Duke of Windsor first learned to know under its fairest, most romantic aspect. It suggests that he often thinks, too, of the feudal splendors of former days, and that his thoughts may be not untinged by remorse. Other Knights of the Garter prefer to show their coats of arms, not on their match covers, but where those chivalresque emblems properly belong, above their stalls in St. George's Chapel, Windsor.

Even simple people, without too many marital problems, sometimes wonder how their lives might have turned out had they remained unmarried. Socrates was once asked by a friend if he would do better to marry or to remain single; and the wisest and wittiest of sages replied: "Whichever you do, you will repent it." The Duke is no exception to the general rule: he is bound to wonder now and then how his life—and the history of the world—might have turned out if Wallis had said "No."

In the course of an interview given on his forty-ninth birthday, June 23, 1943, the Duke was jumped by a clever *Newsweek* reporter: "Sir, a personal question. You mentioned being King a few minutes ago. Have you any regrets for what you did?" The Duke fidgeted, then gulped, and finally answered: "Well, that is rather a personal question, isn't it?"

Even to those who do not take the trouble to read between the lines, this sounds like an admission. Fortunately the Duke is not often caught off his guard.

Windsor in his book claims to be something of a fatalist, saying that man is seldom master of his fate, and that when great issues are invoked, the forces let loose are beyond the limited power of personal decision.

Of what forces is he speaking? Of the whirlwind, the earthquake or the dark Atlantic storm? Of none of these. He is speaking of the great issues of history—the questions that are decided, one way or another, not by the nonrational powers of nature, but by the working of human minds and wills. The forces let loose at such times may indeed be beyond the limited control of any one man, but they are not beyond personal decision. For they are the result of decisions made by thousands, perhaps by millions of human beings: personal resolutions, and as such subject to personal control.

Elsewhere the Duke dismisses the suggestion of the "workings of fate." "The fault was not in my stars but in my genes" (*A King's Story*, Chapter VI). Here is further evidence that one cannot go on living with reproaches and with thoughts of might-have-been—one must seek some rationalization. The excellent foppery of ancient times blamed the stars; the newer plea that the fault lies in one's genes is simply a modern variant on the same theme. One must blame something. Or somebody.

Of course, there is another view. Jean-Paul Sarte, the Existentialist, has many another philosopher with him when he writes: "The free choice which a man makes himself is completely identified with what is called destiny."

Sometimes the note of reminiscence, so obvious on the Duke's matchbook, creeps into his conversation; and he will begin a sentence: "When I was King . . ." As the Windsors so often dine in public, the remark is familiar not only to café society, but also to the waiters and consequently to the world, which is always eager for such intelligence.

On rare occasions the Duke does speak directly to the staff of a restaurant. (After all, New York is not the Court of Queen Victoria, where royal etiquette forbade the Prince of Wales to speak to his own barber; so that a courtier had to be on hand to give instructions.) When recently he discovered that the *sommelier* of a fashionable restaurant, frequently visited by the ducal pair, could speak German, he chatted with him in that language, which he loves to speak. This departure from his usual reserve toward waiters apparently had an upsetting effect upon him; for at the end of the conversation he so

Guess who? . . . The Best Dressed Woman in the World, of course!

The Windsors pose with some of their canine companions.

The Windsors and Miss Elsa Maxwell

far forgot himself as to tip the astounded wine steward, giving him two dollars.

As this happened on All Fools' Day 1952, the *sommelier* naturally thought that the Duke was having his little joke. But then he recognized the miracle for what it was, and so the Duke of Windsor's two dollar bills will never leave their awed recipient. They have been framed and hung above the mantelpiece of a Bronx apartment.

Waiters, captains of waiters and wine stewards do not think that the Windsors are good tippers. "It's the honor," says a suave *maître d'hôtel* mockingly when he talks about serving them, "not the money." One wine steward who for years has helped to quench their thirst, a man well-known for his hypnotic powers over the reluctant bankroll even of a Jack Benny, admitted with a red face that he had never received largesse from the Windsors.

Though the Duke is careful with his tips, once in a while he can be generous in a good cause. For instance, during a charity drive he donated one hundred dollars to the Salvation Army, slipping the bill into his wife's collecting box as she sat in the lobby of the Waldorf. By a coincidence, at that memorable moment a *Daily News* photographer was passing by.

The Duchess is always considerate of those who serve her. When she visits the salons of Mainbocher or Carnegie, Valentina or Mr. John, to sit watching the mannequins as they parade for her, she sometimes says to the saleslady: "Do sit down, please." This is truly humane. But it may have something to do with the fact that she knows she will be shopping for a long, long time . . .

The night clerk of the Tower, a man whose very profession compels him to a certain sycophancy, stubbornly maintains that the Windsors are generous. As he unctuously puts it: "Their Royal Highnesses are very wealthy. Besides, they are extremely kind. Goodhearted. Think only of others . . ."

But people living in the glitter of café society have not only to think of others; they ought also to be mindful of what others think of them. People do not only think evil—they talk. As Louis Sobol put it in his column:

> The Duchess of Windsor has been telling friends: "We no longer care about rumors. We used to be sensitive, but not any more." Nevertheless the rumors have been growing—and among those spreading them are the so-called "friends."
>
> (New York *Journal-American*, January 31, 1951)

The Duchess' statement had a melodramatic flavor and sounded a little improbable, as well, for both she and the Duke seem to care more than ever for popular favor. And can it be said that a lady who is, by all accounts, so exceedingly well set in financial matters, was ever unduly sensitive?

Did the Duchess show any annoyance when in *Life* (June 9, 1951) Janet Flanner wrote:

> He is, according to how people feel about him, the selfish, shallow, pleasure-loving former King Edward VIII of England who let the Empire down and who, enriched with England's money, made English history pay for his marriage bed.

The rumors so assiduously spread by "friends" were denounced by other friends. Thus *The American Weekly* (December 9, 1951) carried a story: "Will the Windsors Ever Separate?" by Elsa Maxwell. But scandalmongers who turned to the article by this famous hostess were disappointed. For Miss Maxwell concluded her outspoken piece:

> It is natural for people to gossip—even when they see the Windsors apart on a single occasion. But remember this man gave up his throne for the woman he loved. She loved him enough to give him up if necessary...Will the Duke and Duchess of Windsor ever separate? No, never!

Russell Nype sufficiently brought out the absurdity of such gossip when he revealed that he was merely the Duchess' mascot—she had nicknamed him "Harvey." "What could there be romantic between a middle-aged Duchess and a young man who reminds her of an invisible rabbit?" was his pertinent question. (New York *Journal-American*, October 19, 1951.)

It is true that when the wiseacres see in the columns that the Duchess again went out with a friend, they remark to each other: "Aha! Here it comes—she is sure to be swept off her feet by that dark man in the cards!" But there is no dark man in the Duchess' deck, and to the thoughtful observer it is obvious that there never will be. A completely complete woman, who is haughty and ambitious, who has always lived for herself, keeps away from the whirlwind of passion. For one thing, it ruffles the hairdo.

Ambition excludes affection. *Affaires de coeur* simply do not happen to people who concentrate on worldly riches, and who take a one-sided view of what makes for happiness. The Duchess finds gratification in recognition and plush security, in ostentation, and in being The Best-Dressed Woman in the World. She had one of the most amazing romances in history, and she intends to hold on to it. Who could come after a King of England! Who could be more eligible than the Duke of Windsor? And who could be more loyal a subject to his queen regnant?

Not that the Duchess is indifferent to men, or that men are indifferent to her. With them, her greatest asset is one of the best-known and most effective weapons in the female armory: she has the gift of making each in turn feel that she is interested only in him, and in what he says. With other fascinating ladies she is naturally and openly antagonistic; and she cannot bear that the flattery and attention she receives from her men friends should be shared by other women. Not long ago a columnist of the New York *Post* asked her, not maliciously either, how she felt about younger women. "Poor dears!" she lamented. "They have all their mistakes before them."

This public statement conveys the idea that the Duchess has learned by experience; also that in private "someone" is held responsible for her "mistake."

A woman who affects to pity but actually dislikes her own sex, especially its younger, good-looking members, firmly believes in sole ownership, insists upon it, and sees that she gets it. Such a woman's avocation is not romance. Far from it.

It is easy to see why the Duke, no longer an adolescent, for some time left the Duchess to her own amusements, to the bantering conversation in which she delights, and to a continual round of pleasure-seeking. It had dawned on the former King that there is consolation in work for nearly every ill.

Embracing one of the few professions open to the unskilled—memoir writing—the Duke labored hard and long on the task of producing *A King's Story*. Every producer must work hard: he has to blend the abilities and various talents of many people into one harmonious whole, for unity must characterize the completed work. As the reader already knows, the Duke had to unify the work of no fewer than thirty-seven people: press lords and politicians, researchers and typists to that number, helped him to remember the facts about his own life and put them down. Above all, he had the able and experienced assistance of the senior editor of a well-known magazine.

Naturally such a project could not be kept secret. The intimate friends of the Duke and Duchess found the news exciting indeed, for some of them were aware that Wallis had written her own version of the World's Greatest Romance. With becoming modesty, Her Grace at that time thought that her story ought not to be made public until both the principals had passed on. She revealed to her Kentucky cousins that the precious manuscript had been deposited in the vault of an American bank, to appear twenty-five years after her own and her husband's death.

But twenty-five years is a long time to wait, even for such a literary titbit. And *A King's Story*, served as a welcome *hors d'oeuvre*, was enough to stimulate the American public's appetite. When the memoirs appeared in serial form, people could hardly wait for Friday morning and their magazine.

The stir caused by these articles must have led to the publication of *A King's Story* in book form, even if there had been no earlier plan to do this. The tedious tasks of revision and proofreading fell partly to the Duke: during the months of hostile publicity already described, in 1950 and 1951, he often stayed at home, foregoing dinner invitations in order to complete his work.

Meanwhile the sight of the Duchess doing the rounds without the Duke set tongues wagging again, and it was whispered that, after all, there might be strife in the Windsor menage. But, as Cholly Knickerbocker assured his readers, nothing could be further from the truth. The Duke's publishers, wrote Cholly, had been after him to deliver the revised manuscript, and were quite put out that the work had not been finished before the holidays. *A King's Story*, being a monumental book, required much work; and accordingly the Duke had resolved never to "hit the sack" later than midnight until the end of the year. But he would not deprive his wife of her usual pleasures, and the Duchess was seen about town, squired by one or other of the Windsors' friends.

The anxiety caused the Duke's publishers by the delay was eventually relieved. *A King's Story* appeared, well heralded and with its cover enriched by three coats of arms—those of Edward Princeps, of Edward Rex Imperator, and of Edward Duke of Windsor. It does not seem likely that the Duke of Norfolk, Earl Marshal of England, and the authority on such matters, was consulted as to the validity of this usage.

The major part of the great publicity was free; and paid advertising was on an appropriate scale, including full-page ads in the book supplements of Sunday papers. The cost to the publishers must have been considerable, but so was the reward. In October 1951 David Dempsey could tell the readers of the New York *Times Book Review* that "*A King's Story* has probably outsold all other books by English royalty combined." That is very likely. The Duke's book spent seven months at the top of the best-seller lists.

Obviously there had to be a literary cocktail party at the Waldorf to bring the book out, with an opportunity for the American press *en masse* to meet the Duke at his best. The New York *Times* commented next morning that the Duke abstained, and this austere newspaper recalled that there had been a time (during the abdication period) when he had not. Other papers did not reach back into the past for such trivial details, but made much of the fact that the Duke's signature, the simple "Edward P." on the front page of his book, enriched Windsor by one hundred dollars per copy.

This inexpensive favor was extended to some three hundred and fifty friends of the Duke, who had been tactfully approached by circular letter to secure the de luxe, limited edition. This differed from that offered to hoi polloi, simply and solely by the addition of the ducal autograph.

The attitude of literary men toward finance is subject to change. Contemplating the $35,000 harvested in one sweep by the Duke of Windsor, one recalls another English author of title. Lord Byron, when he was offered £600 for the copyright of his first great success, "Childe Harold's Pilgrimage," indignantly refused the money, and signed over the copyright to his needy friend Dallas with the words: "I will never receive money for my writings!" He weakened later in this respect, but then this lord, who had so much feeling for *noblesse oblige*, had no obliging family to fall back on.

However, the Duke published in the United States, and in an age in which *noblesse oblige* seems to have been forgotten. He was justified in expecting not only an enthusiastic reception for his book, but also financial rewards for himself. "Childe Harold's Pilgrimage" was child's play compared to *A King's Story*—had not an American woman captured a British King, succeeding where even General Washington had failed? England remained to be conquered by the memoirs, and in the autumn of 1951 *A King's Story* made its London bow, under the chaperonage of a celebrated firm. The public received it with gratifying curiosity—advance sales numbered 59,700 copies. The reviews of the book showed varied reactions. The London *Daily Herald*, as might be expected of Labor's official organ, found it safe to support

an ex-King, enjoying the opportunity to crack even at the long-dead
Conservative administration of 1936. But the general trend of comment was not wholly congratulatory. The New York *Herald Tribune*
summed up perhaps a little too briefly:

> The Press reception [in England] ranged from polite to quite enthu-
> siastic, the reviews saying, in effect, that it's certainly an interesting
> book, but that Prime Minister Baldwin was quite right back in 1936
> when he insisted that Edward VIII couldn't marry Mrs. Simpson and
> stay on his throne.
>
> (October 21, 1951)

Plans were made for the royal author to visit London for the British
publication of his memoirs. As guest of honor at a banquet planned
for September 28, 1951, by the Book Publishers Representatives'
Association, he was to deliver an address which would, it was hoped,
be broadcast. But the British Broadcasting Company refused co-
operation, and so the speech was never made.

The Duke had intended to journey to England via Paris, where the
Duchess would await his return from what both supposed would be a
brief yet profitable business trip. But at Paris alarming news reached
them: King George was ill. In June he was known to be suffering with
lung trouble; now it was announced that he had agreed to be operated
on. On September 23 the operation took place, and by September 24,
when the Duke arrived in London, the doctors could tell an anxious
world that the King had passed a restful night.

It was impossible for the Duke to boost his book and so revive the
delicate question of the abdication at such a time. But as in 1936, so
now, Lord Beaverbrook was at hand to help in his own way. *The
Sunday Express* gave the text of the intended speech. In it, His Royal
Highness showed that he had lost none of his gift for assessing and
challenging public opinion: "It seems in the eyes of some," he gently
complained, "that in writing it I have done something very terrible
. . . It's the first one that gets you into trouble. After a man has
written two or more books people get used to it."

So far as is known, the only trouble caused to the Duke by his first
book has been the filling-in of an author's income tax form under the
capital gains tax or the Margaret Mitchell Law. And he is apparently
determined that people shall get used to it, for six months later the
editor of the New York *Mirror*, Jack Lait, could write in the April 2,
1952 issue that:

> The Duke of Windsor likes authoring. He is already compiling notes
> for his next book and the ghostwriter has been chosen.

Mr. Lait did not tell his readers if the Duke's chief editor was once
again to haunt the Waldorf Tower; and he left them to decide for
themselves how welcome this quasi-royal competition would be to
those professional writers who, not being able to afford ghosts, are
forced to labor over their books themselves.

To return to the undelivered speech, the Duke concluded:

> While "A King's Story" is strictly non-fiction, I do believe that, as
> far as its last chapters are concerned, it is in a personal sense a romance
> . . . I only wish that I had thought to add the old familiar ending of
> all romances: "And they lived happily ever after."

There could be no doubt that the Duchess was living happily.
While the Duke visited his mother, who had been seen passing with
anxious face to and from Buckingham Palace before the operation;
while he waited for admission to the sickroom of his brother and King,
the Duchess found time hanging heavy on her hands. Fortunately
Paris is a place where a gay and amusing lady need not lack for distraction, and Wallis could summon an aide-de-camp of several years'
experience to escort her. Soon Cholly Knickerbocker was informing
his readers that:

> The Duchess of Windsor was recently at *chez* Florence, one of Paris'
> most frequented nite spots, with Jimmy Donahue. He ordered an
> enormous bunch of red roses for her. At the time she was waving a large
> feather fan. She put it on the table and said to the girl with the flowers:
> "Put the flowers on the fan." Isn't it amazing? The Donahue roses on
> the Prince of Wales' feathers!
>
> (New York *Journal-American*, October 15, 1951)

When the Duke returned to Paris, relieved that his brother was now
out of danger, he decided that this was enough of *La Vie Parisienne*.
Her husband longed to be alone with Wallis, away from the city,
from any land even, and so, hiring a smaller yacht than the *Nahlin*,
they went cruising in Southern waters. They had to make the best
of things until they could go back to New York.

6

The Grand Tour

Stick close to your desks, and never go to sea,
And you all may be Rulers of the Queen's Navee.
— GILBERT AND SULLIVAN:
H.M.S. Pinafore

MUCH of the Windsors' energy is spent in going from one place to another. In this respect they do not differ from those other rich people who seek diversion in wandering. But since the Duchess likes the Babel of New York, they always return to the Waldorf, their principal stopover. When going to Europe or coming back to America they do not fly, for though the Duke is fond of air travel the Duchess dislikes it, and so they go by boat, usually by a Cunard liner.

Although they do not own one, they love the exclusive atmosphere of yachts. They have had much experience of yachting, for owners either invite them on cruises, or offer them the use of their vessels. Mr. Axel Wenner-Gren, the Swedish industrialist, was once such a host; the Windsors enjoyed his yacht during their sojourn in the Bahamas. But then this friendship was buffeted by the waves of chance, and finally broke on the rocks of circumstance.

They have also been the guests of Mr. and Mrs. Joe Davies, on their luxurious yacht *Sea Cloud*. However, since 1949, neither the *Sea Cloud*, nor the Davieses have been visited by the ducal couple. Since that year it might have embarrassed them to recall that this yacht owner was formerly Ambassador to the Soviet Union. To be sure, Mr. Davies did an outstanding job in diplomacy, perfectly suited to the period of his appointment, but times have changed, and as so often happens in life, he has had to suffer for having carried out his mission to the best of his ability. So some people who entertain peculiar notions about loyalty and public relations refrained from stepping aboard the *Sea Cloud*, and in 1952 this "floating white elephant," which needs a crew of seventy to operate it at a cost of $1-million a year, was offered for sale.

There were other, perhaps not as grand but untainted yachts the Windsors could sail on, free, such as that of Mr. Wrightsman of oil millions; but an irreverent English lady in 1951 actually insisted on chartering hers to the Windsors for money!

The next best thing to a graceful yacht is a private train. One of the closest American friends of the Windsors is Mr. Robert R. Young, the banker and railroad magnate (who moreover was never Ambassador in Moscow); he often invites and entertains the ducal pair on his train. The exclusive Windsors frequently follow the travel trend of the tourist, except that they tour in a majestic fashion. Going in the Young Pullman to New Orleans or Louisville or the Greenbrier, in Virginia, certainly cannot remind the Duke of his horrible journey through Yugoslavia in 1936.

In 1950, after a hunting trip to Mexico, they returned in the plush train by way of New Orleans, and there stopped to see the famous Carnival and Mardi Gras. Naturally the historic Creole town was happy to see them; and since many doors are open to the Windsors, they soon found a friend there, the celebrated author Frances Parkinson Keyes. The Duke and Duchess were the guests of honor at a mint julep party at the writer's house before attending dinner at Antoine's, this shrine of epicures. Later they all went to the Carnival Ball, where the Duchess dropped a perfect curtsy before the Carnival King, though he was only an elected monarch. Mrs. Keyes, who wrote a report on the Windsors' visit, could tell her readers that New Orleans —a town that showed its partiality for ex-emperors nearly one hundred and forty years ago, when one of its wealthy citizens offered asylum to Napoleon Bonaparte—rang with praise of the Duchess. Native and tourist alike had succumbed completely to the irresistible spell of the lovely lady for whom a real king had willingly relinquished the mightiest throne in the world, declaring ever after that he had never regretted this act.

In the same year, when the people of the United States showed firmly that they would no longer appease Communism—the year in which that "little skirmish" in Korea began—the Windsors supported the popular movement, and openly displayed their anti-Communist feeling. They appeared at a City Hall affair, at which the disturbers of the world were denounced. But this seems to have been almost their only active and public help to democratic propaganda so direly needed nowadays.

Nonpolitical parties were more to the taste of the Windsors; the

Duchess here is in her element and much sought after, together with her *bons mots*. She once arrived at a dinner given by Miss Elsa Maxwell, wearing a black velvet gown without a single jewel! But their absence went unnoticed—as Miss Maxwell pointed out in print—for Wallis' wit sparkled sufficiently.

An unusual event made that mid-century year, 1950, even more memorable—all of a sudden the Duchess dropped out of circulation. Of course soon after the Duchess of Windsor was missing from the Waldorf, the press discovered her: she was in a hospital, awaiting an operation. As has been said before, nearly a dozen eminent physicians and surgeons were called into consultation, with a worried Duke in constant attendance. He was photographed on the steps of the hospital as he went in, and again as he came out. His expression was one of anguish, and he had the full sympathy of the American public. Upstairs, the feeling was different. The Duke sent his wife a daily gift of American Beauty roses, and himself brought caviar, such a welcome food to the jaded palate of the sick. Ailing neighbors of the Duchess could not help overhearing this fragment of conversation:

"This caviar is salty."

"But, darling, this is fresh Beluga."

"It is salty, I tell you!"

"But it's the finest Beluga I could get, darling."

"This caviar is salty!"

"But, darling . . ."

At this point a solicitous nurse closed the Duchess' door.

Fortunately Wallis was soon discharged from the hospital in better health than ever and was brought home to the Waldorf to recuperate. The Duke went to Florida, and of course this trip led to further silly gossip. In fact, when he arrived at Palm Beach he was asked by a fresh newshawk: "And where is the Duchess, hmm?" The Duke was furious. "She is sick in New York!" he shouted. "I wish she could be here with me! It's quite difficult to be without one's wife, and doubly so when she is ill!" However, the day after this outburst, the Duchess was able to appear without assistance or difficulty, at Cartier's on Fifth Avenue.

Traveling has always an element of adventure; one of the most memorable journeys undertaken by the Windsors was made in May 1951. It was a sort of *à là recherche du temps perdu* visit to Louisville, Kentucky, a kind of testing of Southern hospitality, to see if this was the same as ever. The Windsors were invited by Mr. Young to attend the Kentucky Derby at Louisville, traveling in his private train; but the Derby, which is run in May, allows for a traditional display of private trains—well, as many as there are left in the United States, what with heavy taxation and the mounting prices. It is also traditional that those who arrive in these trains do not sleep in their rolling bedrooms, but are invited to the house parties which go on for the whole week. The Windsors slept in their Pullman.

The most famous sportscaster of the United States, who comments on the Derby, a few days before the event phoned the local social arbiter, a racing stable owner and principal shareholder in historic Churchill Downs, suggesting that she give a party in honor of the Windsors. He received a very cold reply. "I will not give a party for them. But here are the telephone numbers of two people who might."

One of the two people happened to be a second cousin of the Duchess. The other was a young matron who, before marrying one of the richest men in the state, had a brief stage experience. When contacted, both agreed to entertain the Windsors. The Duchess' cousin—who also married a millionaire—arranged a dinner for eighteen, and sent to the bank for her gold service. When, at the last moment, instead of eighteen, twenty-four guests turned up, a messenger was despatched posthaste to the bank manager's home, asking him to go back to his vault and dole out six additional gold covers. Thus dinner at eight took place at ten. Otherwise the evening went off without any further mishap.

At the other party there also occurred an embarrassing moment. The society lady with a theatrical background was the only person who curtsied to the Duchess during her entire Kentucky stay; and this is still matter for a smile. One might expect to meet with more curtsying in Kentucky, but owing to the spirit of independence in that state, this ceremony is not observed there.

Another invitation took the Windsors to the *must* party of Derby week, given at the exclusive River Valley Club, immediately after the famous race. The Duchess, when requested to honor this gala with her presence, first resisted, but finally let herself be persuaded. This party is a grand but crowded affair, and seemingly did not please the Duchess; but the Duke, thinking that he might go unnoticed in the crowd, liked it very well. Wallis was vigilant though. Catching her husband several times, she spoke to him in a determined way:

"Put that down!"

"Yes, dear."

"Put it down, I said!"

"Yes, dear."

The Duchess' attempted return to the past was not a notable success, one way or another. The Windsors went back to New York, and as in every year, when the weather changed and early summer brought with it excess humidity, they embarked for France, there to spend some time in their Paris house, 85 Rue de la Faisanderie, near the Bois de Boulogne.

Although the affection felt by the Windsors for France is seasonal and changes with the weather, it is true love. But as the piercing proverb phrases it: "In love, there is always one who loves and one who is loved." The feeling does not seem to be reciprocated. This is the more remarkable, when one compares the indifferent attitude adopted toward the former Edward VIII with the warmth shown to the late Edward VII. The Duke's grandfather was known and welcomed in France as an irresistible and irrepressible Don Juan, who as Prince courted the ladies of Paris, and as King successfully wooed *la belle France;* whose gallantries were the more acceptable, in that they expressed a real sympathy for the French nation, and covered, while they did not disguise, a most able political diplomacy. The Duke, in the role of an obedient middle-class husband, a *bon bourgeois* spouse, presents, to a nation content with the Code Napoleon, a less attractive appearance. With no political compensations whatever.

This indifference is rather ungrateful of the French, for in spite of the acid comments of the people and the press, the Windsors confer benefits by their visits, which never do any harm to the various resorts and hotels they bless by their presence. Far from it. Wherever they go, there is an upward surge in trading. Snob appeal never fails to attract the smart set. People are morbidly curious about royalty, as the Duke sometimes says—though he does nothing to discourage them—and his book of memoirs increased the interest.

But even before the appearance of that remarkable volume, the presence of the Windsors could ensure the success of a season. In the postwar period, for instance, the Basque resort of Biarritz was hoping for a much-needed revival, and invited the Windsors to honor it with a visit. The Duke and Duchess obliged, and Biarritz promptly woke up; as did nearby San Sebastian, whither Mr. Donahue, who now was the constant companion of the Duchess, escorted the Duchess while the Duke played golf or sought other relaxation.

Similarly, when, as occasionally happens, a resort like America's own Greenbrier needs a lift, the Duke is not reluctant to play the eighteen holes there, and one of the heiresses of the Anheuser-Busch beer millions joyously and dutifully holds a parasol over the Duchess' sensitive head as she follows her husband round the links.

However, the Duke's golf playing is not confined to the course at the Greenbrier. He plays wherever he goes. In November 1951 for instance, he went round a Paris course with Mr. Berlin, the *totum factorum* of Hearst publications, and an excellent golfer. Windsor's own game was improving, so much so that he has been mentioned as a possible open tournament player; and he did not choose Mr. Berlin for a partner because he wanted to improve his relations with the press—the relations between the ex-Emperor and the Hearst Empire have always been friendly.

Still, even in the Hearst papers some editorial writers have come out from time to time with unpleasant little pieces. Especially since the more modern and vigorous young "Bill" Hearst inherited his Empire. There was, for instance, the columnist who played on the theme of typical British understatement when he reported the Duke as saying, when asked to dance shortly after his brother's death: "Can't. Death in the family, you know . . ."

Much about the same time another column strongly criticized, on purely professional grounds, the Duke's attempt to play the drum; as a drummer, it was said, he was an amateur.

The Duke, who so vividly described his father's shooting, enjoys this sport as well as golfing and drumming; so in the winter of 1951 he went hunting in Germany. However, his visit to the land of his remote ancestors did not last long, nor was it attended by any great éclat.

For in 1951 the Duchess seemed to regain her calm, and to seek tranquillity and even seclusion.This surprising change in her demeanor might have been due to any one of several reasons, or to a combination of several of them. The illness of King George VI had distressed his brother, and so perhaps the Duke at last exerted himself to tell his wife that in the circumstances, she must not appear in the gay places of Paris with Mr. Donahue. Further, his book had just come out in England, and her conduct might injure the sales. He himself was in need of care, reported to be suffering from stomach ulcers; for worry is a known cause of this particular illness.

However, the most probable and most important reason for the Duchess' discretion was that the Windsors' old champion, Winston Churchill, was now once again in the saddle as a result of the General

Election of 1951, and the Duke was hoping to obtain an official post. What position could be offered no one could guess, but it was rumored that the Windsors thought that the ambassadorship to Washington would be suitable. He most certainly did not want another governorship on a Godforsaken island—on that point his wife was adamant.

But though the Duke went back and forth between London and Paris, he always returned empty-handed. Doubts had again risen about the ceremony of "kissing hands," and the appearance of his lady at Buckingham Palace.

Eventually the Windsor Team reappeared in New York, and as if to show its pleasure at the return of the beloved lovers, the Big Town was friendlier than before. Columnists ceased heckling them, and even the incorruptible Walter Winchell declared an armistice. A New Deal must have been made, probably by one of the Duke's friends, a gentleman of the long robe certainly not less astute and worldly-wise than Sir Walter Monckton had been.

The Windsors were seen everywhere together, even if there were others in the party. On New Year's Eve 1951, before attending the Miller affair, they were at the Sherry Netherland Hotel's Carnival Room, the cynosure of neighboring eyes; as the clock struck midnight, the Duke rose and kissed the Duchess, who responded with a wry smile, half-pleased and half-embarrassed by this public embrace. Afterward the ducal couple did the rounds with Ethel Merman and Russell Nype—the latter's remark about "a middle-aged Duchess" had apparently been forgiven and forgotten.

But though some things had gone down the stream of time, other and pleasanter ones remained. An air of gentle reminiscence hung about their frequent visits to El Morocco, where the Duke asked for certain Viennese songs so old and so little-known that Charles Inwald, the famous Viennese pianist, who remembers all of them, had to pause for recollection. When his evocation of the past had ended, the Duke showed his pleasure by giving a copy of his own bookplate to Mr. Inwald, to be kept carefully in the latter's copy of *A King's Story*—now rendered doubly precious by this unique addition. The plate showed the Duke of Windsor's coat of arms, with the Garter motto and his signature "Edward," all encircled by a gold frame. There was no mention of horsehair or of $100 as this symbol of past chivalry changed hands.

The Duchess, too, has her memories. So varied a life as hers cannot be without "remembrance of things past." Perhaps it was the recollection of an impertinent member of Parliament which about this time led her to limit her innocent pleasure in looking for "something simple" in the shops of the New York dressmakers, milliners and jewelers. Or she restrained herself because Mr. Churchill was on his way over to seek American aid; anything that might be misinterpreted as ostentatious display by the jealous minds of steakless Britons must be avoided.

In this harsh world, however, virtue is not always rewarded, and the Duchess' self-restraint does not seem to have produced the results she was probably hoping for. Mr. Churchill received the Duke of Windsor at Mr. Baruch's house, where the Prime Minister stayed as a guest. Tactfully, the Duke arrived to see the British statesman in an English Rolls-Royce. Onlookers speculated as to the possible owner of this magnificent chariot, and some hinted that it was the property of Thelma Chrysler Foy.

The Duke had promised to the waiting photographers that he would ask Mr. Churchill to pose for them, but he does not seem to have found the Prime Minister in an acquiescent mood, for there were no pictures. And if anything more than cigars and talk passed between the two gentlemen, the press was not admitted to the secret.

However, conjecture on this conference did not last long. For a short time after Mr. Churchill's departure, news of mighty moment involved the Duke in keen personal suffering. King George VI died.

It was noteworthy that the American press did not find it necessary to tell its readers "the King of England is dead." As if there were but one King, those two words "The King" meant, to Americans as to Englishmen, only one man, the irreproachable Monarch.

This fact throws a flood of light upon the mental and political process of democracy. George VI had lived in an age plentifully supplied with upstart rulers who towered above their countries like Colossi, while petty men crept under their huge legs to find themselves graves, frequently compulsory graves. With no *coup d'état* to establish him above the law, with no truncheoned thugs nor secret police to enforce his will, by character alone George VI had so impressed himself upon the mind of his time, that these two words "the King" called forth, from a nation born in war against a king and maintained in war against dictators, a response as immediate and hearty as in any British mess, when the colonel calls for the loyal toast.

America, which has long repudiated the principle of monarchy and now withstands the power of dictatorship, could thus express itself upon the men who in our day variously embodied, or still embody, these various principles:

> He [George VI] his wife and family became the symbols of things
> cruel men must not be permitted to change.
> (New York *Times Magazine*, February 17, 1952)

These words (quoted by the British economist Barbara Ward in an article, "Britain's Timeless Tradition") were taken from a small paper in the American West, the heartland of the United States. They came from the heart.

The Duke received the sorrowful news in his Waldorf Tower apartment, and very shortly left New York on the *Queen Mary* to attend his brother's funeral. On embarking he said that this was indeed a tragic journey, and doubly so because he was not being accompanied by his wife. But he kept in touch with the Duchess by ship-to-shore telephone.

On his arrival at Southampton the Duke read a carefully prepared statement to the waiting pressmen:

> This is indeed a sad arrival in my country. I have crossed the Atlantic
> for the funeral of a dear brother, and to comfort Her Majesty Queen
> Mary, my mother, in the overwhelming sorrow which has overtaken
> my family and the Commonwealth of British Nations.
>
> As we mourn a much-beloved monarch our hearts go out to the
> widowed Queen Mother and her two daughters in their grief.
>
> Youth and courage are great assets in this precarious time in which
> Elizabeth II begins her reign. And at the outset she has the help and
> support of her husband Philip and the loyalty and good wishes of all
> her people.
>
> God save the Queen!

The Duke of Windsor had been accompanied by one of his New York attorneys, Mr. Henry Walter, a fact which aroused speculation about Windsor's financial future. From Southampton he drove to Marlborough House, where he arrived weary and white-faced, to comfort his mother. Later he visited Buckingham Palace, where he was received by the Queen Mother and Queen Elizabeth II. On this sad occasion, the two Queens wished to show all consideration to the self-exiled eldest brother, whom they regarded as one of the chief mourners. While this courtesy meeting was taking place, Britons by

According to rules: the Windsors attend a prize fight with the Marquess of Queensberry.

The Cruising Windsors. The Duke seemed curious—the Duchess was cool and carefree.

When Wallis was counselor at a boarding school.

Wallis Warfield's Biddle Street Home in Baltimore, Md.

the tens of thousands were filing past his brother's coffin. In these vast throngs of grieving subjects, in the murmur of their voices and the rustle of their feet as they moved forward, a few paces at a time, through sleet and rain and snow, could be seen and heard the panegyric of King George VI—not an innovator, not a reformer, simply "George the Good."

Windsor's place in the funeral procession had of course been fixed by ancient etiquette. As one of the four Royal Dukes, he was to walk in line with the Dukes of Edinburgh, Gloucester, and Kent.

But there was one problem to be solved: should he appear in civilian mourning or in uniform? Unfortunately the ex-Emperor was ill-advised. Many thought that the Duke of Windsor, whose uniforms of kingly days had been stored in mothballs at Windsor ever since 1936, should on this sad occasion have shown himself to the nation he had disappointed in civilian clothes. But he chose instead the uniform of an admiral.

On his accession, Edward VIII had automatically become Commander-in-Chief of all the armed forces—Admiral of the Fleet, Field Marshal in the Army, and Air Marshal in the Royal Air Force. By abdicating he had also, automatically, given up these titles, with all others, even if he had signed no separate document to this effect. As a matter of fact, on his return to the Army for a brief period in 1939 he received a new rank: he became a brigadier general, with the right to the appropriate uniform.

This being so, it is perhaps a little curious that the Monarch who had abandoned his country in its greatest peril decided to wear the uniform of an Admiral of the Fleet, the same that he had worn as King at his father's funeral. As though nothing had happened in the intervening fifteen years! But perhaps this decision arose from a modest desire on his part not to compete with his brother, the Duke of Gloucester, who wore the uniform of a general. So the Duke of Windsor marched in the funeral procession in an admiral's uniform, thus outranking the Queen's husband, Lieutenant Commander the Duke of Edinburgh!

Pageantry is a touchy business; while considering the sensibilities of one person, one may unhappily tread on the toes of another. But the Royal Dukes apparently wasted no word on the matter; complete silence reigned between them before, during and after the funeral.

However, the former King was not received in complete silence by his erstwhile subjects. As he reached Marlborough House, a woman had called out: "Welcome home, Eddie," but this sentiment was not at all widespread. The bitterness that in 1936 had uttered itself in the cry, "He let us down!" found expression in 1952. The Duke might or might not be entitled to the uniform he was wearing; the commentators in the crowd did not stress such niceties, and most of them were uninformed on the subject, anyhow. But one London columnist remarked that whereas the greatcoat of Admiral Lord Louis Mountbatten, the hero of the Burmese campaign, was in accord with recent regulations, the Duke's watch coat was not; the writer explained this by pointing out that in fifteen years, the time that had elapsed since the Duke last donned naval uniform, regulations have changed, and the watch coat has become obsolete. This was succinctly put.

Other opinions were more openly expressed, and may be summed up in the words of a highly placed English lady recounting details of the funeral to an American acquaintance:

"Admiral indeed! Everybody knew that the Duke of Windsor threw the Crown of England in the gutter, and that George VI picked it up and polished it."

The British are a cruel race—certain matters they can neither forget nor forgive. Even if they can live and die like Spartans.

So it was not surprising that the Duke made haste to return to the help and support of the woman he loved. When he reached New York on the *Queen Elizabeth*, Wallis was waiting for him, suitably attired in deep mourning.

A little later, the Windsors made a visit to Florida, and the Duke's grief was respected by his friends. Complete retirement, with its opportunities for brooding, might have been very bad for his health; so the ducal couple, while observing the period of mourning decreed by Elizabeth II, permitted themselves some social relaxation. They dined with small groups at first; then, as time went on, the Duke resumed his golf and the Duchess' pink parasol was once more seen about. Old and tried friends gave parties of eighteen or more, at which the Duchess' sprightly charm had full play.

Almost exactly a year after the Duke attended his brother's funeral, very disturbing news reached him from his native land: his oldest and thoroughly reliable friend was seriously ill. This friend, of course, was his mother, Queen Mary, her gracious Majesty. The word "gracious" is used nowadays indiscriminately. Originally this adjective was selected by the compilers of the Prayer Book to typify the virtues and charms of an English Queen; and Queen Mary fully deserved the description.

The Duke of Windsor described his mother as being old-fashioned and clinging to the Victorian traditions. Others, also close to the Queen, people with more acute judgment than the Duke's, said that Her Majesty was familiar with the social outlook of all classes. In her girlhood she even had firsthand knowledge of poverty—her father, the Duke of Teck, was a poor prince; and his mother, the Princess of Cambridge, spent the greater part of the modest amount Parliament granted her, on charity.

The gracious Queen, who, notwithstanding those funny hats and umbrellas, drew a deeper-throated cheer from the usually un-demonstrative English crowds than any other royal personage, was gravely ill. Her son was summoned from the side of his Duchess to the sickbed of his eighty-five-year-old mother.

Queen Mary lingered on for some days and then death came to her while she was asleep, tactfully, almost delicately. The news of her death was learned with universal sorrow; and many British men and women cried, for they had real affection in their hearts for this most gracious Majesty.

Between his mother's death and her funeral the Duke of Windsor hopped over to Paris to take care of some errands for the Duchess.

As Queen Mary's obsequies were not a State occasion but a family affair, organized by the Lord Chamberlain and not by the Earl Marshal, precedence was given to the Duke of Windsor as the late Queen's eldest son. Once again he marched in the procession in the uniform of an admiral, abreast with the other Royal Dukes, Gloucester Edinburgh, and Kent. And as to commemorate the sad event, Gloucester made up with his self-exiled brother, even if only for a few days: for twenty-four hours after the final rites, the Duke of Windsor was already on his way to New York to join his wife.

London press reports about the perennially newsworthy Duke of Windsor were varied, depending on who owned the particular pub-lication. One faction, loyal to the Duke, clamored for his return and for his settling down in England; but it failed to give a single word of advice as to where the Duchess should settle down. The other faction put forth the speculation that with the passing of Queen Mary the Duke's last and strongest connection had been severed and that the Duke will now seldom if ever go back to England.

At any rate, pictures taken at the funeral of his mother show a tragic-faced Duke of Windsor, extremely crushed and broken. A week later when he arrived in New York, at the sight of his waiting Duchess, his expression was joyful and he even managed a big smile for the photo-reporters.

A great and gracious Queen, a kind, strong lady, who always discharged the duties of her high station queenly yet warmheartedly, died . . .

7

A Duchess Is Born

As good luck would have it.
—SHAKESPEARE:
The Merry Wives of Windsor

THE Duchess of Windsor's birthplace is claimed by almost as many communities as is that of Christopher Columbus—she is alleged to have been born near Baltimore, Maryland; in Washington, D. C.; in Monterey, Blue Ridge Summit, Pennsylvania; and even smoky Pittsburgh once had the boldness to contend for the honor!

The most probable place is Monterey, Blue Ridge Summit. Teakle Wallis Warfield, the Duchess' father, came to this mountain health resort a sick man; and with him came his expectant wife.

According to one version, that of the Baltimore *News Post* of November 13, 1936, Mr. Warfield died when the little girl was only a few months old; according to another, she was a posthumous child. Historians will have difficulty in solving the mystery of the Duchess' birth date, for she has a marked objection to speaking of her childhood and youth.

Wallis Windsor is said to have been born on June 19, 1896. Self-styled authorities upon the subject insist that she was born six years earlier, in 1890. (The author has in his possession two letters to this effect—but both are from women who naturally envy a fortunate Duchess.) If she is really over sixty, all women of the same age, and indeed many who are ten years younger, must envy her, for she looks around forty-five.

That her appearance so belies her age is no doubt due to a life of leisure, to her epicurean eating, and to the fastidious care she gives herself. For instance, she enjoys the invigorating services of a masseuse every day; the coiffeur calls twice daily; and there are rumors of visits to the Park Avenue offices of a famous endocrinologist-geriatrician. (The new science of geriatrics is concerned with making people look younger and live longer. Stalin employed a whole academy of endocrinologist-geriatricians.) Add the glamour of a wardrobe rivaling that of Elizabeth Tudor—at least one hundred dresses and suits a year!—and it is not too difficult to account for the Duchess' triumph over time.

After her husband's death Mrs. Alice Warfield—some chroniclers changed the name to Alys when it became news—went through a period of semiprivation. For a while she could not even look after little Bessie (who was later renamed Wallis), and the baby lived with her grandparents or with various relatives. Why mince words? Bessie was born into shabby-genteel poverty, and as a natural result the hunger for security has been a compelling force in her life.

In 1908 Mrs. Warfield married a second time, Mr. John Freeman Raisin, Jr., son of a Baltimore politico. He was well-to-do, as every good politician's son should be, and the standards of Alice and her daughter suddenly changed. Unfortunately Mr. Raisin died two years after the marriage, leaving little or no money. Not until 1923 did Wallis' mother marry again, becoming Mrs. Warfield Raisin Allen. With all these impressive names she obtained a post at the fashionable Chevy Chase Club in Maryland as the club hostess. She had had experience with paying guests before; and this was a great help to her in this position.

It is easy to understand why the Duchess is reluctant to speak of a childhood of so many violent ups and downs. Who can depict the sufferings and longings of a shabby-genteel young girl? The frequent embarrassments, the rankling contrast between her lot and that of others, of a girl whose mother can find just enough money for the "right" school, but not enough for the trimmings that go with it? Baltimore and the milieu of Bessie's life were notably snobbish.

Here was the humiliation, with perhaps slights and snubs like salt rubbed into the wound, that is said to be so important for the development of strength of will, a strength that could remain unbending and stubborn in the midst of the most frightful havoc; or that could be, alternatively, the root of egocentricity, materialism, a determination to succeed hardening into mania, a fanatical longing to become better than anyone around, and to return to the homeland in the role of a fairy queen. The inferiority complex which was to attain such tremendous proportions surely had its birth in Baltimore.

One can picture the teen-age Bessie walking from 212 East Biddle Street, where she lived, to Arundel, a day school which no longer exists. Covering the short distance must have felt to the girl with no money and expensive tastes like running the gantlet—people who knew her saw her in last year's skirt that was too short and therefore outmoded, in a blouse that had shrunk, probably even in darned stockings.

A curious comparison comes into the mind as one learns such details of the Duchess' childhood. Many, many years later there was to be another Bess—a Princess of England. Secure in her lofty position, passing from one romantic castle to another, what could she know of scanty or shabby clothing? Yet the charming young woman who appears in public today, shining in silk and glittering with diamonds, had an experience not unlike that of Bessie Warfield. She too wore old clothes—Miss Crawford, the governess of Princess Elizabeth, tells us that her pupil, in common with her father's subjects, had very few new dresses during the war. "Make-do and mend" was the rule in Buckingham Palace, as it was everywhere else in England. Even in the Princess' first postwar outfit, her evening gowns were hand-me-downs from her mother, and when out stalking on the Scottish moors at Balmoral she wore an old pair of her father's plus fours. And not for fun, either.

Though royal etiquette and pomp demand a frequent change of attire for public appearances, there are no grounds for supposing that the Queen's wardrobe rivals that of the Duchess of Windsor. True, Her Majesty too has magnificent jewels; but none of these caused headaches to the Government or figured as items in the Empire's bills. Many of them were presented to the Queen, when she was still Princess Elizabeth, by older members of the Royal Family, who wisely invested in diamonds before World War I and until the subsequent "Great Slump" called for cuts in the Sovereign's budget.

Unlike her namesake, the shabbily dressed wartime Princess Elizabeth could suffer no slight, no strain of competition, for there could be no "keeping up with" friends whose wealth of coupons was no greater than her own.

Bessie Warfield, in those far-off days before the tiresome phrase "World War" was heard, could and did suffer.

A press clipping from *Cavalcade* of December 12, 1936, helps fill in the picture of her childhood:

> Her mother sent little Bessie to "nice" Arundel School, made ends meet by taking paying guests in her rented brownstone house.

At twelve daughter Bessie gaily wore long curls tied with ribbon of her favorite blue, was delighted when fourteen-year-old Thomas Shryock, son of General Thomas Shryock, slipped her love notes and lace valentines over the back fence of Arundel School. That year, 1908, widowed mother Alice was married to John Freeman Raisin, son of a Maryland politician, was given away by her sister, Mrs. D. Buchanan Merryman (Aunt Bessie), who started to take an interest in young Bessie.

The marriage brought money into the family and Bessie went back to Arundel School a richer girl, let it be known that her name was no longer Bessie but Wallis.

Four years later she went to ride, play golf and tennis, become socially finished, at Oldfields School for Girls, fifteen miles outside Baltimore. Then she was taken under the care of her uncle, Solomon Davies Warfield, wealthy business man who later became president of the Seaboard Air Line Railway.

As this quotation shows, the Duchess of Windsor at the age of twelve had certain traits which remain to this day: she already loved that shade of blue now universally known as Wallis blue; she was delighted by the attention of little men; she disowned the humble "Bessie" for the elegant "Wallis."

As for lessons, the Duchess' biographer, Edwina H. Wilson (in her book *Her Name Was Wallis Warfield*) writes that Wallis studied "arithmetic, spelling, geography, history." (The word "history" covers a lot of ground; it is certain though that English Constitutional History made no part of the curriculum at Arundel or later at Oldfields.)

Other items in the list were "Sums on the blackboard. Transitive verbs and intransitive. Participial phrases and compound sentences. The state of Maryland is bounded on the north by Pennsylvania, on the east by Delaware and the Atlantic Ocean, on the south by Virginia . . ."

This last sentence is not concluded, and Miss Wilson's readers may wonder what had happened to Maryland's western boundary. There is something attractive about vaguely delineated maps; one rebels at the mere thought of confinement, but here, especially, naming the state line is important—for Wallis, the young woman, eventually went west. To California . . .

The whole world—the world of the Social Register, that is— knows that Miss Noland's Foxcroft School for Girls is one of the most stylish institutions of its kind in the United States; or in the crude phrase of the masses, one of the swankiest schools on earth. Here arrive carefully screened pupils, with hunters and grooms and all the paraphernalia necessary for wealthy young amazons. The testing ground for Foxcroft was, at a much earlier period of Miss Noland's career, her Summer Camp at Burland, Virginia. Here Wallis passed two summers as a counselor; and perhaps it was here that, as reminiscent Tom Shryock reported to the Baltimore *News Post* of November 27, 1936, "Wallis took the highest jumps without batting an eyelash."

In his memoirs the Duke asserts, that "Mrs. Simpson did not ride and obviously had no interest in horses, hounds, or hunting in general," when they were together for the first time—according to the Duke—at Melton Mowbray, in England's hunting country. She was not interested in the chase. Not on that occasion, perhaps; not all hunting is done in the field.

But back to those budding days before it seemed possible that Wallis might blossom into a Tudor rose. The childhood attentions of Tom Shryock were followed by the adolescent courtship of a youngster named Lloyd Tabb, aged seventeen. Mr. Tabb's people were affluent, and they had a large Maryland home, "Glenora." Here Wallis was frequently a guest at tennis parties and for Sunday evening meals. These visits were a welcome change from the discipline of Oldfields School, where the future Duchess was required to make her own bed —a task she admittedly loathed.

At the age of eighteen Wallis abruptly quitted Oldfields, and came out at a mass debutante party on December 7, 1914. She made her debut, with forty-eight other girls, at the Baltimore Bachelors' Cotillion Club. Thirty-four of the young ladies, including Wallis, had signed an agreement that they would abstain from rivalry in elegance in social functions, and from all extravagance, because of the outbreak of war.

It is interesting to note that at the same time Wallis' uncle, the wealthy Solomon Davies Warfield, who must have been a busy man, took time out to make a public statement which ran as follows:

> The report that I will give a large ball for my debutante niece, Miss Wallis Warfield, is without foundation in that I do not consider the present a proper time for such festivities, when thousands are being slaughtered in Europe.

It is not known what aggravation moved Mr. Warfield to make this statement. It may be that Wallis bragged a little about the rich

uncle and exaggerated his interest in her. Mr. Warfield himself was
vulnerable—he was the chairman of the Seaboard Railway Company;
but resentful critics said that he had no practical engineering knowledge; that he had been elected solely by reason of his social pretensions.

The third beau in Wallis' life was Carter G. Osburn who, when the
romance faded, retired from the world to a small town in Maryland.
At the time when half the world half-believed in the fantasy that
Wallis might be crowned Queen of England, Mr. Osburn readily
admitted that he had been "badly smitten by the Baltimore heart-
breaker."

Nothing is more understandable—Wallis at that time wore her
hair à la Clèo de Mérode, with very little make-up on her face. Her
nose and chin were less eagle-like than they are now. She often
dressed in a tight-fitting blouse, with an Eton collar and a bow tie
around her neck, and a belt that emphasized her narrow waist. A
long skirt hid her shapely ankles, but allowed a glimpse of sizable
white buckskin shoes with flat heels. Photos of Wallis then do not in
the least resemble modern pictures of the Duchess of Windsor, The
Best-Dressed Woman in the World.

The fourth and fifth romantics to fall for Wallis were Tony Biddle
and Reggie Hutchinson. Whether these two strings to her beaux were
in harmony or syncopation, who knows? Helen Worden, who drew a
most interesting word-portrait of the Duchess in the June 1944 issue
of the *American Mercury*, described Wallis' Baltimore flapper years in
these unromantic terms:

> She was a typical Southern belle who collected scalps. It is unlikely
> that she realized how far the collecting would go. But ambition grew
> with success.

But Wallis was far from being an Indian squaw. Like any other
attractive, vivacious, smart young lady, she must have had a number
of proposals before the urge to marry affected her. And just like other
attractive young ladies, she would not be content with the firstcomer,
but must have resolved to be careful in her choice. For appealing
girls of marriageable age do not dream only of romance; they mingle
prudence with their dreams, and ponder over economics and social
position—unless they have their own money or the ability to earn it.

Of course there is always the possibility of their falling head over
heels in love with someone from across the railroad track. This does

happen. But misalliance in the case of a well-bred girl brings in its
wake the pity of her sisters, a sentiment women do not particularly
care for. However, they are exhilarated by the envy of their own sex,
and both envy and astounded applause greet, in liberal measure, the
heroine of a Cinderella story.

When in 1915 Wallis did away with the Clèo de Mérode coiffure
in favor of the more fashionable Mrs. Vernon Castle hairdo, she took
a trip to the, as yet, socially undiscovered Florida. She went to visit
her relative, Lieutenant Henry Mustin, U.S. Navy, at the Pensacola
Naval Base. There she met Lieutenant E. Winfield Spencer, Jr., a
dashing Navy officer, and a flier to boot, at a time when flying was
still in its exciting heroic age. After the innocent Baltimore flirtations,
young Spencer seemed to be the right man for marriage.

Wallis could not expect to find a happier match: the virile-looking
Spencer's offer promised security, a higher dignity, and a home. His
employer could be trusted, like all good uncles everywhere, and was
known to be quite prompt in paying. There was, of course, love—
the sex urge which, in the case of a good girl, seeks and finds its outlet
in marriage.

So Wallis accepted the lieutenant's proposal. The engagement of
the young couple was announced in the Baltimore newspapers by
Mrs. John Freeman Raisin, Wallis' mother, on September 19, 1915;
and the wedding took place less than two months later, on November
8, at Christ Protestant Episcopal Church, Baltimore. The bride was
given away by her rich uncle, S. Davies Warfield.

The Duchess of Windsor at her first wedding wore a gown of white
panne velvet embroidered with pearls, and about her dark hair was
a coronet of orange blossoms from which fell a tulle veil. Her wedding
bouquet was composed of white orchids and lilies of the valley.

The Spencers' short honeymoon was spent at White Sulphur
Springs, for the bridegroom had to report back to the Pensacola Base,
where they remained until the end of the war. Later they went to the
San Diego, California, Naval Base. It is on record that Wallis designed
and made her own clothes on an old sewing machine; yet she was
the smartest among the Navy wives. Already she was moving into the
spotlight, albeit on a Lilliputian stage; already she was hearing the
first, hesitant claps of applause and the first, faint susurrations of envy:
sounds that, mounting in volume, would follow her throughout her
career.

Wallis' blueprint for marriage proved to be unsound as construction proceeded. The Duchess' biographers put the matter delicately—there were frequent differences and scenes. The union had been a youthful mistake; though a useful one, as later events were to prove. But after long years it is not necessary to dwell on the Duchess' first or even second mistakes in the field of official romance and marriage.

From San Diego the Spencers went to live in Washington. And then suddenly the disagreements came to a halt—Lieutenant Spencer was ordered to duty at Shanghai, and Wallis preferred to stay in the capital. During that time of grass widowhood Mrs. Spencer was not idle. She displayed an impressive capacity for making important friends, coming to know almost everyone worth knowing in Washington. It was a period of champagne-like excitement, the time of No More War and Flaming Youth. Though in Washington society, at least at the embassies, the flames were more controlled, they were not less warm nor burning-bright. At the "Soixante Gourmets" luncheon club Wallis mingled with the members of the various diplomatic corps—Harold Sims of Great Britain; Jules Henry of France; Felipe Espil of Argentina; the Italian ambassador . . . Perhaps she heard the call of the South, of that Latin civilization whose charm she had already encountered in California; but she did not go to South America.

Rather, Europe beckoned to her. In 1923 she sailed with Aunt Bessie Merryman, carrying a sheaf of letters of introduction. Travel broadens the mind; it heals the heart. After a delightful holiday the two left Europe again, vowing to return. However, back in Washington once more Wallis found the scene much changed. Old friends had left. And Felipe Espil had married. The champagne of youth had given way to the wine of bitterness . . .

Under such circumstances the idea of reconciliation appealed to Wallis. She set out for Shanghai. When she announced her plan to her mother (who was now Mrs. Allen and hostess at the Chevy Chase Club) she neither approved nor opposed it. But to a friend she used these significant words: "Shanghai is such a long way and such a strange place. But I would not dream of interfering with Wallis—I have always let her make her own decisions."

There is some uncertainty about the length of Mrs. Spencer's stay in China: good sources mention two years. It is, however, certain that on her return to the States she had resolved upon divorce. She must have communicated this intention to her uncle, who appears to have been as rabid on the subject of divorce as the late King George V; for shortly after, Mr. Warfield, whose heiress she had been considered, changed his will. From the Baltimore *American* of December 6, 1936, comes the following news item relative to the major financial disaster:

> Wallis' first divorce caused her wealthy uncle, S. Davies Warfield, to call in his lawyers and make a new will. There can be no doubt that she was his favorite niece and every one imagined she would inherit the bulk of the Warfield millions. She probably would have been named the principal heir to her uncle's estate if she had not secured that Virginia divorce from Lieutenant Spencer. Uncle Sol had an intense dislike for divorce courts. So one month to the day after Wallis' divorce he drew up a new will, leaving the bulk of his $5-million estate to establish a home for "aged and indigent gentlewomen" as a memorial to his mother.

It is not known to the writer whether the home for aged gentlewomen is still in existence or not. But certainly Uncle Sol underestimated his niece, for he provided that a room should be reserved for Wallis. It is also certain that Mr. Warfield's $5-million had shrunk to a mere $1-million after the lawyers had finished with the litigation arising from the will.

Yet there was a small inheritance for Wallis, a trust fund of $15,000 providing her with a revenue of about $60.00 a month. All in all, Uncle Sol's reaction to her divorce had given her a bitter pill to swallow; but there was a consolation. On December 10, 1927, Judge George L. Fletcher of the Circuit Court awarded her a divorce decree at Warrenton, Virginia. The charge was desertion. Mr. Spencer was still in Shanghai. Wallis had come back from there . . .

Wallis thought of settling in Warrenton. But after her divorce she grew tired of the sleepy little town. So she checked out of the Warren Green Hotel, and went to New York. Here in those crazy Stock Exchange margin-profit days everyone was a millionaire, or about to become one; everyone except a young divorcee, whose only paper was a decree, who was without bondage. It must have been hard for the attractive stranger to make ends meet in the Big City in the speak-easy period. For at that time her only known income was the pittance from the trust fund.

She had no reserves of jewelry yet. From China she had returned with a few jade pieces such as are gathered by every tourist, but nothing resembling "the rain'd gems of the old Tartarean line."

So Wallis *almost* took a job in 1928 in New York.

At a cocktail party one of the guests spoke with enthusiasm about construction elevators, the big money that could be made selling them. And then (as we learn from *Her Name Was Wallis Warfield*) Mrs. Spencer raised her voice:

> "I want a job. There must be something in such a big business that I could do!"
>
> "You—a job?"
>
> "Why, Wallis!"
>
> There were other protests. "What on earth do you want a job for?" "What could you do?" "Honestly, I never *heard* of such a thing!" "Do you really mean it, Wallis?" the man asked doubtfully.
>
> "Certainly I mean it. Why not?"
>
> "By George, I believe you do!" The man before the fireplace turned, studied the face of the woman who had spoken. "You could do it, too!" he announced, snapping his fingers. "By George—of course you could. You've got personality, appearance, enthusiasm!"
>
> "But she's never done anything like that in her life," said one of the others, coming forward. "Wallis, you can't be serious. You don't mean that you really want to go to work!"
>
> Wallis Spencer smiled. "Other people get jobs, don't they?" she said. "Then, why can't I? I do want a job; it's the one thing I do want."

But despite the enigmatic smile, Wallis was fortunately spared the humiliation which some otherwise very nice people think accompanies a wage-earning position. She spent her time in the more readily rewarding and interesting pursuit of happiness. She was addicted to all-night parties; the kind that ended up at dawn with everyone else bedraggled and sleepy while she still bubbled over with bright ideas for borrowing the milkman's horse and driving down Broadway. With such a dazzling personality she attracted many people in New York. Soon she met the Simpsons, Ernest and Dorothea; and she surely saw their four-year-old daughter, Audrey. The three adults became close friends.

But there came a time when the three of them were no longer seen together. Wallis had noted Ernest Simpson's growing interest in her; and so the "unconquerable" woman, as the Duke calls her, once again left for Europe in the company of Aunt Bessie. The Simpsons, too, made moves: toward the divorce court. Thereafter Mr. Simpson's shipping business took him to London, where he came across Wallis. Together they visited Soho's charming little restaurants; and soon explored another part of town, Chelsea, the Greenwich Village of London. Here, in the Registry Office, on July 21, 1928, Mrs. Spencer became Mrs. Simpson.

To end this chapter on a historical note which is also a note of promise, an unhappy prologue to the swelling act of the imperial theme: there was once a Baltimore girl who married the brother of an emperor.

Back in the nineteenth century Elizabeth Patterson (the third Bess in this story) met "the burlesque Bonaparte," Jerome, the youngest (and most worthless) brother of Napoleon I. It was love at first sight, and they married in Baltimore. Napoleon, the Corsican upstart, was furious at Jerome's stooping to a commoner, and when the newly married Bonapartes arrived in Europe Elizabeth was not permitted to land. The brokenhearted lovers were separated. Napoleon went so far as to annul his brother's marriage by an imperial decree. Then he quickly procured for Jerome a new wife, in the person of Princess Catherine of Wurtemberg, and made him King of Westphalia.

Elizabeth returned to the United States and made her home in Baltimore. After her death she served both as the ideal and the model of the young and attractive girls in that city. The story of her love and life, not to mention the social ambition which led her later to tour Europe with her son, a proclaimed Bonaparte, must have made a lasting impression on Wallis. What a strange and beautiful and tragic romance! Meaning tragic for poor Elizabeth Patterson. Wallis' royal road to romance turned out to be quite different. History repeats itself but never with an exact correspondence of detail.

8

A Prince Alive and Kicking

It is a reverend thing to see an ancient castle or building not in decay: or to see a fair timber tree sound and perfect. How much more to behold an ancient and noble family which hath stood against the waves and weathers of time.

—Francis Bacon: *Essays*

History had quite an opportunity to repeat itself during the reign of Queen Victoria, which lasted so long that the beginning had become history before the end was reached. Three times the birth of an heir to the throne was announced to the Queen. The first heir was her son, later Edward VII; the second, Edward's younger son, who would reign as George V; the third, her great-grandson, briefly known as Edward VIII.

After her first look at the future Edward VIII, Queen Victoria described him in her *Journal* as "a strong, fine-looking child." This was an understatement—he was a beautiful baby.

But some of those who had not seen the infant did not share the good Queen's enthusiasm. For example, Keir Hardie, member of Parliament, a crusader for social justice, a champion in the war upon widespread poverty during Victoria's reign, was daringly critical. The Duke mentions Hardie in *A King's Story*. From among the many militant speeches of this parliamentarian, he quotes a part of one delivered at the time of his own birth: a part which predicted, more or less precisely, the Prince's future career, including an attempt at morganatic marriage, with the Empire paying for all his fun.

It is necessary to enlarge here a little on Hardie's—and that interesting era's—attitude: he was nearly skinned alive in the Commons when he suggested that Queen Victoria should send a message of sympathy to the relatives of the two hundred and sixty miners who

Wallis Warfield at Princeton University Prom, 1912

Summer resort cottage in Pennsylvania (Blue Ridge Summit). The Duchess was born here, around 1896.

Fort Belvedere, favorite residence of Edward VIII prior to the abdication

had lost their lives in an explosion at the Albion Colliery, South Wales, on June 23, 1894—which happened to be the very day of the Prince's birth. (It was an ominous coincidence: but a month before the moral death—the abdication—of Edward VIII, the same Albion Colliery once again blew up, with the loss of two hundred and sixty-one lives.)

Hardie later showed want of deference and marked contrariness, for when it was proposed in Parliament that Lords and Commons should unite in sending a loyal address of congratulation to the Queen on the birth of her great-grandson, he opposed the motion, saying that if there were to be no message of sympathy for two hundred and sixty deaths, there ought to be no congratulations upon a single birth.

However, his opinions were not shared by his fellow-parliamentarians. So the little Prince, son of the Duke of York and Princess Victoria Mary of Teck, began his charmed life with the good will of the people, as expressed by Parliament.

He had everything a youngster can desire: yet he does not seem to appreciate the magic of his boyhood. That it was stuffy, restricted, formal, are some of his explanations. The fine-looking child was forever hellbent to show the world that he was different from ordinary royalty. Had he had his own way, he would certainly have gone down in history as "Edward the Innovator." When he became King of England, the Royal Mint was ready with designs for the new coinage; and he was ready with his own. This is what *The New Yorker* said upon that occasion:

> There is a tradition that successive British rulers face in opposite directions on the coins of the realm. Queen Victoria faced left, King Edward VII right, King George V left. The new Edward then should face right, thus showing his right profile. But he doesn't want to. He parts his hair on the left and prefers the left view. This, we have been informed by our British representative, has delayed the new coinage. When they told His Majesty that by not facing about he was breaking an immemorial tradition he replied, "Why shouldn't I?" It is a good answer. And to the average man it suggests, among other possibilities, a cowlick.

Although the King was deeply concerned about his looks, he did not forget his soul. He seems to have read some works about that modern science, psychiatry. This helped him to trace his later tragic mistakes to a thwarted childhood.

Does Windsor know how the universal mind of his old friend and protector, Winston Churchill, treated this topic?

> It is said that famous men are usually the product of unhappy child-hood. The stern compression of circumstances, the twinges of adversity, the spur of slights and taunts in early years, are needed to evoke that ruthless fixity of purpose and tenacious mother-wit without which great actions are seldom accomplished.
> (*Marlborough, His Life and Times*, by Winston S. Churchill, Scribners.)

The Duke of Windsor's childhood could not be called unhappy. Perhaps that's where the trouble started . . .

He was surrounded by a happy family; and unhappily by flattery.

He had younger, less spectacular brothers he could boss and a charming sister who bossed him; a father who took his children's, and particularly his heir's, upbringing most seriously (George V, having seen service in battleships, insisted not only on a spotless exterior, but on an immaculate interior too); and a mother who was indulgent but not overindulgent. His grandfather, Edward VII, was a fasci-nating gentleman, who favored the Prince and was worshiped by him; while his grandmother, Queen Alexandra, downright idolized him. His great-grandmother, Queen Victoria, who to others might appear as embodied history, was to the boy Edward merely an old lady in a lace cap.

It was a nice family circle. Does it suggest any reason for the Duke's later maladjustment?

True, Queen Victoria and even Edward VII still had a funny German accent; and this might have embarrassed an ordinary English-speaking child. But royal children are accustomed to be cousins to the oldest ruling houses, rolling the strangest R's: certainly the Prince had opportunity to hear every kind of accent. For, as he points out, Queen Victoria had an immense family; so much so that she was nicknamed "the grandmother of Europe."

As for the Prince's father, he was as English as a mutton chop; and had, by steady hard work, acquired both naval rank and the naval character, stiff but kindly. He was already, as Chesterton noted many years later, a sea captain, fully able to maintain discipline from the bridge, but with a fund of good stories and benevolence down in his cabin.

The young Prince had three square meals a day; the finest Irish linen sheets on his beds; the handsomest jodhpurs Bombay's best

tailor could cut; a tremendous tub encased in mahogany (Edward
VII had commenced his reign by installing bathrooms in Windsor
Castle). He had obedient Shetland ponies; affectionate terriers;
bunny rabbits at Easter; legions of lead soldiers; railroad sets, tri-
cycles; early cameras and those old-fashioned, honest fountain pens.
And thrilling journeys from one royal home to another.

He had a governess who sometimes found the children beyond her
control, especially when they were with their grandparents; cautious
and friendly tutors who would laugh at practical jokes. Other children
might go down to Buckingham Palace to watch the Changing of the
Guard; but *this* child was saluted by the Household Cavalry, those
dreams and delights of children.

In short, the Prince had the child's paradise so many of his subjects
lacked. He had a better chance to grow up to be the captain of his
own soul than any other boy of his time.

He actually lived in a garden. And what a garden it was!

It was Windsor Great Park, one of the finest in the world, with the
proudest castle in England looking at itself in the Thames. Everything
that could feed the imagination of a boy—or an adult—was there.
The Park and the Castle and the Chapel of St. George, all the various
buildings of the great complex—including Fort Belvedere, the house
that later became the Prince of Wales' private residence—breathed
the spirit of England's glorious or bloody but always interesting past.

The Romans had been at Windsor—very likely Julius Caesar slept
there. Legend said that on Windsor Hill the peerless King Arthur had
held court, surrounded by his Knights of the Round Table. Edward
the Confessor had had a manor at Old "Windleshore" (to use the
old form of a name derived from the graceful windings of the river),
and had bestowed it on the monks of the Abbey Church of St. Peter
at West Minster; but William I got it back in exchange for two
manors elsewhere. Henry III, who rebuilt Westminster Abbey,
erected a chapel in honor of the Confessor in the Castle. Edward III,
who founded the Most Noble Order of the Garter, also built the
original Chapel of St. George as the spiritual home of the Order; and
Edward IV pulled down this chapel to build a more stately mansion
of the soul. Henry VII, Henry VIII, Charles II and other English
rulers went on adding to the splendor of both Castle and Park.

As befits an ancient English home, the place has a full quota
of ghosts: Herne the Hunter, crowned with a hart's skull and
antlers, in the Park; and Catherine Howard, that "rose without

a thorn" beheaded by her deceived husband Henry VIII, in the Castle.

The Castle also has its heroes in history; to mention but one, the thirteenth-century Ingelram de Archie, who at the head of a sixty-man garrison beat off the French forces of the Count de Nevers.

But even today Windsor Castle is commanded by the brave: old Lord Gowrie, who earned the highest military order, the Victoria Cross, was in charge until recently; he was succeeded by that gallant Australian, Lord Freiberg, also holder of the Victoria Cross, and a Jew. The name Windsor was ever associated with the dauntless—men as steadfast and unmovable as the Norman Tower of the Castle.

Windsor has dungeons and a donjon, chapels, cloisters and battlements. It contains the Royal Collection of magnificent paintings by Leonardo da Vinci, Michelangelo, Raphael, Rubens and Van Dyck. There are also rather too many Winterhalters: Queen Victoria had a liking for the "eau sucrée" of this painter, and the Duke seems to inherit her taste for academic bad art.

Here also are many works of Holbein, who preserved for posterity likenesses of some of the heads Henry VIII chopped off—or omitted to. The great painter made eighty-seven portraits at this King's court.

St. George's Chapel contains the most elaborate and interesting ironwork in the world, the masterpiece of Quentin Matsys. Here Henry VIII was buried, at his own wish, beside his third wife, Jane Seymour, mother of his son Edward VI. The tomb of Charles I is near theirs; this unfortunate Sovereign was buried by the Cromwellian rebels, minus his head or the funeral pomp of other kings (in fact, without a service of any kind).

Ancient and stately oaks and elms led the way to Virginia Water, that beautiful artificial lake. And Eton, the famous public school, is just across the river; Henry VI, who founded it, called it "The King's College of Our Lady of Eton so near Windsor." The visitor entering the cloister walk of the school sees under the great archway the memorial tablet to Field Marshal Lord Roberts, V.C., with a quotation from Shakespeare's *Henry V:*

> Awake remembrance of these valiant dead,
> And with your puissant arm renew their feats.

When Prince of Wales, the Duke, who is not an Etonian, predicted the end of the old Eton topper and the collar. Eton, toppers, collars and all, remain. (Edward VII once said that his grandson would be the last King of England. Fortunately, even royal predictions don't always come true.)

The Duke quotes Samuel Pepys, who called Windsor and the Park "the most romantique that is in all the world." It was, and is, the most romantic. And this demiparadise was the home of a Goliath who turned Davey!

But Windsor was far from being a place reserved for scholars and saints. Nell Gwynne, that "true child of the London streets," who never pretended to be anything else although a king was her lover, lived in a house in Windsor town. And so did Jane Seymour before becoming one of Henry VIII's wives. The town had a merry aspect, too—in Shakespeare's time the tiny place boasted seventy inns!

Queen Victoria often resided at Windsor. After she had been buried in her mausoleum near the Castle—for even in death she refused to be under the same roof with "my wicked Hanoverian uncles"— Edward VII moved in. His son and heir, George, lived with his wife Mary and the children not far away, at Frogmore. This place, too, was a little Eden, but a simple house as royal houses go. The garden was full of flowers and well-kept lawns and interesting ponds, with nightingales working overtime as though they knew for whom they sang. The comfort of the family was looked after by a large retinue of royally trained servants.

The Duke of Windsor, today's hotel dweller and wanderer, had a well-ordered boyhood. He was looked after by a servant of his own, Frederick Finch; a tutor, Mr. H. P. Hansell; a governess, Madame Bricka; a French tutor, Monsieur Hua. The great Cecil Sharp, who had rescued the folk songs and dances of Britain from oblivion, taught him folklore and games. After the customary chores of children of his age, he was as free as any to play in the emerald-green setting of Frogmore and explore the whole domain of Windsor with his brothers and sister. It was, unluckily, too happy a life.

In 1907 he entered Osborne, the English preparatory naval college. He was twelve years old. At that age Prince William, later William IV, had been sent to sea by his father, George III; and George V had also gone to Osborne when only twelve.

After two years at Osborne the Prince went on to the Royal Naval College at Dartmouth. These two wonderful schools never fail to build character. Well, hardly ever . . .

Certain important events in the Prince's life took place in 1910 and 1911. His grandfather, Edward VII, died; and his parents were crowned, with all the royal makings of a king and queen. He himself was invested with the Order of the Garter in St. George's Chapel, and was confirmed in the Private Chapel of the Sovereign. These ceremonies signified that the boy was becoming a man; and all the royal relatives present—including the late Empress of Russia—sang lustily: "Fight the Good Fight," and "Jesus, I Have Promised."

Later, Prince Edward was formally invested as Prince of Wales at historic Carnarvon Castle (birthplace of the first Prince of Wales, the ill-fated Edward II). Kneeling before his Sovereign and father, the sixteen-year-old boy was a beautiful sight in his antique robes, with glittering insignia and a coronet on his blond hair.

The Home Secretary, Winston Churchill, read the impressive Letters Patent of the new Prince of Wales, with his voice so cultivated and sonorous in spite of the lisp. The Prince's father and mother beamed with happiness. Contemporary photographs give eloquent testimony of their pride and joy.

The aristocrats present, together with the Prince's Welshmen, looked spellbound at the living symbol of England's future. These two classes, the nobility and the workers, took his later defection the hardest.

A few weeks later the new Prince of Wales sailed for a training cruise in the *Hindustan*, as junior midshipman. After the voyage he went to Paris for a vacation, and on his return took up residence at Oxford, entering one of the most exclusive colleges in the University— Magdalen.

For those who took it seriously, Magdalen was truly a home of learning. Otherwise it taught a fine hot-potato accent, the merits of Audit Ale, the timetable to London, and the truism that one either paid the tailor's bill or ordered more clothes. It also taught the patience to listen to boring conversation while saying at intervals: "Quite!" and thinking of other matters—a revealing "Yes" or "No" would be dangerous. Magdalen championed the middle course: to stick to a job, no matter how tedious it might seem.

Of course the Prince had his equerry with him, his tutor and servants. But he was allowed to live a normal life and to choose his own friends, instead of being cloistered and unhappily isolated like his grandfather, who had had to observe really severe rules. Windsor's Oxford days were undistinguished but happy.

Once when he was visited by his parents, the stately Queen, who was interested in details, even looked into the storeroom where her son bought his cigars and liquor. She examined the cigar boxes minutely and asked the meaning of the different figures on them. The old store-keeper said: "Ma'am, those are the prices of the particular brands." The Queen was amazed. "Good gracious, I always thought that all cigars cost the same price!"

The King meanwhile went over the young Prince's expense ac-counts. When he saw an item of a few pence recurring too frequently His Majesty asked what it represented. It turned out to be the apple which the careful Prince bought each morning. He then already had the large income from his properties of the Duchy of Cornwall, but with praiseworthy foresight seemed to be saving his money for a later, rainier day.

A paragraph from the book *H.R.H. The Prince of Wales*, by W. and L. Townsend, Macmillan, 1929, runs as follows:

> There was great danger, not unknown to his parents, that the Prince, in his earnest desire to be "one of the crowd," might please a certain section of His Majesty's subjects, yet might, from the viewpoint of the great Colonies, and even other European countries, belittle the dignity of the Crown.

While at Oxford, incognito, as the Earl of Chester, he spent two vacations with his German relatives. Kaiser Wilhelm showed off his soldiers and aircraft, the cannon and zeppelins that in "Big Willie's" overheated imagination were the "shining armor" of Germania. The naive Prince of Wales agreed with his uncle, whom he admired.

"Bookish he will never be . . . still less a British Solomon," was the guarded but weighty verdict of the President of Magdalen when at the end of two years the Prince of Wales left the University, un-steeped in the classics, untouched by the atmosphere of this old seat of learning, and without a sense of history but with a flair for the banjo. It was also said by the historian, David Churchill Somervell, that in his youth the Prince had shown intelligence but not much capacity for concentration.

So he could not be blamed for being glad when the First World War interrupted his studies. He had been a member of the University Officers' Training Corps, and now told Lord Kitchener, Field Marshal and Secretary of War, that he wanted to go to the Western Front; adding, with the wonderful bravado of any twenty-year-old, that it would be quite all right if he died. The succession was assured, for he had brothers. Lord Kitchener replied calmly that he could not permit His Royal Highness to go to the front, saying:

> If I were certain that you would be shot I don't think I would restrain you. What I cannot permit is the chance of the enemy taking you prisoner. You have a lot to learn about soldiering yet.

The moustachioed Kitchener seems to have been an uncommonly frank individual.

The changing of a royal person from a Navy officer to an Army officer takes only a minute. So when at the end of 1914 the Prince of Wales at last arrived in France, he was an Army officer. He joined headquarters staff as aide-de-camp to General Sir John French. Sir John, Sir Charles Munro, and the Earl of Cavan had the task—not an easy one—of looking after his safety.

> Whatever the private wishes of the Prince, no unnecessary risk could be taken with the life of the Heir Apparent to the Throne. Certainly, as the Prince himself had pointed out, there were four brothers to follow him, but it had to be taken into account that should any harm befall the young Prince, the first to ask why his life had not been more strictly safeguarded would be the people themselves. Truly, the authorities were in an unenviable position! Then, too, there was the added risk that the Prince of Wales might be taken a prisoner of war in France. The result on the morale of the British troops if the Prince of Wales had been in the enemy's hands would have been disastrous.
>
> (*The Prince of Wales*, by W. and L. Townsend, Macmillan, 1929)

In spite of their constant surveillance, the Prince once disappeared from General Headquarters on a foolhardy escapade which led to a resounding scandal. He ordered a dispatch rider off his motorcycle, and seating himself in the saddle rode off at top speed toward the front lines. Bewildered staff officers drove after him in powerful cars, in a wildly exciting chase. Finally they found him, covered from head to foot in mud, playing cards with some French officers on the roadside. Nearby was the wreck of the motorcycle—the Prince had struck a shell hole. The shivering British officers succeeded in persuading him to return to General Headquarters.

A legend grew up that the Prince of Wales was the bravest of the brave. He came to be regarded almost as reverently as St. George, the patron saint of England. Men who are in constant danger of sudden death naturally become superstitious, but the dread of impending tragedy can be lessened and soothed by idolatry. The British forces had urgent need of an ideal, and here was an ideal by divine right.

Most of the Prince of Wales' war years really amounted to a sort of glorified, military-like camping, and moving around from one sector to another. After some time he left France and the Western Front to join the Mediterranean Expeditionary Force as one of the staff officers. Then the young Prince went to Italy, where he met King Victor Emmanuel III, a Monarch who through all the years of the war never left his soldiers except for his annual leave of two weeks, and who, when asked to be more careful of himself simply replied, without childish bravado: "I am but one link in a chain, and if I am killed there is somebody younger and more able to take my place."

From Rome the Prince returned to France, where he served with the Fourteenth Corps during the Battle of the Somme. After another jaunt to Italy, he was recalled to France. At last, unbelievably, the war that was the forerunner of another one was over, and he could return to England.

He had won the First World War. Or so it seemed to his people, who were more in need of an ideal than ever before.

9

What Led Up to It All

Well born, well dressed, and moderately learned.
—Statute of Oxford University, defining a
gentleman, A.D. 1440

A SOLDIER no longer belongs to his family. A young veteran, returning from the war, wishes for complete independence. He must be left in peace, for his mind may be dwelling on grim memories. Or memoirs. The Duke of Windsor waited with them rather longer than many of his contemporaries—the brilliant Charles Graves, for instance, brought out a first instalment of his autobiography when he was forty; and Erich Maria Remarque was not yet thirty when his autobiographical novel, *All Quiet on the Western Front,* created such a stir. There are many other examples of self-revelations in literature. It might reasonably be expected that in 1951, after fifteen years of reflection, the Duke would review past events with detachment, or at least that he would take the trouble to look up the facts in some reliable works of reference.

He recalls that at the end of World War I, the Prime Minister, David Lloyd George, told the country that "the power of every land has been drained," and that "all nations have been bled at every vein." He might have added that Lloyd George discredited himself by promising the moon to the demobilized armies of Great Britain: among this irresponsible, flamboyant politician's major commitments being the all important postwar problem of housing. "Slums would be swept away," he promised his hearers, "and homes fit for heroes constructed in their place."

The Prince of Wales did have a home fit for a hero: York House, a historic edifice built by that Michelangelo of London, Sir Christopher Wren, within the confines of St. James' Palace. Here the Prince enjoyed his freedom.

Unfortunately, it soon became apparent to his father that now a gulf had opened between them; that the honest and kind parental advice was going in at one ear and out at the other. The differences between the King and his heir were such as seem inevitable between fathers and sons; and the outward signs were trivial. For instance, the conservative habits of King George V and his staid court were symbolized by the Monarch's beard.

There was a craze, one of the many in postwar England of the 1920's, for a game called "Beaver." This betting game was played between friends who would stroll down the street, alert to spot bearded men, shouting "Beaver!" when they did so. Many of the despised beards were leftovers from the war. But the razor-saving habit had also spread to the arty, a growing postwar group which affected togas and sandals, spinning and sex freedoms, and pretended to go back to the land. As a rule, members of this strange group could be found strolling in the pastoral region of Regent Street, or in Chelsea's rural purlieus around bohemian Cheyne Walk.

Beards were so cruelly mocked at, however, by the "Beaver" playing folk that they were soon laughed out of fashion. Thereafter one could see only white beards in London, for "Polar Beavers," as they were called, were still respected. And, of course, so was King George's beard. No one cried "Beaver!" when they saw him.

But it became "the thing" to try to look like the handsome young Prince, if in nothing else, at least in point of being clean-shaven.

"The loud wave that travels round the world" was already in motion, with the Prince of Wales carried on its crest. For nearly two centuries writers had played up successive Princes of Wales; and when the efforts of the movies and the radio were added to those of the press, this propaganda became gigantic in scope. The heir's youthful good looks, his charm, his seriousness of outlook befitting a man mature in years—these were the continual theme of discussion. Every detail of his waking life was canvassed; every item of his dress was news; every incident the basis of an anecdote. Did the Prince wear a turtle-necked sweater? Turtle-necked sweaters became the fashion. Did he appear in suede shoes? The fashion was assured. Everybody imitated his tie-knot, his bowler, and turned up the cuffs of their trousers as he did his.

King George had patronized various tailors: the famous Davies, and Son, the firm of Poole, and Lesley and Roberts (Poole made clothes for the dandy Edward VII, Davies and Son for George V, and Lesley and Roberts for George VI). The Prince of Wales discovered new. and more modern ones: Kilgour and French and

Anderson and Shepard. But certain Italian tailors also received the royal command.

Such little things as these went to fill in the broad outlines of the Prince's picture, as it was drawn by the guides of public opinion. They were reported as faithfully as were his more important doings.

It surely need not be said that his speeches were invariably first-class news. And yet it must be said; for at that time they still made sense. As the postwar disillusion deepened—as it became plainer that neither peace abroad nor plenty at home was to follow war as inevitably as spring follows winter—these speeches appeared to be torches in the gloom. Though the religion of inevitable progress was breaking down, there remained a tendency to hope that the future must be better than the past; there was the popular sentiment which so often gathers around a young heir, the mingling of too-optimistic hope, expectancy and idolatry that gleamed around Frederick, Prince of Wales, father of George III, and the young George IV, to name but two.

Moreover, this modern Prince so perfectly fulfilled the role of a Prince of Wales. He represented the younger generation, was characteristic of it, and that to a greater degree than any of his predecessors. They had been at once the models and the leaders of the highly placed; but the future Edward VIII, in uniform in his teens, seen often among the *jeunesse dorée* in the night clubs, and once in a while in the filth and murk of some industrial slum, was at once the paragon and the type of a greater number of Englishmen than any Prince before. He was an ex-serviceman, in a land of ex-servicemen; so like any ordinary man, at a time when the ordinary was steadily mounting in social status; modestly nervous, when modesty was decreed moral dress, and panache might even be resented, his appeal was to the masses even more than to the classes. Was he gay at the Kit Kat Club?—a young man, back from the wrecked cities and misery of war, must have some fun.

People derived an intense, vicarious pleasure from reading of his social life. After a hard day of riding, and dancing late into the night, he got up to explore the dying towns, the sullen misery of Lancashire or Wales. He demonstrated that his was not a life of purely selfish pleasure. To all appearances, he was gaining a wider knowledge of his people, an understanding that would guide him when his hour came to reign. Gradually, and with the aid of the press, there was building up to superhuman heights the figure of a *preux chevalier*, a Patriot King who would not simply seek to preserve the status quo, but who would reign with wisdom and power for the good of all.

Prince Edward, the individualist, refused to limit himself to the well-defined routine of British royalty. He made up his own schedule. It was frequently most embarrassing to the Government. At a later period this obstinacy was to be held against him. Thus *Time*, considering the Prince's fraternizing in retrospect, wrote that:

> The ever-young Prince of Wales visibly lacked manner, interest in the actual proposals and specific complaints drawn up by the leaders of the masses—such as shop councils and aldermanic bodies of depression-stricken towns.
>
> (*Time*, November 30, 1936)

After the war, manners and interests changed. And women and those older men who had not fought commiserated with the homecoming soldiers: "You poor boys!" was the lament. "You have lost four long years."

The Duke's generation was dubbed the Lost Generation. There had been other wars, but no previous struggle had resulted in massneurasthenia. Now great numbers of ex-servicemen were suffering from shell shock—and the vast extent and complexity of the field of psychic injury covered by this term was not yet comprehended. Pity for the veterans was undoubtedly in order, even in victorious and still solvent England. (Yes, Lloyd George's slums remained, but there was still money in the country.) Many of the affluent, "the bright young things," played on this public sympathy as they proceeded to make up for the lost time. Not by going back to the universities, or by entering business or politics to help their country, but by turning life into one long party.

Night clubs became the rage of the young British elite. London's Kit Kat Club counted thirty peers of the realm among its members. Obviously the Prince of Wales had to belong to it. The Night Light Club had two princesses and four dukes on its board. Mrs. Kate Meyrick was the acknowledged night club queen. She owned several places, among them the 43 Club, where the Prince would do a little serious drinking when he was not drinking at the Kit Kat or at the Embassy.

Eventually Mrs. Meyrick went to jail, once for six months and again for fifteen. No one was surprised to learn that liquor had been served in her clubs; it also emerged that dope had been handed out—of

course, quite without her knowledge. And the Bank of England
absurdly disapproved of the night club queen's habit of mixing fake
bank notes with good ones. But before the lady took her well-deserved
rest from the din of the world, her three daughters were already
safely married to outstanding members of the peerage, to Lord
Kinnoull, Lord de Clifford, and the Earl of Craven. And Kate was
regarded as a sort of martyr who sacrificed herself for the sake of
giving a good time to the Lost Generation.

The popular choice of dope was cocaine, to be had by the initiated
for the asking. Those who did not take it were satisfied with the new,
relatively harmless stimulant of benzedrine topped off with sleeping
pills, regardless of the vicious circle thus created. The new, the Lost
Generation, thought that it needed hopping up.

As to alcohol, the ordinary Englishman thirsted for beer; but the
newly established partial prohibition permitted drinking only between
certain hours; while at the night clubs and in the mansions liquor
flowed in rivers. The Prince was a brandy man, while his father liked
a little whisky now and then.

A block or so away from the Prince's York House was a rambling
hotel, which was in fact the luxurious house of assignation of the Lost
Generation. Here the gilded youth of England breakfasted on
champagne, and then went upstairs "to take a little nap."

It was the Jazz Age, complete with drums, bells, whistles, banjos,
trumpets, saxophones, and frantic noises. Everyone was a jazz maniac,
including the Prince of Wales. He liked to play the drum, and this
liking persisted even as late as 1952, when he was already past middle
age. When the Duke was staying at the Greenbrier, Virginia, in May
of that year, he was asked "to join the band" for the evening, and to
the delight of the Duchess and their friends agreed to perform. But
unfortunately he was out of practice, and dropped the sticks.

In the 1920's he was much more skilful with them.

Back in those days the United States was represented in England
by Tallulah Bankhead, who may therefore be thought of as anticipat-
ing Mrs. Mesta, as America's first ambassadress. Miss Bankhead was
unaccredited, to be sure, but still very important in the eyes of the
Lost Generation. She heralded the coming of the American Woman.
It may even be said that she began a fashion for a female type till
then unknown to Europe: elegant, self-possessed, independent, blessed
with sex appeal and a wisecracking wit. The demure, coy, clinging
vine woman went out of fashion.

It was the era of Michael Arlen and his amusing novels about languid degenerates. When Elinor Glyn's *Three Weeks* was still considered sensational. When James Joyce was known only for his *Dubliners*. When a young American expatriate, T.S. Eliot, worked in a bank in the daytime and wrote bitter verses at night and had not yet thought of *The Cocktail Party*.

It was the time when the cocktail party was still a novelty; when Professor Freud's work was first popularized, and such strange, till then unheard-of words as "psychoanalysis," "repression," "rejection," "the id," "inhibition," "inferiority complex," and "sexual self-expression" were freely flung around. The users of these terms might have no very profound understanding of their meaning, but they furnished fine-sounding rationalizations for conduct that helped to pass the time, in an age when the art of conversation went into decline.

The oddest behavior of the returned heroes was excused by the plea that they were the Lost Generation. They needed analysis; they must achieve a release of the subliminal consciousness, by continuous confessions to a doctor, or devouring books on analysis.

Professor Krafft-Ebing's book of case histories on sexual aberrations was in great demand. But almost every week there appeared a new book, purporting to give the layman information on this new science, so intriguingly related to the mysteries of sex. This literature also expressed strong views on children—for example, an ambitious woman psychoanalyst created a sensation with her volume on child libido. A case in it told of a little boy whom she had been treating. At one session the child lifted up the skirt of a chair's slip cover and looked underneath (perhaps for imaginary tigers). The analyst asked: "Why are you doing that? Isn't it really that you want to lift up my skirt and see what's hidden there?" She concluded her story by claiming that her subsequent treatment assured the little boy of perfect sex happiness in his more mature years.

A woman who paid daily visits to a psychoanalyst shot herself in Mayfair in broad daylight. The famous Ingleby Oddie, who conducted the inquest, was horrified after listening to the analyst's long, Freudian explanation, and commented: "I am not a scientific person, but it sounds to me like gibberish."

In this "uninhibited" postwar world, one well-known Mayfair meeting place was The Running Horse saloon; another, the Ritz Hotel. Inside were the Lost Generation, catching up on lost time; outside were the homeless, sleeping under the arcades of that same Ritz,

with newspapers for covering. Unemployment had never been so high
in England as in this strange period; the country had to spend many
millions of pounds on relief. Social life was humbug, with misery beneath the glitter.

England no longer had faith. The gilded youth and their leader,
the Prince of Wales, seldom went to church. This latest generation of
the ruling, supposedly "best" class, had never read, or had forgotten,
the words of Carlyle: "The best class of people are the religious people."

This ruling class also took delight in being, or at least sounding,
unpatriotic. It became an English gentleman's snobbish whim to
speak ill of England: "Boring, awful place. Rain. Fog. The Prince
can't stand the climate either," they would say.

There was a certain amount of truth in this remark: the Prince of
Wales spent most of his time abroad. He was the Empire Salesman,
and as such was constantly held up as an example to the playboys
and girls of the younger generation.

In this confused, bittersweet, empty-headed, lighthearted, fermenting, nihilistic era, a letter, by current standards a strange letter,
appeared in the London *Times* (June 23, 1919). It was signed only
with the initials "F.S.T." and was accompanied by a teller's check
in the amount of £120,000, which, translated into gold dollars, represented $700,000 at the then rate of exchange.

" 'F.S.T.' stands for 'Fellow, Surely Tipsy,' " said a pretty girl at
The Running Horse, attempting to solve the initial puzzle with a
silly joke. It was years before people found out that "F.S.T." actually
stood for Financial Secretary to the Treasury; and that this official
was the then rather obscure Stanley Baldwin.

A study of Mr. Baldwin's letter will perhaps help to an understanding of the man, and of his actions at a later date, when obscurity was
exchanged for the arc lights of world publicity.

> Sir—It is now a truism to say that in August, 1914, the nation was
> face to face with the greatest crisis in her history. She was saved by the
> freewill offerings of her people. The best of her men rushed to the colors;
> the best of her women left their homes to spend and be spent; the best
> of her older men worked as they had never worked before, to a common
> end, and with a sense of unity and fellowship as new as it was exhila-
> rating. It may be that in four and a half years the ideals of many became
> dim, but the spiritual impetus of those early days carried the country
> through to the end.
>
> *It is so easy to play; so hard to learn that you cannot play for long without
> work. A fool's paradise is only the ante-room to a fool's hell.*

George V and Queen Mary a year before Edward VIII's succession

WHEN ROYAL BROTHERS WERE UNITED

Princess Yolanda of Italy, whose name was once linked romantically with the Prince of Wales

Ingrid, Queen of Denmark. Another lovely royal princess Windsor could have married.

How can the nation be made to understand the gravity of the financial situation; *that love of country is better than love of money?* This can only
be done by example, and the wealthy classes have today an opportunity
of service which can never recur.

They know the danger of the present debt; they know the weight of
it in the years to come. They know the practical difficulties of a universal statutory capital levy. Let them impose upon themselves, each
as he is able, a voluntary levy. It should be possible to pay to the
Exchequer within twelve months such a sum as would save the taxpayer 50 millions a year.

I have been considering this matter for nearly two years, but my
mind moves slowly; I dislike publicity, and I hoped that some one else
might lead the way. I have made as accurate an estimate as I am able
of the value of my own estate and have arrived at a total of about
£580,000. I have decided to realize 20 percent of that amount, or, say,
£120,000, which will purchase £150,000 of the new War Loan, and
present it to the Government for cancellation.

I give this portion of my estate as a thank-offering in the firm con-
viction that never again shall we have such a chance of giving our
country that form of help which is so vital at the present time.

Yours, etc.
F.S.T.

The Lost Generation affected not to hear Mr. Baldwin's grave
warning, and the money to match his financial sacrifice was not forthcoming, either. Gold was needed for better things than to steady a
shaky empire.

Who taxed himself to help England, Lloyd George or Stanley
Baldwin? In *A King's Story* the Duke confuses the two Prime Ministers.
Lloyd George only *spent* the country's money. Thus, at the end of the
war there arose strong opposition to the antiquated practice of making
special payments to military leaders—Lloyd George forced the payment of £585,000 to the generals and admirals concerned, with the
abandonment of an irresponsible steward who is liberal with his
master's money.

"F.S.T." had not the flamboyance of "the Welsh Wizard."

That honorary Welshman, the Prince, lacked the flamboyance but
had something of the wizardry. He charmed all manner of men: those
in the society of the great world, those in the little world of Society,
and some of the half-world. And it was a cause of some anxiety to his
family. The King worried about his son's behavior and health. He
had "a" serious talk with the Prince, this leader of the Lost Generation. "The war has made it possible for you to mix with all manner of

people," George V told his heir, "but don't think that this means that you can now act like other people."

At least the royal father was careful in his choice of words. How could he put it? That the Prince had been a visitor at the Kit Kat a mere twenty-four hours before it was raided by the police? (An over-ambitious bobby once arrested Sir Basil Thompson, head of Scotland Yard, in a like situation.) Or that he must not make friends with certain types. Or that reckless riding was not a suitable hobby for the Heir Apparent?

The Prince's feats of equitation later became less startling, after a Conservative member had raised the matter in the House of Commons. Public alarm had been aroused by an accident at an Army race, when the Prince fell and suffered a concussion which laid him up for a month.

But the demands of a prospective kingly career were not to go un-satisfied. With no theoretical or practical control of their govern-ments, with no military or naval power capable of coercing them, Great Britain had yet grappled the Dominions beyond the seas to her very soul, as with hooks of steel. An immense surge of strong personal feeling had brought them into battle at her side in 1914, as it was to bring them again in 1939, "to the last man and the last shilling." To the support of that feeling the Prince of Wales now devoted himself. He must see the Empire. The project had, could not but have, hearty approval. It was right that the future King-Emperor should know the lands he was to rule; it was wholly desirable that the Dominions should be helped to fix their loyalty upon their prospective ruler. Not only must he see the Empire: the Empire must see him. And travel would afford a useful outlet to his restlessness.

The Prince wanted to go to India, as his grandfather had gone in 1875. This visit of an earlier Heir Apparent to a country where government was still largely a matter of personal princely respon-sibility, had paved the way for the proclamation of the Imperial title "Empress of India" in the following year. And in 1911 King George and Queen Mary had been crowned at Delhi, during a magnificent Durbar. The royal homes of England contained many proofs of the bond between the little green island and the great subcontinent. Was not the wonderful Peacock Throne, in the great hall at Osborne, the work of Indian craftsmen? That alone might have wakened in any boy's mind dreams of "the gorgeous East," whose "richest hand showers on her kings barbaric pearl and gold."

But in 1919 the terrible epidemic of Spanish flu had killed nearly ten million Indians in two months, and the idea of this dangerous journey was therefore put aside.

Canada was chosen for the first of the Empire tours; a brief surprise visit to the United States followed. Here, too, others had preceded the Prince. Prince William of England (later William IV) had charmed the Tory New Yorkers. And Edward VII, traveling as Baron Renfrew, had visited both Canada and the United States.

So, following their example, the Prince of Wales embarked in the battle cruiser *Renown* for the New World. The Empire's First Salesman had commenced his career. He had a fair salary and, of course, expense account.

10

The Hope of an Empire and Beyond

Why are you shoving away, little master? You see everybody is standing still. What do you want to push for?

— TOLSTOY: *War and Peace*

THE Canadians were delirious about the forthcoming visit of the Prince, the mere mention of whose name was at that time enough to turn their heads.

Twenty years later, when Windsor entertained high hopes of becoming their Governor General, the Canadians wanted no part of him.

The young Prince of Wales was accompanied on his Canadian tour by a suite of 23, including valets, orderlies, secretaries and equerries; and detectives from Scotland Yard. He was escorted by two admirals; and by the captain and officers, and the thousand-odd sailors comprising the personnel of the *Renown*.

In Newfoundland he discovered the New World. Here, he records, a garish triumphal arch had been erected in his honor. Although he was used to such odd constructions (once, when he visited a silk stocking factory in England, the girls toiled day and night to put up an arch of triumph made ingeniously of stockings), the Duke says that he was astonished to see that the Newfoundland arch was built of drums of cod-liver oil and dried codfish!

Francis Joseph, the emperor of Austria-Hungary, was astonished, too, when he shot his first eagle. "It's an eagle, that I know. But where is its other head?" he asked his courtiers. For Austria's emblem was a two-headed eagle. In a way, that emperor could have been forgiven for his idiocy: he was only eighteen.

The Prince of Wales, when he felt astonished at the sight of the oil drums and codfish, was nearly twenty-five. What, had he supposed, were the chief industries, the ancient pride of Newfoundland, which was a nursery of the British Navy?

The island was discovered five years after Columbus had sighted America, by the Venetian John Cabot, who set sail from Bristol under the patronage of Henry VII. Cabot returned home with the news that he had claimed this "new found land" for the King, who received him graciously and rewarded him with the sum of £12. Within a few years, the English were "lords of the harbors," and of the thriving fishing trade carried on by men from Devon, Brittany and the Basque coast.

Lord Baltimore, the founder of Maryland, set up an inland colony, only to see it destroyed by the French. At last the victories of John Churchill secured the sovereignty of England here, as elsewhere. And in 1900 the Admiralty set up in the Colony a branch of the Imperial Naval Reserve, of such importance that it was treated as a special imperial undertaking.

To their nautical habits the people of Newfoundland added a strong spirit of independence; or perhaps this feeling derived from their seagoing—seamen of all kinds are notoriously unbiddable. For a long time they refused to confederate with Canada. This plan fell through at the time, but since then they have become the tenth province of Canada.

In his *A King's Story* the Duke refers to the Canadians, and to most of the people he reigned over for such a short time, as being mainly interested in burlesque!

"As Lloyd George had shrewdly surmised," the Duke writes, "the Dominions wanted, if not a vaudeville show, then a first-class carnival in which the Prince of Wales should play a gay, many-sided and natural role."

No one would dispute the Welsh shrewdness of David Lloyd George. No one denies that the Prince played the prescribed gay, multifarious and natural role. But that charming, irresponsible politician, Lloyd George, had often been criticized for his love of showmanship at the taxpayer's expense. The Prince had a natural inclination to follow the ideas of the Prime Minister on this score.

A certain type of mind is acutely sensitive to fame—and to the lack of it. The desire of fame is not only the last infirmity of noble minds, but also, as Ruskin tartly remarked, the first of little minds.

A friend who had visited Tennyson in the Isle of Wight remarked that "Tennyson is much annoyed by people hanging about his garden gate." The cynical listener replied: "He'd be much more annoyed if they didn't!"

Famous actors have the same difficulty; and in this respect a prince
is like a famous actor. He may appear to hate attention; but if people
do not notice him, he wonders what has happened. The young
Prince of Wales responded to his unprecedented popularity with the
sensitiveness of a seismograph. But his waywardness showed itself in
his desire to "run his own show"—an impossibility for persons in
public life.

In the daytime he dazzled the good Canadians, reading a speech
so that they could hear his voice: "I come to you as the King's eldest
son, heir to a throne that stands for a heritage of common aims
and ideals . . ."

Above his blond head, the wind rippled his own personal banner,
displaying the ancient pledge *Ich Dien* beneath the coat of arms.
"Ich Dien" his enraptured hearers repeated the motto to themselves,
translating it in their minds: "I Serve!" They were mad about their
Prince; and were delighted if he spoke even briefly. Nor was there
any doubt in their minds that the pledge conveyed by the motto, and
in the speeches, would be fulfilled to the uttermost.

But soon as he could do so, the Prince escaped business and went
dancing. Whether aboard H.M.S. *Renown* or H.M.S. *Repulse*, in the
United States or in South Africa, in Australia or Japan, no evening
passed without his dancing; and, of course, there was strenuous entertainment. In his command panegyric, *The Tour of the Prince of Wales
to Africa and South America*, Ralph Deakin remarked that "He danced
almost every night while H.M.S. *Repulse* lay in harbor." On his thirty-
first birthday, for instance, he whirled around with a special abandon,
late into the night; and when the electricity suddenly failed, he did
not need to stop his fox trot—the royal retinue stood round with
lighted candles. He never let slip opportunities to exhibit to the public
his terpsichorean abilities.

"My education," says the Duke in *A King's Story*, "was completed
on the trade routes of the world. That strikes me as a happy judgment." It was an expensive education. And the unhappy results do
not seem to have justified the price.

Having traveled 10,000 miles in Canada, the Prince went on to
visit the United States. New York's welcome was of the sort given a
conquering general. Here was the answer to the American hero-
worshiper's prayer! This fairy Prince aroused all the snobbish
romanticism of the great American Republic. The scenes of universal

joy on his arrival were little short of lunatic; and there was much private entertaining.

The future King also went to see the dying President. Woodrow Wilson was already ill, lying in the very bed in which Lincoln had slept, or frequently lain awake, during the struggle to preserve the Union.

In the course of the Prince's travels across this Union, on November 11, 1919, at 11 A.M. his train suddenly halted at—of all towns, Baltimore! It was Armistice Day. The Prince stood in silence for two minutes, at the station of a town that meant nothing to him then, but which would later mean more to him than the whole British Empire.

Before his departure, his parents had dropped a quiet hint (already quoted in a previous chapter) to a member of the Prince's suite: "If David found a suitable wife in America, they would be delighted." No one can doubt that, on both personal and political grounds, they would have been pleased. David was twenty-five, surely it was time for him to marry. A union between the future King of Canada and one of his subjects would cause jubilation not in Canada alone, but throughout the Empire; while a beautiful, highly bred American lady might well help her royal husband to undo some of the mischief done by George III.

It is interesting to speculate on the mental state of George V and Queen Mary, could they at that time have looked into the future, and in a single flash seen Wallis Spencer curtsying before the Prince at Coronado Beach during his second visit to the United States in 1920, and Wallis Simpson marrying the Duke of Windsor at the Castle of Candé in 1937 . . .

The Prince of Wales returned to England later in November 1919, and his welcome there too was like that tendered a conquering hero. The King gave a banquet for him, as did the Lord Mayor of London, and he was showered with praise and attention for his splendid work.

The town of Windsor bestowed upon him its greatest honor: it made him a Freeman. On that occasion he took the ancient, solemn oath, "I promise not to do anything whereby this town or the freedom thereof may be damnified. And if I happen to know any conspiracy or mischief contemplated against the borough I would speedily disclose same to the mayor." His Fort Belvedere, scene of later conspiracy and mischief, was in the borough of Windsor . . .

King George of course wanted to hear all about David's travels.

The King's ideas of the United States had been derived, in the main, from his contacts with such highly placed persons as the successive ambassadors and their families; and with Americans well-known in international society, like the Vanderbilts and Astors. He was now curious to receive his son's livelier and worldlier impressions, being especially interested to learn how prohibition was working out. Abstemious himself, the King considered it outrageous for the government of any country to attempt to regulate the drinking habits of its citizens. And he was accordingly delighted with a little rime imported by David from the United States:

> Four and twenty Yankees, feeling very dry,
> Went across the border to get a drink of rye,
> When the rye was opened, the Yanks began to sing
> "God bless America, but God save the King!"

Could it be that George V forgot that there was prohibition in England, too, even if it was only partial? Either the King, or the Duke, neglected to consider the Licensing Acts of the era. The liquor consumption of Britons was regulated, all right, but very wisely no attempt was made to abolish it. The hours of drinking in public places were strictly enforced, and steep taxation of alcoholic beverages had already started. There is a little ditty of this period, not quite as gay as the Duke's:

> They're taxing Ale again, I hear,
> A penny more the can;
> They're taxing poor old Ale again,
> The only honest man.

Having spent a few months in England, the Prince of Wales again started on an Empire tour. This, indeed, was to be the pattern of his life for some years to come. Extensive and expensive tours, dignified by all the panoply and ceremonial due to the heir of so many kings, colored by the Prince's often disconcerting informality, followed upon each other: Australasia, South Africa and Spanish America, India were all visited in turn. Every such tour contributed to the Prince's mounting popularity at home and abroad; and every return contributed to the anxiety of his family and the inner circle.

For the Prince of Wales, during his periods in England, would vary the dignified and admittedly dull routine of royal life by falling in love—with the wrong ladies. He was young, and youth is the time for love. And had all the romantic trappings of the Prince of Wales been stripped away, leaving, say, a bank clerk, still the personal charm, gaiety and good looks of David Windsor would yet have been sufficient to attract.

"There had been moments of tenderness, even enchantment," admits the Duke in his memoirs. Unfortunately, as so often happens in real life as in the best fairy stories, the enchantment was all too frequently of an undesirable kind. Rumor was hard at work, hinting that the Prince was interested in a Kensington schoolteacher; that he had been attracted by a fascinating Irishwoman; that an actress, or a peeress, had captured his attention. Some of these ladies had a chance of marrying Prince Edward, long before Wallis reappeared from Coronado via China and the Chelsea Registry Office.

During one of the intervals between tours the Prince met Mrs. Frieda Dudley Ward, the charming, pretty, very witty, freedom-loving wife of a fellow-Guardsman. (Another version of the story has it that their friendship began during his Oxford days.) The Prince and his friend's wife seemed inseparable. She felt very deeply for him. But when he urged her to seek a divorce and marry him, the wellborn Englishwoman knew her station. "Sir," she probably told him, without the *arrière pensee* of the lady who eventually succeeded her in his affections, "I'm a subject of His Majesty, your royal father. He would never consent to your marriage with a divorcée. And even were you to succeed him tomorrow, how could I be your Queen? A divorced woman! It would never do. David—please let me go." She went to Canada, to get away from it all. And, as they say, she lived happily ever after.

One of these predecessors of the Duchess of Windsor recalls how the Prince, sobbing bitterly at the parting, left for a tour of duty as the First Salesman of the Empire (for, like some *jeune fille de bonne famille* sent on a long voyage to forget the wrong heartbeat, he was frequently going abroad). While away from England he sent her innumerable cablegrams, many of them dealing with the doings of the little dog she had given him to remember her by.

In 1920 the Prince was off again, this time to New Zealand and Australia, then through the Panama Canal to San Diego. The mayor of San Diego, Louis J. Wilde, gave a brilliant party in the Prince's honor at the Hotel del Coronado, on Coronado Beach. After the dinner, the Prince held court. Two thousand guests passed before

him, the women executing neat and recently learned curtsies; among
them the wife of a Naval lieutenant, Mrs. Earl Winfield Spencer. If
she was there (as some of her biographers assert) she must have looked
long at the blond, frail Prince Charming. And he must have looked
at her with no premonition. True, it was a balmy evening at Coronado
Beach. An enchanted evening, fit setting for one of those moments of
tenderness. But there were so many ladies present . . . Such real
beauties.

The return home brought no lessening of work. The apologists of
the Duke can bring many items to show that he was a good Prince of
Wales, always on the job. One night, after *a* night, he visited St.
Martin's, in Trafalgar Square. This famous church is the parish
church of the Royal Family, for Buckingham Palace is within the
parish boundaries; and George III (whose statue, in Roman armor,
stands nearby, with Mr. Washington tucked safely across the road on
the lawn of the National Gallery) was proud to be a parishioner.

But by the 1920's St. Martin's was famous less for its connection
with royalty than for the character and writings of its pastor, Canon
Dick Sheppard. St. Martin, the soldier-saint not yet baptized, had
shared his cloak with a beggar: a scene depicted on the lampposts of
the neighborhood. And mindful of the charity of St. Martin, Canon
Sheppard had opened the crypt of the church as a temporary, overnight refuge—it unfortunately could be no more—for the homeless.
Here one night the Prince appeared, and talked to the men who
harbored there. He also invaded the homes of the workers—in Wales
he waded ankle-deep in mud to enter one miserable hovel, and there
an unemployed miner began (not surprisingly!) to complain of the
miseries of his life. His mother silenced him, and turned to the then
still rational royal visitor with words that must have affected him
more strongly than any congratulatory address delivered by the
well-fed: "We are very pleased to see you, Prince."

Certain *bon mots* are attributed to the Prince who at one time
pleased so. The late Will Rogers wrote that he asked H.R.H., when
he was mad about steeplechasing and the horse had once again
finished without the rider: "How are you falling, Prince?" "All over
the place!" came the royal crack, or so the generous Will Rogers said
in his inimitable column. Another anecdote-monger relates that when,
early one morning in Mayfair, the Prince was being helped from his
car by a footman, a tramp loitering nearby bitterly exclaimed: "Idle

rich!" The Prince fired back: "Rich, but not so idle!" This sounds like early Noel Coward. Curiously enough, clever sayings seem to come to royal lips with far greater ease than to those of ordinary people. One day, as he left York House, the Prince allegedly quipped to the press photographers: "Gentlemen, here I am—the raw material of your industry."

Any item about the Prince of Wales was the raw material of the press. That he liked to play the banjo, or beat the jazz band's drum; that he was shy, and enjoyed laughter; that he hated banquets. His good looks were a great help—they contributed to the popularity which was his asset. And his danger. With that popularity as weapon, there was nothing he might not have done, even to the restoration of strong monarchy in England; there was nothing, his people believed, that he would not do when the right time came.

On his third trip to the United States, the Prince mixed too much with members of the "international set" on Long Island. His parents, who sensed—rightly, as it proved—that these associations might eventually lead to disaster, made unremitting efforts to draw him away from such society. King George was both shocked and indignant at the freedom, or rather freedoms, of the American press (but then, what King of England before him had been confronted with headlines commenting on his son's pajamas?). The old New York *World* was painfully blunt in its comments:

> He managed by his choice of friends and diversions to provoke an exhibition of social climbing on the part of a few Americans which has added nothing to his prestige nor to the prestige of royalty in general. In fact, he managed to demonstrate to Americans, grown tolerant of the business of royalty, that it is, whatever his personal democracy may be, in fact a pyramid of snobbery.

It must be remembered that these words were written long before the United States became the last best hope, not merely of the common people throughout the world, but of deposed royalty and nobility.

There were indications on his Empire Tour in 1932 that the people also were beginning to be worried about their Prince's playboy interest in hilarity. For his future subjects now sang lustily and with some judgment a verse to the tune of "Three Blind Mice":

> Here's our Prince!
> See how he smiles!
> Did you ever see such a smile in your life!
> Lucky the princess he takes to wife!
> Amongst all the girls there's a deadly strife
> For our Prince!

From 1925 on, marriage for the Prince of Wales was always a subject of the greatest interest to the British people. A woman's magazine
was merely taking advantage of a deeply rooted emotion when it
published an article on "What Would Happen to You If You Became
Engaged to the Prince of Wales." It described, among other things,
the ordeal by publicity which would immediately follow upon the
announcement: every camera lens in the world would be turned upon
her. But most probably this article was never read by the lady who
did become engaged to the Prince of Wales; and who was thereupon
naively distressed to find her own face upon the front pages of a
picture paper.

The home life of a monarch is the particular concern of his subjects.
This may be proved by numerous instances in monarchical history.
From Agnes Sorel the "Lady of Beauty" to Madame Du Barry, many
"Queens of the Left Hand," mistresses of the Kings of France,
exercised a great, often an evil influence, over the fortunes of their
country. The infatuation of the feeble Emperor Hsien Feng for his
concubine Orchid, who became Empress of the West, led to the
destruction of the Imperial Dynasty of China. The Queens of England
often played a decisive part; nor were they usually chosen by mere
personal whim. English kings were expected to marry for the benefit
to the country; and high birth, beauty, and a rich dower were deemed
essential qualifications in the bride. Kings who ignored these rules
did so at their peril.

In this connection may be quoted a passage from the Malmesbury
Diaries by that great eighteenth-century diplomatist, the Earl of
Malmesbury, which perfectly illustrates public feeling in England as
it was and remains. The following dialogue took place between the
Prince of Wales (later George IV) and Malmesbury, in May 1785.

LORD MALMESBURY: May I suggest, Sir, the idea of your marrying?
It would, I should think, be most agreeable to the King and, I am
certain, most grateful to the nation.
THE PRINCE (with vehemence): I never will marry! My resolution

is taken on the subject. I have settled it with Frederick (his brother, the Duke of York). No! I will never marry.

LORD MALMESBURY: Give me leave, Sir, to say most respectfully that you cannot have really come to such a resolution. You *must* marry, Sir. You owe it to the country, to the King, to yourself.

THE PRINCE: I owe nothing to the King. Frederick will marry, and the Crown will descend to his children; and, as for myself, I do not see how it affects me.

LORD MALMESBURY: Till you are married, Sir, and have children, you have no solid hold on the affections of the people, even while you are Prince of Wales. But if you come to the throne a bachelor, and his royal highness the Duke of York is married, and has sons to succeed you, your situation when King will be more painful than it is at this moment. Our own history furnishes strong examples of the truth of what I say.

In the eyes of his subjects the public and private life of a future king are almost inseparable. The office of *maîtresse en titre* has been no part of British public life; and favorites, male and female, have often been the targets of bitter criticism, sometimes on moral grounds and usually because of their cost. Queen consorts, and future queen consorts, have been the objects of even more jealous and possessive scrutiny. In times when government was by the personal will of the Sovereign, the character of his wife, who shared and often wielded the power of her lord, was of the first importance to the nation.

And now that the British Monarchy wields a moral power alone, it is character alone that counts; for character is the root of moral power. Unhappily, the Prince of Wales forgot this, and King Edward VIII was dismayed to find that his people remembered it.

11

The First Round

THERE are many versions as to when and under what circumstances the Duke of Windsor met the Duchess. His Royal Highness might be expected to give the world firsthand information on this matter, but for the unfortunate fact that he does not, or does not wish to, remember certain tremendous trifles precisely. It will therefore be necessary to report what some others say concerning this memorable first meeting.

As has already been mentioned, Mrs. Spencer probably paid her homage to the Prince of Wales at Coronado Beach when he visited the United States in 1920. This brief encounter may be crossed off—hundreds of other ladies curtsied to the Prince that evening.

The next date comes from an issue of *Cavalcade*, the British news magazine, which reported in 1937 that the Duchess, while married to her second husband, Ernest Aldrich Simpson, was presented at Court in 1926. This was an error; in 1926 Mrs. Simpson was still Mrs. Spencer, and in fact she was not presented at Court until June 10, 1931.

On June 19, 1926, Mrs. Spencer had just arrived at Warrenton, Virginia, from China, and taken up residence at the Warren Green Hotel. This hotel actually faces the Court—the little Court House of Fauquier County, Virginia.

In the summer of 1931 the Prince of Wales did not know Mrs. Simpson. Or in his own words, knew her only slightly. How then can her presentation be accounted for?

Presentation to the Sovereign is a focal and formal part of Court and society life; consequently the honor is sought, every year, by a great number of women. Both as a social event and as involving many people, it needs regulation. The Lord Chamberlain makes the rules, which, although reasonable, call for strict compliance. They are published some months before the Presentation Parties begin, in order that both the Court and the presentees may have sufficient time to make their preparations.

A lady cannot ask to be received. She must first find a sponsor, a *married* woman who has herself been presented to the Sovereign; and she, on her protégée's behalf, makes application to the Lord Chamberlain's office for an invitation.

This office has the task of scrutinizing the list of would-be presentees, to make certain that no divorced person or bankrupt—in other words, nobody who has admitted to the world that she has broken her word —shall be admitted to Buckingham Palace. The Lord Chamberlain does not take it into account that the divorce was granted on account of the husband's fault. In Palace circles a divorce is a divorce. And bankrupts are not barred because of their poverty, but because a Declaration of Bankruptcy reflects on their character.

The Parties take place in the State rooms of the Palace, where the appointments, of great beauty and splendor, provide a suitable setting for the majesty of the Sovereign, and the dignity of the occasion. The Monarch, enthroned in a splendid gilt chair upon a dais, is surrounded by the Honourable Corps of the Gentlemen-at-Arms, in picturesque crimson-and-gold uniforms and hats adorned with white plumes.

The presentees move in line toward the throne; as each approaches, her name is pronounced aloud. She curtsies to the Monarch, and to the consort if there is one; then moves on, still in line, to take tea in an adjoining drawing room.

At the court of King George V the few hundred ladies received had to submit to a most searching scrutiny. The late King, and the late Queen Mary as well, always insisted that women who had been divorced should never be permitted to enter the Presence.

This inflexible rule was made not only because their Majesties regarded their own marriage vows as sacred, but also because they knew extremely well the feeling of the British masses on the subject of divorce.

Yet Mrs. Simpson slipped through the gates of Buckingham Palace! At sight of this lovely lady, demure as though she had never been divorced, the wrought-iron British lions on the gates seemed more like purring kittens.

Again, how is it possible to explain the allegation that, when the presentations were over, Mr. and Mrs. Simpson were driven home to their Bryanston Court apartment by the newly met Prince of Wales? Is it likely that immediately after a stiff and ceremonious assembly-line introduction the heir to the throne would taxi home the obscure couple he had never seen before?

Among the countless stories of the first meeting, one, a supposed dialogue between the Prince of Wales and the old Duke of Connaught, is almost too good to be true. The author of *Her Name Was Wallis Warfield*, describes this conversation as having taken place just before the Buckingham Palace reception. According to this writer, the two Royal Princes were standing near to the throne of George V, enjoying a little chat:

> Said the Duke, in discreetly muffled tones to the Prince:
> "Are there any good numbers tonight?"
> Said the Prince, smiling, "I hear that Mrs. Simpson is a very attractive American and I hope to meet her afterward."

It is sufficiently startling to find the Duke of Connaught, a son of Queen Victoria, speaking good American slang, but there are more important questions to be asked regarding this report. One would like to know who could have eavesdropped at this "discreetly muffled" conversation. Is it possible that King George squealed? Or did a publicity-wise lackey offer the information to the chroniclers?

Another story claims that the World's Greatest Romance began, like that of Romeo and Juliet, at a private ball. After the Presentation Thelma Lady Furness gave a party. In a variant of this tale, the hostess was her sister, Mrs. Benjamin Thaw, whose husband was attached to the United States Embassy in London. At any rate, the story goes that they met at a ball, and here it was that Wales could say with Romeo:

> Did my heart till now! forswear it, sight!
> For I ne'er saw true beauty till this night.

It is possible that the Prince, meeting Mrs. Simpson before the

International News Photo

A Great Lady with Her Son

When the World still thought of the beloved Prince as "Number One Boy."

The Windsors at the ruins of Pompeii before Fascism also crumbled

Presentation, was already attracted to her; and that, when she casually mentioned that "just for fun" she would like to be presented at Court, he first tried to secure admission for her through the officials of Buckingham Palace.

When he found that as usual the King and Queen had combed the list of presentees with the diligence of proofreaders, the Prince may have given his parents an ultimatum: Mrs. Simpson must be presented in spite of the fact that she had been divorced.

No one knows in what terms this alleged edict was delivered. But the Prince's obstinacy and his peremptory nature must be considered, as must the fact that in his relations with comely women this supposedly mature man could still summon up an adolescent's hysteria. But however it happened, Mrs. Ernest A. Simpson, the divorcée, was presented at Court to that King and Queen who simply did not wish to receive divorcées.

Also in the book *Her Name Was Wallis Warfield* (which appeared in 1936) occurs this amusing story about the Presentation:

> There wasn't any one she (Mrs. Simpson) wanted to impress and she wasn't a social climber. Why should she don plumes and court train and set out for the palace?
> At last, though, she was persuaded. "Very well," she said, "I'll do it, if it doesn't cost anything."
> And she did. From one friend she borrowed the gown with the court train and from another the three white plumes for her hair. She bought a band of aquamarines to hold the plumes in place, and then—at the last minute—saw a beautiful aquamarine cross. It was four inches long and made of gorgeous stones, and Wallis had a weakness for aquamarines. She bought it, spending more than she might have on an entire court costume, and wore the cross suspended from a cord about her throat, with her borrowed finery.

In the Duke's memoirs there is a photograph of Mrs. Simpson in those clothes "only lent," together with the plumes in her hair and with an impressively large cross dangling from her neck. In the *Life* version the caption under the photo read: "Wallis Simpson was presented to my parents at a Court in the early thirties and this photograph of her in her Presentation gown was taken at the time. We were then almost strangers." (In the book the caption was changed to read: "Wallis was presented at a Court June 10, 1931.")

In the calendar year there are two winter seasons, the first from January to March, the second including November and December.

The Prince spent fifteen days of January 1931 in England, for on the morning of January 16 he left on an extended tour to South America, and did not return until April 29 of the same year. By this date, of course, winter was well over. It was not, then, during the earlier winter period that he met Wallis Simpson.

For in his own, discrepant story as to how and when he met Mrs. Simpson, the Duke himself writes: "We first met during the winter *after* my return from South America in 1931." (Author's italics.)

According to the Duke they were almost strangers in June, yet they never met until the winter of the same year!

Where are the facts the ex-King promised to give as a "duty to history"? Or is it possible that he doesn't know that summer precedes, as well as follows, winter?

How could he forget the date of a meeting which was all-important to himself, and which led to catastrophic results? The date and circumstances of the encounter must be established.

Here are some more of the Duke's "facts."

By his account, the winter meeting took place at Melton Mowbray, the heart of England's hunting district. The Prince and the Simpsons were guests in one of the elegant houses of the neighborhood. "Wallis did not ride, and obviously had no interest in horses, hounds or hunting in general," says the Duke in the memoirs.

It has already been shown that the Duchess of Windsor used to be extremely fond of horses and riding and, in fact, possessed a pluck in the saddle which was the envy of accomplished male riders. The Prince, too, adored the chase, and indeed all forms of horsemanship; though the pleas of his family and friends had induced him to give up steeplechasing with its attendant risks. His riding had been reckless— an expert might have called it clumsy—and neither his parents, nor the Government, nor the people liked that. But he could still follow hounds if only he rode with care.

Yet the Prince and Mrs. Simpson were among the few members of the house party who gave up the pleasures of the chase, the chief admitted reason for visiting Melton Mowbray. Mrs. Simpson had a good excuse: she had a bad cold. But in spite of this the "almost strangers" began to talk; and following the rule that royalty must take the lead, the Prince asked the American lady if she did not miss the comfort of central heating?

Mrs. Simpson pounced upon the opening, for she knew an opportunity when she saw one.

"I am sorry, Sir," she said. "But you have disappointed me."

"In what way?"

"Every American woman who comes to your country is always asked the same question. I had hoped for something more original from the Prince of Wales."

"I moved away to talk to the other guests, but the echoes of the passage lingered," writes the Duke nostalgically of this occasion.

To the disciple of Stendhal, acknowledged the foremost theorist of love, or to the reader of Weininger (author of that extremely interesting pioneer work, *Sex and Character*) this last remark is a revelation indeed. It shows that the Duke was knocked out—in the first round.

Mrs. Simpson had perhaps never heard of Stendhal; nor ever read his masterpiece, *De l'Amour*. But with marvelous feminine intuition she had spontaneously acted on a main Stendhalian principle: that in certain situations love can, and even must, be started with a terrific impact, a spiritual slap on the face. This, wrote Stendhal, is a method especially successful with a naive, unsophisticated and inexperienced lover, the sentimental soul. Or with a man who is jaded by the quick surrender of many, too-willing women.

At this first meeting Mrs. Simpson showed rare penetration. She recognized immediately that feminine element in the Prince's character which responded to her own masculinity.

In his book, *Sex and Character*, Weininger pointed out that every man has a certain degree of femininity in him, and every woman a certain amount of masculinity. If in a man and a woman these percentages add up to one hundred, the cycle is completed and the two become one, a unit. It is to be doubted if Mrs. Simpson had ever read Weininger's book or even heard of his theory, and this renders her strategy all the more commendable.

Whether she acts upon the spur of the moment or follows a planned course, the woman who is determined to attract a much-sought-after man must be exceedingly versatile as well as instinctively clever. Mrs. Simpson's conduct at Melton Mowbray showed her to be greatly gifted in both respects. She put into practice the theories of two great authorities on love, though perhaps she had never read a line of either.

She used the so-called "chill treatment," a hazardous undertaking at a first meeting, but one which may prove greatly rewarding. Like poker playing, this method requires coolness, strength of character, and the skill of an expert. Later events showed that Mrs. Simpson certainly had all these qualities, for she succeeded in her attempt to fix the Prince's attention. This was due to her ability, conscious or unconscious, in exhibiting her positive (masculine) as well as her negative (feminine) elements; plus her very pleasing features.

The Prince might not know it, but can anyone doubt the lady was hunting at Melton Mowbray?

Of course, as in any love story of poignant interest, there were from the start obstacles to be overcome. On December 12, 1936, the Baltimore *News Post*, the Duchess' home-town gazette, endeavored to pierce with one dazzling beam the fog that veiled the beginning of the World's Greatest Romance:

> Thelma Lady Furness came to America (from England) to assist her sister in the custody trial involving her sister's little daughter Gloria Vanderbilt. While in America Thelma fell in love with Ali Khan— but she had nightly telephone calls from the Prince of Wales' St. James' Palace. Ali Khan went back to England on the same boat with Thelma. In Southampton there was a message from the Prince of Wales—would she stop at Fort Belvedere for tea on her way up to London?
>
> It was a meeting Thelma dreaded. For she had decided to tell the Prince of Wales that she had fallen hopelessly in love with Ali Khan. The reunion of the Prince and Lady Furness at Fort Belvedere was therefore not very pleasant. However, before she departed from the Fort, Thelma had promised to return for the weekend.
>
> During that weekend at Fort Belvedere, Thelma was alone with the Prince, except for his aide-de-camp, General Trotter, who acted as chaperon. The Prince was coldly polite, Thelma was the same, and the general tried to thaw out the atmosphere.
>
> The following Monday Thelma dined with her friends the Simpsons and Ali Khan, and she swore that she would never spend another unhappy weekend at Fort Belvedere.
>
> "Why not have us down as referees?" suggested at that dinner Ernest Simpson. So shortly afterwards when the Prince invited Thelma to the Fort again, she suggested bringing the Simpsons. She reminded the Prince that he had met Mrs. Simpson with her on several occasions. The Prince reluctantly consented to the Simpsons' visit. That was the first time Wallis was the Prince's guest. Thelma, who imagined that the Prince of Wales was trying to put obstacles in the way of her marriage with Ali Khan, was most ungracious throughout the week-end—and Wally was graciousness personified. Thelma retired early with a cold, leaving Wally to talk to the Prince while her husband talked to General Trotter.
>
> Before they retired, they made a pilgrimage to the kitchens of Fort Belvedere. Wally suggested that she scramble eggs in the American fashion for the Prince. That was the last time that Thelma was a guest at Fort Belvedere. She completely faded away from the royal horizon.

It is not necessary to dwell any longer upon the volatile friendship between the Prince of Wales and Thelma Lady Furness, nor on the newspaper's hard-to-prove statement that "the Prince consented *reluctantly* to the Simpsons' visit." Nor is it pertinent to this account that once upon a time Lady Furness and Ali Khan, later Rita Hayworth's husband, once had a mind to marry. But it is amusing to read that an early bond between the Duke and the Duchess was a culinary one.

Is it possible that King Edward VIII sold his birthright for a plate of scrambled eggs? In a way it is. The Duke remarks that food at the Simpsons' apartment in Bryanston Court was the best in London and that Wallis had an expert knowledge of cooking. And he hints that this was one of his reasons for dropping in. This is quite a confession, though it can hardly please various *cordons bleu* in the royal kitchens back in England to learn that their former master had to seek his gastronomical content elsewhere.

But it helps to show that the great also are human, and that the way to their hearts is through their stomachs. Even Julius Caesar was supposed to have said, on invading England for the second time, that his reason for seeking to conquer the foggy land was the excellence of the native oysters.

At Mrs. Simpson's salon there was conversation: "The talk was witty and crackling with the new ideas that were bubbling up furiously in the world of Hitler, Mussolini, Stalin, the New Deal, and Chiang Kai-shek," recalls the royal author. This is a curiously mixed grill. From the outset people talked with abhorrence of many of those "new ideas," and the passing of time has brought melancholy comment on them.

Besides, the Duke might have ended the list where it began—with the name of Hitler. For Herr von Ribbentrop, the unwelcome German envoy to the Court of St. James, the *alter ego* of Hitler, was among the Simpsons' guests. So frequently, in fact, that when later the Cabinet put the King's ladylove under the microscope, weighing all the evidence about her gathered by the British Secret Service (and also by the agents of other major powers who now regarded the King's friend as a factor in the balance of peace or war), the association with Ribbentrop was one of the reasons for the Government's adamantine attitude toward the projected marriage.

The Prince and Mrs. Simpson often worked on jigsaw puzzles, at which she reportedly excelled. It is not known if Ribbentrop joined

them in the game, or if one of the puzzles was a map of the Commonwealth—but certainly the German envoy was there. And this high-
ranking Nazi must already have been familiar with Hitler's plans.

It is probable that both the informal Prince and the well-informed
Mrs. Simpson heard the little ditty so popular at that time in certain
British circles:

> With crude commodities as rare,
> As spokesmen of Das Reich declare,
> How can the Fatherland afford
> To ship Von Ribbentrop abroad,
> To Bryanston Court . . . ?

The Duke claims for Mrs. Simpson that she was surprisingly well-
informed about politics and current affairs. This is doubtful. If she
were, she did not really believe in England's invincibility. Or, perhaps,
wishing to serve "her" England, she was going to get Ribbentrop to
tell her the Nazis' secrets. The Duke says that he was impressed by
her habit of reading four newspapers every day from cover to cover.
If she really did, she must have seen on the front pages what a worried
Stanley Baldwin said in the spring of 1934:

> The white cliffs of Dover are no longer the frontiers of England—
> now in the new airplane age our frontiers are on the Rhine.

Yet Mrs. Simpson, who was so well-informed and worldly, entertained the arrogant, goose-stepping former champagne salesman, who
despised Great Britain and democracy. She was indiscreet enough to
bring him together with the heir to the throne! The favorite was
furthering a friendship between the First Gentleman of the Empire
and a scoundrel who was thoroughly mistrusted by every honest and
foresighted person in British public life.

Here was a woman "surprisingly well-informed about politics and
current affairs"! Yet she so little appreciated the position of the Prince
of Wales or his place in the world scheme of things that she could
allow herself to bring him together with a man like Ribbentrop! One
cannot help wondering what she gained from reading four newspapers
a day. And what exactly were the advantages to be gained by the
soon-to-be-King's meeting with the soon-to-be-hung Nazi?

Who was fooling whom?

She must have seen in those four papers that Hitler's Germany was beginning to be a menace to England, now her home, and to the peace of the world. That German forces had remilitarized the Rhineland, and that Hitler had restored conscription as of March 1935, while England had no conscription; that Russia had 7,000 combat planes, Germany had about 10,000, and England was proposing to build 820 *in the coming five years*. There was grumbling that there was not as yet a single gas mask in England, and even supplies of pikes for the future Home Guard had not been procured. The plight of democratic countries was grave, and it was plain to see even by those who were not so well-informed.

But at this time Mrs. Simpson's conversation, whether on politics or less dangerous subjects, such as books or the theater, fashion or gastronomy, was "deft and amusing"! And she had that elementary but most potent gift of seeming to be genuinely interested in the work of those with whom she was conversing. This, writes the Duke, was her greatest charm. Truly amazing! Having gone through the finishing school of two marriages, she could hardly *not* have known what to talk about with a man, even if that man was the Heir Apparent.

She also knew, much better than many merely royal persons, how to grant favors, and, what may often be more important, how to refuse them. She could appear to be interested in the Prince; but she knew better than to seem aware of his interest. For a long time she was unaffected—such at least was the Duke's impression. And the reader is tacitly called upon to share it.

Windsor confesses that the hope imperceptibly formed that one day he might be able to share his life with her, though he did not know how this could happen.

When a man is getting into such a state, he seizes on anything as a cause for hope. Glances, actions which may be contained in a moment or spread over days, raise his hopes and at the same time strengthen his desires. Then he seeks greater proofs of love, and becomes eager to enjoy his happiness immediately. But "too easy a victory soon robs love of its charm." This rule, already enunciated by a twelfth-century Court of Love, is instinctively understood by clever women. They know that obstacles increase the value of a thing difficult to attain, and are accordingly aware that at this stage coldness, or a rebuff, will produce surprising results. It will not repel the would-be lover; but by awaking a doubt of success in his mind, it will make that success appear even more desirable.

A clever woman, therefore, will often affect a certain indifference toward a man, being very well aware that even a slight show of kindness on her part will cure his despair and renew his ardor.

European society in the 1930's included a group of American women who, by instinct or training, were learned in these matters. They knew the art of attracting a man's attention by encouraging him, and then making him suffer by some snub. To hang up the telephone, perhaps after a cold word, when the victim called; to be seen in some public place with another man; to fail him at the *rendezvous;* and when they had thus rendered him unhappy, to become kinder and more encouraging—these were tricks they understood very well.

Stendhal held that a love revived after suffering is much stronger than that love which precedes the pain; and long before Stendhal, Shakespeare had expressed similar views. His Cleopatra delights in tormenting Antony:

> If you find him sad,
> Say I am dancing; if in mirth, report
> That I am sudden sick.

And when in the same scene Charmian urges her to give way to Antony in everything, she cries: "Thou teachest like a fool; the way to lose him." Until disaster renders Antony terrible, she maintains her ascendancy over him by opposing him in everything.

Shakespeare and Stendhal wrote from their knowledge of the human heart. They copied nature; and in writing as they did, simply reproduced the traits of a certain type of woman as she has existed through centuries and generations—as she was long before Cleopatra ascended the ancient throne of the Pharaohs, and as she will no doubt be long after Paris has ceased to reckon its millennia.

As such women have been known to every period, so they may be found in every land. Frequently they prefer a foreign country, and move in the smart international set. In England and in France, between the two world wars, the American female was still a novelty, with a particular spice of her own, a sparkle, a raciness which delighted by its difference. What in a European woman might have provoked anger, in an American woman was accepted as a facet of the national character, as a feminine version of American forthrightness and independence. In this, as in so much else, Mrs. Simpson was true to type—she had these characteristics in the highest degree. The Duke records that he found her not only complex and elusive, but also the most independent woman he had ever met; and he ascribes this to the Revolution of 1776!

It was perhaps to this independence that he imputed her seeming indifference to his "interest."

But is it possible to believe in her indifference? Can one imagine the Prince of Wales besieging an impenetrable fortress? Can one picture him cajoling and persuading with the poesy of a Shelley, or the Latin urgency of a Don Juan? Begging the lady of his heart to heal the intolerable suffering caused by unrequited love?

Yes, one can.

For Mrs. Simpson seems to have been a most dexterous lady, endowed with the talent to make a man happy or miserable, just as she willed. She prolonged and obstructed his courtship.

It was not the first time in English history that such a situation had arisen. When Henry VIII sought Mary Boleyn, she was quite ready to yield to the royal condescension, and to be married off later to a mere gentleman. But when the Monarch turned to Mary's sister, Anne proved less pliable. Not that she was unwilling to heal the King's hurt: on the contrary, Anne was determined to have him, even if at the price of her life, that her children might be royal. But for this, nothing less than marriage would serve. For eight years she kept the King on the rack of his desires, while the Holy Roman Empire, the Catholic Church, and the people of England obligingly provided a series of obstructions past which Henry fought his way. When at last her goal, "the sweet fruition on an earthly crown," was in sight, Anne could allow the King to reach *his* goal. Elizabeth Tudor was conceived; and Henry hurriedly married Anne, who was thereafter crowned and beheaded within the space of two years.

But the Prince of Wales did not have to wait eight years, which was fortunate; for he was less successful than Henry in the struggle with an Empire and a Church. Before he could pine away altogether, Mrs. Simpson must have become aware of his unhappiness. For in the summer of 1934, when the Prince went cruising on the yacht *Rosaura* in southern French waters, among the guests was Wallis Simpson, very properly chaperoned by her aunt, Mrs. Bessie Merryman, of Washington, D.C. In the newspapers of Europe and the United States there appeared, on September 12, 1934, a short news report:

> The Prince of Wales is evidently enjoying his sojourn in Cannes. To the delight of hundreds of onlookers, last night the Prince danced the

rumba with an American woman identified as a Mrs. Simpson. Although it had been announced that the Prince would stay aboard the yacht *Rosaura*, he came ashore yesterday afternoon and shortly before midnight he appeared at the Palm Beach Casino with Mrs. Simpson.

Not a word was said about Mr. Simpson.

Apparently the impression of Mrs. Simpson's indifference had already been removed. Now the Prince could be allowed to think that *he* had conquered her. Herein lay the superb artistry of the lady.

According to the memoirs, the idea of giving up everything for the woman whom chance ("that happeneth to them all," Ecclesiastes 9:11) had thrown in his way, had already formed in the mind of this unlucky man. He took comfort in the thought that if the worst happened, there was "my brother Bertie," the late King George VI, who was a devoted family man, "a quality that goes a long way for a king in a constitutional Monarchy." How unfortunate for the world that this observation was made so late!

Speaking generally, it is obvious that some men give little thought to such trifling matters as an afflicted world or the welfare of their country, or indeed to any other matter after they meet *the* woman, after their heads are turned.

For soon:

> She spoke. And both her snowy arms outflung
> Around him, she embraced the Sire;
> And softly fondling him she clung
> With all her melting charms that so inspire.
>   —Virgil

Momentous happenings can always be illuminated by a quotation from the ancients. By some passage beautiful and romantic, or hard and sober. For instance, Montaigne—on whose shoulders both Stendhal and Weininger stood—opines that women never really love princes.

12

The Royal Marriage Market

Louis XIV's attachment to Marie Mancini (niece of the Cardinal Mazarin) was an important matter, because he loved her sufficiently to wish to marry her, and because he was sufficiently master of himself to consent to a separation. This victory gained over his passion was the first act which displayed the greatness of his character . . . He married, for his country's good, the Infanta Maria Theresa.
— VOLTAIRE: *Siècle de Louis XIV*

I N THE late thirties the people of the Empire lost some of their traditional reverence for the Royal Family. One reason for this was that the heir to the throne was still playing time and a half and was still unmarried. The popular song of the day ran:

> England's Virgin Queen was Bess,
> I'll be Virgin King, I guess,
> And the greatest sport in Merrie England.

That great idealist, the Duke of Windsor, shares with ordinary mortals his thoughts on marriage at that time. The idea of an arranged marriage was, he says, altogether repugnant to him; he was determined under no circumstances to contract a loveless marriage; and he was also determined that his choice of a wife should be dictated "*not by considerations of state,*" but by his heart.

This is a most important statement. It is an open, almost brazen, admission that there was once a King of England who put his own "heart" above the interest of his country.

It is also a confession that this Prince was an ardent believer in the Hollywood romantic dream, so different from the serious business of marriage; and ignorant of the philosophy of worth-while counselors such as Hegel, Count Keyserling, Rabindranath Tagore, and a host of others.

Hegel, the German philosopher who had mesmerized so many British intellectuals during the nineteenth century, said that the healthiest approach to marriage lay in a good moral choice; that then affection and friendship and partnership would naturally follow; that the individual preference was a secondary element—one does not marry a woman simply in order to "possess" her. Marriage is mainly for the sake of stability and the unity of man and woman, with the aim of founding a family. Time has sifted out many of Hegel's doctrines; but others, as sound as the one quoted, still remain.

Keyserling, a lifelong student of marriage in all its aspects, emphasizes in his *The Book of Marriage* that common experience unfortunately goes to prove that love is not a guarantee of a happy marriage. Keyserling thought fit to underline the following passage in his chapter "The Proper Choice of Partners": "*It is an essential condition for the proper choice of partners that both should be on the same plane of existence, for equality in birth is not only absolutely justified but imperative.*" Keyserling was not thinking of royalty when he wrote this.

That romantic Hindu, the great poet, Rabindranath Tagore, when it comes to the serious business of marriage suddenly becomes prosaic. He points out that his people, Brahman or outcast, from time immemorial were extremely suspicious about the dictates of the heart in marriage. He said, among other things: "The way to marriage which is shown by the torchlight of passion has not for its goal the welfare of society, but the satisfaction of selfish desire."

But here was the Prince of Wales abandoning himself to his desire for a married woman, when for more than ten years his parents and the half-billion people of the Empire had been hoping that he would marry according to the rule of princes. That is, without selfish desires. His father and grandfather had both contracted marriages in obedience to popular demand.

The marriage of George V had been dutiful if curious. When his elder brother the Duke of Clarence, heir to the throne and already engaged to the very pleasing, very reputable Princess Mary of Teck, suddenly died, George V promptly stepped into his place—the peoples of the Empire must not be disappointed. George was then a young Prince, a naval officer serving in foreign waters. He was devoted to his profession, but he obediently returned to England and married Princess Mary. Here was a glowing example of how to keep

faith with the people. And the marriage of George and Mary turned
out to be very happy, despite the fact that it had been arranged.

Edward VII, that irresistible, charming bounder, that born Don
Juan, at the age of twenty-two married Alexandra of Denmark.
Thereafter he lived a gallant life, to the diversion of his subjects. He
knew that nobody would interfere with his personal pleasures as long
as he did his duties. Queen Alexandra, as is well-known, was most
understanding. In *The Edwardian Era*, André Maurois writes that:

> When Queen Alexandra saw that there was no hope (*for Edward
> VII on his deathbed*) she sent for Mrs. Keppel (*one of her husband's favorites*)
> to come to the palace, and herself led Mrs. Keppel by the hand to
> the dying king.

At one time the name of the Prince of Wales had been linked with
that of a king's daughter. When in May 1918 he paid a semi-official
visit to Italy, a ripple of rumor ran round the Continent—he was
about to become affianced to Princess Yolanda of Savoy! The advantages of such a match were eagerly canvassed. Of the friendly relations
between the two countries there could be no doubt. Italy had been
the mistress of England in arts, and her comrade in arms. It was of
the greatest moment to both countries to maintain this friendship,
and to make it even stronger, for both had vital interests in the
Mediterranean.

A royal romance, coming at that moment, would have set a lasting
seal upon Anglo-Italian relations. It would have provided a welcome
note of joy after the war, somber even in the case of victorious nations.
And it might have brought into the British Royal Family a share in
those high gifts of statesmanship for which the House of Savoy was
famed.

There was, of course, the question of religion. Princess Yolanda,
a Catholic, might be received into the Church of England; but if she
would not consent to this, might not the Pope be willing to grant a
dispensation for a mixed marriage? The times were evil: the Catholic
Church, which had suffered so greatly as a result of the war and the
advent of Communism, would be only too pleased to secure the support of the British Empire, hoping that the King-Emperor might
assume the character once played by Constantine and Charlemagne,
of protector of the Church. The Church of England might accept
even a mixed marriage in the hope of that reunion of the Churches
toward which many learned men had been working.

The Empire, too, might hope to benefit: the Catholic populations of, say, Ireland and Canada would be delighted by the match. It might, also, indirectly have a very favorable effect on American public opinion—many Americans of Italian and of Irish extraction would be led to view England with a friendly eye.

But all these exciting speculations were dashed by one look at the law of England: the Act of Settlement provided that any member of the Royal Family becoming a Catholic, or marrying a Catholic, should forfeit all right and title to the throne of Great Britain.

Might not the British Parliament, hopefully inquired the romantics, be willing to repeal this part of the Act?

An immediate "No" would be the reply of anyone acquainted with England—particularly with England as it was in those days. Educated persons might feel it highly desirable to amend the Act, in such a way as to leave the Prince of Wales (not to mention future generations) a wider field of choice in wives. But anti-Catholic feeling of a certain kind was still alive; and it is possible that any attempt to amend the Act of Settlement would have produced its own defeat. So the idea of an Italo-English royal romance was regretfully dismissed by even the most romantic. Rumor and argument seemed only to have ended in nothing; but the chatter of the amateur marriage brokers may have started the Prince in his determination to show his independence concerning marriage.

For he says in his memoirs that as a result of his travels, and ever since his return from his first Empire voyage, he no longer shared the outlook of his family. He now wanted to marry only for love.

The Duke also points out that whereas Russia and Germany had for some centuries provided consorts for members of the British Royal Family, this could no longer be the case, since the Russian Royal Family had been murdered, and after the war of 1914-1918 a German bride would hardly have been acceptable to the British. Even so, the press during the summer months of 1936 remarked that "intimate friends of King Edward say he will marry soon," *Cavalcade* adding on July 18, 1936, that Princess Cecile Victoria was a possible royal bride.

And who was Princess Cecile Victoria? She was the daughter of ex-Crown Prince Wilhelm—the Kaiser's granddaughter!

This was not the first time *Cavalcade* had tried to play the role of matchmaker. In May 1936 it had reported that certain officials

;... are saying to discreet friends that when King Edward is crowned he will have a consort at his side.

This may be considered the first intimation that Wallis Simpson might wear a crown.

A picture of Mrs. Simpson appeared in *Cavalcade* of June 6, 1936. The same number bore on its cover a photograph of Princess Alexandrina Louise of Denmark, with the caption: "Chosen to Marry King Edward." The Princess was the youngest daughter of Prince Harald, brother of King Christian of Denmark; and rumor had it that her uncle and King George of England had hoped to arrange a marriage between her and the Prince of Wales. As Princess Alexandrina had been born in 1914, her age, as well as her station, rendered her a suitable consort; not to mention either of her two elder sisters, Theodora born in 1910, or Carolina Matilda born in 1912.

There were other Scandinavian princesses. Over in Sweden King Gustav V had one daughter Ingrid, born in 1910 (she eventually married King Frederik of Denmark); and the King's brother, Carl, had three: Margarita, born in 1899; Maartha, born in 1901; and Astrid, born in 1905.

Of the three young women, the press favored Princess Maartha: in the twenties there appeared a notice in the papers:

> The Prince of Wales is now reported engaged to Princess Maartha of Sweden, niece of the Swedish King. Due to his going on his present South American and South African trip, the official announcement will not be made until his return.

The press might also have mentioned the name of Princess Frederika of Brunswick-Lunebourg, a very good-looking, very able royal lady, who has since acquired renown in her own right. She became Queen of Greece, a tower of strength to her husband and her subjects in all the cruel sufferings of the years after World War II.

Of course the Prince of Wales might have looked farther for a wife, without encountering any dynastic or religious difficulties. The two Rumanian princesses—Marie, later Queen of the Yugoslavs, and Ileana, who married Anton, Archduke of Habsburg and still later became Mrs. Habsburg of America—were not Catholics. Either one of them would have been made welcome in England.

The Habsburgs were of course rulers of Austria-Hungary; but their greatest subjects were themselves often of royal blood. The Counts of Transylvania, the Telekys, the Bethlens, the Banffys, were of kingly descent and Protestant faith. The ladies of these quasi-princely houses had their fair share of the beauty for which the women of Hungary are so renowned: a beauty perfected by that touch of the exotic, which is the fruit of a rich and ancient culture.

This list does not exhaust the possibility of a suitable marriage for the King of England. For besides the reigning houses of Europe there were families of great and ancient renown, now fallen on evil times: for the nobility of Russia had not all been destroyed by the assassin's bullet, or by worse than bullets. Some fifty of these families had escaped abroad. They had suffered all the privations experienced by the gently born who by one stroke of fortune lose all. Of these people "the marrying Mdivanis" were the best-known, but certainly not the most typical. The typical exiles had worked—or starved—in silence. They were governesses; they were translators; they were waitresses or secretaries. They could be found on lecture platforms, or behind the counters of shops.

Had Edward, whether as Prince or King, met and loved one of these ladies, the sentimental English would have taken her to their hearts. This is plain from the reception given to Princess Marina of Greece in 1934. A royal wedding always provides a good excuse for junketing, but this royal wedding had a touch of its own. The Duke of Kent appeared in a gallant light as the Prince who had had the sense and spirit to seize upon his fairest princess, who was most rich, being poor; and the remarkable elegance and beauty of the bride justified his choice.

For a Queen of England high birth had been, always, a *sine qua non*, partly as a result of the strange medieval *mystique* of noble blood at which Shakespeare had tilted:

> . . . Strange is it that our bloods,
> Of colour, weight, and heat, pour'd all together,
> Would quite confound distinction, yet stand off
> In differences so mighty
>   . . . honours thrive
> When rather from our acts we them derive
> Than our foregoers.

And partly by reason of the political and other advantages to be derived from such a choice. Wealth and beauty were also looked for.

Nowadays a different set of rules obtains. Beauty, "that hook of wiving," is still as desirable as ever, and much more easily found than formerly: with modern beauty culture what it is, even an ugly woman *soignée* and well-dressed, may be more attractive than one

Sir Walter Monckton, adviser to
Edward VIII

Thelma Lady Furness

Lord Hardinge, the faithful Private Secretary of Edward VIII, and his bride.
The Hardinge family motto is: "For King and Country."

This palatial yacht "Nahlin" took Edward VIII and Mrs. Simpson on a memorable vacation.

Another floating palace. Mr. and Mrs. Axel Wenner-Gren, owners of the yacht, "Southern Cross," entertain the Duke of Windsor, Governor-General of the Bahamas, and his Duchess.

dowered only with unaided good looks. But a Queen Consort must not be lowborn; she must not be scandalous; and her marriage to the King must not involve England in foreign entanglements.

This last requirement is of such weight that it was one of the reasons which persuaded that sapient princess, Elizabeth Tudor, Queen Elizabeth I, to remain unmarried.

And of course it was quite possible for King Edward VIII to marry within the realm, as had happened before in his family. Queen Victoria had allowed her daughter, Princess Louise, to marry the Marquis of Lorne, later Duke of Argyll; Edward VII had allowed *his* daughter Louise, the Princess Royal, to marry the Duke of Fife. Both these marriages had been popular, and the lesson had not been forgotten. The Prince of Wales' brother (later George VI) and his sister, Princess Mary, had married commoners, and this had paved the way for him to contract a nondynastic marriage, should he so wish.

It is unthinkable that, during those postwar years, there could not have been found, among the ladies of Britain, one fitted by birth and beauty to be Princess of Wales. There were peeresses in their own right, ladies of high title. London was teeming with aristocratic girls, wealthy, interesting, and charged with sex appeal. The Prince of Wales had plenty of opportunity for selection—he danced with them. In those days Elsa Lanchester, wife of Charles Laughton, made popular a song entitled: "I Danced With a Man Who Danced With the Girl Who Danced With the Prince of Wales."

Of course there is still a faction, particularly in the United States, which sanctions Edward's insistence on a love match. "Every one must marry only for love," is the tenet of this group.

It is therefore interesting to find an outstanding American man of letters who holds otherwise. In that outspoken book *In Defense of Women*, the unusually clearheaded thinker and writer—perhaps the most brilliant in America—H. L. Mencken, expresses ideas very different from those of the "marry-for-love" group.

Mr. Mencken praises the French and Jewish custom of arranged marriages, as assuring lasting contentment and even happiness. He says that the love match almost inevitably deteriorates into boredom and unhappiness. Women, he declares, are born for the business of marriage, and they pursue their end with apparent sentimentality, but actually with all the precision of a calculating machine; they never, even for a second, allow their emotions to interfere until the quarry is seized, their chief device being to play hard-to-get. Mr.

Mencken further declares that every man is transformed into so much
putty in the hands of the woman who has made up her mind to marry
him. The American woman, especially, has for her principal goal in
life the altar, and rolls her efficiently amorous eyes toward the man
on top of the ladder, since she always hopes to re-enact the story of
Cinderella and Prince Charming.

Mr. Mencken goes on to say:

> I propose the prohibition of sentimental marriages by law, and the
> substitution of matchmaking by the common hangman. For one thing,
> it would purge the serious business of marriage of the romantic fol-de-
> rol that now corrupts it, and so make for peace and happiness.

Of course Mr. Mencken is joking. But in between the sardonic lines,
the champions of Marriage for Love Alone may be able to trace a
wise meaning.

But the present work is concerned with the love match of an ex-King
and not an ordinary man. So here may be quoted a few words from
the chapter, "Of Love," in Francis Bacon's *Essays:*

> You may observe, that, amongst all the great and worthy persons
> there is not one that hath been transported to the mad degree of love,
> which shows that great spirits and great business do keep out this
> passion . . . It is a strange thing to note the excess of this passion, and
> how it braves the nature and value of things . . . There was never proud
> man thought so absurdly well of himself as the lover doth of the person
> loved . . . They do best who, if they cannot but admit love, yet make
> it keep quarter, and sever it wholly from their serious affairs and
> actions of life.

The Prince who so longed to be "transported to the mad degree of
love" that he was ready to barter his honor for it, and jilt the millions
who had placed their faith in him, no longer shared the rational view-
point of his family—his companions, an extremely fast set, saw to that.
Nor is it probable that the Harlem dancing girls he knew and also
danced with, in London and Paris, taught him the proper steps,
except perhaps those of the Black Bottom (which, as he says in his
memoirs, for some time he regarded as America's greatest export).

He was, then, already determined not to sacrifice anything for his
people, nor even to undertake the very natural *mariage de convenance*,
one of the easiest duties of rulers. When he writes of the lack of
"eligible royal princesses of pure stock" one is forced to wonder if his

own stock was so pure. Does he not recall his predecessors, the debauchee George, the idiot George, the mad George, the no-account George? There were many other ineligibles in his family album. His great-grandmother, Victoria, was perhaps the first person of character in a crazily alloyed family.

His brother, the late King George VI, and his sister Mary and brother George of Gloucester had married commoners, it is true. That is, if the petty Hanoverian Guelphs, or the Saxe-Coburg-Gothas, can call the Bowes-Lyons, the Lascelles and the Montagu-Douglas-Scotts, three of Britain's finest families, commoners. But assume that they were commoners; the younger princes and princesses in the British Royal Family may marry at will, since they are of less importance. But the eldest son—that's quite another matter! The Princess of Wales, who will become Queen of England, *must* be somebody.

Windsor hints in the memoirs that he was concerned with the purity of the succession; that he wished to improve the royal stock, thus assuring the nation of a perfect heir. Does it seem probable that he ever really thought of any such momentous matters?

Was this hapless person—of whom it was said that "King Edward was a distraught, unreasonable man during the days before his abdication, and negotiations with the King would have been impossible"—capable of any kind of reflection? Was the marriage with Mrs. Simpson, which he tried to force on the nation, likely to assure a wonderful progeny?

As it is, the Windsors have no children—and whether they are both at fault, or only one of them, would be impossible to determine without complete data. So, events or rather the lack of events, would soon have shown this to be an idle excuse.

The English would have accepted an American-born Queen. Such a marriage would have been regarded by many of them as timely, modern and as providing a firm bond between the two nations. An American girl who had no past and no divorce in her life would have been welcome as a Queen of England. She would not have had to be the daughter of a president, a Morgan, an Astor or a Vanderbilt. Just a nice American girl. Not even a movie star, as *The New Yorker* at one time jocosely suggested:

> The yearning for royalty and royal romance is not a laudable human passion maybe, but it is a real one, all right. "Shall the new king marry?" is the question which upsets the world. The *Daily News* sent

its Inquiring Reporter out to stop people and ask; and the other day a woman who lives on Delancey Street in Philadelphia wrote WOR making a tangible suggestion which expresses the heart of America. "Yes, the new King, Edward VIII, should marry," she wrote. "It would make his subjects so happy, and the girl should be none other than Greta Garbo. With her beside him, he would rule the world. What a king and what a queen! As you probably know, Garbo has blue blood in her ancestry far back. It would be like a dream if something like this would happen. Both have had a rough time with love."

It would be like a dream indeed. It would be the greatest thing since Lindbergh's flight.

But it seems that what Edward really wanted was a woman far below him in rank, with whom he could play the role of King Cophetua. Any psychologist could have explained that he was suffering from the "Drang nach Unten" complex of the *grand seigneur* who thought he had everything—until he encountered the maid who refused to grant him even a smile.

No, Greta Garbo wouldn't do. What this royal Narcissus needed was a mirror.

13

Lively Skeletons in the Closet

He who serves his country well has no need of ancestors.
—Voltaire

If it were not for Winston Churchill's ancestor, John Churchill, a poor country boy who began his career at Court as a page and eventually became the Duke of Marlborough, there wouldn't have been a Duke of Windsor.

Handsome John Churchill showed unmistakable signs of his genius in practical matters at an early age: with forty-five hundred of the five thousand pounds he received as a gift for a single night from the Duchess of Cleveland, who was one of Charles II's favorite mistresses, he purchased an annuity from Lord Halifax. In old England aristocrats were the insurance brokers.

Back in those days of war and unknown bacteria, men died young. Halifax, pocketing Churchill's money, rubbed his hands joyfully— John was off to the wars and would be cut down in no time. But Halifax was fooled: John Churchill went on cashing his annuity for half a century!

Not only did the great Duke of Marlborough win the war of sex and economics. He was the foremost general of his time, indeed of all time, one general who never lost a battle—nor his temper. Once, when his orderly was insolent to him, he merely said with a smile to his aide-de-camp: "I wouldn't have this man's temper for all the money in the world." And he was a most able statesman. However, his interest in money matters sometimes got the better of him. When George Guelph, an insignificant ruler of the tiny principality of Hanover in Germany, sent his mercenaries to help Marlborough's troops at the Battle of Blenheim, and paid the expenses out of his own pocket, the thrifty English leader never forgot this generosity: he determined to support George's pretensions to the English throne.

But in order to win this battle, too, when heirless Queen Anne

Stuart was dying, Marlborough had to think, and act, quickly. George, to be sure, had a just if slight claim: his grandmother, Elizabeth, Queen of Bohemia, was the daughter of James I of England and sister of the beheaded Charles I. But the son of James II, the Old Pretender, had a better claim than George, if lineage be regarded as the overruling factor. So far as the bulk of the English nation was concerned, the matter had been decided by the Act of Settlement of 1701, which gave the crowns of England, Scotland and Ireland to George's mother, Sophia of Hanover, daughter of Elizabeth of Bohemia, and to her descendants. But it was a case of touch-and-go: there was in Scotland a considerable, and even in England minority, support for the Old Pretender. Powerful, patient and perfidious Marlborough, who had first upheld and then abandoned the Stuarts, came out for the Guelphs, and so in 1714 a German became King of England.

The fact that George's wife was languishing in prison (altogether thirty-two years), having been put there by her sex-maniac husband when he discovered that his unhappy wife had taken a lover, Count Königsmark, did not seem to matter in the new King's new country.

And don't immigrants mend their ways in their adopted land? They do, if they learn the language and have the proper influence—preferably gentle, feminine influence.

George I of England brought with him his own female entourage. He needed companionship. As he could not speak a word of English, it was natural that for conversation's sake, he should have in his train a few ladies. Two of the German *Hausfraus* he imported into his new country were noted for their extreme ugliness. So, probably to cover up this greatest of sins, he created them duchesses.

George I was constantly homesick; and consequently he spent most of his time in Germany. Besides, he had certain dislikes—he hated England, the English, and his son and heir, who warmly reciprocated the feeling. But of course George could do nothing to prevent the accession of his son to the throne.

George II was not exactly an English scholar, either. When the Prime Minister, Horace Walpole, told him that his father was dead, he couldn't believe it: "Dat isz van bik lie!" he replied, so the good news had to be repeated.

He followed in his father's footsteps. George II also had numerous mistresses, and, like his father, hated England and loved Hanover.

But he hated so many things and people that it would be impossible to list all his pet aversions.

However, it is easy to name his one ruling passion: money. He would sit for hours counting his gold, piece by piece.

The reign of this ancestor of the Duke of Windsor can be summed up with a neat zero. It amounted to nothing.

George III was the son of George II's eldest son, Frederick Prince of Wales, who predeceased his father. This George, too, was a strange fellow, who suffered from long periods of madness; the loss of his American colonies, and the conduct of his children, were thought to contribute to his illness. When he was in an unbalanced state, he sometimes had to be put in a strait jacket. There he sat, poor King, in Windsor Castle, singing the melodies of Handel; or, when he was taken out for exercise, engaging in serious conversation with an oak tree.

Mad George had fifteen children. True to his family tradition, he could not stand his eldest son and heir. After a brief sketch of the other children has been given, it will be possible to consider the Prince of Wales, later George IV, more at length.

Prince Octavius and Prince Alfred died in infancy (of cerebral meningitis). Frederick, Duke of York, contracted a marriage—with Princess Frederica of Prussia—which lasted less than a year. The Duke of Clarence, who eventually became William IV, set up house with an actress; Edward, Duke of Kent, lived with a Canadian lady; the Duke of Cumberland married Frederica, the widowed Princess of Solms-Braunfels, and later, upon the accession of Victoria, became King of Hanover;* the Duke of Sussex twice married commoners. Long after the death of George III, the Duke of Clarence and the Duke of Kent also married, but not their mistresses.

The daughters of George III were the victims of parental tyranny. The Princess Royal, his eldest daughter, escaped at last, by negotiating a marriage with the Prince of Würtemberg; Princess Mary, at the

---

* Hanover was subject to the Salic Law, which does not allow a woman to inherit the Crown. A son's son may succeed, but not a son's daughter. Consequently, the title to the throne of Hanover did not descend from the Duke of Kent to his daughter Victoria, but passed to the nearest male heir, his younger brother Ernest, Duke of Cumberland. Ernest's son George was defeated and dethroned by Prussia at the battle of Langensalza, in 1866, and Hanover was annexed to Prussia, ceasing to be an independent kingdom.

age of forty, succeeded in marrying her cousin, the Duke of Gloucester; Princess Elizabeth waited even longer—at forty-nine, she became the Landgravine of Hesse-Homburg.

Three of the daughters sought solace in love affairs. Princess Augusta was in love with the Court physician. Princess Sophia was said to have married, secretly, one of the King's equerries, and when she was with child by him, the mad King was told that she had dropsy. Princess Amelia had an unhappy romance with Charles Fitzroy, another equerry, a man twice her age. She wanted to elope with him, but the thing never came off. It was rumored that Fitzroy himself was an illegitimate son of George III, and consequently the half brother of the girl who was in love with him.

As if he had premonitions, George III, while still a sane young man, insisted on the passing of the Royal Marriages Act of 1772, in his determination to control the marriages of the Royal Family.

To return to his eldest son, later George IV. It is easy to describe this Monarch, for no prince was so frequently painted. He too was a beautiful baby. And he too grew up to be a handsome youth, with blond hair, smooth skin, a Windsorian nose, a tight and stubborn upper lip, and a well-proportioned figure. As he grew older he became very fat, for dieting was not yet in fashion. "Prinny has now taken off his corset, and let his belly fall to his knees," was the acid comment of Beau Brummell, a former friend who for some years was copied and envied by George IV. After the rupture, the Prince, while walking in Piccadilly with another friend, cut the Beau dead; but it was not easy to ignore Brummell. "Who is your fat friend, Alvanley?" he asked aloud of the Prince's companion.

The Duke of Windsor, when Prince of Wales, gained fame by inventing a new kind of tie knot. The incomparable George IV, who was in all seriousness called "the First Gentleman of Europe," as a prince invented a shoe buckle. He thought up an entirely new kind of shoe buckle, all by himself! That's about all that he himself gave to England, Europe and the world.

On the other side of the ledger: he drained the coffers of the treasury. His yearly income was gradually advanced. First it was £62,000, then £70,000 then £100,000 and £120,000. He borrowed vast sums abroad. He also asked Parliament that the nation should pay his debts of £160,000 and of £650,000. He built a semi-Oriental palace in Brighton, where he sojourned frequently. This edifice cost the nation half a million pounds; and was so encrusted with domes and cupolas

that the witty Sidney Smith, Dean of St. Paul's, said that it looked as if
St. Paul's Cathedral had gone down to Brighton and pupped there.

In 1785 the Prince secretly married Mrs. Maria Fitzherbert. She
was beautiful, "the store of refined good humor, and good nature."
When he first proposed a marriage that, in view of the Royal
Marriages Act, would be illegal, she refused. George exhausted every
argument known to lovers. He then wept hysterically before her;
created scenes; and threatened suicide. Finally she agreed to an
engagement.

But Mrs. Fitzherbert was a sensible woman, and she had misgivings.
She knew that great evils might result from a marriage. Without the
need of any warning from a Private Secretary, she went abroad and
remained away for nearly a year. But her wealth and her beauty made
her the target of adventurers; besides, George bombarded her with
letters. So she returned to England, and to the Prince.

Ten days before the wedding took place, George had received a
warning from the great Charles James Fox, who was devoted to him.
This marriage, said Fox, would be the worst thing that even his
enemies could suggest to the Prince. As for the lady,

> . . . if I were Mrs. Fitzherbert's father or brother, I would advise her
> not by any means to agree to it, and to prefer any other species of
> connection with you to one leading to such misery and mischief.

Fox was not a man indifferent to the claims of the human heart,
or the individual's right to liberty. During the War of Independence,
for instance, he declared that if he were an American he would never
surrender. This English patriot also lauded George Washington to
the skies! But he, like Mrs. Fitzherbert, was a responsibly minded
person; and so he penned his warning.

From this marriage arose a very peculiar situation: by the Act of
Settlement of 1701 any royal person becoming a Catholic or contracting marriage with a Catholic, forfeited all title to the throne; however,
by the Royal Marriages Act of 1772, the marriage was legally null
and void. By insisting on the passage of the latter Act, thirteen years
before, George III had lost the satisfaction of seeing his hated heir
lose the throne!

Immediately after the marriage the Prince swore to Fox that he was
not married, and he continued to lie in the matter to this loyal supporter for nearly two years. Relying on the Prince's word, Fox in turn

swore to a restive House of Commons that the alleged marriage was "neither a legal nor a canonical fact."

The extravagant Prince of Wales was often in need of money; and though he was really in love with Mrs. Fitzherbert—mainly because she resisted him—her possession of a personal fortune cannot have harmed her in his eyes. This fortune she brought into their common purse. But she too had expensive tastes. One day a bailiff arrived at her house with a warrant for her arrest for the sum of £1,825. She offered her own jewels in payment, but these were not accepted. The Prince, who was present, then came to his wife's rescue and raised the money on his own jewels from a well-known pawnbroker of Fleet Street.

At one time the Prince made showy efforts to cut down his expenses. He abruptly stopped work on his London mansion, Carlton House, which he had been building at public expense; and proposed to live abroad. To his adviser, Sir James Harris, he suggested that he might live at the smaller Courts of Europe, incognito. Harris was firm in his reply:

> "Impossible, Sir. The title of the Earl of Chester will be only a mask which covers the Prince of Wales, and as such, your actions will ever be judged."
> "You think I mean to go to France? I shall keep to the Empire,* and perhaps to Italy."
> —*The Life of George IV*, by P. Fitzgerald, M. A. Harper & Bros., 1881

By a coincidence, Mrs. Fitzherbert was living in Holland at the time that the Prince suggested his scheme to Harris. This proposal to go abroad was to have a curious parallel in the life of the Duke of Windsor.

It is also a curious parallel that neither prince resisted temptation. George IV spent £10,000 a year for his coats alone, at a time when £10,000 represented more than $50,000 and a man's coat could be bought for twenty-five dollars. The Windsor temptation came at an even more expensive rate. "Who can find a virtuous woman? for her price is far above rubies."

George also had musical gifts—he loved to play the flute and sing. And by George! he did sing. He sang to his friends, the parasites and

---

*The Empire referred to was, of course, the Holy Roman Empire, which had become a loose federation of the German principalities, under the presidency of the House of Habsburg. It came to an end in 1806, when Francis II resigned the Imperial title.

the prostitutes. In that age of urbanity neither of Windsor's favorite instruments—the bagpipes and the banjo—would have been *bon ton*.

Photography had not yet been invented, so George IV posed patiently in that golden age of English portraitists. In this he was impelled partly by vanity, but also by his wish to patronize art. For this bad King, who was a bigamist, liar, spendthrift, at least behaved with some generosity to artists, writers and composers. He collected the Dutch and Flemish masters, and at his command the famous Sir Thomas Lawrence painted some portraits for the adornment of Windsor Castle.

George, unlike Windsor, also gave some money to music and literature. He sent £200 to help Beethoven. He gave £1,000 a year to the Royal Society of Literature. He bestowed a baronetcy on Sir Walter Scott, which the latter treasured far more than money. He doted on the works of Jane Austen, and never traveled without a set of her novels.

Another great writer to come under royal notice was Charlotte Brontë—in 1934. When the Prince of Wales once asked for something to read, he was handed a volume of *Jane Eyre*. "What is this appalling stuff?" exclaimed the Prince after reading a dozen pages, "and who is this Charlotte *Bront?*" "One of the greatest of English novelists, Sir," gravely replied a courtier.

George married money though, unlike Windsor—when his debts became insupportable he secured their payment by consenting to marry a German princess, Caroline of Brunswick; in spite of the fact that he already had a wife. At the wedding he was so drunk on brandy that two dukes had to hold him up. The unhappy couple lived together for a year, during which time the Princess of Wales gave birth to a daughter, Princess Charlotte.

Charlotte grew up to be an attractive woman, and wonderful to relate! contracted a happy marriage with Leopold, the future King of the Belgians. But the Princess died in childbirth two years later. Thereupon her uncles, Duke William, Duke Edward and Duke Frederick, hastily married: after all, one of their legitimate children might inherit the crown. George III was still living, but who knew how long the mad King would last?

He lasted another three years, and thereafter his hated heir celebrated a long-delayed accession with the costliest coronation in English history—near a quarter-million pounds were spent!

Subjects are ready to forgive the youthful irregularities of an heir, whether he is called George or Edward. Princes must sow their wild oats, and have a little royal fun. But George IV tormented the nation nearly half a century, and when he died the people of England sighed with relief. There followed the short reign of his brother William IV who was succeeded in 1837 by the young Victoria.

Victoria was the daughter of Edward, Duke of Kent, fourth son of George III. Canadians may remember him for his brutality: one deserter received a sentence of 999 lashes, another was sentenced to death, marched for miles in his shroud and finally reprieved at the graveside. The Duke lived with a Canadian woman, Madame St. Laurent, for twenty-seven years; and upon the Duke's marriage the discarded mistress went into a convent.

The new Queen was a level-headed young woman, who had the good sense to place herself in the hands of two of the most intelligent men of the epoch: her Uncle Leopold, King of the Belgians, and Lord Melbourne. Leopold's instruction was of the mail-order variety —until her accession; Melbourne directed her until her marriage with Albert. It was, of course, Uncle Leopold who conjured up Victoria's cousin, Prince Albert, as a suitable husband. The choice proved to be a good one for both Queen and country. But even here scandal crept in: it was rumored, perhaps quite wrongly, that Albert was not the son of his father.

On the other hand, the eccentricity of his mother was not a matter of mere gossip. After being divorced by the Duke of Coburg she married a Count Pölzig; and at her death it was discovered that she had left him a large sum of money in trust, on condition that he would have her body nicely embalmed and would never part with it.

One cannot blame Pölzig for marrying again; but it was unfortunate that while on his honeymoon he lost the duchess' body.

Queen Victoria was as good as a queen-bee—industrious, fertile and long-lived. Nor was she as strait-laced as history sometimes makes her out to be. Her married life was happy, and its effects were felt beyond the family circle—nine times the British taxpayer was informed that "the measure of the Queen's domestic felicity is now full." Unfortunately this happiness was not extended to all her nine children. But in spite of the severity of his upbringing, "dear Bertie" (King Edward VII) was not a moral copy of his "dearest father"; indeed, in his youth he seemed almost like a throwback to his Hanoverian ancestors. Thoughtful persons might feel that the upbringing itself had had something to do with this: that the history of her own family, a mere generation before, should have taught the Queen that cruelty would defeat its own aims. "A stupid German sergeant system of discipline . . . rigorously applied" had in part been the cause of her wicked uncles' wickedness; it had failed to cure the natural weakness of George IV. If his environment did not produce the same results in Edward VII, this was mainly because he had a wonderful character.

When at last Edward VII succeeded he revealed himself as a Monarch who possessed the rare, unique power of combining dignity with bonhomie. He had very great charm; he had tact and poise, good sense and judgment, and to a very high degree a gift most valuable to a Sovereign, the feeling for ceremonial. He would go out of his way to please individuals, and always said the right thing at the right time. He side-stepped mistakes with the dexterity of a polo pony.

The misfortune or unhappiness of anyone he knew caused him the greatest distress, and he would do anything in his power to relieve it; while the good fortune of a friend gave him the utmost pleasure. He was warmhearted, human and kind. He adored beautiful women because he liked beauty in general and had an immense capacity for enjoying life. But he also had a positive and strong desire that everyone else should enjoy life, too.

His was indeed a great personality. He was a vital asset to national stability, and especially in time of crisis proved himself of inestimable value. (His sound feeling in public affairs was passed on to his son, George V.) The majority of his subjects sympathized, for there was a great community of feeling between the King and the nation.

But despite his nearness to the people, Edward VII never lost his dignity. He once acted as godfather to the child of a Sandringham gamekeeper: but there could be no question of undue freedom on one side or the other, for the positions of both father and godfather were too well defined in the social hierarchy.

No one, ever, with impunity took liberties with Edward VII. He was more strait-laced than would at first appear. At a Court party he called over a pretty noblewoman, and delivered a smiling rebuke of a too-daring dress: "You must be mistaken—this is the Court, not the tennis court." On another occasion, at one of his informal dinners, the beautiful Jersey Lily, his mistress of seven years' standing, slipped some strawberry ice cream down his back. The King did not so much as turn toward the practical joker, continuing the conversation with his neighbor as if nothing had happened. But he never saw Lily Langtry again.

The death of such a man must have been keenly felt, even if it had not occurred at a time of political strife: the eloquent and truculent David Lloyd George was laying the foundations of the Welfare State. It took time for the nation to appreciate that George V had inherited his father's sterling qualities, with some of his own added. He was a devoted husband, and in public life lived up to the example of Edward VII. His faithfulness to national tradition, and his very strict observance of every duty, were his most marked characteristics. He was a true patriot, as English as a mutton chop, as has been said before.

The Hanoverian blood had apparently been purified. Victoria, Edward VII, and George V were good, constitutional, public-spirited rulers. George VI was cut to the same pattern: a family man, obedient, dutiful, hard-working, not given to dramatics. Though George VI had to struggle against weaknesses of health.

It is perhaps not so well-known that the Duke of Windsor also had difficulties of the same sort. As a child he suffered from such ordinary troubles as measles and colds. Then something happened to one of his ears, and he often traveled to Vienna to have it attended to by the famous Professor Neumann. It is not known if while there he consulted any psychiatrist in respect to his neurasthenic tendencies. As Prince of Wales, he had many falls from his horse—unnecessary falls, for (as has been remarked) a good rider acquires a solid seat in the saddle at the outset of his career. Once the Prince fell really hard and was laid up for a month with concussion of the brain. And later in his life the anxieties usually accompanying exile or unhappy wedlock seem to have affected his stomach.

14

The King Is Dead — Long Live the King!

Our duty is to England always.
— KING GEORGE V

*A wise king must do less in altering his laws than
he may; for new government is ever dangerous.*
— FRANCIS BACON:
Essays

H AD *A King's Story* not been written, future historians might
have had but an incomplete picture of the former King's character.
But the publication of this book did away with the possibility that his
complex nature might remain a mystery. Some of his basic traits,
including those which prompted him to give up the kingship less than
a year after he inherited it, are unwittingly revealed in the memoirs.

Death, whose powers are even greater than those of a "relentless"
Archbishop or a "ruthless" Prime Minister, forced George V to give
up his throne on January 20, 1936. The passing of kings is a matter
of high ceremony, where every detail demands forethought; for instance, when in 1928 King George was ill, Lord Stamfordham, his
Private Secretary, corresponded with the Archbishop of Canterbury,
the Most Reverend Cosmo Gordon Lang, discussing the right and
duty of the Primate to be present should the King die. Now, eight
years later, Dr. Lang was present. To Edward, the Primate might
appear as a noiseless specter, but to King George V he was the friend
of thirty-eight years' standing, who was, moreover, bringing spiritual
support to the dying sovereign.

The Duke of Windsor hints that if the Archbishop of Canterbury

had not "insisted" on his sick father's taking part in the exhausting
ceremonies of the Silver Jubilee in 1935, George V might have lived
longer. But the Duke's enemies whispered that his father's demise
was hastened by worry over his son's friendship with Mrs. Simpson,
which, to the old King, seemed a mere courting of disaster. (Speculations of this sort are always rampant when a king dies—in 1952
Londoners, gathered to gossip in the pubs after the funeral of George
VI, said that, had he been spared the burden of kingship imposed on
him by the abdication, he might have lived longer than to fifty-six.)
As George V reached the ripe age of seventy-one, it is possible that
both suggestions were mistaken.

Now, as the old King's life moved peacefully to its close, the four
Princes were visibly suffering; but their great mother, "calm and
strong . . . amazingly self-controlled," as Dr. Lang noted in his diary,
upheld them. After her husband breathed his last, Queen Mary bent,
and kissed the hand of the new King, her eldest son, Edward VIII.
For nothing, not death itself, could make Queen Mary forget her high
concept of kingship. Sixteen years later her conduct was the same:
she was driven to Clarence House to make her curtsy to the new
Queen, Elizabeth II. This eighty-five-year-old Royal lady did not
claim the privilege of age to wait until her granddaughter could come
to her—*she* went to "kiss hands."

Back in 1936 the example of Queen Mary was followed by her
younger sons. Unfortunately, the man who received this act of
homage could not appreciate it: he could not bring himself to believe,
he claims, that other people ought to humble themselves before him
in this way. He failed to perceive that his mother and his brothers
were doing reverence not to the individual but to that which he
embodied: the ideal of the Monarchy as the unceasing life of England.
The King was dead? In England the King is *never* dead. It is a maxim
of English law that the Throne does not remain vacant, even for a
moment.

With the homage of a loving mother and dutiful brothers began
the reign that Edward's trusting subjects thought would be the most
glorious in the annals of England and the Empire. Those who knew
the King personally, and some who did not, but who were acquainted
with his peculiar tastes and his unkingly outlook, trembled for him
and hoped for the best.

Trembling was in order—the new King soon began to break the
rules and traditions so deeply rooted in the English heart. It was a

Principals in a Bahamas mystery. The daughter of Sir Harry Oakes and her former husband, de Marigny.

Queen Frederica of Greece—one of the score of lovely princesses the Prince of Wales could have married

The King had all the locomotion . . .

small thing first, but a significant one: by King George's wish all the clocks at his beloved Sandringham had kept a special "Sandringham Time," half an hour in advance of the time elsewhere, to allow a little longer for the pleasures of country life. The night of his father's death, Edward abolished this innocent old custom. "He had put back the clocks! I wonder what other customs will be put back also!" wrote the apprehensive Archbishop in his diary.

The ability to attend to small details even at a time of grief seems characteristic of the Duke. On the death of his father he attended to clocks; two days after the passing of his brother he attended to shirts.

En route for England and the funeral of George VI aboard the *Queen Mary*, the Duke discovered that while in London he could order a certain type of shirt for evening wear. Rather than tell his steward that the ex-King of England could not spell the King's English, he called up the Duchess on the ship-to-shore phone, at two dollars a minute, to ask: "Darling, how do you spell piqué?" Wallis obliged— after thirty minutes.

Miss Elsa Maxwell reported this touching story of wifely help in her syndicated "Log." Unfortunately, everybody concerned forgot the accent over the "e," so important in this harmless word of French origin, which without the accent becomes the dangerous "pique." And Miss Maxwell's readers were thus reminded that the Prince of Wales' pique at a challenging snub had first fixed his attention on Wallis. Later, of course, he had discovered her weightier qualities.

More important things than spelling occupied the Court and the Government in 1936. To them, it was quite disturbing that, the morning after King George's death, King Edward flew in his private plane from Sandringham to London, to meet the Accession Privy Council. In the eyes of the Government this was an imprudent journey—rapid movements had never contributed to royal dignity, nor is Sandringham as far from London as is Kenya. (Nor was an accident impossible. In later years George VI always took the precaution, when flying, of dividing the royal party, with himself and Princess Margaret Rose in one plane, and the Queen and Princess Elizabeth in another.) Imprudence, of course, at this time was synonymous with lack of ceremonial feeling.

The ceremonies of accession in England were arranged centuries ago, and ancient precedent is not to be lightly set aside. The accession is a highly organized business; and any improvisation would be resented. All sorts of difficulties can be caused to those concerned by even a slight departure from custom. But Edward VIII did not worry about the difficulties of others. So he descended on his capital from the air a few hours after he succeeded. This was a mistake, though not a grave one. And his admirers were ready with the plea that in his bereavement King Edward sought to steady his nerves by quick travel.

Obviously the new King mourned his father; although it was well-known that George V and his heir had not seen eye to eye for a long time. Authorities on the subject of these royal differences claimed that the Prince of Wales had no great liking for the King, chiefly because the older and more experienced man tried to steer his son in what he thought was the right direction.

Here is what Margaret Case Harriman wrote about these disagreements in her piece, "The King and the Girl from Baltimore," in the volume *The Aspirin Age* (Simon & Schuster):

> "My father doesn't like me," Wales sometimes told his closest friends with an air of gentle sorrow. "Not at all sure I particularly like him," he would occasionally add, perhaps after a second brandy.

But thinking of himself as modern and efficient, the Empire Salesman just had to get to London quickly to start "this king business" with his Government. The trouble was that he did not take his business as seriously as had his father.

The same day, Edward VIII's accession was proclaimed at a meeting of His Majesty's Most Honourable Privy Council. This Council is composed of the Princes of the Blood, and the most distinguished and able personages of the land, for Great Britain protects its constitution not only by normal Parliamentary procedure, but also by having a group of the mightiest and cleverest standing behind the Throne. Nearly three hundred people who fill or have filled high positions in the realm, either in Great Britain or elsewhere in the Empire, with, occasionally, eminent men of science and letters, are appointed by the King to membership of the Privy Council. They are banded together to serve the Sovereign and uphold that sense of devotion to duty, morality and religion, without which the state would fall apart.

The Duke of Windsor proudly quotes in his memoirs the fine speech he made to the Privy Council:

> When my Father spoke here twenty-six years ago he declared that one of the objects of his life would be to uphold constitutional govern-

ment. *In this I am determined to follow in my Father's footsteps and to work as he did throughout his life for the happiness and welfare of all classes of my Subjects.*

I place my reliance upon the loyalty and affection of my peoples throughout the Empire, and upon the wisdom of their Parliaments, to support me in this heavy task, and I pray God will guide me to perform it.

Hearing such a speech, delivered with the gravity of a solemn promise, the high dignitaries, many of whom knew of Edward's unfortunate attachment, were reassured. They could have sworn that their new King's words were serious; that for the sake of his calling he would let his wildness die, and would put the happiness of his subjects first.

In the evening the King dined with Mrs. Simpson. Was she more in need of company and consolation than his widowed mother?

And probably that same night the Prime Minister, Edward's "enemy," worked over an enthusiastic speech which he delivered in the House of Commons on January 23. Baldwin said:

> King Edward VIII brings to the altar of public service a personality richly endowed with the fruits of travel and universal good will. He has the secret of youth in the prime of age. He has a wider and more intimate knowledge of all classes of his subjects, not only at home but also throughout the Dominions and India, than any of his predecessors.
>
> We all look forward with confidence and assurance to the new reign. Under God's providence, Edward VIII will establish the throne more firmly than ever on its surest and only foundations—the hearts of his people.

Did this sound like a Prime Minister who was seeking to undermine his King? Although Stanley Baldwin already knew more about him than anyone else in the kingdom . . .

Edward continued to commit breaches of tradition. Contrary to custom, he watched the Proclamation of his titles as King-Emperor. But Wallis being one of a select little party in a window of St. James' Palace, overlooking Friary Court, he simply could not resist being near her, and looking at her with pride as the Garter King of Arms proclaimed the friend of Mrs. Simpson:

"By the grace of God . . . of Great Britain, Ireland, and the British Dominions beyond the seas, King, Defender of the Faith, Emperor of India."

The earthly remains of the King-Emperor who had departed were brought in a train, slowly and with dignity, from Sandringham to London. The simple, unvarnished coffin was placed on a gun carriage and taken to Westminster Hall. King Edward VIII followed with his brothers, on foot. Upon the Royal Standard, the Sovereign's personal flag, covering the coffin, was the Imperial Crown. On top of this Crown—which, save for some of the jewels, is not an ancient one; the original regalia of England was destroyed in Cromwell's time—is a Maltese cross, set with precious stones.

This scene of a Sovereign's last pomp, the gun carriage with sailors at the dragropes, the display of crown jewels, the splendid uniforms, is a familiar one. It was re-enacted at the funeral of George VI. It is a marvel of *mise-en-scène*, better directed than any film. But at the funeral of George V that Fate on which the Duke of Windsor leans so heavily in his memoirs showed its hand and disturbed the meticulous arrangements—the cross broke off the Crown and fell into the mud!

It may be repeated here that the new King, seeing the precious jewel drop, uttered a startled cry. A Guardsman walking just before him quickly stooped down, picked up the cross, and put it in his pocket. The people knew nothing of this, though to many of them it would have seemed like an omen.

Nor did they know of an irreverent alteration attempted by King Edward. Having changed "Sandringham Time," the King wanted to change something much more important: he told the Archbishop of Canterbury that he did not want any religious service to be held after his father's coffin had been placed in Westminster Hall. As he said to the Archbishop, he wished to spare Queen Mary.

Now the King of England, as Head of the Church of England, is expected to suit his behavior to that role. The English sometimes boast of their inconsistency: "We are not a logical nation." And consistently with that inconsistency, even those Britons who are not churchgoers themselves like their King to be one. The idea of the Royal Family walking to church on Sunday morning in the country is part of the national tradition, for people many of whom have no religious practice.

For the British demand from their kings two major virtues: regard and affection for the religion and the constitution of their country. And if he does not possess and show these two essential qualities, their absence will only be emphasized by the King's other, lesser virtues.

The profound religious sentiment and unfailing practices of King George and Queen Mary were known, not only to their subjects, but to the world at large. Everybody knew that George V was a habitual Bible reader. He had been trained in the Navy, where religion is a part of daily life, and where His Majesty's ships display the words of St. Peter: "Fear God and honour the King." It is easy to imagine what comment George V, the Sailor King, would have made on a Lying-in-State without a religious service.

On both official and personal grounds, the Archbishop could do no less than insist that there must be some service in Westminster Hall. He decided to draw up a short form which included the Lesser Litany, the Lord's Prayer, and a hymn: "Praise My Soul, the King of Heaven." He showed it to Queen Mary, who sanctioned it; and from this it is easy to see what she thought about the matter.

Five kings and a host of lesser dignitaries had come to England for the funeral of George V, among them the Nazis, Baron von Neurath and General von Rundstedt. To these representatives of the new Germany King Edward was markedly attentive at the State Banquet customary on such an occasion. This was quite consistent with his behavior as Prince of Wales: he had, in 1935, addressed a speech to a British Legion deputation en route to Berlin, pleading for fair play for Germany! When Germany was already prepared to play unfair with Britain and the world.

Now the friendly attitude adopted by the King at the banquet was especially agreeable to certain London bankers, as well as to some members of the upper classes. Although Churchill was warning England, apparently in vain, with all the power of his eloquence based on knowledge. Baldwin, too, spoke of the gathering storm. The working classes had already sized up Hitler. The pro-German attitude of King Edward could not be welcome to the majority of his subjects.

Events were soon to show how ill-judged and ill-timed was this affability toward the enemies of peace. The banquet took place on January 28; five weeks later, on March 9, German troops entered the demilitarized zone of the Rhineland.

This was a major crisis in European affairs, and as such it receives some attention in the Duke's memoirs. The situation was one in which an informed Monarch could have played an important, perhaps a decisive part. Constitutionally, of course, the King of England takes no part in politics: he acts by the advice of his ministers. But they also act by his advice: thus in 1945 George VI secured the appointment of Ernest Bevin to the Foreign Office, simply by telling Mr. Attlee that this post must go to the best man in the Cabinet.

King Edward asked the opinions of visiting European statesmen as to what should be done about Hitler's defiant gesture. It does not appear that he gave emergency audiences to his Ministers, who did not want to involve this Monarch in such an immense and controversial issue anyhow.

Some of the visitors thought that Great Britain should oppose the Nazis; others wanted no such thing. And Edward—he now says— saw the pros and cons of both courses of action, yet was not convinced that either would lead to a peaceful solution. Then follows his admission that he felt that war was on its way. The ex-King of England openly confesses that he knew a war imperiling his country was coming—yet he left!

A display of firmness on the part of Edward VIII might have resolved the vacillation of England, who wanted France to act first; and thus indirectly resolved the vacillation of France, who was waiting for England. But what action, if any, was taken by King Edward on this occasion, is unknown. What is common knowledge now, of course, is that in March 1936 England and France lost the last opportunity of staving off war.

However, on that January evening the coming coup, and all its terrible consequences, were unthought of. The stately ceremonial went forward, and the funeral of George V ended as the Garter King of Arms, after proclaiming the name and titles of the dead Monarch, uttered the joyful prayer:

"And now let us humbly beseech Almighty God to bless . . . our Sovereign Lord, King Edward VIII."

It was the beginning of a new era for Great Britain, an odd, a unique one.

Windsor says in his memoirs that he wanted to bring a fresh and original mind to the old picture of kingship. Yet he also says that he had no desire to go down in history as "Edward the Reformer"; that "Edward the Innovator" would do. This was an unhappy choice of words—reform means change for the better, innovation only means change, which may be for the worse.

Edward VIII, the great popular idol, *could* have been "Edward the Reformer." The presence of this frail, slender, remarkably youthful-looking man exhilarated his people, as that of Napoleon is said to have exhilarated the French. There was a time when the English would have done anything for Edward. A fleeting glimpse of him through the windows of the royal car caused his phlegmatic subjects to cheer happily.

Although Mrs. Simpson had sold him on the excellence of American cars, willy-nilly the King used one of the family Daimlers, that stately, specially designed, high-roofed automobile in which the Royal Family had always motored, and which in point of quality is on a level with the Rolls-Royce. It was said that in the early days of the Rolls-Royce company George V had a slight disagreement with that august corporation, and thereafter insisted on using the product of the other august corporation. To Edward the family car was "the Crystal Palace," and he did not like it. There was some justification for this: royal persons must always present an immaculate appearance, without a hair out of place; hence the windows of their cars remain closed, often with intense discomfort to the passengers. King Edward would have preferred to walk, but, as he says, he knew better than to do so.

One day, however, he broke his own rule. Together with Rear-Admiral Sir Lionel Halsey, his old chaperon of Canadian days, he walked from Buckingham Palace to a council meeting of his Duchy of Cornwall estates. It was raining, and King and Admiral carried umbrellas. The next morning the papers ran a picture of the two gentlemen walking in the rain.

A few days later, Mrs. Simpson was invited to a dinner where she sat next to an important member of the Conservative Party. This man said to her: "I am told that you know the King." Wallis said yes. The Conservative thereupon burst forth: "Did you see that newspaper photograph of His Majesty walking from the Palace in the rain? That umbrella! Since you know the King, won't you ask him to be more careful in the future how he is photographed?"

Wallis replied that it would be presumptuous of her, an American, to advise the King of England upon a point of behavior so patently British! This was unusual modesty on her part: she had by now been the King's adviser for a long time. And had she not informed him, when they first met, that his references to such patently British subjects as the climate were boring?

Mrs. Simpson, when she told King Edward what the Conservative member had said at the dinner party, seems to have recalled the politician's words with surprising exactness: "The Monarchy must remain on its pedestal, above the commonplace. We can't have the King doing this kind of thing. He has the Daimler."

Those who know the London scene will agree with the Conservative. The appearance of any member of the Royal Family in the street is the signal for a crowd to gather, and a crowd does gather, immediately. It has always been so. And consequently few kings of England ever walked on the streets of London.

About this time there took place a graver encounter than that of Mrs. Simpson and the Conservative M.P. The new Head of the Church of England granted an audience to the Archbishop of Canterbury, his spiritual subordinate. Though he had known the Primate since his own childhood, the Duke admits to having received him coldly. Earlier in life he had liked the Archbishop, but gradually changed in feeling, because for a prelate Dr. Lang was "almost too polished, too worldly."

Henry II called his Primate a "turbulent priest"; Elizabeth I reduced hers to tears; George III wrote a letter of strong rebuke to his Primate, Dr. Cornwallis, condemning Mrs. Cornwallis' gay parties. Even George V had a disagreement with Dr. Lang the first time they met. But Edward VIII is perhaps the only British Monarch to complain of his Archbishop's being "too polished."

And what exactly does the Duke mean by that word "worldly"? Was Dr. Lang a member of the Kit Kat Club or the Embassy? Not very likely. He had been Dean of Oxford and of St. Paul's, "the Cathedral of the British Empire." He had written ponderous, perhaps tedious, books on intellectual subjects. In 1912, as a member of a Royal Commission, he was partly responsible for modernizing the inhuman English divorce laws. He spoke well at public dinners—but it is not alleged that he dined or wined too well.

These are hardly grounds for an accusation of worldliness, but there is another and more surprising source of dissatisfaction. It seems that the Duke detected worldliness in Dr. Lang's conduct of public worship.

Now there were not too many occasions on which the King watched Dr. Lang, or any other cleric, conduct a church service; for His Majesty's absence from church was a matter of comment. It was indeed one of the most striking points of contrast between King George and his eldest son. True, Dr. Lang had a great feeling for religious ceremonial, not only for itself but for what it conveyed. But that it should be possible to detect "worldliness" in a cleric conducting a service as it should be conducted is certainly a matter for some surprise.

The Duke of Windsor writes but briefly of the Archbishop's visit. Dr. Lang said: "I want you to know that whenever the King questioned your conduct I tried in your interest to present it in the most favorable light."

"My conduct, I wondered. What was Dr. Lang driving at?" The Duke answers his own question on the next page of the memoirs. The Primate had for some time been aware of the friendship with Mrs. Simpson. In 1935 he had had a long and intimate talk with King George on the matter, nor had this been their only discussion of the Prince's affairs. Dr. Lang knew, and frankly said to King Edward, that he feared this had set the new King against him; and he hoped to overcome this feeling. But his eloquence in this case did not have a happy effect. To his hearer these talks seemed to hint at Mrs. Simpson, to suggest that the friendship ought not to continue. For the first time it occurred to Edward that he might have difficulty in carrying out his plan to marry. But the Majesty of England was now dedicated to this scheme, and the earlier, the right and natural dedication to his people had already been set aside.

So the King turned the conversation to another subject: his new task as Head of the Church of England. Here, he complains, he could not seem to impress the Primate. Dr. Lang's diary, to the contrary, speaks of his being impressed by the King's alertness and obvious eagerness to learn; though clearly he knew little, and perhaps cared little, about Church affairs. He asked Dr. Lang how bishops were appointed! As Windsor remarks, the Primate no doubt left the audience with a feeling of relief.

The moral conduct of the Sovereign was the prelate's business, in spite of the King's own view that he had a right to compose his life on the Throne in terms of his own philosophy. (Some idea of this philosophy has already been given.) Windsor claims that at the time of his accession he was a man with a profound faith in God and the highest sense of duty! Yet he had given no public evidence of his faith: and paid no heed to the Primate, who dared to speak to him for his own good.

Another, far more fantastic audience was granted by the new King soon after his proclamation; Edward received with all imperial grace the Soviet ambassador, M. Litvinoff.

King George V hated the Communist and would never permit this

representative of the Russian Government in his presence: these were
the people who had murdered his relatives, the Russian Royal Family.
And for the attitude of King George, as for so much else in the British
Monarchy, there was precedent. In 1903 King Alexander Obrenovic
of Serbia began to rule as dictator. He had already affronted public
opinion by marrying and crowning his mistress, a woman older than
himself. A group of disaffected army officers murdered the King and
his Queen, Draga, in a shockingly brutal manner, and then enthroned
a member of the Karageorgevic dynasty. King Edward VII refused
to receive an envoy of the new Serbian government; and when approached upon the matter, uttered the famous words: "*J'ai mon
métier du roi*," also intimating that kings must be loyal to their caste.

But here, as elsewhere, Edward VIII showed himself an innovator.
The King and the representative of Joseph Stalin were closeted for a
long time. When Litvinoff left the Palace, newsmen asked about the
conversation. The Communist described King Edward as saying that
his father would have been delighted to receive him. He had had a
talk with the diplomat about Russia: the King asked for and M.
Litvinoff had obliged with a resumé of recent Russian history, explaining, in answer to a further question, why it had been necessary
for his fellow-Communists to murder Edward's cousins, the Tsar II,
his wife Alexandra (granddaughter of Queen Victoria) and their
children.

In thus reporting what, he alleged, had passed between himself and
King Edward, M. Litvinoff was also acting as an innovator. Revelations of a private conversation between a head of State, and an
Ambassador, by that Ambassador, are in flagrant violation of diplomatic usage. Only a Soviet envoy could get away with it. But worse
was to come. One of the reporters asked M. Litvinoff what he thought
of the new King.

"He impressed me as a mediocre Englishman who glances at one
newspaper a day," replied the diplomat. (*Time*, February 10, 1936.)

A few weeks later the unhappy little Emperor of Abyssinia pleaded
in vain for an interview with His Majesty, his powerful cousin, for
by this term kings formally address each other.

Edward and his apologists always protest that he was for the underdog. There was no more unfortunate underdog in England at this
time than the melancholy Emperor, the reputed descendant of King
Solomon and the Queen of Sheba. The Italians had then already
ravaged Abyssinia and Haile Selassie was the pathetic, exiled ruler of

a conquered land. Eden asked the King to see him, and when His Majesty demurred, said that it would be a popular gesture. "Popular with whom? Certainly not with the Italians!" the King replied.

But the fortunes of princes and countries often change. In 1951 the once-rejected Emperor of Abyssinia was back on his throne, thanks to the Allied victories in North Africa; and was able to send troops to Korea to help fight the Communists.

So each day the new King, who should constitutionally have kept out of controversy and politics, offered a new surprise to his admiring subjects. There was, for instance, the matter of the Privileged Bodies, whom the Duke of Windsor gracefully describes as "the so-called 'Privileged Bodies.' "

He did not know what they were!

The Privileged Bodies include the Corporation of the City of London, the Archbishop and clergy of the Province of Canterbury, the Governor and Company of the Bank of England, the Universities of Oxford, Cambridge and Edinburgh, the Royal Academy of Arts, the Royal Society of London for Improving Natural Knowledge (usually referred to as "the Royal Society"), and various religious groups. It will be seen that they represent the authority, the religion, the wealth, the arts and sciences of Great Britain: they are the spokesmen of the nation. Membership of any one of them is a matter for pride, and no mere sinecure. Thus to be a member of the Royal Society is to belong to one of the oldest scientific groups in Europe.

These Privileged Bodies have each the right of audience with the King on his accession, ostensibly to present a loyal address; but also to bring Sovereign and people into touch with each other. King Edward proposed to abrogate these rights, and to receive all twenty groups at once! This might be a snappy and business-like proceeding, but it was undoubtedly very bad manners. It is not surprising that the Lord Mayor of London, at least, would not submit to such treatment.

To understand the magnitude of the insult which King Edward proposed to inflict on the City of London, in the persons of its Lord Mayor and Corporation, it is necessary to understand something of that city's peculiar position in the national life. The City of London, "the square mile" at the heart of the great sprawl called London, is the capital of England; *it is not the royal city*.

The City of London, grouped round the "East Minster," St. Paul's Cathedral, is the capital of England; the City of Westminster, with its Collegiate Church of St. Peter—"Westminster Abbey"—is the King's city. And the King of England can enter the capital of England only by the consent of the citizens; a fact symbolized (needless to say) by ancient rite. When the reigning Monarch wishes to enter the City of London, he (or she) is met at Temple Bar, the City limit, by the Lord Mayor of London, who presents the sword of the City, the symbol of its authority, in token of homage.

There have been monarchs who disdained the citizens of London, to their own harm. Eight hundred years ago the heiress to the Crown of England, Maud, the daughter of Henry I, insulted them. They refused to acknowledge her sovereignty, and she lost a kingdom. As other past events show, whoever holds London holds England. That is why, a mere four years after the "unimportant incident" so lightly dismissed by the Duke of Windsor, Churchill proposed to fight "in the streets" of London, if need be; and four years later still, cried of the great city now throned with Troy beyond the wreck of Time: "She will not fail, nor will her glory fade!"

Compared with London, other European capitals are ghosts or newcomers. As the heart of England, the heart's heart of an Empire, in tradition, in wealth, and now in martial glory, the City of London has few equals and no superiors. For an Englishman there are no honors greater than those conferred by the City of London, save those conferred by the hand of the Sovereign.

Consistently with the worth of the city, the chief citizen (for the time being) of London is not merely a mayor: he is the Lord Mayor of London. He is always a person of worth and standing, a wealthy, often a self-made man, who is knighted when he enters upon his one year of office.

A former Lord Mayor of London, William Beckford, once rebuked George III for invading the rights of the City. It may be conjectured that there was something behind the modern Lord Mayor's final consent to be placated, by a reception of himself and the Corporation in an anteroom.

The attitude taken up by King Edward to the Privileged Bodies typified one of his failings. He did not work as his father had done, perhaps could not; his inability to concentrate, commented on during his Oxford period, had not changed.

The transition from one reign to another always makes itself felt in a multitude of ways, small as well as great. King Edward's innovations ensured that the change should be felt by the greatest number of people. He altered all around him, in small things as in great. He had been affable to the Nazis; he had condescended to the Communists; he had cold-shouldered his fellow-Monarch and the Primate. He had also changed the clocks at Sandringham, and now he proceeded to turn the sheep off the lawns of Windsor. They were ordered to be sent to the Zoo.

The King's private frolicking, his nonchalant disregard of dignity —his own and that of others—his depriving the populace of pomp and pageantry, was tolerated with benign smiles. But the banishment of the sheep hurt the Londoners deeply. They love a pastoral scene and the sight of old pets, even if the gamboling lambs don't belong to them.

So it went on. Each day the new King offered a new surprise to his subjects. Yet the personal mesmerism of Edward VIII was still so strong that had he called his people to arms, every one of them would have been willing to die fighting for him. He counted on that immense popularity to support him in other matters.

Now, writing after the event, the Duke claims that he was not deceived by the eulogies of press or politicians: he knew that popular devotion was by no means uncritical. This is hardly consistent with his remark reported by Lord Beaverbrook, and referred to in a previous chapter: "I thought I could get away with it . . ."

For the nation's devotion to Edward VIII amounted to adoration. True, it did not find the same extravagant, puerile expression as that of the American bobby soxer for a crooner, but it was greater, and not at all superficial. Whatever might be said by those in or near the Court and Government, whatever might be known to journalists or foreign nations, still for the mass of the people King Edward was their heart's darling, their hope, their future.

So it was as with the shock of a thunderbolt, or of the more modern flying bomb, that they opened their newspapers one day to find that a turbulent priest had criticized their King. The Bishop of Bradford, addressing his Diocesan Conference, had urged his hearers to pray for the King, who with his great responsibilities had so much need of God's grace. This was quite in order; but unfortunately Dr. Blunt had seen fit to add: "Some of us wish that he showed more awareness of his need."

But that was still to come. Ten months had to elapse before Dr. Blunt would light his fuse, and it is necessary to take a look at some of the events which occurred during that time.

15

The Voyage of the *Nahlin*

I love to sail forbidden seas, and land on barbarous coasts.
—HERMAN MELVILLE: *Moby Dick*

"Ah, your honor!" said Pugachov the Pretender, "come and be my guest; here is a place for you, you are very welcome."
—PUSHKIN: *The Captain's Daughter*

THE new King disliked the official royal residence, Buckingham Palace, and this is hardly surprising, for it is an ugly house.

Yet his father, grandfather and great-grandmother, endured it for brief sojourns, and regarded a stay there as one of the duties of the Sovereign. They knew Londoners like to feel that once in a while the paterfamilias is among them, and when they spy the royal standard on the Palace's mast say contentedly to one another: "The King's at home."

But Edward VIII cared little for the small joys of his subjects. And he much preferred his own house, Fort Belvedere, built in the somber style of eighteenth-century Gothic by the cruel "Butcher" Cumberland, who had his own secrets to keep. Edward had turned this toy castle, with its donjon and battlements, into a bohemian hideaway.

Time reported (October 26, 1936) that Mrs. Simpson was spending nearly every night in the King's suburban snuggery at Fort Belvedere, and it was definitely established that His Majesty had not slept in Buckingham Palace since he returned from the Balkans.

But this is looking too far ahead. It is necessary to go back to the spring of 1936, to March—proverbially a crazy month, and not for hares only—when the King sent a neat little memo to Parliament. This note dealt with the royal finances.

From the eighteenth century on, the Crown was dependent for its upkeep on the Lords and Commons, who voted on the Civil List and the Privy Purse at the commencement of a reign, and on additional supplies as occasion required. The Kings of England had only to give a bill to Parliament naming the extra sum they needed or would need in the near future. The lawmakers then considered, debated, and voted—either favorably or unfavorably.

In that crazy month of 1936, King Edward asked, among other things, that provision be made for a fixed income for his future queen, and suggested $200,000 per year (50,000 pounds sterling at the then rate of exchange) as a suitable sum. If the bill on finances including this provision had proved acceptable to both Houses of Parliament, it would have been signed by Edward under the words "le roy le veult," a venerable phrase which has been used since Norman times: "The King Wishes It." But Parliament, the representatives of the people, most emphatically did not wish it. They refused to vote money for the as yet unnamed majesty. Most Members knew about Mrs. Simpson; and although they thought her both improbable and impossible as queen, they were not uninformed as to the King's wishful thinking.

The actions of the Sovereign disturbed the Members, too; and they found his disregard for the dignity of the Crown quite bewildering. The King was often markedly lacking in reserve when reserve was needed. Gleefully H. G. Wells wisecracked: "Nowadays princes come plain—like chicken without stuffing." King Edward's deportment was becoming the talk of official and socialite London. One night a peer jokingly complained to the King that only that same day a royal car had nearly run him down. King Edward reportedly replied: "Couldn't have been me. It must have been Lascelles. (Lord Lascelles, his brother-in-law.) He's the one who drives around in state. You know—he's getting royaler and royaler while I'm getting commoner and commoner."

Fort Belvedere was liberty hall. The faster people were, the sooner they got to the Fort. Americans and married women had first preference on the bachelor King of England's invitation list; and in their case the royal summons was most informal, often issued as a hasty telephone call in the morning—please come to dinner this evening. With members of the Household things stood on quite another footing; as the Duke reveals in his memoirs, no member of the Household was allowed at the Fort save by appointment! (The author had a friend who was invited so much on the spur of the moment that

he did not even have time to pack an overnight bag. On arrival at
the Fort he found that he might have to sleep in the raw. It was
summer, but he had the soul of a Beau Brummell. He mentioned his
plight to a valet, who obliged him with a pair of the King's pale blue
silk pajamas.)

August in England is a wonderful month, balmy and sweet of scent,
with romantic evenings and comfortably warm nights. This month,
renamed to honor Augustus Caesar, had previously been called by
the Romans *Sextilis*, or the sixth from March; and perhaps because
of such associations it brought restlessness to this particular Caesar.
He had been confined by business, working like a slave, for eight
months without a vacation! So he chartered Lady Yule's palatial
yacht, the *Nahlin*, and invited a party of twelve tired friends to keep
him company on a Mediterranean and Adriatic cruise.

The crew of the *Nahlin* handled the party's baggage with due care.
One batch of suitcases and trunks was marked: "Duke of Lancaster,"
the easy incognito of their King-Emperor. Another and large pile of
luggage was marked in eight-inch-high letters: "Mrs. Ernest A.
Simpson"—Wallis' incognito. But though she was the guest of honor,
her name—strange as it may sound—did not appear on the sailing
list. Neither did that of Mr. Simpson; and the censorious might find
this even more strange. For in August 1936, he was still the husband
of Wallis. But in his case not only the listing was lacking—he himself
was not there.

The tolerant explained Mr. Simpson's absenteeism easily by saying
that it would have been simply impossible to invite him, for he would
have brought the number of guests to thirteen. However, he was
probably not missed in a party which included such a light of beauty
as Lady Diana Duff-Cooper and her husband—Lord Brownlow and
his wife—the sparkling Mrs. Evelyn Fitzgerald—and the famous
Lady Emerald Cunard. This latter noblewoman not only lent the
final note of *bon ton* to the voyage: she also possessed a sense of rhythm
acquired from exotic dancing partners. So the King, an eager dancer,
could always be sure of an outstanding Black Bottomer who was con-
tinually in training. But none of these guests were slaves to conven-
tion; in view of the deep incognito, what need was there to observe
vexatious rules while on a holiday?

For it was to be a holiday indeed! Onlookers wondered why the
books were unloaded from the yacht's library, and came to the conclusion that lighter literature had been removed to make way for

Bride for the first time, 1916

First husband, the late E. Winfield
Spencer

Second Husband, Ernest Aldrich Simpson

Dr. Cosmo Gordon Lang, Archbishop of Canterbury, merely an anxious bystander

The man who saved a kingdom: Baldwin, Earl of Bewdley.

scholarly reading matter and piles of State papers. But the onlookers
were mistaken. The library had simply been changed into a bedroom,
and moreover space had had to be found for a cargo of liquor, not to
mention 3,000 golf balls, with a strange destiny which will be mentioned later in this chapter.

Youth at the prow, the gilded vessel glided off. The Duke of
Lancaster was not aboard—he was going to join the vacationists at
Venice, flying there in his private plane. But at the last moment Mr.
Anthony Eden, who was then Foreign Secretary, spoiled this part of
the itinerary. Mr. Eden pleaded with the King not to go to Fascist
Italy. Employing all his persuasive powers, the Foreign Secretary
succeeded in making His Majesty alter his course and agree to meet
the *Nahlin* in Yugoslavian waters. The last part of the Duke of
Lancaster's journey to the Dalmatian port of Sibernik was undertaken
in a train, and there is a vivid description of the clanking and jolting
he endured as the stiff price of bending his plans to the expediencies
of British foreign policy.

Probably that Walpurgis night conditioned the King. For throughout the voyage of the *Nahlin* he never again bent his plans to suit the
exigencies of his country's foreign policy. On the contrary. He upset
them by visiting dictators or would-be dictators whose ideologies
were totally opposed to the lofty democratic ideals of Great Britain.

> When plans for my trip were announced, my Ambassador at Ankara
> urged the Foreign Office to propose to me that, as a gesture of friend-
> ship, I extend my cruise in order to pay a call on the Ghazi at Istanbul.
> This I was ready to do.
>
> (*A King's Story*, Chapter 18, Page 308)

The turn of phrase will not be lost on readers who know that a
constitutional Monarch can act only through his ministers; and the
recommendations of a representative abroad may not prove acceptable to the Cabinet at home. True, the Ambassador is the man on the
spot; but in an important matter like this a full Cabinet has the task
of evaluating his report, and making decisions with a view to the
effect on the political situation as a whole. The presence of Duff-
Cooper—who was then the War Minister—aboard the *Nahlin*
afforded not the slightest guarantee of the Constitution, for he was
there in a purely private capacity.

Under Kemal Atatürk, Turkey's half-moon emblem somewhat

resembled the swastika; and the Cabinet would never have "advised" the King to see the man who "did a Hitler" on Great Britain when he occupied the Dardanelles in 1922.

However, the visit to Kemal Atatürk went off very well. The great Turk received graciously the most noble, puissant and Christian Prince Edward, Duke of Lancaster; and Wallis Simpson. According to her friends, Wallis has never been too shy to do anything that occurred to her; apparently it did not occur to this daughter of democracy to shy away from the dictator. Perhaps she, who had come from a country where women are dominant, saw in Kemal less the dictator of Turkey than the emancipator of Turkish womanhood. Kemal had a sharp Oriental eye for both women and politics; in Wallis he saw them fused. And with an eye to future relations, both political and personal, he treated her as if she were already married to the King.

In Hungary wily Admiral Horthy, semidictator, closed his eyes. He went even further—he closed his ears when one early morning a frail, blond man, leaning out of a window of the Hotel Ritz, shot out some of the street lights lining the Danube embankment. The King loved that bottled dynamite, *barack*, the smooth Hungarian peach brandy.

Budapest was at that time the gayest capital in Europe, and the King and his party loved its way of life. Wallis did not yet impose restrictions on the King's fun as she did after their marriage; he was allowed to imbibe all he liked. The demure lady sipped and praised the cocktails the King made for his friends in the bar of the Ritz, to the utter dismay of Ilonka, the barmaid, who had till then prided herself on being called the queen of mixed drinks. Later in the evening, sparkling and splendid in a dinner coat of spun and woven glass, an enormous diamond glittering in her hair, Wallis romped through a gypsy czardas with the Duke of Lancaster. "What a man! A real king! But who can the lady be?" cried the gilded youth of Hungary, where no one knew Mrs. Simpson. And when the young men heard that the King had driven those 3,000 golf balls off the *Nahlin's* deck into the sea to keep in practice, exclaiming: "I love a splash!" their admiration knew no bounds. So great, indeed, was that admiration that, the day after King Edward went hatless round the shops, the dandies of Budapest appeared bareheaded—they, who till then had changed hats three times a day in obeying the rigors of fashion!

No, the voyage of the *Nahlin* was not uneventful. True, no new flora or fauna were discovered, nor were the habits of foreign countries' natives studied in order to add valuable data to anthropology. However, heads of state were very much on the King's schedule. He visited the Greek dictator, Metaxas; and also Prince Paul of Yugoslavia, another notorious Nazi sympathizer, who had been his friend in Oxford days. These odd visits to disorderly dictators by a constitutional Monarch bewildered the Cabinet and the Foreign Office of an orderly nation. So, naturally, His Majesty's Ministers in that summer of 1936, studying the reports and the pictures of the *Nahlin's* party joyously junketing round Europe, must have been staggered, and wondered which constitution would give first—the personal or the political, Edward's own or England's.

The time was ill-chosen, to say the least of it, for these brotherly visits by a mighty emperor. The unwise politics of that fumbling wizard, David Lloyd George, for whom Edward had—and has—the greatest admiration, had putrified Europe; and their results were now emerging.

Hitler had just been declared Fuehrer; his friends—for instance, Storm Trooper General Roehm—had just been liquidated on his orders in the terrible night of the "Long Knives." A few months earlier Prince Stahremberg had bombed the workers' homes in Vienna; and subsequently Chancellor Dollfuss had been murdered by Nazis who seized the Cabinet Buildings. (In this turbulent Vienna the royal vacationist also made a stopover.) Italy had raped and annexed Abyssinia. The Spanish Civil War had, only a month before, broken out into open, antireligious savagery. Tyranny and unrest ruled in the Balkans. And on their way home from the restaurant where they had admired the King, the gay dandies of Budapest stopped early morning citizens hurrying to work, stripped them, and beat those who were circumcised. No, no bullets yet—that came a bit later.

The King and his visits to these fermenting lands were criticized in his own country only in whispers; but the press abroad took off its muzzle. For example, the *Deutsche Allgemeine Zeitung*, not yet Nazi-trained, permitted itself this bark:

> King Edward VIII does as he wishes. It would have been unthinkable, during the reign of King George V, that a divorced woman

should be received at Court. It is well known that the views of the Church of England are very strong about divorced women. The King is only a few months on the throne, but one has no doubt that it will be an extraordinary reign.

This journal might have gone farther. After reminding its readers that "In England the King reigns—he does not rule," it might have asked: "Will Edward reign or rule?" At least one English review of the right wing had suggested the desirability of greater power for the Crown; the thing was definitely in the air. Did not the King of England tower over such rulers of the time as the frustrated Austrian water-color "artist" (a paper hanger later turned hangman); an Italian reporter; a Georgian peasant? If they had done so much, what could not be done by one born to power? However, the speculations of the European press did not proceed so far.

This was the realistic picture as the King's sentimental journey drew to its close: he had drawn on himself the suspicious eyes of foreign observers; he had alienated his family; the Church of England; the politicians; the statesmen and diplomats; and the aristocrats. There remained yet another important group to be annoyed: the manufacturers of England. King Edward obliged. When he came back from his voyage and his private plane landed on home soil, he was driven to Fort Belvedere in a brand-new Buick, registered in Mrs. Simpson's name. The English makers of fine automobiles must indeed have been dismayed by the pictures in their morning papers of His Majesty in the Buick, the favorite make of his favorite.

16

Who Was Baldwin?

Land of our Birth, we pledge to thee
Our love and toil in the years to be; . . .
When we are grown and take our place,
As men and women with our race.
— RUDYARD KIPLING: *The Children's Song*

H IS Majesty's Prime Minister bounced about in a ridiculously small English car. Anything written about Stanley Baldwin, the man who helped save the British Monarchy, must come dangerously near to sounding like an enthusiastic schoolboy's composition. The most diligent research cannot unearth a mean action in this man's life, which was clean to the point of dullness. Admittedly, Baldwin made mistakes. But he never wilfully endangered the country which he loved with the passion of a poet.

He never forgot that the difference between public and private affairs is as great as that between sky and earth; that devoting oneself to public life entails thinking about the good of others, while confining oneself to private affairs means nothing more than egocentric concentration on personal interest and advantage.

Baldwin might truly be called Defender of the Faith, for he kept faith with his country when it was imperiled by the private affairs of Edward VIII.

For Baldwin was, first and foremost, a patriot. And he, too, was an important heir. Neither royal nor noble, merely an industrial one. He inherited from his father a busy steel mill and collieries, which he boosted to an empire known as "Baldwins Limited."

Although born in the Victorian era, Baldwin grew up to be a modern-minded man—while other rich industrialists in England had a tendency to treat their employees like slaves, he treated his as though they were part of his family.

At the turn of the century, many English manufacturers still behaved as if they and their workers were two different breeds. This inhuman attitude was repulsive to the mind of Stanley Baldwin, who curiously combined a liberal outlook with deeply rooted conservatism. He reaped profits, yet worked as hard as any of his men, and he had sufficient cunning, combined with compassion, to share his profits. At one time the workers of Baldwins Limited were ordered on strike by the allied industries, and naturally wages were suspended for the period of the walkout. Except by Baldwins Limited—Stanley, the boss, paid for every idle hour out of his own pocket. It is easy to guess how much his employees liked such an employer.

But Stanley Baldwin was not only an industrial leader. His forefathers having been small landowners in Worcestershire, he also knew all about the soil. He was an expert gentleman farmer.

As though these two accomplishments weren't enough, the "Nemesis" of Edward VIII had also a talent for writing. But like many a born writer, he thought little of his own ability. Besides, Rudyard Kipling was his cousin, and who would want to compete with this genius? asked Baldwin. According to Kipling, his kinsman could have done so easily. "Stanley is the real literary member of the family," said the author of the *Jungle Book* and *Kim* and a score of other masterpieces.

But Baldwin had no urge to show off. The "literary member of the family" was content to go on reading in his library at Bewdley, in the house in which he had been born. He loved other people's literature. The great public school, Harrow on its hill, gave him his first view of the written "realms of gold," and his years at old Cambridge, where new ideas were bubbling up furiously at the end of the Victorian era, further whetted his appetite for the classics.

There is a much more surprising instance of Baldwin's literary powers. Winston Churchill more than once submitted his writings— for instance, his six-volume biography of his ancestor, the Duke of Marlborough—to the scrutiny of Stanley Baldwin, for criticism and correction. Churchill knew what a stylist "the Old Man" was.

Baldwin, the industrialist, when not farming found time to read and edit. He was also an unpaid magistrate. As a side line he did some gardening. And in his spare time learned all about the habits of the birds on his estate.

He was Chairman of the Board of the Great Western Railway, but he owned no luxurious special train. In fact, he seldom rode in trains, preferring to tramp the countryside, enjoying the beauty of nature, and possibly reflecting on the perversity of human affairs.

The marathon walker was also a great anonymous giver. Once, while hiking in Gloucestershire, he heard of two old ladies who had spent their last penny supporting an asylum for the feeble-minded. Now that they had come to the end of their resources, the home would have to be closed. Having listened to this bit of local gossip, Stanley Baldwin walked on apparently unmoved. He never stopped until he reached a distant town, called Stroud, where he found a bank. He wrote out a check for five hundred pounds, asking the teller for the dirtiest, oldest bank notes. Then he scribbled a note to the old ladies, in the style of the semiliterate. He described himself as a tramp who happened to have some money, and who had heard that they needed funds for their asylum, where, who knows, he might become an inmate himself in the not too distant future.

Having wrapped the money and the note in a newspaper, this latter-day Diogenes strolled out in search of an honest-looking man. When he finally found one, he handed him the packet. The man promised to paint the sender in dingy colors, and went off on his bicycle to the old ladies. Of course, it wasn't long before the "tramp" was identified; the bank teller told all.

This anecdote merely serves to show that Baldwin hated publicity or ostentation of any sort, and took an almost childish delight in obscuring himself. Certain honors, however, even he could not reject. He could not well refuse the Chancellorship of Cambridge University, or the Presidency of his county's Council.

In 1908 Baldwin thought that the time was ripe for him to serve his country in a wider field, and so he entered Parliament. He left his own domain with an easy conscience: he had done a good job at home, and wealth gave him the independence so desirable in a politician. In Britain, affluence or disinterest in one's financial gain has always been regarded as one requisite of a public servant in the higher echelons.

The theme of his maiden speech was not a popular one. The new member had the audacity to feel himself qualified, as a fifth generation member of a family of coal mine owners, to champion the eight-hour-day law for miners! But as an orator he was applauded. For this, he did not greatly care. "I have never yet known a good worker who could talk, and I have never known a good talker who was a good workman," he used to say. Stanley Baldwin seemed to be the exception to his own rule.

He had that wonderful gift, in speaking, of making the hearer feel that he was thinking aloud. Baldwin had nothing to hide—he *was* thinking aloud. He impressed even his critics as a completely open and honest man. Once in a while he would say: "When I deal with a matter of principle, I would rather go to the stake than give way." Again: "If I make sure that what I believe is right, I stick to my belief without faltering." And he meant what he said.

Here was a plain, simple, true man, who was always ready to spend himself and spare others, a rare virtue among men and especially among politicians. In one speech he said: "It is one thing to do good to your own soul by giving away your worldly goods, and it is quite another thing to persuade others to renounce them."

This odd, homespun character sat in the House on a back bench where no one would notice him. He dressed quietly, appearing every day in a black suit. The majority of Members did not even know him. The curious fellow was devoid of petty political ambitions; he was there to serve his country, but not by vaudeville and merry-go-round propaganda at public expense, in the manner of David Lloyd George.

T. P. O'Connor, the Nestor of the House of Commons, once wrote:

> Mr. Baldwin is a modest and a shy and a very simple man . . . There is no more thoroughly English Englishman in the House of Commons, and Englishmen rarely lose the splendid tradition of self-control and the saving humour which restrain them from vehemence of expression, or give them that sense of proportion which does not allow them to take things tragically. Like most Englishmen he is saved from excess of emotion or expression by the keen and ever-present sense of humour which sent the Tommy with a joke over the top, and ends a scene of tragic passion in the House with universal laughter.

In spite of himself, almost against his own wish, Baldwin began to climb in politics. In vain he insisted that he had "only second-class brains compared to Winston Churchill's hundred horsepower brain." (Someone answered that Baldwin had a first-class character—never mind that explosive gray matter of Winston's.) He feared Churchill's bellicose nature, because his own temperament was that of a calm, cool negotiator. He had had a good deal of practice in straightening things out amicably at his steel mills and collieries.

Yet when Baldwin became Prime Minister in 1923 for the first time, he at once asked Churchill to join his Cabinet, and allowed him to run things almost as if Churchill himself were Premier. Then came the General Strike in 1926, and Baldwin's exit. One of the world's least biased newspapers, the *Manchester Guardian*, spoke succinctly on his dismissal:

> We are heading steadily towards a real and passionate conflict of class. We are, in fact, in sight of the very catastrophe of which Mr. Baldwin warned us, when he became Prime Minister, saying that we need not be afraid as long as he was in office pursuing his policy of conciliation.

Churchill was an aristocrat, the descendant of one of the ablest generals England has ever had. As such, he proved himself in 1940 the natural leader of that forlorn hope which later blazed into victorious achievement. Baldwin was the mirror of the middle class, the landed gentry of Great Britain, a combination of Shropshire squire and cockney.

Churchill was great from the start: from his earliest youth he was plunged into adventure, both gallant and military. He was a formidable practitioner of "our fine language and beautiful expressions," of which Baldwin professed to be only the slave. Churchill was a born and practicing *grand seigneur*, despite his being so human, so close to people and life. Yet perhaps, aside from their different political views, he might even have had a certain scorn for the country bumpkin, Baldwin.

At any rate, the faults of the various Baldwin administrations, grandiose mistakes of little Cabinet Ministers, were often laid squarely on Baldwin's strong shoulders. He never whimpered. He bore the weight of accusation patiently, because he was a man in whom patience had been highly developed. He was further than a mouse from being a dictator; he just could not lay down the law to his fellow-Ministers.

This gentleness turned out to be his principal trouble. He was unable to deal with the intrigues and jealousies of his colleagues, as a political boss is expected to do. Once he said laughingly: "Some of my colleagues think I am a half-wit; others, that I am not even a quarter-wit. I can quite understand that. What I cannot understand is why they insist on remaining in the Cabinet of such an idiot."

This "idiot," this patriot and poet, this unassuming, unselfish

English gentleman, was in and out of the Prime Minister's chair. The press ganged up on him, particularly the papers of the late Lord Rothermere. The other great newspaper lord, Beaverbrook, also opposed Baldwin; yet the Prime Minister respected the eager Beaver's patriotism. Only the *Times* evaluated Baldwin properly; perceiving behind his shy, simple demeanor a sterling character that would stand the shock of the most fearful crisis. The *Times* proved to be right.

Stanley Baldwin arrived at the doubtfully satisfying Olympus of British politics a wealthy man. When he left 10 Downing Street, in 1929, he was a poor man. It was said that for every pound he owned when he came into office a shilling remained when he left it! He set about recouping his fortune, but when he was recalled to the Premiership in 1935, he was still a poor man. Only his soul was richer, his patriotic spirit had been forged to steel, his insight seemed to penetrate deeper. The people of Great Britain recalled his earlier words: "A Prime Minister sees human nature bared to the bone."

There he was, the most stolid of Englishmen, back again to serve the nation, without craving notoriety or plaudits, at an age when most men long to retire. At sixty-eight Baldwin, with his pipe, his "second-class" brain, his keen sense of humor, his unemotional, steadying influence, his tenacity, were there again in the troubled English scene. His sure and pure instincts, his unselfishness, his sober judgment, his honesty, would soon be direly needed.

The Empire had its humble servant back. King George V had his old friend back. And the future Edward VIII, too, had his friend back, one of the few truthful friends he ever had.

Of course, the runaway Sovereign had not the faintest idea of this—he thought, and thinks even today, that romantic but righteous Stanley Baldwin was his enemy.

But in its fair criticism of *A King's Story*, the London *Times* commented that at a certain point in the drama of 1936, Baldwin suddenly stopped begging Edward VIII to stay on the Throne. It was the day after Edward told his mother that he must marry Mrs. Simpson on the throne or abdicate.

Long years after there was to be a pregnant contact of certain principals of that drama, not in their persons but in their pictures. In October 1946, *Life*, highlighting the news of the world, showed its readers Earl Baldwin of Bewdley at the University of Cambridge. Above the dignity of the Chancellor's gown, with its long train and gold-embroidered sleeves, rose the face of the elder statesman, carved and hollowed by pain: the illness which was shortly to kill him had bitten deep into the earl's physiognomy. It was the last public appearance of Stanley Baldwin.

Immediately below appeared a photo of the Duchess of Windsor, radiant, chic in elegantly simple traveling attire; at her side the Duke. They were making their first visit to England since 1936.

Elsewhere in the same issue of *Life* was a picture recalling that earlier period of the Duchess' career when, as Mrs. Simpson, she had conducted her *salon* at Bryanston Court. The drawing depicted one of her best-known guests, surrounded by soldiers, doctors, and hangmen.

The caption under this picture read: "Ribbentrop Was First to Hang."

17

A Friend in Need

It is a heavy burden to bear a name that is too famous.
—VOLTAIRE

M R. BALDWIN had assured Parliament that the reign of Edward VIII would be a brilliant one. That ancient native name, meaning "rich, happy, and guardian," itself seemed ominous of good.

Edward the Elder, King of the Angles and the chosen father of Scotland, first bore it over a thousand years ago. Then virtuous, monkish Edward the Confessor made it famous. There was an early, unhappy Edward surnamed the Martyr. But that strong king, Edward I, after being

> Renowned for his deeds as far from home,—
> For Christian service and true chivalry,—
> As is the sepulchre in stubborn Jewry
> Of the world's ransom, blessed Mary's Son ، ; ;

had reigned as the "Justinian of England."

True, Edward II had perished miserably as a result of a bad choice of an adviser and a worse choice of wife. But his son, the liberal, kindly Edward III, had achieved military glory in France, and at home founded the Most Noble Order of the Garter to signalize the triumph of chastity and chivalry over temptation. The strenuous sex life of handsome, charming, hot-tempered Edward IV had been blazoned through England, but it had never weakened his grip upon the scepter. That chubby child, Edward V, had no time to assert himself: his life and his reign were the shortest of those of all the English kings. Nor was the reign of intelligent, scholarly, myopic Edward VI long—a mere six years, time enough for the boy-king to champion education in his realm.

Nearly five centuries after the gallant Edward IV, another Edward, equally gallant—the King's own grandfather—had earned the title

of "The Peacemaker." With such examples to follow what might
not *this* Edward achieve?

Yet soon after his accession the Prime Minister was shaking like
a leaf; for he, unlike the ordinary Englishman, saw behind the scenes.
He knew what Edward had so far accomplished—suspicion, dis-
pleasure, annoyance, and even alarm among leading Englishmen.
And Mr. Baldwin also knew that a woman was reigning at the
bachelor King's Fort Belvedere.

Wallis was now the chief ornament of the Fort. She ran the King's
establishment, she acted as hostess, she had the decorations changed,
and as *Time* pointed out (in its January 4, 1937 issue) when "she
caught His Majesty's servants spending too much for things like bath
soap, King Edward sacked old retainers right and left on her slightest
say-so." After all, one had to economize somewhere in order to pay
for gems and gowns.

But it was not only servants who incurred the royal wrath. Brigadier-
General Trotter, who had been the King's aide—his "wet-nurse" as
the rest of the courtiers affectionately called him—for nearly a quarter
of a century, became all of a sudden *persona non grata*. The dismissal
took place the morning after General Trotter had dined at the Savoy
Hotel with an American lady, a friend of the King in pre-Mrs.
Simpson days. Wallis reportedly was furious: Savoy society might
have thought that the other lady's appearance with the King's aide
meant that the former bond had not yet been severed. The new
Sovereign and the old soldier had a short interview, according to
those in the know: "Trotter, you dined with Mrs.——at the Savoy
last night?" "Yes, sir." "You are no longer in my service."

Perhaps in order to dispel the hope that there might be someone
else in the picture, Mrs. Simpson exhibited in public the heart-
warming interest of the ordinary housewife in her man's appearance—
she would pull the King's hat to a rakish angle, remove lint from his
blue serge, and even straighten that famous tie. Outwardly it was
all very cozy. But in private Wallis must have thought of finances,
as is the way of realistic women. For she seemed to be aspiring to
the high and useful office of Keeper of the Privy Purse, too, as witness
the following excerpt (also from that after-the-abdication account of
Time, January 4, 1937):

> Mrs. Simpson from the moment King George died began to "help"
> Edward VIII according to her lights. She helped him to spend thou-

sands of guineas royally, imperially, wildly; she helped him to pinch
pennies, convincing His Majesty that in housekeeping she is most
economical. Together they cruised the Balkans in one of the world's
costliest yachts; they ransacked Cartier's in Paris for diadems in
October; they picked out ermine skins recently made up in London
for Mrs. Simpson's Christmas.

This was a far cry from those sewing machine days, self-made
dresses, and the tiny jade Buddhas that tourists bring home from
China!

Yet despite the *Nahlin* voyage the ordinary people of England still
did not know about the King's love affair, and those in high places
did not realize how serious it really was. But the American papers
wrote freely about the forthcoming Simpson divorce, and predicted
that the King would marry Wallis. Thus the *New York Journal-
American*, organ of the powerful Hearst press, naively declared that:

> In all human probability, in June 1937, one month after the cere-
> monies of the coronation, will follow the festivities of the marriage (of
> King Edward VIII) to the very charming and intelligent Mrs. Ernest
> Simpson, of Baltimore, Maryland, U.S.A.
>
>   (October 26, 1936)

The incomprehension of the English character shown in this reference
to human probabilities is curious, but not too remarkable in an
American paper; but if—as has been suggested even by pro-Windsor
authors—King Edward himself had inspired this prenuptial announcement, then the passage is indeed remarkable and revealing.

Other papers were less restrained in their handling of the strange
theme. One cartoon showed the royal arms of England with the
supporters, the lion and the unicorn—but not in their usual caracoling
attitudes. The unicorn, wearing that unmistakable "Have-you-heard-
this?" look of the born gossip-geyser, was stretching out a long neck
to whisper in the ear of the lion, whose expression was that of a
dowager eagerly listening halfway between horror and delight. But
such papers were censored and clipped for English consumption.
That fussy, finger-snapping (a habit of the Prime Minister the King
hated) old Baldwin saw to that . . .

Stanley Baldwin reflected on the situation in silence, not sharing
his anguished thoughts with a living soul. But he felt grave misgivings, not only for the personal dignity of the man Edward, but
also for the dignity of the Crown of England. In the Sovereign these

two are inseparable. Baldwin feared for the stability of the Throne. He had constantly in mind the thought that the first duty of the King's first servant—for what else does the title "Prime Minister" signify?—is always to the Monarchy; to the Monarchy, even more than to the Monarch. His great predecessors of previous reigns— Melbourne, Peel, Palmerston, Disraeli—the first servants of Queen Victoria; Lord Grey of Fallodon who had served Edward VII; even Lloyd George on occasion, not to mention Asquith and Balfour—had from their wealth of experience repeatedly stressed this duty: respectful but absolute frankness to the Sovereign in all important matters, public or private, is the *sine qua non* of the First Servant. Lord Grey summed up admirably this ideal relation when he wrote:

> Certain conditions must be present in a Sovereign—he must be aloof from controversy. He must maintain the ceremonial side of the Crown with dignity. There must be nothing done by the Sovereign to weaken or undermine the position of his Prime Minister or Ministers. In return, their attitude to him must be one of respect as well as frankness—they must be careful and zealous to protect the Monarchy and observe its forms.

Like other people Mr. Baldwin had noted the change in the King's demeanor. He could hardly avoid doing so. King Edward, who had been so youthful and gay, now looked haggard and distraught. Incessantly he fumbled with his tie; and not only did he seem not to hear what was said to him, but his absent-mindedness extended even to the beautiful little nieces to whom he had formerly given so much affection. "He made plans with the children," laments Miss Crawford in *The Little Princesses*, "and then forgot them."

Beside the change in the King's personality, Mr. Baldwin had to consider the change in public opinion. He knew of the "Misters of England." (This was the name of a movement, an exclusive faction, with a well-known young peer at its head, entertaining the fantastic notion that it could depose Edward VIII and substitute for the rightful Monarch the extremely popular Duke of Kent.) He was aware that any publication of the facts must result in swift, perhaps disastrous, weakening of the Monarch's popularity. His fears were eventually justified by the fact. Stocks are not the only things to decline on a panicky Stock Exchange—when the news reached that delicate register of opinion, the brokers remarked that King Edward's decline in his people's favor was amazing.

While pondering over this bewildering situation, Mr. Baldwin must often have taken from the shelves of his library at Bewdley the incomparable volume of Montaigne; for his conduct at this time certainly befitted a disciple of that sage. Now that he was about to seek an interview which would be the most painful of his long career, he perhaps turned to the passage where that formidable essayist, as if foreseeing the conjunction of Edward VIII and Baldwin, wrote this directive:

> A king is not to be trusted if he cannot, for his own good and improvement, stand the liberty of speech of a friend, which has no other power but to penetrate his ear, the rest of its effect being in the King's own hand.
>
> Now there is no kind of man that stands in such great need of true and sincere warning as a king. He has to endure to live in the public eye, and to satisfy the notions of so many onlookers. Those about him are wont to conceal from him everything that frustrates his plans. And he might find himself involved, without being conscious of it, in the hatred and devastation of his people, often on grounds he might have avoided even without prejudice to his own pleasures, if he had been set right in time.
>
> Indeed, most of the duties of true friendship towards the sovereign are put to a rude and dangerous test—so that there is need, not only of great affection and freedom, but also of courage on the part of an honest adviser.

Thus strengthened, Mr. Baldwin on the thirteenth of October, 1936, begged an audience of His Majesty, pleading that his mission was both very urgent and most secret.

The Duke's account of this momentous meeting betrays a certain confusion. Windsor wrote—in the serial which preceded his *A King's Story*—that he received the request on a Sunday at Sandringham, and that he made an appointment for the following Tuesday at Fort Belvedere. He went on to say that Mr. Baldwin's sudden intrusion perplexed him; that he wondered if the Prime Minister intended to advise him officially concerning Wallis, and if so, how far Baldwin would go. In the book, however, Windsor no longer regards Baldwin's request for an interview merely as "a sudden intrusion"; quite the contrary. He says that he at once invited the Prime Minister to join the royal house party (which of course included Wallis) at Sandringham, and that Mr. Baldwin—who had known and loved this favorite

Lord Justice Hawke, three days before he granted a decree *nisi* to Mrs. Simpson

The Prince of Wales and Mrs. Simpson holidaying in Biarritz, 1934.

A candid shot of the Windsors

country home of George V—declined the invitation because of the
need for secrecy.

At any rate, it was not until October 20, seven days after the
Prime Minister's request had been addressed to him, that he permitted Mr. Baldwin to leap over the wall of Fort Belvedere to speak
of this "very urgent" matter.*

Windsor allots some terse paragraphs to this visit. He describes
the arrival of the portly Mr. Baldwin: "He crunched up the driveway
in a tiny black motorcar that didn't seem half big enough for him."

The King, with his income of $10-million per year, had easy access
to every kind of locomotion, such as a fleet of Government and private
cars, including the stately Daimler he so despised. He had the famous
Windsor grays, thoroughbred bays, innumerable other nags, airplanes
(with a Captain of the King's Flight), cruisers, yachts, bicycles,
perhaps even roller skates! In short, he had all the get-there-quick
magic carpets an adolescent can dream of.

The sole vehicle at Mr. Baldwin's command was a tiny black
Austin car, the sturdy, swift, cheap-to-run baby car so many Britons
own and so many long for. This Austin had been lent to Mr. Baldwin
by the police. Although he was then a very sick man, he refused to
ride in anything more comfortable. More comfort meant more
expense, and he was determined to save money, if not on bath soap,
on gasoline, and for the country.

Throughout the memoirs the Duke ridicules Mr. Baldwin's modest
vehicle, calling it a "sinister and purposeful little black beetle," and
recounting how he watched his Prime Minister "wriggle into the
same undersized little black box in which he had made his first
descent upon the Fort." Harmless objects like a baby car become
charged with symbolism and share in the rationalizing which is so
prevalent in *A King's Story.*

In the account of this momentous interview, Windsor deals another
blow at Bad Boy Baldwin. When the visitor, not yet completely
recovered from a serious illness, came to see his King on that fateful
October day, he shiveringly asked for a drink, although it was only
ten o'clock in the morning. The gracious Monarch commanded his
butler to bring some whisky; apparently there were two glasses on
the tray; for when it arrived Mr. Baldwin, about to pour, courteously
enquired: "Sir, when?"

---

*The Baldwin family motto is: "By the help of my God, I will leap over a wall."

With a decorous disapproval which would have been applauded at a Sons of Temperance meeting, King Edward replied:

"No, thank you, Mr. Baldwin, I never take a drink before seven o'clock in the evening."

Yet as early as 1926 there had been an interpellation made in Parliament that the Prince of Wales drank too much. And almost two months after Baldwin's visit, this is what the usually reliable *Time* had to say about the King and potables (in the December 21, 1936 issue):

> So much brandy and soda was continually taken by His Majesty during the early stage of the crisis . . . that the work of the Prime Minister was really of heart-breaking difficulty. It was necessary once to apply the stomach pump. (On December 4, by Lord Horder . . .)

What happened at the first meeting between the King and Baldwin is matter of history: the Prime Minister gave a full report of it to the world through his speech in Parliament. But he made only one of the tête-à-tête. It would indeed be of prime interest to read the other party's side of the story, and such an account might reasonably be hoped for in a book which professes to be written as "a duty" (*A King's Story, Foreword*). But such hopes are not fulfilled.

Clio can hardly be supposed to share Windsor's obsession with Mr. Baldwin's whisky: she would prefer his filling in the details and coloring of his delicate outline:

> Mr. Baldwin's business did indeed concern my friendship with Wallis; and, in justifying his intervention in this most delicate matter, he hastened to say that he had been moved to do so not alone in his Prime Ministerial capacity but also as a friend who was anxious to help. The rumors and criticism appearing in the American and Canadian press had given him great anxiety; if continued, they might, he said, endanger the position of the Monarchy.
>
> (*A King's Story*, Chapter XIX, page 319)

Mr. Baldwin's intervention needed no justification from himself; it was already, and amply, justified by his position as Prime Minister. His bare duty imperiously dictated his speaking. Only silence could have required "justification," i.e., self-defense. He might, if he had pleased, have defended his speaking even on "this most delicate matter" by pointing out that the marriage of the Monarch can never be a private matter, but concerns even the humblest subject. He might also have defended his action on a broad historical basis.

King Richard II had regarded his marriage as a private affair. Heartbroken by the death of his beloved wife, "the good Queen Anne" of Bohemia, he had long refused to marry again, even to provide an heir; and this refusal, followed by his union to a child of seven, had helped to undermine his popularity and sweep him from the throne. The deposition had led directly to the Wars of the Roses. Later, Elizabeth Tudor savagely snubbed anyone who ventured to mention the word "marriage" to her: indeed, her unfortunate Archbishop of Canterbury was reduced to tears by this virginal virago; and the latter part of her reign was darkened by her subjects' fear of another civil war. Still later, at a period not so remote from our own, George IV when Prince of Wales was seriously warned by his chief adviser that he would have no solid hold upon the affections of his people until he was married; as Lord Malmesbury pointed out, the history of England would by itself have furnished many examples of this truth.

The Prime Minister, like the noble lord, may have had in mind those "many examples" of which only three have been cited.

Mr. Baldwin might have adopted a merely official attitude, that of the King's First Servant. And merely had in mind to tell his Sovereign that the people still expected the Royal Family to have the representative virtues. But he was a happily married man, a man of generous sentiment; and so he came as an older and wiser friend anxious to help. He wished to warn King Edward that the growing public resentment of Mrs. Simpson was already expressing itself even in epithets scrawled on walls. It would later reach such a pitch that in December the Government could not even guarantee her personal safety.

Mr. Baldwin told the King that he and his Cabinet colleagues, and Members of Parliament as well, had been deluged by poison-pen letters for months. He pointed out that the rumors and criticism of the North American press might jeopardize the Throne; and well they might! One example of the style of comment appearing has already been given; and another may be here anticipated. Within a short time a banner headline in the United States would read: "King's Moll Renoed at Ipswich."

The Duke of Windsor claims to be telling "the facts as I know them." In carrying out this self-imposed task, he had achieved such a degree of self-exposure as must give pain to any considering reader. In a single page of the memoirs he reveals his own unworthiness of his high calling (*A King's Story*, page 319). A King on being told that his conduct is endangering the Crown might be expected to make some response, whether of self-accusation or of indignant denial. He might at least be expected to ask on what basis such an accusation could be made.

For the Crown of England is not a private possession, to be accepted or abandoned as its wearer chooses. It is the repository of the English tradition, the epitome of all that is meant by the word "England": ". . . this land of such dear souls, this dear, dear land," of Alfred the Great, of Shakespeare, of "the English poor, who in 1914 entered history to the sound of trumpets," and who were shortly to re-enter to the mingled strain of the evening siren and the *Trumpet Voluntary*. The coronation procession is not a mere piece of fancy dress: it is a review of English history.

The man who is anointed in the making of a King at Westminster receives the Crown as a trust from his predecessors, which he in turn must pass on to those who come after him.

> It is an honour longing to our house,
> Bequeathed down from many ancestors,
> Which were the greatest obloquy i' the world
> In me to lose.
>
> (*All's Well That Ends Well*)

But the Crown means even more than this. It epitomizes the history not alone of England, but of a large part of mankind. Thousands of years of the human story are contained within "the round of sovereignty." He who sees the Sovereign of England with a flash of imagination sees also, down the long vista of the centuries, the Symbol, the Sacred Man, crowned and anointed, by whose intercession with the gods his people were maintained in well-being; him by whom the rains fell, the crops grew, the fish were increased in the river; he who, if need were, had to offer his life or his son's life as a sacrifice for the good of all; the man who, in Christian tradition, is represented by that King who received tithes of Abraham.

Furthermore the Throne of Great Britain seems to have a more solid foundation than any other. As even ex-King Farouk remarked prior to the death of King George VI, there are really only five monarchs left: the King of Hearts, the King of Diamonds, the King of Spades, the King of Clubs, and the King of England!

More than ever before, the Crown of England is also an exemplification of the Christian view of man, which considers man not as the mere drudge of a Monarch, not as a cog in a machine called The State, but as *homo liber et legalis*—man free and law-abiding, who by a free choice of will abides by the good because it is good. Other members of government represent a part of the national life: the Christian king represents the whole nation of free and law-abiding men. His office evokes the faith and loyalty of his people, those safeguards of the nation. He is the shepherd, exercising over his flock that rule for which he must one day answer to the King of Kings.

When Edward VIII rejected the advice of Baldwin, as a step toward abandoning his charge for purely selfish reasons, he struck such a blow at the Christian conception of man, faced with the onslaught of atheistic dictatorship both black and red, as a recreant in battle might strike at comrades who refused to bolt with him. This was realized at the time. When all was over, Beverley Baxter, the Canadian who sat in the English Parliament to represent the London borough of Wood Green, bitterly recorded that Prince Edward's last broadcast sounded like the deserter from the line— offering to help in the next war.

But even if he did not at the time give any thought to public matters, now, at this later time, and in his personal memoir, he might have adverted to them. For decorum's sake, for the sake of history, he might have admitted that when confronted with two great issues, his own happiness and the well-being of his people, he found the former the more important of the two.

But to return to the interview. Mr. Baldwin must have felt acutely the difficulty of speaking, for

> . . . although he never came right out and asked me in so many words to do so, it slowly dawned on me that his real object was to persuade me to prevail upon Wallis to withdraw her divorce petition. With Wallis's petition not yet heard, I could not at this stage allow myself to be drawn into a discussion of my hopes. Finally the Prime Minister asked almost bluntly, "Must this case really go on?"
>
> "Mr. Baldwin," I said, doing my best to hide my feelings, "I have no right to interfere with the affairs of an individual. It would be wrong were I to attempt to influence Mrs. Simpson just because she happens to be a friend of the King's."
>
> (*A King's Story*, page 319)

One cannot believe that the King deceived either his hearer or himself by these words. He *was* not being invited, as King, to issue to the wife of a subject his royal command in the polite form of a request; nor was he being asked, as Supreme Magistrate, to override the law. But as an individual intimately concerned with the outcome of the divorce suit, he was being pleaded with to tell Wallis that the hopes they should never have entertained must be forgotten.

Mr. Baldwin knew, and King Edward knew that he knew, the insincerity of these words; but what comment could the Prime Minister make? It was impossible for him to give his King the lie. He left, with a parting compliment on the beauty of the garden, and an excellent suggestion for spring planting. The "cruel" Baldwin had been unable to hide his romantic and sentimental nature. Moreover, in speaking of flowers springing for the delight of his Sovereign in a future season, the old friend and First Servant implied that Edward would then be at his Fort. As Baldwin later said to friends, he had always loved Edward VIII as though the King had been his own son. This sentiment was not reciprocated, to put it mildly.

There is a curious illustration in the unexpurgated American version of *A King's Story*. In it Prime Minister Baldwin, shovel in hand, plants a tree to commemorate something. He is bent over. Directly behind him stands Edward VIII, contemplating Mr. Baldwin's considerable posterior. The picture is illuminated by the following caption from the pen of the Duke of Windsor: "Never again did I observe Mr. Baldwin at such a disadvantage."

At any rate, exactly seven days after the Fort Belvedere conversation, a King's friend in need of a decree *nisi* was granted one at Ipswich Assizes.

18

Love's Labor Lost

Law is king.
—Latin proverb

WHEN EDWARD VII was Prince of Wales and Lily Langtry, the beautiful Jersey Lily, was his mistress, the following line appeared in the columns of a gossipy London weekly: "There is nothing whatever between the Prince of Wales and Lily Langtry." In the next issue of the paper, in exactly the same place, there was an apparently unrelated remark: "Not even a sheet."

Edward VII, the able diplomat, in private as in public life, affected not to care what the papers or the people said about his personal affairs. In fact, he once gave evidence in open court in a notorious gambling scandal that should have remained private (but Lady Brooke babbled).

On another occasion he was named as corespondent by Sir Charles Mordaunt. Edward went to court and swore that "There is nothing whatever between Lady Mordaunt and myself." He added no fillip, either then or a week afterward.

This great King was safely married and had safe mistresses. He would never have dreamed of marrying in a whimsical way or of tossing his ancestral trust to the winds. Unlike his grandson, who does not seem to know the meaning of the word "trust."

In the autumn of 1936, King Edward VIII feared the press and public opinion, because he had every reason to fear them: the divorce action of the woman he had determined to marry was scheduled for hearing.

The doings of Edward VIII and Wallis Simpson had for some time past been the subject of the plainest possible comment in all sections of the American press, and a matter of enraptured interest to American readers. In June, *Cavalcade* referred decorously to the King's "old friends, Mr. and Mrs. Simpson" who had, on May 27,

been guests at a dinner party at St. James' Palace, along with—
Mr. and Mrs. Stanley Baldwin! Very different was the style of
comment in the United States, particularly after the voyage of the
Nahlin. Thus Miss Gretta Palmer variously speculated in the September 23, 1936 issue of the *New York Woman* that:

> Mr. Simpson will soon sail for America incognito to divorce his wife,
> who will become England's morganatic queen.

> Mr. Simpson will not divorce his wife, in spite of the earnest pleas of
> his family, because he enjoys the royal circles to which his wife's charms
> have admitted him.

> Mr. Simpson would dearly love a divorce in England naming His
> Majesty as corespondent, if it were not for the law that one cannot
> sue the King. By not suing while Edward was still Prince of Wales,
> Mr. Simpson has clearly missed the boat.

Miss Palmer seems to have written in equal ignorance of Mr. Simpson's intentions and the British Constitution. Her article did not
explain what a morganatic *queen* might be; presumably she meant
morganatic *wife*. Mr. Baldwin had to tell King Edward that Mrs.
Simpson could not be a morganatic wife, because the King of England's wife, according to the Constitution, must be Queen. However,
a busy lady journalist cannot be expected to be as well acquainted
as a Prime Minister, with the niceties, the sometimes bewildering
niceties, of English constitutional practice.

While the American journalists were thus making hay of the
juiciest sort of sensation under the sun, the English press found itself
in a position of no little difficulty. The English tradition of decency
decreed that there should be no attack upon the Monarch, who
could make no reply; but publication of anything relating to King
Edward's private life, as he was known to be living it, would inevitably
be construed as, or at least made the basis of, attack. Excited, but
still cautious, Fleet Street turned to the Cabinet for directives, but
His Majesty's Ministers were so embarrassed that they declined to
offer any kind of official suggestion. Unofficially, they continued to
keep a ring fence round England.

By July a divorce suit at the town of Ipswich was known to be
pending. And it was then, of course, as Winston Churchill was
to point out, that advice should first have been tendered to His
Majesty. Mr. Baldwin cannot have failed to see, in the sacred Court
Circular of July 9, 1936, that Mrs. Simpson had been present, without

Mr. Simpson, at a royal dinner party at York House. Had he then suggested that Mr. Simpson should take a holiday—say, a yachting cruise, a form of vacation surely suitable to a shipping magnate— with Mrs. Simpson, his advice might not have been taken: just as, at a much later date, and under much more dangerous conditions, Major Hardinge's most urgent advice was angrily rejected. But there would have remained on record the fact that the Prime Minister had acted at once. And herein lay Mr. Baldwin's sole fault in the "King versus Prime Minister struggle." He was naive enough to believe that the King's infatuation would die away, as other, similar infatuations had died.

But from the beginning the Simpson matter was different. It was the King who acted, pulled wires, "advised." For instance, knowing that adverse publicity might break out, he had, at an early stage, approached the press lords. He sent for Lord Beaverbrook, the proprietor of the *Daily Express*, and for the Honourable Esmond Harmsworth (now Lord Rothermere), whose father owned the *Daily Mail*. The King requested these gentlemen to curb their own reporters, as their action (or inaction) would be followed by the other papers; and save for the inevitable two-line announcement that the divorce had been granted—for who could doubt that it would be granted?— no report would appear. There must be no unsavory revelations.

A royal request is of course a polite command. Consequently both Beaverbrook and Harmsworth behaved like loyal lords. They said that they would ensure the silence that the King hoped for. Presumably the Fleet Street newshawks who would be sent to Ipswich to cover the case would not even be allowed to take pencil or paper with them.

Ipswich is a good hour's drive from London, even for the King's chauffeur driving Mrs. Simpson's high-powered American car. It is a town about the size of Portland, Maine, or Phoenix, Arizona.

But Ipswich is rather older than either of these American towns. A Roman villa has been discovered there. After the Romans came the Saxons, who gave the town its name; and the place was later the scene of Viking raids. The grant of the local grammar school dates from the fifteenth century, and the interesting art gallery was housed for a long time in a Tudor mansion. Cardinal Wolsey was born here; and here he maintained one of "those twins of learning, Oxford and Ipswich," a preparatory school from which gifted boys were sent to Christ Church, the college he erected and endowed at

Oxford. The river Gipping flows lazily by to join the sea north of the town, near Felixstowe.

Ipswich is the seat of an Anglican bishopric; and also of a district court, the Circuit Court of Assizes, where judges arrive four times yearly to deliver their verdicts on cases that have arisen in the county of Suffolk.

On October 27, 1936, there appeared on the desk of the Assize Court's clerk a file marked "Simpson W. vs. Simpson E.A." It was the first case on the afternoon calendar. As soon as the judge had seated himself in his tall-backed, carved oak chair, the clerk handed him the file.

Mr. Justice Hawke had the typical face of so many English jurists; stern, solemn, keenly concentrated, its ruddiness brought out by the yellowish-white, full-bottom wig; and with broad-rimmed eyeglasses on the tip of the nose. He was protected by a baldachin above his head; his formidable weapon, a quill pen, towered from the inkwell; and the dark oak paneling served admirably as a background for the ancient picture. Next to the justice sat the county's High Sheriff in his full regalia. The spectacle was as rich, as traditional, as it must have been in the time of Judge Jeffreys.

But this was no Bloody Assizes. And Mr. Justice Hawke presumably had no stones cutting into his kidneys, like Jeffreys, who was said to have meted out justice according to the intensity of his pain.

Mr. Justice Hawke had not even been personally acquainted with the lady who, at that moment, stood near the oaken witness box. True, she was the King's great and good friend, but judges are not now accustomed to hobnob with them, as they did under the Stuarts or the Tudors.

A bespectacled and bewigged lean man with a hawk's nose, wearing an ample black silk robe, stood up. He was Mr. Norman Birkett, K.C. (now Lord Chief Justice of England), the two letters indicating that he was a King's Counsel, one of the few hundred outstanding legal lights so honored in Great Britain. Mr. Justice Hawke was also a King's Counsel. Both judge and lawyer were Benchers (Fellows) of the Inner Temple, the august legal comradeship of England.

"My Lord," began Mr. Norman Birkett, "I appear in the case, Simpson W. vs. Simpson E.A., with my learned friend, Mr. Frampton. I assure you, My Lord, that we will not impose upon your

time. I shall proceed with the petitioner at once." He then turned
to Mrs. Simpson and directed her, with whispers and gestures, into
the witness box.

One of the velvet-jacketed bailiffs, with fine lace cuffs showing
below his sleeves, put before the King's friend a Bible. Simpson W.,
as she was named on top of the file, placed her hand on the Book.
The bailiff mumbled, "I swear by Almighty God that the evidence
I give to this court shall be the truth, the whole truth, and nothing
but the truth." Mrs. Ernest A. Simpson repeated the oath, fixing
her clear blue eyes on the bailiff's. Then she sat down.

"My Lord, this is an undefended case," said Mr. Birkett.

The King's Counsel, who was now really, actually that, spoke as
though Mr. Justice Hawke had just come down through the chimney
and had not the slightest idea as to the nature of the case. But the
judge asked in a very pointed way:

"Why has the case been brought *here?*"

No one replied. Mr. Birkett fidgeted with his papers.

Later, when the news broke and the divorce was discussed by
Londoners in retrospect, even little people, with very limited legal
knowledge, commented: "The case reeked of collusion! Imagine a
woman of her position getting a divorce in a place like Ipswich."

"Proceed, Mr. Birkett," said Mr. Justice Hawke finally in a grave
tone. He reached for his quill, and perhaps made a few arabesques
on the foolscap before him.

"Is your name Wallis Simpson?" asked Mr. Birkett of the lady
in the witness box.

"Yes," answered Mrs. Simpson.

"Do you reside at Beach House, Felixstowe?"

"Yes, I do."

Now at this point, if the famed Judge Jeffreys, that relentless
and cruel cross-examiner, had been sitting on the bench instead of
Mr. Justice Hawke, there might have been some trouble. For Mrs.
Simpson did not actually *reside* at Beach House, Felixstowe—she
lived chiefly at Fort Belvedere, Windsor Great Park.

Mr. Birkett went on.

"You also have a town address, Mrs. Simpson?"

"Yes."

"Is it 16 Cumberland Terrace, Regent's Park, London?"

"Yes."

"You were married to Ernest Aldrich Simpson on the twenty-first of July, 1928, at the Registry Office, in the district of Chelsea, London?"

"Yes."

"Afterwards you lived with him at 12 Upper Berkeley Street, and also at Bryanston Court, both addresses in London?"

"Yes."

"Were you happy with Mr. Simpson until the autumn of 1934?"

"Yes."

"But then came a change. Please tell us what that change was."

"He was indifferent. Very often he went away for weekends. Alone."

"Did you complain to him about this matter?"

"I did complain."

"And yet he continued to do what you complain of? Going away alone, and staying away for whole weekends?"

"Yes, he did."

"Now, on Christmas Day, 1934, did you find a note lying on your dressing table?"

"Yes."

Norman Birkett opened his brief case and pulled from it a pale blue letter. A bailiff took it from him and handed it to the clerk of the court. The clerk placed the note before the judge, who began reading it intently. While he read, Mr. Birkett continued his questions.

"Has there been another letter?"

"Yes. A letter came to our house around Easter time this year. It *seemed* to have been addressed to *me*, but when I opened it I found that the contents could have been meant *only for my husband*."

"Having read the contents of that letter, did you consult your solicitors? And upon your instructions, did your solicitors keep observation upon your husband?"

"Yes."

"What was the result of that observation?"

"Certain information which made me bring this divorce action."

Birkett now paused. Then he opened his brief case again and produced yet another letter.

"On the twenty-third of July 1934, did you write to your husband the letter I now hold in my hand?"

"Yes," said Mrs. Simpson.

The lawyer arched himself over his desk and gave the letter to his client. He could just make it.

"Read the letter," he said.

Mrs. Simpson first looked at the letter. To make sure, no doubt. She then started to read it very slowly and distinctly. People in the court listened attentively. They rather liked the American tone, the strange and pleasing accent.

"Dear Ernest," began Mrs. Simpson, "I have just learned that while you have been away, instead of being on business as you led me to believe, you have been staying at the Hotel Bray with a lady. I am sure you realize this is conduct which I cannot possibly overlook and must insist you do not continue to live here with me. This only confirms the suspicions I have had for a long time. I am therefore instructing my solicitors to take proceedings for a divorce."

This formal letter did not sound at all like the notes exchanged between married couples, even if they are on the threshhold of divorce. It sounded like a letter written by an experienced hand, by someone who had paid great attention to simplicity and clarity, sentence construction, and economy in punctuation. With or without intent, one insignificant mistake appeared in the note—the reference to the hotel in Bray-on-Thames as Hotel Bray, when it was actually the Hotel de Paris. With legal foresight—as first advocated by Francis Bacon, Lord Chief Justice of England—the all-important message, "This only confirms the suspicions I have had for a long time," came as the last sentence but one, so that it would remain in the mind of an audience when read aloud. All in all, it was an excellent letter, perfect for its purpose. It was to the point, cool, stating facts, with no animosity or hurt feelings. The letter also had its own witness— a registration from His Majesty's Post Office, requesting a return receipt, signed by the recipient. This form was shown to Mrs. Simpson by Mr. Birkett.

"Please look at this registration form. In whose handwriting is the signature on that form?"

"Mr. Simpson's," said the petitioner.

"You mean Ernest Aldrich Simpson?" asked the lawyer. Nothing must be left to chance in this most important business. No half sentences, no vagueness as to names, must remain to give some crank the opportunity of causing embarrassment.

Of course there were no cranks in this solemn courtroom. Apart from the formidable legal talent, there were present thirteen policemen, four plain-clothes men from Scotland Yard never taking their eyes off the spectators; as though a heavy sentence was about to be pronounced, and the confederates of the prisoner must be prevented from assaulting the judge, in a vain and foolish attempt to rescue the culprit.

The officers of the law had nothing so fantastic on their minds; they watched simply to ensure that no pictures should be taken of Mrs. Simpson. Back in 1936 candid cameras were a novelty and, like children with a new toy, people were anxious to try them out on memorable occasions. But no camera could have been smuggled into this courtroom. Five policemen, headed by an inspector, had scrutinized everyone at the door before permitting them to enter. Ipswich, the assizes, the courtroom, had never appeared so important.

"That is all, Mrs. Simpson. Thank you," Mr. Birkett said. The King's friend walked to the spectators' bench and sat down.

Three witnesses were called. They were dealt with by Mr. Frampton, Mr. Birkett's learned friend, for they were small fry, the usual witnesses in these stereotyped divorce cases. Two were waiters at the Hotel de Paris in Bray-on-Thames, Archibald Travers and Dante Buscalia, whose names and uncanny memories for trivia seemed to be their most striking characteristics. Both swore that they waited on Ernest Aldrich Simpson in Room No. 4, Hotel de Paris, Bray-on-Thames, on the 21st and 23rd of July, 1936. Mr. Simpson was staying there with a lady. No, positively not with Mrs. Simpson. Mr. Frampton produced a small group photograph and asked Signor Dante Buscalia if he could identify Mr. Simpson in that group. Dante instantly picked out the gentleman without the least trouble.

Christian Haesler, the hall porter of the hotel, coming last in this pageant of witnesses, concluded the overwhelming evidence. He deposed that he saw Mr. Simpson and a lady arrive at the hotel on the night of July 21, and that Mr. Simpson signed the register. Mr. Frampton showed him a sheet of paper, pointing to an entry. "Is this the signature?"

"Yes."

Christian then joined Archibald and Dante on the witnesses' bench, no doubt to enjoy a well-earned rest. Mr. Frampton sat down with a satisfied expression.

So far there had been nothing unusual about the case. "Mr. Simpson had just done what any disgruntled English husband does who wishes to spare his wife's name," said *Time* (October 26, 1936). And then the periodical went on to point out to its readers that

Ernest was not the first member of the Simpson menage to stay at a hotel in recognizable company:

> The story of the King and Mrs. Simpson last week was plain and simple. Under English law a man who makes a trip in company with another man's wife, the two stopping at the same hotels, has in fact given the husband opportunity to sue the wife for divorce on the ground of adultery. The King has just made an extended yachting trip in company with Mrs. Simpson and notably in Vienna they stopped at the same hotel.

But no one in the Ipswich courtroom was so tactless as to cry "Veto!" or to mention Vienna. Silence reigned on the legal stage. Only, Mr. Norman Birkett coughed a little and came to his feet again.

"Upon that evidence," he said, "I ask Your Lordship for a decree *nisi* with costs."

Did the last word mean that Mr. Simpson had to pay Birkett's retainer of at least a hundred guineas, which in 1936 stood for five hundred and fifty still powerful dollars? Plus Mr. Frampton's fee, all the costs of the court and the witnesses' expenses, including travel and their rooms and hearty meals at the local inn? Yes, it did.

"Well," said Mr. Justice Hawke at last, "I suppose I must come to the conclusion that there was adultery in this case. But there is one question I should have liked to ask you. I suppose, Mr. Birkett, you know that question."

"That the name of the lady who stayed with petitioner's husband has not been mentioned here?" asked the lawyer brightly. "But, My Lord, the name of the lady is plainly disclosed in the petition and the lady has been served with a copy of the petition."

"That was what was in my mind, Mr. Birkett," replied the judge. The modulation expressed satisfaction. And well might Mr. Justice Hawke be satisfied: he was as well acquainted as any other judge with the activities of the professional corespondent, and there was no question of such a thing here.

"If Your Lordship pleases, decree *nisi?*" continued Mr. Birkett. "With costs?"

Poor Mr. Simpson!

"Very well," said the judge, "decree *nisi*. Unusual circumstances. So you may have it." Then he added, "With costs, I am afraid. Unusual circumstances."

The newly divorced lady was already at the door. One of the
bailiffs opened it and she slid out. The reporters of foreign newspapers galloped after her. But when they reached the same door,
they found it locked! And no bailiff offered to unlock it. They ran
to another door. That too was locked! The reporters gave voice to
their indignation. "Why can't we get out of here?" shouted one
especially obnoxious fellow. But the others, too, began to talk loudly.
Mr. Justice Hawke gave them an icy stare. "Silence! Silence!
Silence!" cried the bailiff. Newspapermen don't particularly care to
be cited for contempt of court; the impatient reporters did not relish
the idea of spending a night in an Ipswich cell.

When at last the doors were unlocked and the eager pressmen
rushed into the street, Mrs. Simpson was gone. The newshawks could
only hope that the photographers whom they had stationed outside
the court had been on the job. They had been on the job—but so
had the police. However, only cameras were smashed, not heads.
This happened in England, not under a dictatorship . . .

The place was not Reno, either. So the former Mrs. Simpson did
not command the King's chauffeur to drive to the River Gipping in
order that she might jubilantly throw her second ex-husband's ring
into it. She first drove to Felixstowe, where she picked up her personal
belongings. She was able to take all her effects in one single trip, in
a limousine, without the aid of station wagons and trucks, although
her wardrobe was already known to be one of the largest in the world.
So this one trip goes to show just how long had been her residence at
Beach House, Felixstowe.

The automobile and its precious cargo had a swift journey back
to London—Scotland Yard saw to that. At strategical points there
was a police ban: the Yard had blocked all London-bound traffic.
Who knows? Perhaps the future Queen of England was sitting in
that car . . .

No interdict was placarded, no anathema was pronounced, no
libel suit was threatened against Margaret Case Harriman, in the
wake of certain relevant passages in her piece, "The King and the
Girl from Baltimore":

> . . . However, in 1931, all such cozy domestic bliss seemed far away.
> The Prince of Wales was thirty-seven years old, and he had just met
> a lovely American lady . . . Here is the groundwork for high romance
> and deep tragedy. Unfortunately, there is an interlude of pure, shriek-
> ing farce.

Mrs. Simpson's famous trousseau, "The semblance of a form divine."

Wallis' third marriage

FAREWELL

Lady Furness, through whom Wales first met Mrs. Simpson, had been well known in London as the Prince's favorite dinner and dancing companion. But she had another suitor, one Ali Khan, a son of the Aga Khan. She had an engagement to dine with him in Paris on the very evening, as it happened . . . that Syrie Maugham, Somerset Maugham's ex-wife, had asked her to dine in London. After Lady Furness had wired her regrets from Paris, the dinner date with Ali Khan somehow fell through, so Lady Furness took the next plane back to London and turned up at Mrs. Maugham's party after all. "Where is David?" she asked the moment she swept through the front door. "I'll find him for you," said Mrs. Maugham quickly, but not quickly enough. Lady Furness hurried past her down a corridor, threw open a door she seemed to know well, and sure enough, David, Prince of Wales, was in the small library quite alone, except for Mrs. Simpson. Sensation!

(*The Aspirin Age*, Simon & Schuster)

This episode, described by a keen observer of international society, took place then apparently in 1931, but not later than 1932. According to court records, Mr. Simpson turned up with that unnamed lady at the Hotel de Paris at Bray-on-Thames at least two years later, in 1934! The arrangement concerning the Simpson W. vs. Simpson E.A. divorce surely does not call for further comment. Except that not so long after the assizes, Mr. Norman Birkett was knighted.

And, since this is not a book of fiction, but a book of facts, written to analyze that "pure, shrieking farce," a significant paragraph may be quoted from that excellent book, *The Long Week End*, *A Social History of Great Britain, 1918-39*, by Robert Graves and Alan Hodge (The Macmillan Company, New York):

In 1926, when King Carol renounced the throne of Rumania, though some papers took the line "Royal Romance," others knew their public well enough to title the story "Carol the Cad." His caddishness was assessed by the number of women in the case. If he had separated from Princess Helen because he wished to rejoin the morganatic wife whom he had been forced, for dynastic reasons, to abandon, it would have been a romance; actually, he went to live with a third person, Madame Lupescu. Public opinion now condoned a single change of heart, but not more; as the police-court ruling branded a woman who took more than a single lover as a common prostitute. This principle was applied in 1936 in the Mrs. Simpson case: she was a twice-divorced woman.

But of course readers—like the judge—will wish to know the name of the corespondent in the Simpson case: it was a Miss "Buttercup" Kennedy, a name impressive even if not famous.

19

The Letter

In a man's letters his soul lies naked.
—SAMUEL JOHNSON

The language of truth is simple.
—SENECA

THE DUKE in his autobiography explains in detail the importance of the post of His Majesty's Private Secretary. He emphasizes that the Private Secretary of the King of England is the only channel of communication between the Sovereign and his Ministers; and is responsible for the good public relations of the Monarch. As Windsor puts it, "He, the King's Private Secretary, should keep his ear to the ground so as to *advise his master in the moulding of royal policy*." (Our italics.) The Private Secretary must be unswervingly loyal, and must possess a rare combination of personal gifts in tact, political sagacity, and knowledge of constitutional procedure. Boldness and benevolence—in Plato's view the virtues most needed in a king's adviser—are not mentioned in the Duke's list of desiderata for a Private Secretary.

The importance of the post may be further gauged from George V's remark about Lord Stamfordham, his own Private Secretary: "He taught me how to be a King."

The appointment of a suitable Secretary naturally received the King's attention early in the reign. After much deliberation he chose for this onerous post Major the Honourable Alexander (now Lord) Hardinge.

Major Hardinge already had behind him sixteen years' experience as a member of the *Comus Regis*, the King's Household or Court, having been Assistant Private Secretary to George V since 1920. The Hardinge family motto ran: "For King and Country." Major Hardinge's father, Lord Hardinge of Penshurst, had been Viceroy of India, Ambassador to Russia and to France, and Permanent Under

Secretary of State. His great-grandfather fought heroically throughout the Peninsular War, where he lost an arm; and after the Battle of Waterloo was presented by the Duke of Wellington himself with the sword of Napoleon. This Viscount Hardinge eventually became a field marshal and later the very popular Governor General of India.

Major Hardinge's ancestry and upbringing, not to mention his own outstanding record in World War I—his decorations included the Military Cross—were a guarantee of his integrity and zeal in the service of the Monarch. Secure in the fidelity of this gentleman, so well equipped to handle the most delicate affairs, King Edward might be at ease; knowing that any follies of his would be transmuted to wisdom in their passage through the hands of his Private Secretary to the world, while all outside happenings of moment to His Majesty would be realistically transmitted to him by the same loyal servant. Whose ear was—as specified by the Duke—always to the ground.

Yet the instant Hardinge was put to the test, and attempted to report underground grumblings, he incurred the anger and the enmity of his master. The Duke speaks with just appreciation of the devotion shown by all around him at the time of the crisis, from press lords down to the telephone operator at the Fort. But for those who served him most faithfully he not only has no thanks, but he has misrepresentation. Of all those concerned in the handling of the crisis, Mr. Baldwin and Major Hardinge had the heaviest burden. No man will readily take upon himself the task of telling another man that his fiancée is unwelcome to his family, the nation; the Prime Minister and the Private Secretary had to do this, and in doing it they had also, by implication, to criticize their Monarch. The pain felt by Mr. Baldwin in discharging this duty is sufficiently shown by the delicate indirection of his language, for which most men would be grateful, but which for the Duke is simply further matter of offense. As to Major Hardinge's feelings there is no evidence, direct or indirect; but they may be guessed at.

In going about his business—which was of course the King's business—Major Hardinge at his listening post had long been aware that there was opposition to the friendship between King Edward and Mrs. Simpson. Owing to the self-imposed silence of the press, the amount of opposition was not large, at least among the general body of people; but such as existed was like the snowball that starts the avalanche. When that strained silence (requested by the King) could no longer be maintained—and Hardinge knew that it must soon break—when the knowledge of a comparatively small group should become public property—then the avalanche of popular disfavor would crash forward, perhaps carrying away the Throne in its great movement.

The weight of anxiety on Hardinge's mind must have been crushing. But the Private Secretary's duty was clear: he must warn his master. However, the King was safely ensconced behind the walls of Fort Belvedere, and so inaccessible to the members of his Household. The Private Secretary was therefore compelled to convey his warning by a letter, necessarily sent in a Royal dispatch box labeled URGENT AND CONFIDENTIAL.

The contents of royal dispatch boxes are of course official communications to the Sovereign, and as such employ a phraseology fixed for them by court etiquette, which bears to political life much the same relationship that military etiquette bears to army life: it is a means of externalizing discipline so as to enforce and maintain it. A certain deference of bearing and language is rightly exacted from those who approach the Sovereign and his family (and Monarchs who forget this do so at their own peril). Hence when Major Hardinge addressed himself to King Edward, it was "with humble duty."

There is a curious interest in the Duke's manner of treating this letter: it is described as briefly, though much more emotionally, as the interviews with Mr. Baldwin.

The memoirs were allegedly written to tell the facts, before time and repetition could sanction misconceptions. But how little does the Duke tell us of the facts, though he assumes public interest in, and anxiety to know them! Historians in the future will be even more anxious than readers at present to learn what happened. Yet the first discussion with the Prime Minister is covered in little more than a page; and this brevity is defended by referring the reader to Mr. Baldwin's report to the Commons. There was no comparable report on Major Hardinge's letter. The present generation at least must learn of its contents from the Duke, or remain uninformed. Unfortunately this letter is only summarized as to its more important part: the most dangerous political situation developing behind the scenes. That situation was shortly to burst forth as a public crisis—as Major Hardinge accurately predicted—of the first magnitude, and with an éclat that startled the world. The Private Secretary's letter was therefore a historical document of prime interest and importance, and its last home would properly be in the national archives. (Whether

it did eventually, or ever will, find its way there, the Duke does not
say.) In the interim, before the elapse of the "closed period" usual
for such documents, might not the publication of its contents in full
serve to destroy such misconceptions as that King Edward VIII was
forced into an apparent abdication, "secretely, at dead of night," by
a group of sinister politicians?

But though brief the political summary, the paragraph which no
doubt packs the punch for an emotional public is given in full, and
may be quoted here:

> If Your Majesty will permit me to say so, there is only one step which
> holds out any prospect of avoiding this dangerous situation, and that
> is for Mrs. Simpson to go abroad *without further delay*, and I would *beg*
> Your Majesty to give this proposal your earnest consideration before
> the position has become inevitable. Owing to the changing attitude
> of the Press the matter has become one of great urgency.
>
> (*A King's Story*, page 327)

According to the Duke, this letter left him shocked and angry; he
further admits that it struck at the roots of his pride—that is, at his
known obstinacy, the dogged obstinacy of a weak man.

In this matter of personal feeling, Edward VIII contrasts strangely
with his immediate predecessors. It is impossible to imagine King
George V, "the little sea-captain," as G. K. Chesterton once called
him, asking to be handled with kid gloves; most probably he would
have exclaimed:

> Who tells me true, though in his tale lie death,
> I hear him as he flatter'd.
>
> (*Antony and Cleopatra*)

Edward VIII, when once in Antony's position, could not bring himself to speak in Antony's phrase; or to insist to his Private Secretary,
as his grandfather had done: "Tell me the truth, even if it is cruel."

This Private Secretary to Edward VII, Lord Knollys, was not only
the depository of his master's secrets, but also a personal friend, who
went on, one might almost say was passed on, as a sort of living
heirloom, to the service of George V. He had the task of repeating
unpleasant things to King Edward; but it is not related that this
King required to be comforted, even when hearing Nephew Willie's

(Kaiser Wilhelm) sneer that "The King of England is boating with his grocer!" (Sir Thomas Lipton.)

Why should Hardinge's letter have shocked Edward VIII? Mr. Baldwin had already advised him that his actions might endanger the Throne. Tradition, precedence, usage and his own years of travel among the peoples of Great Britain and the Commonwealth should have taught him something: the least observant of men might and should have known that his subjects would never accept, as the King of England's wife, a woman with two husbands still living.

However astonishing the letter to King Edward, his own reaction to its contents is more astonishing still. He graciously concedes that his Private Secretary-Public Relations Counsel had both the right and the duty to warn him. In the same paragraph he describes himself as puzzled by the motives that could have prompted Major Hardinge to write! Such a degree of obtuseness will be credible only to the moronic. Hardinge had a motive which must be all-compelling to an English gentleman in his position: his duty to his Sovereign. Mr. Baldwin had "justified" his "intervention"—another man than the Duke might have said "explained his speaking"—by his Ministerial position. Major Hardinge attempted no justification—his position precluded any self-defense. In truth no more than the Prime Minister's did his act call for justification. A failure to act would indeed have been near treasonable. There was no failure. The motto "For King and Country" was not written only on Alec Hardinge's escutcheon.

From the "mystery" of Major Hardinge's motives the Duke turns to his own feelings. Plaintively he describes himself as being hurt by the cold formality with which a personal matter, affecting his happiness, had been broached.

If he means that his Private Secretary should have told him all, in person, face to face, covering the cold, hard facts with flowery phrases delivered in a voice modulated to velvet softness, then it must be pointed out that at that time it was not easy to see His Majesty alone. Or if he is suggesting that the letter should have been commiserating and sentimental, advocating the adoption of easy courses, he forgets the stoic qualities of an English gentleman. Neither does he consider the responsibility weighing down a king's Councillor. *

---

*Major Hardinge had been sworn a Member of the Privy Council October 27, 1936, on which day Mrs. Simpson received her decree *nisi* at Ipswich.

Nor does he recall that plain-spoken letters, advising of imminent danger, had been sent to former Monarchs.

What other than a formal tone could Major Hardinge with propriety have adopted? He was a subject addressing his Sovereign; moreover he was not writing fiction. The very first sentence of his letter read: "As Your Majesty's Private Secretary I feel it my duty to bring to your notice the following facts . . ."

Major Hardinge then proceeded to give a warning that should never have been needed by a man to all appearances adult. There are some things a person of forty-two should know, without having to be told; there are some things he should be able to face, without asking to be wept over. It is, in any case, hard to detect the coldness with which Hardinge is charged: the urgency of the language used, emphasized by italics, shows that he felt keenly the threat to the Throne, to the man filling it, and even to the lady involved. A Secretary coldly indifferent might correctly have "begged" the King to act; such a man would not "*beg*" him to consider a proposal.

What was that proposal? That His Majesty should send from his land, his realm, the woman he intended to marry. But was Major Hardinge informed of that intention? It was not, apparently, a habit of the King's to carve on every tree of Fort Belvedere "the fair, the chaste, the inexpressive she" who walked with him in its garden. Hardinge was surely acquainted with the speculations of the American press; he must have read that curious article in which the New York *Journal-American* announced the forthcoming marriage, "one month after the ceremonies of the coronation." But he cannot be supposed to have taken such things seriously. The marriage of the King, or of any member of the Royal Family, is not made known to the members of the Royal Household through the medium of the foreign press.

The Duke says that he was nonplussed as to Hardinge's motive. Had King Edward adopted the natural and reasonable course of summoning Hardinge and asking him to state his "motive" the Secretary might have further explained his self-explanatory letter:

"Sir, I had three imperative reasons for writing. First, my duty to Your Majesty obliges me to inform you of a political situation endangering your Crown. Secondly, Your Majesty's personal interests and feelings are involved. I have the responsibility of guiding public opinion, but without Your Majesty's support I am unable to act. Third, the personal safety of the lady is now at stake."

At this stage it is essential to bear in mind that the King had

concealed from everybody—including his family and his advisers—
his intention of marrying Mrs. Simpson, though he and Wallis had
for a long time determined to marry, "come what may." On the
other hand, their mode of life was anything but secret. Naturally
Hardinge, whose task it was to "listen in," was not ignorant of the
state of feeling prevailing in the various circles where the friendship
was known. He knew that Fleet Street was "roaring to go"; that press
lords got to be press lords because they had the gift of perfidy at the
right time; he knew that the quarter-century of propaganda which
had raised Edward to the dizziest heights in history, was in danger of
collapsing like a castle built of cards. Hardinge listened while people
talked.

That Nestor of journalism, Sir Philip Gibbs, writing on the heels
of the crisis, reports one of Wallis' compatriots as saying, "She ought
to be taken for a ride," and "You people ought to bump her off!"
The visitor, a Virginian, spoke from knowledge of a country where
the art of assassination was at that time on a pretty high level; where
Murder, Inc. was flourishing; where the methods of the Renaissance
had been revived; where persons, prominent or obscure, *were* taken
for a ride, or bumped off, or lowered in the river encased in cement.

But this was England. A small country, where an assassin would
have been quickly caught and hanged, even if he had been a Chicago
beer baron; where a policeman's only weapon is a rubber truncheon;
where people are unaccustomed to the idea of assassination. But, even
so, a country that is not wholly without its lofty-minded maniacs:
persons who would think of themselves as doing a public service by
killing one who, to their twisted way of thinking, was a danger to
the common good.

There were cranks in England, too, as in any other country. King
Edward knew that from experience; and even if in his case the gun,
unloaded, was merely thrown under his horse's hoofs, what was the
guarantee that the next gun would also be unloaded and only thrown
for the purpose of demonstrating a real or imaginary grievance? And
whose number would it be next time? Kings have always been
vulnerable targets for cranks. But in the London of 1936 it was the
King's friend who seemed to have been singled out—in her recently
acquired, luxurious house, at aristocratic Cumberland Terrace, every
single windowpane had been smashed.

Hardinge knew that too. If His Majesty's Private Secretary, who
was trusted to keep a close watch on popular feeling, used his common

sense—and as his letter shows, he did—he must have realized that the bricks and stones hurled by the indignant masses at Mrs. Simpson's windows were not meant for the glass, but for someone behind it. The throwers did not know that she was not in residence. But crowds are sometimes carried away by anger, and were the public once to get out of hand it might be impossible to stop them. Bullets are not the only things that kill: a well-aimed or even a stray stone can do that. Major Hardinge was probably among the first to know that Scotland Yard could not and would not guarantee Mrs. Simpson's safety. There was only one way to prevent a tragedy—by Mrs. Simpson's leaving the country.

To be sure, remarks such as those reported by Sir Philip were crude. But it would have been sheer irresponsibility not to take them seriously, and that in time. In view of the damage done at Cumberland Terrace, Major Hardinge would have deserved to be branded a disloyal Secretary and a worthless friend had he not sounded the alarm.

Was it "coldness" on the part of Hardinge that he endeavored, by a recital of unpalatable fact, to save his master—who was apparently living in a dream world—his master's friend—supposedly so well-informed yet in the event stunned by the public reaction—and more important still, the Throne and the Empire? Hardinge must have felt that any harm done to the woman would react most terribly on the man—and had his letter not been written, the King might have been really hurt. So he suggested the one expedient which, if adopted, would avert the peril threatening the Crown, his master, and his master's friend.

The Duke hints that Hardinge wrote his letter at the instigation of Mr. Baldwin. That may be so. But did not the broken glass speak with more eloquence than any Prime Minister ever could? The speedy departure of Wallis for the Continent was the only sound advice, the only wise course to follow. After all, the separation might be but temporary. Besides, Major Hardinge knew that Mrs. Simpson was a much-traveled lady, who had never lived long in any one city. Neither was it unreasonable to suggest that a divorcée should travel abroad. Foreign travel is indeed a recognized and recommended specific for mending hearts; and Mrs. Simpson had already had experience of its therapeutic value—disappointment in Washington had been followed by a trip to Shanghai; and divorce in Virginia by high life in New York. But what was most important was that Mrs. Simpson should no longer expose her life to danger: Major Hardinge's sugges-

tion must have appeared eminently reasonable to everybody but the
man to whom it had been made for his own good. Three weeks later
Mrs. Simpson was to leave the realm of the man she intended to
marry with much greater celerity than that advised by Major
Hardinge. The timely Hardinge plan would have at least made it
possible for her to pack her belongings.

From the Duke's delineation of his own past thoughts and feelings
it is clear that he not only regarded his friendship with Mrs. Simpson
as a purely private affair, but looked on official intervention very
much as a cocky youth looks on the advice of the heavy uncle warning
him against his fiancée: as an impertinence. He seems to have been
overcome with very genuine surprise and dismay by the discovery
that this friendship could be a matter of concern to both Mr. Baldwin
and Major Hardinge, as if they were motivated by personal disapproval and were meddling in a matter which could be none of their
business; though they both had plainly referred to the danger to the
Throne, which was certainly their duty and therefore their business.

In a work crammed with astounding things, this is perhaps the
most astounding portion. Profoundly interesting is the psychology
revealed here—a matter of the utmost public importance is treated
as a struggle between individuals! Edward wrestling, in the manner
of the Greek heroic age, for the possession of the unparalleled Briseis.
The word "challenge" is freely used, and the Duke pictures himself
as bracing himself for battle and hoping to defeat Mr. Baldwin. As
if he were the hero of some cloak-and-dagger novel, he speaks of
coming to grips with the Prime Minister and the nebulous figures
around him (the group naturally including the Archbishop of
Canterbury).

At this point in *A King's Story* Major Hardinge drops out. (In this
book, however, it will be necessary to refer to him again.) The man
through whom His Majesty should, constitutionally speaking, have
maintained contact with his Government, simply disappears; and
there enters instead the interesting figure of Mr. Walter Monckton,
K.C. (now the Right Honourable Sir Walter Monckton).

Interesting, from more than one consideration. Mr. Monckton had
of course at that time no Ministerial position whatever: he was not
even a Privy Councillor. True, he had been Attorney General to the
Prince of Wales, and was legal adviser to the Duchy of Cornwall.
But this latter employment gave him no political position such as
properly belongs to His Majesty's Private Secretary, no official stand-

ing. It speaks volumes for the Cabinet, and for their desire to keep
Edward VIII on the Throne, that they were willing to accept a private
person (in relation to the constitutional struggle), a mere *amicus
curiae*, as the negotiator between the King and themselves.

Mr. Monckton proves as interesting—and as accommodating—in
his personal as in his unofficial relation with the Duke. According to
Windsor, this brilliant barrister was as much shocked by Hardinge's
letter as he himself had been. The sophisticated, worldly-wise lawyer,
who could not have been ignorant of the facts, was "shocked" by the
advice which he must have known was justified by Hardinge's position
and by the real danger of the situation. A pretty picture, indeed!

The reader will recall the extremely frank words of Lord Malmesbury to the Prince of Wales, later George IV; Mrs. Fitzherbert was
already chosen, so naturally the Prince replied that he did not wish
to be King, and that his younger brother could succeed in his place.
When Edward VIII told Mr. Monckton that he did not think he
was the kind of King his people wanted, and "there is my brother
Bertie," Mr. Monckton ventured no advice. Yet the situation was
still fluid; and this brilliant barrister was perhaps the only person to
whom His Majesty would have listened. He, with his shrewd legal
mind, combining that light touch—which in diplomacy sometimes
works wonders—with the frankness of a privileged friend, could have
urged the King down the right path of history. Mr. Monckton
apparently did not attempt the task. He merely acquiesced.

The King's mother did not. This great lady, who by her husband's
deathbed had kissed the hand of the new Sovereign, was appalled
when the 59th King of England—who was of course to be the most
glorious of all—told her that he would abdicate if he could not
otherwise marry Wallis Simpson. The old lady spoke of duty, and
probably of many other "unpleasant" matters. She did not speak
against her son's friendship; but she rejected all entreaties to meet
the friend.

She spoke of another's duty while doing her own. It was her duty
to sustain the Monarchy; and a fortunate accident helped her to do
so. The Crystal Palace was burned down.

The loss of that landmark, wonder glasshouse of a Victorian prosperity so long vanished that it now seems a dream like the dreams of
peace it once nourished, came a day or two after the news of the
proposed marriage broke upon the stupefied public. But when the
fires were out there appeared upon the scene a famous figure. Gracious

and serene, Queen Mary came and surveyed the smoking ruin. All
round the placards flared; all round the talk bubbled much more
furiously than ever in Bryanston Square; from Budleigh Salterton to
Berwick on Tweed and beyond Englishmen—nay more, Scotsmen!—
spoke to other Englishmen—and Scotsmen—to whom they had never
been introduced; and discussed with perfect strangers matters which
had seemed as settled as the weather. But "there is a saving grace
in dull routine"; and Queen Mary knew it. With the major portion
of the globe buzzing like a hornet's nest, the lady most nearly concerned—yes, far more intimately concerned than Mrs. Simpson—
moved in calm dignity. Panic was impossible in that presence; and
watching the stately figure moving on the slope of Sydenham, or
seeing it in the press photos, it was possible to believe that life would
again be normal.

When it did become normal again, upon the accession of King
George VI, the man who forgot the dictum that it is just as dangerous
to tell the truth to a Monarch as to serve him badly, was recalled—
the Right Honourable the Major Alexander Hardinge resumed his
duties. He filled once more his important position in the *Comus Regis*,
along with great noblemen having less exacting duties, such as the
Duke of Norfolk (hereditary Earl Marshal), the Duke of Saint-Albans
(Grand Falconer), the Duke of Buccleuch (Lord Steward), and the
Duke of Beaufort (Master of the Horse).

It is not known where the Private Secretary secluded himself during
the crisis which burst out soon after his prophetic letter reached
Edward. Perhaps in his London mansion or on one of his estates.
In olden days, as a result of having caused his King much pain, he
would have found himself in the Tower; in this modern era he merely
finds himself in *A King's Story*. Lord Hardinge has the distinction of
being among those whom the Duke castigates in the story of his
abdication, his abandonment of his kingdom when it was starting on
its perilous and swift descent from prosperity to adversity, from cakes
and ale to a weekly egg.

20

The Great Decision

It is always thus, impelled by a state of mind which is destined not to last, that we make our irrevocable decisions.
—MARCEL PROUST: *Remembrance of Things Past*

THE great decision was mine and mine alone," says the Duke of Windsor in his memoirs, excerpting the phrase from the epoch-making farewell speech he broadcast at the time of his abdication.

George Bernard Shaw also spoke at the time. Jocularly, to be sure. The only serious sentence in the puckish statement of the old sage aroused attention though—he said that the abdication of Edward VIII was the severest jolt the British Throne had ever had.

It is not possible to believe that the great decision to bring about this great calamity was the King's alone. He only *thought* that the decision was his, just as he imagined that it was *he* who had conquered Mrs. Simpson.

The power of a woman who has gained mastery over a man is proverbial. She can make him do *anything*. Even remain on the Throne . . .

As one views this major catastrophe in the history of England in retrospect, it emerges that Mrs. Simpson, or even an adventuress, for that matter, albeit in possession of all this galvanizing governing power, would have been unable to rise to the greatness of the occasion. Despite woman's wonderful native intelligence, which men call, depreciatingly, feminine intuition.

But this situation was far too formidable to be handled by a lady who had been accustomed to cope realistically with other, much lesser, intrigues and predicaments.

It seems that Mrs. Simpson, who had had till December 1936, the perception to size up situations and men accurately, temporarily lost this ability at the most critical time in her life, for two main reasons.

First, she still continued to act as if playing a game of chess, with the determination to take the King on the board according to her self-established rules. Second, she had no well-informed man in her entourage courageous enough to advise and enlighten her.

Here is a fine example that in certain cases even the most intuitive and unemotional woman must enlist the help of male logic. Plus a man's knowledge of history.

Mrs. Simpson also may have been terrified that in the midst of the raging storm, despite the desperate love of the King, much more powerful, secret forces might carry her off the stage altogether.

Here she was, a member of the frailer sex, battling fiercely against the will, and the wrath, of almost every power in England. True, the King, who loved her to distraction, was fighting beside her. But Mrs. Simpson, like other women, knew love's ups and downs; she knew that the most ardent love may be sometimes extinguished by the slightest breeze. Or destroyed by titanic, far-reaching exigencies. And, since women—most women—can see through men as if through a glass of water, she knew that the King's stubborn and contrary nature was alloyed with mushy, and therefore uncertain, sentimentality. ("Stay me with flagons, comfort me with apples; for I am sick of love," it is writ in the Song of Songs.)

The most eligible man in the world was intoxicated by love for her. But Mrs. Simpson looked at the thing with the inherent realism of women and did not consider this miraculous luck as complete victory: for woman, only marriage is complete victory. She had and had not. And so she could not relax.

Here she was at Fort Belvedere, chaperoned by her aunt. And probably advised by her. Mrs. Bessie Merryman from Baltimore may have been elated by her niece's almost unbelievable good fortune; but still she measured love, no matter how exalted the lover, with the yardstick of a decent, provincial middle-class woman, to whom all love not leading to the altar must seem repugnant.

Even if not in so many words—for there is a kind of freemasonry among women on the subject of marriage—worldly Mrs. Simpson wholeheartedly agreed with her aunt's view. Wallis, too, judged that the situation would remain insecure and uncertain until marriage vows should be exchanged.

No man took it upon himself to warn her of pitfalls, or to impress upon her, by recounting a score of historical precedents, that royal favorites often thrived while the commoner wives of sovereigns often came to grief.

There wasn't a single cultivated, tactful man who would ask Mrs. Simpson whether she was familiar with the tragedy of Edward IV, or to hand her a volume of the History of England, suggesting that she read a passage relating to a certain comely lady, Elizabeth Woodeville.

> Elizabeth perceived that the impression which she had made on Edward IV was so deep as to give her hopes of obtaining the highest elevation. She obstinately refused to gratify his passion; and all the endearments, caresses, and importunities of the young and amiable Edward proved fruitless against her rigid and inflexible virtue. His passion, irritated by opposition and increased by his veneration for such honorable sentiments, carried him, at last, beyond all bounds of reason; and he offered to share his throne, as well as his heart, with the woman. . . . The marriage was privately celebrated at Grafton . . . This step, later, proved to be dangerous and imprudent to the highest degree.
> —HUME
> (*History of England*)

Elizabeth Woodeville's challenging and, as history proved, unfortunate, words which made Edward IV behave exactly as she wanted him to behave, are famous: "I know that I am not good enough to be your queen. But I am too good to be your mistress!"

The twice-divorced lady did not say this to Edward VIII. How could she? Rational Mrs. Simpson would not descend to anticlimax. But a look into the soul of Mrs. Simpson at an early stage of her friendship with the King would probably have revealed her determination to marry him soon after she knew that he was in love with her.

For the great decision to marry does not depend on the man. Even if that man happens to be a king. He is merely permitted to think that she yielded to his fervent proposals; that he was triumphant in breaking down her reluctance; and that, like St. George, he cut off the heads of all the horrible dragons opposing him in his march to victory. A subtle and clever woman creates her man's illusions, for she knows that he is in love with illusions.

Long before "his great decision" the couple had made up their minds to marry, come what might.

Come what might!

Edward VIII, himself, should have consulted the history books of his country at the onset of the crisis. And he should have asked the lady from Baltimore to look over them, too, instead of devouring her four newspapers a day.

They would have found that when a King of England tries to upset the Constitution, he is killed, or deposed and exiled, his posterity also being excluded from the throne. But Edward thought, in his fantastic conceit, that England would never allow its most popular King to leave, and that, to make him stay, the British would put up with any queen he selected . . .

"It was in the early evening of December 2, 1936, that I informed the Prime Minister, Mr. Stanley Baldwin, of my resolve to abdicate, harrowing though the decision would be, if the Cabinet would not countenance my marriage to Wallis Simpson," says the Duke of Windsor in his memoirs.

This statement should be borne in mind—here he says *he* informed Mr. Baldwin of *his* resolve to abdicate unless he could marry Mrs. Simpson on the throne.

He had already told the Prime Minister this two weeks earlier, on the 16th of November.

But to go on punching holes in Windsor's "historical document"— the ex-King says that the same evening, December 2, 1936, he returned from London to his Fort, and not wishing to alarm Aunt Bessie, did not during dinner say anything of the conversation between himself and Mr. Baldwin. So he proposed a little after-dinner walk with Wallis in the garden, to break the bad news to her away from the delicate ears of Mrs. Merryman.

He withdrew his compassion from his family and his subjects, yet he admits his deep concern for the Aunt from Baltimore! Ever since his mother, the widowed Queen of England, had told him, the King of England, that she did not care to know Mrs. Simpson, he had not been near her. He totally ignored her. While for another old lady, a stranger, he showed the utmost solicitude. (But there was perhaps a very good reason for his avoidance of his mother—he was about to risk dynamiting the Windsor dynasty off the face of the earth.)

Perhaps the King of England was afraid of meeting Warfield family opposition; a possible impetuous decision on the part of the two ladies, aunt and niece, to pack at once, to take to the road, making a vow never to spend another night under the roof of a man who could not fulfil his promise of marriage.

"It has been a bad day," the Duke writes he said to Wallis, that

Combine Photos   *International News Photo*

The Duke of Windsor with the late Dr. Ley, Labor Front Leader of Nazi Germany (left). The Windsors on a friendly visit (right).

British Press Combine

London or Berlin? It is England. Faithful followers saluting the would-be fuehrer, Sir Oswald Mosley, who urged Edward VIII to make Mrs. Simpson queen.

The former King of England inspects a Nazi "honor" guard at a time when "Operation Sea-Lion" (the contemplated assault on England) had already been blueprinted.

The Duke of Windsor at the funeral of his brother. The missing button on the Admiral's coat acted as a reminder . . .

evening in the garden. "I have seen Mr. Baldwin. He leaves me no choice. Either I must give you up or abdicate."

The reader will recall that a couple of paragraphs earlier Windsor declared that *he* was the one to give the ultimatum to Baldwin. Now he says that he told Wallis that it was *Baldwin* who delivered the ultimatum. These seemingly insignificant inconsistencies do considerable harm to the Duke's claim that he is revealing the historical facts about his abdication "for the first time."

From the Windsor narrative it appears that after the King had made a clean breast of it, Wallis became solicitous. She said that the King must do what was best for him!

Has the reader ever been told, by the woman he blindly loves, in spite of all, that he must do what is best for him? How did he respond? Did he actually go ahead and do what seemed best? How far did his legs carry him? Did he turn around, after taking a few uncertain steps, and run back to her? And did he beg to be taken back?

Many questions arise when it comes to that famed feminine device, "Do what's best for you." And there are some wise answers, for example this one:

> Take no repulse, whatever she doth say;
> For "get you gone," she doth not mean "away!"
> (Shakespeare, *Two Gentlemen of Verona*)

Mrs. Simpson also told him, the Duke writes, that he ought to remain on the Throne.

Now, in such declarations it is not only the words that count; but also the intonation, the facial expression, a mascara-threatening teardrop on long lashes, a slight inclination of the head, an almost imperceptible shrug of the shoulders, a motion of the hand, a sudden halt of dainty feet, and many other things very difficult to observe, interpret, and remember.

"You should remain on the Throne," can be said in a thousand different ways. It can even be said in that sort of tone which implies: "I dare you to!"

At any rate, it is now known how effectively the woman who ruled the man who ruled an empire said it.

The Duke at this point speaks pathetically of his feeling of responsibility for the trouble that his love was bringing on Wallis.

Was Mrs. Simpson really in such a predicament? Was her situation really so unbearable? Two short quotations will show that this lady was most familiar with the sort of trouble men's love often brings upon the head of attractive women.

> Wallis Warfield resolved early to make men her career and in forty years reached the top—or almost.
>
> (*Time*, January 4, 1937)

The King of England felt responsible for the woman who, according to best-informed sources, made up her mind when young to rise in the world through men. For Wallis who, a decade before her present "trouble," had already been around a little, according to *Cavalcade*, the British counterpart of *Time*.

> In Manhattan at 1331 Madison Avenue was discovered by U. S. newshawks the first Mrs. Simpson, divorced by Ernest for Wally. She and attractive daughter Audrey were poorly off for money. Said the first Mrs. Simpson: "If what newspapers say of my former husband's financial standing is true, Audrey and I wish he could find it possible to provide for our maintenance. The present Mrs. Simpson has enough of what it takes to steal a man—Mr. Simpson walked out on me while I was ill in a hospital."
>
> (*Cavalcade*, December 12, 1936)

During their walk on this December evening in the Fort's garden, Edward warned Wallis of possible newspaper attacks, pointing out that Fleet Street was ready to let the cat out of the bag, and she must expect to be a target.

This seems to have been too much for Mrs. Simpson to bear. She was disturbed. Besides, De La Rochefoucauld in his "Maxims" said that absence increases great passions. So it was at this point that Mrs. Simpson hinted to her fiancé that probably it would be best for her to leave England.

The Duke writes that he was glad of her decision to leave. He wished, he says, to protect Wallis, to remove her from the path of the main attack, and so it was gratifying that the suggestion of departure came from her.

Mrs. Simpson was at this time over forty. She had been married twice. Between times she had pluckily conducted her career without the assistance of a champion. Yet the King's only thought was to shield this highly courageous lady, who had so successfully covered up her courage with an appearance of becoming maidenly modesty. Why, Mrs. Simpson had proved herself perfectly capable of taking care of herself in any and every situation, whether in the asphalt jungle of New York, in the Oriental setting of China, or in the labyrinths of Washington. Whether facing the anguish of husbands or the fury of wives.

Yet Windsor speaks of her as though she were then seventeen years old and had just come out of a convent school!

He felt responsible for the trouble his love had caused, and wished to defend her. Yet he could feel no responsibility for his subjects and the civilized world, then sitting on top of a barrel of gunpowder, in profound trouble, in the gravest danger! The King-Emperor was willing to expose the whole world to ruin in order to protect a single, extremely astute, highly sophisticated woman!

He says that the press observed silence because the exalted position of the Monarchy must be held above all criticism.

But he, himself, wanted the silence for quite a different reason— his one and only desire was to protect the exalted person of Mrs. Simpson from sensational publicity.

The Sentinel was getting ready to leave the battle station.

A prophetic, timely editorial appeared about this time in the leading newspaper of the Duchess' home town:

> . . . At home the government was manufacturing 40-million gas masks, one for each inhabitant, expecting poison gas to drop; it was building war planes feverishly, putting tens of thousands of men at work. It had just heard from Stalin that "Russia has thousands of planes, many submarines, thousands of tanks—look out for yourselves!" Hitler was combining with Japan a danger to England in the Far East; Mussolini and Hitler were helping to establish a Fascist dictatorship in Spain . . . England had ceased to be an island, for the atmosphere was to be the scene of battle in future wars . . . Britain never faced a more critical situation, but all that was forgotten—the King of England wanted to marry an American woman. That menace must be disposed of first, though explosive bombs and the heavens themselves should fall.
> (Baltimore *News Post*, December 7, 1936)

The memoirs at this point fill one with bitterness and indignation. It is not necessary to live according to the dicta of the Spanish Jesuit, severe Baltasar Gracian, author of *The Art of Worldly Wisdom*, in order to appreciate his saying that "Love and honor make poor companions." And where were

> The king-becoming graces,
> As justice, verity, temperance, stableness,
> Bounty, perseverance, mercy, lowliness,
> Devotion, patience, courage, fortitude . . .

Where were they, the reader asks?

Edward apparently had no relish for such virtues. What this Monarch, this supreme governor of an empire so vast, swore allegiance to, was a woman ten years past the Balzacian age. He was occupied solely with her welfare and virtues. His mercy was denied his half-billion subjects and was bestowed wholly upon a woman who invoked the age-old method of saying to the love-befogged man, "Do what's best for you!"

She read the King's nature, so headstrong and contrary, like a book. But she ought to have also read *A Child's History of England* by Charles Dickens.

21

Mrs. Simpson, Meet Britannia

Neither does it appear how a prince's abdication can make any other sort of vacancy in the throne, than would be caused by his death.

—Jonathan Swift

To his readers, the Duke speaks more openly of his marriage plans than ever he did to Mr. Baldwin. Six months must elapse before Mrs. Simpson's divorce would become final; she would then be free at the end of April 1937. The coronation was scheduled to take place on May 12 of the same year. Therefore, as the Duke records, he thought he had plenty of time to "work things out."

The naiveté of this statement is almost past belief! The six months' period would allow time to build up a favorable picture of Mrs. Simpson and the intended marriage. That is, if nothing interfered— if a decorous silence reigned unbroken over that portion of society which had long since (noting the dead-pan countenance of Mr. Simpson) cracked the inevitable weary joke about the "Importance of Being Ernest"; if the Church of England refrained from "Blunt words"; if the Dominions made no open criticism or protest; if the British public could be sold on the idea; and if—most important of all—Queen Mary could be induced to receive Wallis.

It seemed unlikely that Queen Mary, for whom duty had always been the paramount consideration, would abandon the rule of a lifetime, and permit a doubly-divorced woman to approach her. And that, not merely at a formal function, but as the King's, her son's fiancée!

But once again American romanticism matched itself against reality. Journals in the United States informed their readers that Queen Mary had approved the proposed marriage, and had promised to help iron out the difficulties of State.

It did not apparently occur to the editors of these papers that

Queen Mary, being herself a subject, and voteless, might have less to say in the matter than her own maid—who could vote.

The American press may be pardoned for a misjudgment of the constitutional problems of another nation; for in those days it was trigger-happy, punch-drunk with the biggest romance ever. Elsewhere, there was less excusable error.

The Duke thought it quite in order to seek his mother's acceptance of this fantastic marriage.

There is no question here of imagination. The Duke, by his own account, sought to bring about this impossible meeting. In *A King's Story* he describes his attempt; and appears distressed that, despite his arguments, Queen Mary refused to meet Wallis Simpson. But then he explains her attitude by pointing out that her ideas of kingship and of duty were Victorian; she was much too correct and unbending, with no understanding of the weaknesses of the human heart.

Anyone acquainted with the history of the Victorian era—with the characters of the great men and women who were produced by this same sense of duty—will realize that in using these words, the Duke unwittingly lays a garland of honor at the feet of his late mother. The word "duty," he writes, fell between them. Indeed it did! It fell between them like the scalpel of the surgeon, severing this Prince, for the term of his natural life, from his own family and from that larger family which is England.

The members of this great family, the people, were still for the most part ignorant of the fantasies of the American press, and the true state of the King's affairs. After all, Baldwin had been busy with the scissors, and the Blunt bishop had not yet spoken out. One illustration of the general unawareness in England at this time may be given: in this same month of November 1936, an author who seems to have had access to confidential information, preparing a book of comment on Edward VIII for popular reading, could in all sincerity write that the tittle-tattle about the King was "trivial to a degree." He went on to say:

> Yet it holds a hint of drama, even of tragedy, because, however *remote* certain of the possibilities it criminally toys with, these would be tremendous and England-shaking if Fate turned them into fact.
> (*Coronation Commentary*, Geoffrey Dennis, Dodd, Mead & Co. 1937)

While Mr. Dennis was thus defending Edward VIII, the King

himself—not fate—was preparing to turn the possibilities here hinted at, into fact. Mrs. Simpson was of course helping him according to her lights—and so he was about to tell Mr. Baldwin that he would marry "on or off the throne."

But before he should again confront Mr. Baldwin, King Edward had to confront Mrs. Simpson, and with *the* letter. He also told her that if the Government continued its opposition to their marriage, he would abdicate.

Wallis was stunned.

Both by Hardinge's plea, and by the King's threat that he would give up the Throne; with the dreadful result, naturally, that she would not be Queen of England.

"There must be some other way," she said. Obviously thinking they could eat their cake and have it. Her words: "There must be some other way," might be translated as: "There must be some loophole in the law. Get a clever lawyer quickly and he will find it."

Mrs. Simpson had been living for some years in England; she had been moving in London society; she had contrived to be presented at a Court where divorcées were not permitted. Yet she had failed utterly to grasp the inner reality of the world into which she had entered. She had supposed, it would seem, that marriage with Edward would follow his proposal as easily as marriage with Earl or marriage with Ernest had followed their proposals.

She had imagined that the mere wish of the King would marshal her on her way to a third marriage and to the Throne. The power of the Government, the advice of Ministers, simply had not entered into her calculations. She had equally failed to reckon with public opinion and with the views of the masses. So that when harsh reality crashed into her fairy-tale view of the near future, "she was stunned"!

Cinderella, discovering that the fairy godmother's wand would not work, could not have been more dismayed. She had neither the knowledge nor the honesty of Major Hardinge; she had not the pliability of Mr. Monckton. She grasped at the one thing she did know and could count on, the impetuous character of her fiancé. In her words: "There must be some other way," came out, too, that naive romanticism of so many Americans, who seem to picture the King as a demigod who can control all things in England (excepting the weather).

In this matter, Edward seems to have been better informed than Wallis. He declared that if the Government did not approve the

projected marriage, he would abdicate. He knew that he might have
to; but he gambled on the chance. And in this frame of mind he
confronted Stanley Baldwin, saying: "I am going to marry Mrs.
Simpson and I am prepared to go."

With more reason than Mrs. Simpson, the Prime Minister, too,
was stunned. He replied with a tremor in his voice: "That is most
grievous news, Sir, and I cannot comment on it today."

The day was November 16, 1936. Mr. Baldwin temporized. He
may have thought that this nightmare-like discussion was due to a
royal whim; that the King would surely change his mind and remain
at his post. He knew that other kings had threatened abdication, or
flight, or dismissal of their Ministers. For dismissal he was prepared:
he knew that no other Government could be formed. As for flight
or abdication, "there was example for't."

Other kings of England had made such threats. When George IV
tried to get rid of his legal wife, to whom he referred as "that damned
Princess of Wales," he made use of a convenient ally and instrument—
an accommodating lawyer, perhaps the only man of position and
ability who favored his schemes. This was Leach, already his Chancellor of Cornwall, and now his *âme damnée*, who was sent to frighten
the Cabinet with threats of the King's retirement to Hanover, unless
the Cabinet complied with his wishes. The Ministers refused to be
frightened; and arguments about the King's health, and pleas on
behalf of his peace of mind, left them unmoved. They almost apologized for their firmness; but they remained firm.

George IV had tried to divorce a wife. Edward VIII wished to
take to wife a divorcée. The one was to be as unsuccessful as the
other had been.

But neither the example of George IV, nor that of other Monarchs
who had differed with their ministries, seems to have suggested to
Edward that in a struggle between the King and the Government,
the Government would in all probability win. Edward VIII knew
that he was the most beloved King in the long history of England;
and perhaps Hector Bolitho was right in saying in his biography of
this King that: "He relied upon the role of popular Monarch . . . He
imagined a state of royal dictatorship without a Constitution—a
giddy and unreasonable interpretation to put upon his own powers."

While the secret combat went on within doors, the public life of
the King had also to continue. Plans had been made for him to tour
the distressed areas of South Wales: the program had to be carried

out. Confronted once again with the depressed towns amid their
slag heaps, the well-nigh hopeless people, King Edward said: "Something must be done."

This happened three days after he told Baldwin that if he were
not permitted to marry Mrs. Simpson he would abdicate! Trusting
in the adage that "a Sovereign's word is more than a subject's oath,"
the Welsh miners had new hope—for a week. Afterward, the former
King's promises rang for a long time in their ears. They could not
forget that their own Prince, then their King, had said: "Something
must be done," and yet did nothing for them.

Other Britons who were young then remember too—for it has been
said that the most melancholy aspect of Edward's running away
from his duty was the breaking of the many promises he had made
to youth. They wondered how their King and Defender could take
the fatal decision to leave them in their most miserable hour.

But the hour of decision had not come yet; there were still some
days to go before "his" Welsh miners, or the nation at large, would
hear about the King's lady. The unhappy politicians, who followed
him round the Valley of Humiliation, might seem to be troubled
only by the suffering they saw all around them—or for their own
careers. Actually, they carried a heavier burden: a very little might
suffice to turn the sullen misery of the miners into revolt that would
destroy the Throne itself, and all Britain with it; if the King now
walking among them, the last hope of these sufferers, were to make
a certain choice . . . what would happen?

As they returned to London, Mr. Baldwin and his companions
may have thought that the spectacle set before the King on that visit
would turn the heart of Edward back to his people. And indeed for
a little while it appeared that this might happen. For, after the Wales
visit, Mr. Baldwin told the Archbishop of Canterbury that the King
had been much moved by his reception, and consequently the whole
situation was once more unsettled. The Prime Minister hoped
against hope.

In confiding in Dr. Lang, Mr. Baldwin was seeking the moral
support of a man, a leader among those leaders of the country who
had not been affected by a certain corruption of the times. For both
men were well aware that great and unhappy changes had taken
place, after World War I, in British society. "Honor is but ancient
riches"—perhaps. But the once honorable ranks of the great families
had been invaded by the newly-rich, whose money could apparently

buy everything. They had filled the chief places in society; certain "old" families in the peerage were three-quarters foreign, and some of the new families completely so. In a country thus in danger of corrosion from within, the unprecedented act of the Sovereign might spell the end of Monarchy in England—extreme situations lead to extreme reactions, which often come with lightning speed. Mr. Baldwin and his fellow-Ministers had before them the melancholy example of Spain, then crucified in a bloody civil war, to which the destruction of the Spanish Monarchy—it had disappeared within twenty-four hours!—had opened the way.

For a further week of anxiety, Mr. Baldwin awaited the breaking of the storm; thereafter to be faced with yet another proposed innovation, one which, if carried out, would have world-wide effects. For when at last public opinion was brought face to face with the shocking reality, and Edward VIII with public opinion, the King produced a new plan, suggested to him by a friend: morganatic marriage.

At a later date King Edward was prepared to argue that neither he nor Mrs. Simpson had ever insisted that she should be Queen. All they desired (he claimed) was that their married happiness should carry with it a proper title and dignity for her, one befitting the King's wife.

The American papers had already selected a title: Wallis was to be Countess of Renfrew (they ignored the fact that this particular royal title was "Baron Renfrew"). Shortly after, the *News Chronicle* of London, organ of the rump Liberal Party, suggested that His Majesty might marry as Duke of Cornwall; and Edward himself proposed that he should marry as Duke of Lancaster. (How the Duchy of Cornwall, the County of Renfrew, or the town of Lancaster, would have reacted to the new peeress' title was not canvassed.)

This proposal formed part of an address, never actually delivered, which the King hoped that he might broadcast to the nation; and it is interesting to consider the historical background.

Before the Conquest the title of "queen" was not in general use in England: the King's wife was referred to as the "King's Lady." After the Conquest it was understood that, though the King's wife was always Queen, she was *crowned* Queen only at her husband's will and pleasure. Thus, Henry VIII crowned only two of his six wives: Katherine of Aragon, and Anne Boleyn, who was to bring him the much-desired son—only she didn't. Perhaps it was this disappointment

with his second wife which made Henry decide against other corona-
tions. At a later date George IV refused to crown his official wife,
Caroline. But crowned or not crowned, the King of England's wife was
Queen. The convenient device of morganatic marriage, sometimes
used by Monarchs in Europe, is not available to the Kings of England.

Such was the unpromising background of King Edward's proposal.
At first sight it looks well—there is an air of sweet reasonableness and
sincerity about the suggestion that the King might fulfil his public
tasks; and thereafter, in the quiet of his own home, enjoy domestic
bliss with Wallis.

But on second thought, certain unpleasant questions obtrude themselves. Is it true that neither the King nor Mrs. Simpson had ever
sought to insist that she should be Queen? Careful consideration
suggests that they never sought to insist because they had throughout
assumed that she *would* be Queen, and crowned Queen at that. The
plan for morganatic marriage came from Esmond Harmsworth (now
Lord Rothermere), who had the idea from his father, the newspaper
magnate Lord Rothermere.

It is worth-while to pause on this part of *A King's Story*, and reflect
on the implications of the conversations there reported. Esmond
Harmsworth took Wallis to lunch at Claridge's, and without warning
asked if she had ever thought of marrying the King morganatically?

"Morganatically?" she asked. "What do you mean?"

Mr. Harmsworth thereupon gave her a detailed explanation of the
term. If Mrs. Simpson had indeed contemplated becoming simply
Edward's wife but not his Queen, would she have needed this briefing?
Would she have needed to be told that "morganatic marriage"
means the legal marriage of a royal person with a commoner? She
becoming his wife in every sense, except that she has to be satisfied
with the lowly coronet of a duchess or a countess, and the children,
if any, may not inherit the father's rank.

Mr. Harmsworth broached the idea to Wallis; thus educated, Wallis
broached it to the King, who asked her:

"What do you think of it?"

The lady from Baltimore was ready with the answer: "*It sounds
strange and almost inhuman.*"

Even if the italics are the writer's, these six memorable words are
not—they were written down in all gravity by the former King of
England and originally uttered by Wallis Warfield Spencer Simpson.

As Mrs. Simpson did not care for morganatic marriage, it is not surprising that King Edward, too, quickly found the idea distasteful.

And here the memoirs provide a study in self-betrayal deserving of pages of comment. The Duke says that he was, at this stage, willing to consider any sensible scheme that might help him to marry as King, without bringing about a political struggle; if the difficulties could be swept aside by his giving up for Wallis the state and title that properly belong to the King's wife, then a morganatic marriage might solve their problems.

It is clear from this passage that King Edward had believed, at least for some time, that he could make Mrs. Simpson, who used to be Mrs. Spencer, who used to be Bessie Warfield, Queen of Great Britain, and Empress of India! Had he not proceeded on this assumption, the scheme put forward by Mr. Harmsworth would surely have been present to his own mind at an early stage; he would not have needed to receive a suggestion from a third party. A king planning such a marriage (as, for instance, King Leopold of the Belgians married the Princess de Réthy) would not have had a "first reaction," nor required "further consideration." Still less would he have needed to send a personal friend, as Edward sent Harmsworth, hotfoot and privately, to the Ministers with whom he was already embroiled, that they in turn might study the proposal.

Mr. Baldwin's own reaction to the plan could astonish no one acquainted with British history, or with the personal history of King Edward's not-too-remote ancestors. The Prime Minister knew that history and understandably he was surprised. When the King summoned him to discuss the matter, he hinted—justifiably, as events were to prove—that neither Cabinet nor Parliament would be likely to approve a morganatic marriage. The Dominions too must be consulted. Supposing that, in spite of all, such a marriage had taken place, inevitably the question would have been raised: "Why is not the King of England's wife his Queen?"

What answer could have been returned? As the veteran author Hugh Walpole said at the time: "It is not because Mrs. Simpson is an American that England would spurn her as a Queen. It is because the Crown, that very sensitive and vulnerable ideal, would lose caste by union with a woman twice divorced."

The tangible possessions of princes remain their own (as remarked earlier, this is one of the few pieces of privacy allowed them); but their reputation, like their public life, belongs to their country. For the international standing of a nation may well be affected by the personal prestige of its rulers; and this is especially true of Great Britain, whose King is also the King of realms beyond the seas.

In order that the American reader should fully understand this overseas king business, it must be explained that the British Commonwealth of Nations (to give it its official title) is regulated in its internal relations principally by the Statute of Westminster, of 1931. That Statute leaves the Crown as the one remaining link between Great Britain and her daughter nations. For England does not *own* Northern Ireland, Canada, Australia, New Zealand, and South Africa. The conception of colonies as the property of the mother country, governed largely from afar, received its deathblow in the snows of Valley Forge. By the mid-nineteenth century a wider view obtained.

The mature political wisdom of England found a middle path between the extreme of total political and economic dependence and that of independence (perhaps preceded by rebellion) and complete disassociation. The realization grew that as the greater colonies expanded in population and in wealth, so also they might develop politically. Historically speaking they were young countries; but their new settlers were the heirs of a long political tradition. This was the new ideal: Dominion status. As each colony advanced on the road to nationhood, it attained self-government. Canada was the first self-governing Dominion.

Constitutionally the Sovereign of England is also King (or Queen Regnant) of Scotland and Northern Ireland, reigning by consent of the Lords and Commons in council assembled. But the King, or Queen Regnant, of England is also the Sovereign of Canada, reigning over a country ruled by its own Parliament quite independently of the Government in England. The same is true of Australia, New Zealand and South Africa. It is not true of India, which has declared itself a Republic within the Commonwealth, but which regards the Monarch as the Head of the Commonwealth and its First Citizen.

Queen Elizabeth II was formally proclaimed as Queen of South Africa and Queen of Canada even before she was proclaimed in her "royal throne of kings," England.

In absentia, the Monarch is represented in the Dominions by a Governor General, a person of honor and distinction, frequently a member of the immediate Royal Family. (It has recently been suggested, for instance, that Elizabeth the Queen Mother should hold the post of a Governor General.) On a visit to any one of the

Dominions, the Monarch appears there as the King, or Queen, of that Dominion, and maintains royal state and holds court.

This being the relation of the British Monarchy to the Dominions beyond the seas, they have naturally just as much interest in a Sovereign's marriage as have the people of Britain.

This interest is not merely a matter of sentiment: it is also a matter of law. The Statute of Westminster provided that any change affecting the royal style and titles, or the succession to the throne, must receive the assent not merely of the British Parliament, but also of the Parliaments of the great Dominions.

So that for King Edward to contract a morganatic marriage, one of which the hypothetical children should have no right to succeed to the Throne, legislation would be necessary in every Parliament of the Commonwealth. This point does not receive sufficient attention in *A King's Story*.

The Duke emphasizes that, as the Crown is the sole remaining link between the nations of the Commonwealth, it is the King's right, his sole prerogative, to approach each Dominion through his personal representative, the Governor General; and that the Prime Minister had no authority to make such an approach.

But did Mr. Baldwin communicate with the Dominions without any right invested in him? The Duke himself answers the question. It was the Prime Minister, he says, who reminded him that the proposal for morganatic marriage must be submitted to the Dominions Cabinets, and he asked if the King really wished this to be done.

Edward's answer was an absolute "yes."

Thus on one page of *A King's Story* the Duke depicts himself as commanding Mr. Baldwin to take those steps which, he says on the next page, the Prime Minister had no authority to take! It is these contradictions which make the autobiography such fascinating reading.

Windsor claims that the matter was too personal and delicate for him to handle it himself. But if he would do nothing, and if the Prime Minister had no right to act—in spite of having been told to do so—what was to happen? Affairs could hardly remain forever in a state of deadlock! Sooner or later the truth must have burst forth to public knowledge, probably sooner rather than later. Already Miss Ellen Wilkinson had asked, in the House of Commons, why American magazines were being censored on entering Britain.

The drafting of the necessary legislation, and its passage through five Parliaments, would of course take some time, thus prolonging the period of crisis and of weakness. During the interval every aspect of the proposed marriage would be matter for emotional and embittered debate, public and private. The political, dynastic, and moral questions raised would have furnished fuel to the fire. Governments would have to weigh the effect, on peoples so widely different as French Canadians or Hindus, of a special law enabling the King to marry a twice-divorced woman. That effect might be political disaster. (To take an earlier example from near home, the winning of Irish liberty had been delayed for a generation by the marriage of Parnell, "the uncrowned king of Ireland," to the divorced Kitty O'Shea.) It is not surprising that, a little later, Mr. Baldwin warned Edward that if the uncertainty continued, a dangerous constitutional situation would arise not only in Britain but throughout the Empire. What *is* surprising is that the Duke reports the remark. For in that one sentence he condemns himself.

A King's Story is a masterpiece of unintended self-exposure.

Even were disaster avoided, even if the Monarchy had not disappeared, very bad results would certainly have followed a prolongation of the crisis. The Crown, the golden link of the Commonwealth, would have ceased to be a bond of unity, and would have become a storm center. And it would have sunk immeasurably in the esteem of all its subjects.

It is not wonderful that Mr. Baldwin hesitated to commit himself on a proposal that, if carried into practice, must have had such results. Still the King urged the "strange, inhuman and distasteful thing," so that Baldwin offered to examine the proposal formally, that is, not as a private person, but as the King's First Minister consulting with Governments in four continents.

Thus the discussion of the marriage was now passing beyond that personal and private level at which Mr. Baldwin had so far kept it. Formal examination of the matter meant that personal counsel would become ministerial advice; the affair was entering that public domain where a constitutional Monarch must act according to the advice of his Ministers, or seek new Ministers.

The Prime Minister, therefore, as requested by the King, approached the various Governments of the Dominions. The result was as had been foreseen. Mr. Baldwin's honesty impelled him to make a statement in the House of Commons, and to history, pointing out that:

> The King himself requires no consent from any other authority to make his marriage legal.
>
> But, as I have said, the lady whom he marries, by the fact of her marriage to the King, necessarily becomes Queen . . .
>
> The only way in which this result could be avoided would be by legislation dealing with a particular case.

And, as Mr. Baldwin went on to say, neither the English Government, nor any of the Dominions Governments, were prepared to introduce such legislation.

The Cabinet had done all that it could do to protect the Monarchy in its seat of Britain; but no screen had been interposed abroad. American books, magazines and papers, with their strange mingling of sentimentality and scandal, of romantic and snobbish reverence for Monarchy, had flowed freely into Canada, Australia and New Zealand. The masses in the Dominions knew things of which the Londoner never dreamed; their Governments knew much more. The people of the United States read of the cruise of the *Nahlin*, and of many other matters; and passed on their knowledge, not without embellishment, to the people of the Commonwealth.

His Majesty's Ministers at home and abroad could not feel happy as they looked into the *salon* of Bryanston Square where talk was of the "new ideas." And when they heard that they were being asked to legislate in order that the King might contract a morganatic marriage with the lady of the *salon*, they felt even more unhappy. They could return but one reply.

By the time that the verdict was rendered, the people of England had already, and for some days past, known that the King and his Cabinet were deadlocked. For on December 4, the British press at last made public what it had for so long concealed. It was inevitable that the truth should come out; and the remarks of Dr. Blunt to his Diocesan Conference had simply been the occasion of its doing so.

Much has been made of the fact that the abdication crisis was of such brief duration—that all was over, so far as the public was concerned, within ten days. It has been claimed that the people of England were rushed off their feet, that the sheer suddenness with which the storm first blew up, then blew over, deprived them of opportunity for full consideration and temperate judgment. Undoubtedly there had been ignorance, and a terrible sense of shock when the truth became known. The Archbishop of Canterbury remarked in his diary that those who had known the whole business, as

The late Pierre Laval, with the King of England

God Save the Queen—and Her Consort

he had, for two years past, could scarcely realize the effect of the sudden crisis "on minds wholly unprepared for it and ignorant of all that had led up to it."

The Archbishop, indeed, in *A King's Story*, is made to appear as one of the principal villains of the piece. The Duke speaks of him in a manner that suggests a malignant ghost. There is no justification for this picture. Dr. Lang had been much troubled in conscience as the affair developed; but after long and painful consideration he had determined to crown the King, knowing that if he declined the duty some other bishop might take his place. But he had a presentiment that the final decision might not rest with him.

Now he repeatedly requested that he might be permittted to see King Edward, but all to no avail. The King said emphatically that he would listen to nobody but Mr. Baldwin, who had a right to speak to him, and advise him. In saying this, he apparently forgot that the Archbishop himself had a moral right to speak to, and advise, the head of the Church of England. Quite apart from that legal tie between Church and State, Dr. Lang might claim to be heard as a man of God, bound to uphold the moral law. But he was less fortunate than the Prophet Nathan in seeking the ear of his David.

So that if the Archbishop remained "a shadowy, hovering presence," it was by the King's own choice. The prelate was informed of all that went on; he discussed the matter only with two other Protestant leaders, the Moderator and the Secretary of the Federal Council of Evangelical Free Churches.* But this was all that he could do.

The three clergymen agreed that while the mass of the people would support the Government, still a large number, especially among the younger folk, would rather side with the King—partly from sentimental considerations, partly from ignorance of the real state of affairs.

This widespread ignorance was, of course, one of the factors making the situation potentially so dangerous. But Baldwin, who had often managed to steer England out of trouble and away from war, was determined that the possible danger should not become an actuality. He had made up his strong mind that the Monarchy should survive in England.

It is interesting to see what a British publication, *Cavalcade*, had to report on the subject of the last disputes between unreasonable Master and the Servant striving to reason with him:

---

*Representing the major Protestant churches, other than the Church of England.

A slightly built man paced the room, ran his fingers through his fair hair as he raged and swore.

Sitting uncomfortably in a chair was a heavily built man with grey-streaked hair and a lined face which twitched with tension.

The words of King Edward VIII were a torrent of anger and anguish. ; . . . The most stolid of all Britishers looked on.

At one point the King's abuse must have gone too far. The most stolid of all Britons was near to tears as he protested: "Sir, no one ever called me that." But despite the cursing, the old and ill servant of his country remained firm. He was determined to save the ancient institution of England, the Crown, and with it the Commonwealth.

Even if this meant that the idol of the nation had to go.

22

A Royal Exit

I give this heavy weight from off my head,
And this unwieldy sceptre from my hand,
The pride of kingly sway from out my heart; . . .
With mine own hands I give away my crown,
With mine own tongue deny my sacred state.
—SHAKESPEARE: *Richard II*

Is it for this you propose to fling away the ancient
heritage bequeathed to us by the architects of our
magnitude and renown?
—WINSTON CHURCHILL, *at a Party meeting*

SOME time ago four ladies were having their luncheon at a renowned New York café. Between lamb chops they talked. One of them was a famous English actress (born in Windsor) and a close friend of grand old Queen Mary. The three others included a successful writer who probably knows more about men's likes and dislikes than they do themselves, and two supercilious editors of a fashion magazine which devotes most of its pages to advertisements.

When stage and style gossip had been exhausted, the talk turned to the Windsors. The editors, who were enthusiastic about the famed couple, lamented the unpleasant publicity they had recently been receiving. The Englishwoman listened patiently for some time. She then attempted to correct the ideas of the arch-sycophants. Only one portion of her lecture need be repeated:

When the King told his mother that if he was not allowed to marry Mrs. Simpson, he would abdicate, Queen Mary answered, "My son, then you must abdicate, because if such a thing is in your mind, you are not fit to rule the British Empire."

The two editors started busily on their second chops . . .

Reference has already been made to Dr. Blunt, the Bishop of Brad-ford, who late in 1936 took it upon himself to criticize the erring King of England before an audience. After that it was impossible for the press to remain silent. The scandal was getting beyond control, not because the King had a lady love but because he was determined to marry her.

The fact, suddenly blazoned across every paper in the country, affected the nation more than an earthquake would have done. It was, in fact, a moral earthquake. The King wanted to marry a divorcée, on or off the Throne! To the people of England, the masses, the idea of abdication was unbelievable. To others, it was fantastic.

Disgusted, scared, miserable, the people began to bombard the King, the newspapers, the Cabinet, the Members of Parliament, with demanding or pitiful letters. Something must be done, they insisted, to make the King stay. Some of the correspondents wrote in this vein:

> Our King is being asked to give up the woman he loves that the Empire may still be on solid ground. In the war many thousands of men gave up the women they loved and much more than the King is asked to—some gave up everything. I cannot believe that the King we have always loved and looked up to can fail to do the same thing for the British Empire.

The *Sunday Pictorial* remarked that "there ought to be a solution for a simple problem set by the facts that the King wants Mrs. Simpson and we want the King." But the situation was not quite so simple as the writer imagined. As one correspondent commented, the marriage of the King to a woman with two other husbands still living would work havoc with England's reputation in the Dominions.

And not only in the Domininions.

England's anger against the woman who had so bewitched the King that he was ready to abdicate mounted to fury. The public temper may be partly gauged from an incident of the time described by Miss Marion Crawford, in her book *The Little Princesses*. She was waiting, on the steps of the Duke of York's house in Piccadilly, for a taxi. In those few moments a hostile crowd gathered—someone shouted "Mrs. Simpson," and boos followed. Miss Crawford beat a hasty retreat.

For some time past Mrs. Simpson had been living in Cumberland Terrace, with Aunt Bessie for companion. The American public was gravely informed that she lived there "secure and serene," observing "the conditions of her divorce—and six months from October 27, 1936, if the King's Proctor finds no cause otherwise, the decree *nisi* will be made final." (*Her Name Was Wallis Warfield*, Edwina H. Wilson.) The security and serenity were not so evident in Cumberland Terrace: as the Duke says delicately, the house was now a focus of curiosity, and even shopping had become unpleasant. (One wonders for what Mrs. Simpson could have been shopping in those days. She was already well supplied with clothes, furs and jewels, and surely she cannot have been carrying her own groceries home.)

The Duke's careful understatement conceals the real state of affairs at Cumberland Terrace. It was such that under cover of the November twilight Wallis and Aunt Bessie slipped out, entered the car in which King Edward sat waiting for them, and were driven down to Fort Belvedere. Thus Wallis was now living in the house of the man whom she was known to be intending to marry. This was a situation that in the case of any other person would have aroused the interest of the King's Proctor, a legal personage who represented the Crown in the Divorce Court, and whose chief duty was to prevent the obtaining of a final divorce decree by collusion.

Whatever serenity had reigned in Cumberland Terrace was now destroyed by those stones that broke the windows of Mrs. Simpson's house. Meanwhile, epithets had been scribbled in red paint on the walls of London buildings and of buildings in the provinces. And more was to come.

On December 3 the leading article in the London *Times* demanded an act or statement which would put an end to the damaging campaign of scandal against the Monarch, referred to its serious effect in Canada and other Dominions, and reminded its readers that:

> Events in the world outside have imposed as never before upon the British monarchy the duty to stand as a rock amid the seething tides of communism and dictatorship. So it stood a year ago. So let us hope it will stand a year hence, when the new reign has been hallowed by the Coronation. But the public need some definite reassurance if the rock is not to be shaken.

Instead of the desired reassurance came the truth; and the couple down at Fort Belvedere were naively astonished to find themselves a storm center of unfavorable criticism. Wallis saw her picture in the papers. "I had no idea that it would be anything like this," she wailed.

It is not known how Mrs. Simpson thought of hitting the front page. But it seems safe to assume that she dreamed of seeing herself pictured in every paper in the world, wearing the Queen's crown and an ermine cape designed by Mainbocher, with the caption: "Queen Wallis, crowned in Westminster Abbey."

The real thing distressed her. And the Duke apparently considers this distress a proof of ladylike delicacy, for he tenderly comments that a sensitive woman can receive few worse shocks than to see her own face, greatly enlarged, upon the front pages of the sensational press.

This is rather surprising: for the sensitive woman had seen her picture, long before this, in American, European, Australian, and even Chinese papers and magazines. It is hardly likely that the King's mail arrived with holes in the periodicals.

Now there is no reason to believe that the other inhabitants of Cumberland Terrace were less sensitive than Mrs. Simpson. It is probable that they, too, experienced some shock on seeing their former neighbor's face in the daily paper, and it may be granted that they suffered less than she did. It is unimportant now; for within a very few years of Wallis' feeling a shock than which few could be worse (according to the Duke), the women of Cumberland Terrace had their own brand of unpleasantness to contend with, and it came in the form of high explosive.

There are no doubt refined souls who would choose death rather than adverse publicity, or indeed any publicity at all. But the majority of gross mortals—including perhaps the residents of Cumberland Terrace—would prefer their trouble to come in the shape of newsprint, rather than as a calling card from Hitler in the shape of, say, a two-hundred-kilo bomb. However, by the time that this was happening, Wallis was far removed from the scene of such discomfort, for she was dwelling in the almost too-placid atmosphere of the Bahamas.

Back in 1936 Mrs. Simpson did not seek publicity; but her actions had not been calculated to ensure its absence. She had been protected from its glare in England by the gentlemanly conduct of the politicians and the press, anxious to preserve the Monarchy from harm and the Monarch from embarrassment. But facts had now come out, as almost anybody but the bemused couple most concerned might have seen would happen.

The principal effect produced on the mind by this part of *A King's Story* is one of utter bewilderment. King Edward from babyhood had been beheld of all beholders; but he was overwhelmed, as much as Wallis, by the sensationalism of the reports. How could he have thought it would be otherwise? As if the behavior of these two people had been anything less than sensational!

Equally interesting is another reaction of Mrs. Simpson's. "I wish that I had had a clearer understanding of the constitutional questions."

This remark makes plain that she, who had expected to fill the foremost female role on the world's stage—that of the Queen of England—had taken no steps to prepare herself for the role. She was also unacquainted with the wise dictum, that when one is confronted with a crisis, it is well to read, not the ephemeral and perhaps ill-informed press of the day, but some book of an earlier decade. Mrs. Simpson need not have gone back quite so far; there were knowledge-able, yet readable, books of recent date, that might have given her some understanding of the constitutional history of her adopted country, and of the issues involved in royal marriages. But she had kept to her newspapers, which had for so long been engaged in pro-tecting her from some, at least, of the consequences of her own actions.

The King's reply to her lament, "I thought it could be managed," is even more interesting. It anticipates (and supports) Lord Beaver-brook's report that he later said: "I thought I could get away with it."

Wallis had awakened, like Byron, to find herself famous overnight. Byron had not, but she and the King had been warned that this would be the case. The warning had been dismissed, with its author. Now, confronted with the situation that she had been told would arise, she had one thought—escape. Already she had suggested going abroad. Now she declared:

"I cannot stay here another day, with all this going on. I must leave England this afternoon!"

Mrs. Simpson was staying at Fort Belvedere, a royal dwelling deep in the beautiful Berkshire countryside, surrounded by trees, and by walls pierced only by two locked and guarded gates. Needless to say, the Fort was watched night and day by detectives and policemen.

Before long it was to be in a state of actual siege from the press. And pressmen might not be the only visitors. The King's lady was by now the least loved woman in England. She had left her house because of the danger; and suddenly she felt that even a royal resi-dence might not protect her. The trees that screened so many enter-prising photographers might also hide a man armed with something more deadly than even a candid camera.

So Mrs. Simpson must leave the society of the man she had planned to marry. "All this" would still be going on after she had left. King Edward would still have to face the Prime Minister and the Government. He would be confined to a house now denied even an elementary degree of privacy by the intrusion of the press. Above all, he would be alone with his own soul.

It was an agonizing situation. Many men have faced agonizing situations, and many women have faced them with their men. But when Mrs. Simpson herself found out, she quickly said:

"I must leave England at once! This afternoon."

Whether fear or guilt, or a mixture of both, prompted these words, is not known; but such, in the hour of a King's necessity, was the help and support given him by the woman he loved.

King Edward had found the suggestion of Wallis' departure, coming from his Private Secretary, an outrage. Only twenty-one days later, when it came from Mrs. Simpson herself, he jumped at the idea! Had Major Hardinge's advice been taken, the lady could have retired in safety, and with some semblance of dignity and decency. Its rejection meant that she fled, under cover of night, and in conditions of indignity and terror. As *Time* reported:

> Candidate for honors as "the Englishman who most dislikes Mrs. Simpson" is the detective who was assigned to escort her on her flight to France. He rode in a speeding, zigzagging Buick for some twenty-three hours with the exasperated, nerve-wracked American whose lover was about to abdicate, and who kept telling the detective he was a stupid Scotland Yard flatfoot, who had not been smart enough to enable her to give reporters the slip.
>
> (*Time*, March 29, 1937)

Meanwhile in England a so-called "King's Party" arose. One of the outstanding figures in this loose, extremely vague faction—which was of course never a party in the true sense of the word—was the notorious Sir Oswald Mosley, leader of the impotent British Fascists. "How would you like a Cabinet of our busybodies to choose your girl for you?" was the absurd question addressed by this absurd man to the crowds. Sir Oswald, that fantastic figure—but not of fun—perhaps hoped to achieve power through the "King's business." He may have fancied himself, followed by his Blackshirts, marching on Buckingham Palace in a manner calculated to frighten the very ducks off the pond in St. James' Park.

But it is not necessary to follow further the delusions of *this* King's

Party. Another one, Mr. William Gallacher, M.P.—"Our Willie"—remains to be considered. Mr. Gallacher saw no reason why the King should not marry Mrs. Simpson, even if she was an American; he considered it was no offense to be an American.

"We Communists," loftily continued Mr. Gallacher, "certainly should not worry about it. If he wants to marry her, as far as I am concerned I will say, 'Good luck to him and good luck to her.' We ought to get socialism and have no King, and when the system goes, so will the King." (*Time*, November 16, 1936.)

Mr. Gallacher's speech provided one of the few laughs of the crisis. "We Communists" aroused, among 45-million Britons, so high a degree of enthusiasm that they had sent *one* Party member to Westminster; and Mr. Gallacher's supporter, the *Daily Worker*, kept itself in being, not by its appeal to the broad masses, but by its hold on the sympathies of a small number of working people, who responded to continual, frantically phrased appeals for money. The *Daily Worker* was (and is) the best begging-letter writer in the British Isles.

Fortunately the nation was not left to such guides as Mosley and Gallacher, to waver in doubts which might have led to serious division.

It was King Edward who proposed to leave the nation to waver.

That is his own account of the matter. In *A King's Story* he writes that he wanted to make a broadcast, presenting his problem in its true light. Not merely as a constitutional question, but as a call of the heart. He would then withdraw briefly from an overheated atmosphere, leaving the nation and the Empire to fight out the question of the marriage. He would go to Belgium, there to await the crystallization of public opinion, and the delivery of the popular verdict.

Meanwhile, how was the business of government to be carried on? Oh, that, it seemed to the King, could quite easily have been arranged —a Council of State would have been set up, as had been done twice in the previous reign, during the serious illnesses of George V.

How simple it sounds! And how far removed it is from any consideration of reality.

In the reign of George V the Councils of State were set up, not because the King had left the country when that country was in ever-increasing danger of faction; but because the King, though remaining at his post, was unable to carry on. King Edward proposed to leave England, still reeling from the shock of discovery, and allow his people to thrash out the problem: abdication or marriage on the Throne? Regardless of consequences.

There is, of course, no way of telling what might have happened had the joint plan of Wallis and Edward for a broadcast, and withdrawal, been carried out. Historical might-have-beens necessarily remain in the realm of pure speculation. But one thing is certain: the Monarchy would have been greatly, perhaps irreparably, weakened.

Speculation as to the judgment of Edward's equals is not necessary, for there are means of knowing what it was. For instance, Queen Mary is reported to have told the Royal Family that the stability and authority of the Throne was at stake (*Cavalcade*, May 27, 1937). And the comment of a member of another Royal Family is painfully revealing. At the time of the crisis, the Crown Prince (now King) of Sweden was visiting England. On the day that the true state of the King's affairs was first made public, Gustaf Adolf lunched at the home of the Swedish Minister, where the Archbishop of Canterbury was also a guest. The two gentlemen had a long talk about current events. The Swedish Prince was much distressed. The matter, he declared, was one which affected not only England, and the Empire, but also all countries where Monarchy survived. Such was the opinion of one who stood on Edward's level.

It is conceivable that the withdrawal of King Edward from England might have led to results even more untoward than those of a national split, and perhaps premature succession.* It might have resulted in the disappearance of the Monarchy. It is one thing for the officers to take over when the captain is sick; and quite another for the captain to jump ship.

There was no protraction of the crisis, such as King Edward could then, and the Duke of Windsor can now, contemplate with such ill-judging calm; nor any possibility of a real "King's Party."

The Duke represents himself as having been hard-pressed by his Ministers. On December 6, 1936, Mr. Walter Monckton was summoned to Downing Street, in order to discuss two bills; the Bill of Abdication, and another which, by rendering Mrs. Simpson's divorce immediately absolute, would have enabled her to marry Edward without further delay. When discussion was going on, Mr. Monckton was dismayed to hear Mr. Baldwin say that the business of the abdication must be finished before Christmas; and disgusted by the remark of Mr. Chamberlain that "the continued uncertainty had

---

*At one point it was hinted that, in view of the Duke of York's delicate health, the ten-year-old Princess Elizabeth might succeed at once, with a Council of Regency to act for her.

already hurt the Christmas trade." Of this the Duke says mildly that the Chancellor of the Exchequer was being a trifle more mercenary than was necessary. But it may be that Mr. Chamberlain, that narrow-minded but upright Midlander, was thinking of little people whose incomes, not princely, were derived from little shops.

Moreover, the Ministers were not handling a private matter: they were dealing with the present and the future of great nations. Mr. Monckton might advance the preposterous plea that the Empire should be kept waiting while King Edward dallied with a question which should never have arisen; but the suggestion was dismissed by the grave men around the table as it deserved to be.

Why should Mr. Monckton have said on December 6, 1936, that the King might need "weeks" for consideration, when he knew the King's determination, and had known it for weeks—since November 13, 1936. For on that day King Edward had said to him: "If he [Baldwin] and the Government are against my marrying Mrs. Simpson I am prepared to go." And the resolution had been repeated. Edward said peremptorily: "No marriage—no coronation."

Mr. Monckton is described in *A King's Story* as "a brilliant barrister." His brilliance seems to have suffered a temporary eclipse, or he would have appreciated that, as Mr. Baldwin told the House of Commons: "Considerable prolongation of the present state of suspense would involve the risk of gravest injury to the national and Imperial interests."

To this risk Edward VIII was willing to expose the nations of which he was supposedly the guardian!

The Duke claims of the Edward-Wallis section of public opinion that had he but made one move, it might have grown and grown, and he might still be sitting on the throne, with Wallis at his side. He also points out that numbers of his supporters were recruited from the younger generation, who argued that if the King wanted to marry the woman he loved, why shouldn't he do so? "They seemed to see the issue in simple terms," writes the Duke. Unfortunately those simple terms did not correspond to the facts of the situation. The younger people did not consider the probable effect on world opinion, of a King of England's marriage with a Mrs. Simpson.

Nor had they that information about Mrs. Simpson which might have helped them to assess more justly the possible results to England of this union. They could not, for instance, listen to the conversations going on between Fort Belvedere and the Villa Lou Viei, Cannes (where Mrs. Simpson had found refuge with her friends, the Herman Rogers), such as this one:

> When the King telephoned to Cannes to tell the lady for whom he was giving up his throne that his decision had been taken and he would abdicate, she answered with her slightly drawling southern accent, "But, David, can't you remain Emperor of India even if you are no longer King of England?"
>
> (The New York *Times*, January 22, 1939)

The *Times* remarked that the report did not seem credible; nevertheless it was printed.

A King's Story makes it plain that Mrs. Simpson—who was not a girl, but an experienced middle-aged woman—had made her way, assisted but not thrown by fortune, into high social circles, without in the least understanding the true temper of England; and remaining, until the latest moment, not contemptuous but wholly unaware of any difficulties that might lie in her path to marriage with England's King. The strange world of Dr. Lang and Mr. Baldwin—the world of a civilized country's ordered public life—had been steadily developing for nineteen hundred years before Britannia suffered the momentary surprise of seeing a Mrs. Simpson near the Throne. The incomprehension which the *Times* found almost normal in the American was not shared by the other party to the clash.

With greater perception than the Duchess or his admirers, the Duke of Windsor says that the price of his marriage on the Throne might have been a civil war, not less damaging because it would have been a war of words and not of blood; but "Wallis and I could not hope to find happiness under such conditions." Of course, the Duke is writing of a might-have-been.

Those few who regarded the issue as a personal one between the Monarch and his Prime Minister were mistaken. And the Duke misleads his readers when he says that his was a struggle with Baldwin; and that the King was bound to be the loser because of the greater power of the politician.

Windsor implies that the issue boiled down to a choice between the King and a cunning politico, and that the politico was certain to win because he was ruthless and determined to stay in politics. It has been shown how much Stanley Baldwin cared for power and personal interests! At the age of sixty-nine—his age at the time of the abdication

—he carried on with his duties, which to him meant doing everything for England.

But the reader must decide for himself who was right—the King, who left when he was so much needed, to satisfy himself; or the Prime Minister, who ran to the rescue and saw to it that an ancient institution did not end in shame and chaos on account of a woman. One man spent his time trying to prove that he was the king of playboys; the other strained with all his might to keep the Kingdom from dissolution. An old Premier represented the interests of the people; a man in his prime championed the cause of "the stranger against whom every hand in Britain seemed turned."

Winston Churchill sided with the King. It has been conjectured that this was because Churchill was out of power and would not have minded getting back. The suggestion is absurd. Mr. Churchill is certainly "the foremost man of all this world." But even he could not have formed a Government of one man, nor can he have deluded himself with the hope of doing so.

In a long statement to the press, Mr. Churchill urged patience, saying that:

> For the Sovereign to abdicate in the present circumstances would inflict an injury upon the constitutional position of the monarchy which is measureless and cannot fail to be grievous to the institution itself.

The great Winston always enjoyed fighting for the weak. He had had his own romantic parents to teach him, his own experience with recalcitrant offspring; he knew life's every phase; and he, too, believed in waiting. Wait, he advised—probably hoping secretly that time would cure the King's sick heart; or that the vision of England's greatness and her glory, the determination to secure her welfare, which have been the beacon lights of his own great life, would illumine yet more brightly the spiritual sight of him who had inherited "the lineal state and glory of the land."

Baldwin and Churchill were summoned alternately by the King. "The prayer of Your Majesty's servant is that you may change your mind," said Baldwin. "Lock yourself in Windsor Castle and let Baldwin figure out the next step," said Churchill. The joke was significant —Churchill knew that everything would soon be over, so he sought at least to inject a bit of humor into the grim business. Meanwhile

Baldwin was attending to the actual business. He directed the Cabinet to make one last effort, and accordingly an Address was drawn up and sent to the King:

> Ministers are reluctant to believe that Your Majesty's resolve is irrevocable, and still venture to hope that, before Your Majesty pronounces any formal decision, Your Majesty may be pleased to reconsider an intention which must so deeply distress and so vitally affect all Your Majesty's subjects.

The King did not waste as many words in his reply as his Ministers did in their plea:

> His Majesty has given the matter his further consideration, but regrets he is unable to alter his decision.

When Churchill saw Edward at Fort Belvedere for the last time, he recited two lines from Marvell's poem on the death of Charles I, another king who lost his head:

> He nothing common did, or mean,
> Upon that memorable scene.

Baldwin rather preferred to point out a King's obligations, in words taken from *Hamlet*, when, the next day, he announced the abdication to an amazed and grieving House of Commons:

> . . . His will is not his own,
> For he himself is subject to his birth;
> He may not, as unvalu'd persons do,
> Carve for himself, for on his choice depends
> The safety and the health of the whole state.

Lord Salisbury expressed himself with even greater gravity when, in the House of Lords, he declared on December 10, 1936:

> The abdication of the Sovereign is a desperate act. It leaves the body politic mutilated. It is a disaster . . .

Salisbury perhaps recalled the disasters that had befallen England after the dethronement of other kings: Richard II and, nearly three hundred years later, James II. Although neither of them can be said to have abdicated in the full sense of the word (James II indeed never performed any act of abdication); both in turn were driven from the Throne by combinations of force and fraud, that were raised against them partly as a result of their own folly and wrongdoing. Edward VIII is the only King of England of whom it can be truly said that he *abdicated:* that of his own free will he gave away his crown.

It must be borne in mind that Lord Salisbury spoke from a family tradition of four centuries' standing. His family name is Cecil, and the Cecils have been playing a most important part in the Government of England since the days of that first Cecil, "Kingdom's Care," who was the Minister of Queen Elizabeth I.

Many of the noble lords perhaps had in mind, on this occasion, the words of George Wyndham, the famous British soldier, courtier and scholar: "The gentlemen of England must never abdicate." They did not do so in that hour of greatest peril which was so soon to overtake them.

But Sir Philip Gibbs, the dean of British journalists and writers, summed up the widespread opinion of the abdication:

> There was a scene in a mess of the Royal Air Force on the afternoon of abdication (December 10, 1936). The young pilots of bombing machines had been crowding around the wireless which gave them the news. Suddenly they all started shouting, and arguing, and cursing.
>
> "He has let us down," they shouted. "He has thrown up the sponge. He preferred that damn woman to England and the whole blinking Empire. He ought to have held on to his job, even if it meant chucking that wench. Aren't we asked to risk our lives every day for him? For King and Country, by God! In time of war we should be asked to give up our wives and women for the country's sake: to do our duty and die like little gentlemen. But that fellow wouldn't give a woman the go-by —or keep her in her proper place—for the sake of the whole crowd of us ... He ought to have kept his job. A fellow doesn't chuck his job like that if he's King-Emperor—or a clerk in a city office!"

"Shouts We Doubt Ever Got Shouted" commented *The New Yorker* in 1951, when this entertaining weekly, usually flawlessly edited, quoted the above passage from Sir Philip Gibbs' book *Ordeal in England*. For some reason *The New Yorker* waited fifteen years to make this comment—until, that is, the danger of any very peremptory contradiction had died away. By 1951, many of these young men who did (or according to *The New Yorker*, did not) shout in 1936, had risked and lost their lives in defense of their country.

It may be thought that an author, writing at the time, was somewhat better qualified to judge what happened in England in 1936 than an American journal making a random comment in 1951. In any case, Sir Philip has never been sued, prosecuted, thrown into the calaboose, or otherwise dealt with, although the libel laws of England are rather stringent.

It is not necessary to quote the ex-King's Farewell Speech, made over the radio on December 11, 1936. The writing of this speech was at first attributed to Mr. Churchill. The Duke of Windsor, however, assures his readers that he himself was the author, and that Churchill merely did a little editing. On the other hand, some people in the business—not the *métier* of kingship but of writing—were led by certain rumors to believe that the first draft of the speech was the work of Mr. Harold Nicholson, M.P., the writer.

Queen Mary begged her son not to deliver that last radio address, a mixture of anguish, anger and sentimentality. But the ex-King, conscientious to the last, was determined not to go without telling the world why he was going.

Queen Mary did not herself go to the microphone: it would not have been consistent with the reticence of a royal lady for her to do so. But once again the power of her calming influence was felt when, on the morning of December 12, 1936, her words appeared in the English papers:

> I need not speak to you of the distress which fills a mother's heart when I think that my dear son has deemed it to be his duty to lay down his charge, and that the reign which had begun with so much hope and promise has so suddenly ended.
>
> I know that you will realize what it has cost him to come to this decision; and that, remembering the years in which he tried so eagerly to serve and help his country and Empire, you will keep a grateful remembrance of him in your hearts.
>
> I commend to you his brother, summoned so unexpectedly and in circumstances so painful, to take his place . . . With him I commend my dear daughter-in-law, who will be his Queen.

Queen Mary's message did take some of the smart away. But Edward's speech provoked others to bid him farewell: "English people are sound in peril," said the Chaplain of the King, the Bishop of Portsmouth. "They would not stand for evil things, indecency, wild conduct and smugness. They have a sense of propriety in great

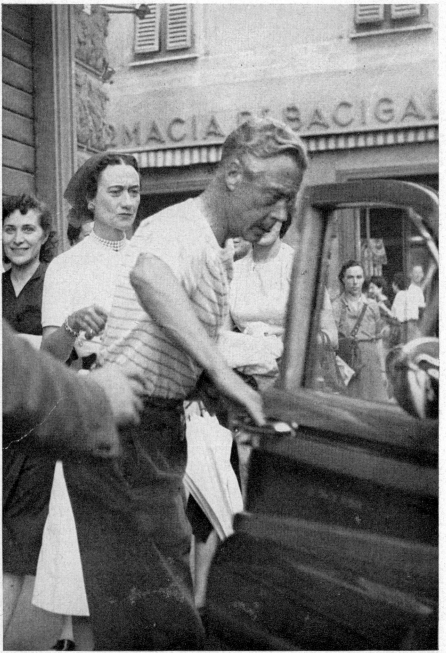

Incognito: the royal station wagon is stamped with the Duke's name.

Government House in Nassau, when the Duke was Governor-General of the Bahamas

One of the Paris houses the Windsors lived in after his abdication

places, and in great affairs, and will not tolerate headlong slips into the abyss of shamefulness."

And here is the good-by that the Archbishop of Canterbury uttered to the former Supreme Head of the Church of England:

> He had a craving for private happiness. Strange and sad that for such a selfish motive he should have disappointed hopes so high, abandoned trust so great. We have loved our King. Let the odd circle which got him away from us, stand rebuked by the nation.

There were other words spoken when the First Gentleman made his exit. For example, Baldwin spoke up, demanding the immediate manufacture and distribution of two million gas masks per month; plans for shelters in Hyde Park were drawn up; Bofor guns were bargained for.

Guns did not speak as yet. But the late Duke of Kent, the favorite brother of the ex-King, not only spoke but cried when it came to the adieus of the Royal Family. (The Duke of Gloucester was absent for reasons best known to himself.) But heedless of family or national reaction, the bridegroom was off. Despite the bride's feverish long-distance entreaties for him to remain on the Throne. "If you don't renounce me, I will renounce you!" came Wallis' anticlimactic threat from France. She would go to the United States; she would go to China; she was willing to withdraw from a situation which had been rendered unhappy and untenable.

Wallis' protestations are among Famous Last Words—by then all was over.

"Halt! Who's there?" shouted the sentry at Portsmouth Harbor as the automobile of Prince Edward (the dukedom was not created until the next day) drove up to the naval gate toward daybreak.

"The King," answered the Scotland Yard detective who sat next to the chauffeur. "I mean . . . can't you see who is sitting in this car?"

The appropriately named destroyer *Fury* carried the has-been across the Channel.

The well-known face was not destined to go down in history the way kings' faces usually do—in the short reign of 325 days no coin was struck bearing the head of this Monarch. And since no such proof remains that he ever reigned, some absurd Englishmen may one day deny that there was an Edward VIII.

Speaking of money, the London Stock Exchange rallied from a

disastrous slump the day after the abdication. And millions of pounds sterling were donated by private persons to the Government in recognition of Stanley Baldwin's successful efforts to save the Crown. For instance, the automobile magnate Baron Nuffield (who has been called "the Henry Ford of Great Britain") made a gift to the Exchequer of £10-million—$50-million at the then rate of exchange. He did this in order to "give practical shape to current expressions of goodwill to King George VI, and at the same time do anything I can to support the National Government, particularly Prime Minister Stanley Baldwin."

23

Master of Castle Enzesfeld

Visits always give pleasure—if not the coming, then the going.

—Portuguese *proverb*

It is a pity that the Duke of Windsor ends his story as abruptly as he ended his reign. For after the abdication his mode of living changed suddenly and completely. It must indeed have been difficult for a former King of England to adjust himself to the status of a mere private individual, and this in a foreign land, in poverty-ridden little Austria. For that is where the Duke of Windsor went after divesting himself of all his grandeur.

He would have liked to join Wallis, who was the guest of her friends, Mr. and Mrs. Herman Rogers, in the south of France, but this was impossible. An obscure fellow in England decided to use any British subject's prerogative, and argued with the King's Proctor that Wallis' divorce should not be made absolute. Of course it wasn't too difficult to shake off this would-be kill-joy; but to prevent any further such attempts during the waiting period of six months which must elapse between the judge's pronouncement of the divorce and the final decree, it was arranged that the affianced pair should live far away from one another until June 1937.

It was easy for Mrs. Simpson to find a retreat for herself. But for a former King of England who had abdicated amid such universal upheaval, the selecting of even a temporary home was truly a task.

And so the ironical thing happened—the recent owner of so many palaces (and theoretically of all the soil of England besides) had no place to go; until Mrs. Simpson's good friend, the late Elsie de Wolfe, Lady Mendl, came to the rescue. She volunteered to find for the Duke an agreeable spot where the pangs of separation might be endured. Lady Mendl telephoned her friend, Baroness Kitty de Rothschild, who was then sojourning in her Paris mansion, and told her of the ex-King's predicament. The Baroness at once offered to lend her castle, Enzesfeld, near Vienna, as a royal refuge. And as she had not visited the castle for several years, she telephoned her estate manager at Enzesfeld and ordered him to get the place ready.

The castle was a beautiful baroque hunting lodge, large enough for a stranger to lose his way in, and of regal splendor. At that time there were thousands of former Austrian Imperial servants unemployed in Vienna, and so it was easy to engage an adequate staff at a moment's notice. But Baroness Rothschild, feeling the historical importance of the Duke's stay at her castle, went even further; and by the time the celebrated guest arrived, the boxes in the stables, so long unused, were populated with snow-white Lippiza carriage horses and low-chested Irish hunters, while green-uniformed *jaegers* were instructed to keep a sharp watch on the game in the Rothschild forests for a possible royal hunt.

Baron Eugene de Rothschild, the husband of Kitty, was a wealthy man. But he had also other qualities making him a unique member of the Austrian aristocracy. He had a certain Edwardian (Edward the Seventh, that is) elegance, an engaging personality, and was a reserve officer in the exclusive cavalry regiment, the Black Dragoons. In short, in spite of being a Jew, he was on an equality with the most ancient Austrian nobility.

Or perhaps on a higher level—the majority of Austrian aristocrats had Jewish blood, and were forever trying to conceal the fact. There was only one pure Jewish noble family in Austria, a famous clan proud of its Jewish blood, never relinquishing the ancient faith: the Rothschilds.

Baroness Kitty de Rothschild was amusing, amazing and beautiful. Her career had been not unlike that of Mrs. Simpson: both turned precedent and society upside down. Kitty Wolff was the daughter of a Philadelphia dentist. A girl of adventurous spirit, she had started to travel around at an early age, and in the course of her travels had contracted three marriages. Two of them had been annulled. She had also had extensive religious experience. First married to a Mr. Spotswood, she became an Episcopalian; on her marriage to Count Schönborn she became a Catholic; and when she married the Baron de Rothschild she again embraced her original Judaism. From the humble background of a middle-class Philadelphia suburb, she rose to the dizzy height of leadership in the international set, with fine palaces in the various capitals of Europe. Eventually she died of cancer in her Long Island mansion.

The Duke of Windsor arrived in Vienna, to find Sir Walford Selby, the British Minister, waiting for his former King-Emperor at the railroad station. It was a bleak December morning. After the brief exchange of greetings the Duke expressed a wish for the photographers to come and snap him. This wish having been eagerly complied with, he motored with his suite of eleven—aides-de-camp, equerries, a financial aide, a butler, valet, chauffeur, and a Scotland Yard inspector, plus a precious private cellar—to the nearby castle. He had had only two days to familiarize himself with his new surroundings when Baroness de Rothschild, his hostess, arrived too.

The Duke and the Baroness met. Perhaps because of the coldness of the weather the initial encounter was not too warm; but even after that the Duke conducted his life as though the chatelaine were absent. Baroness Kitty simply was not invited to the royal table. It should, however, be added that the Duke was quite busy—he was on the telephone. He called Wallis in Cannes several times a day; then he talked to London; to his ranch in Calgary, Canada; and to other distant points in the world. No one can censure him for these costly conversations. Only a few days before he had been King, and a Sovereign's mind certainly is not occupied with picayune things like telephone bills. Now it needed the fortune of a Rothschild to foot them, and toward the end of the Duke's stay the outspoken, incorrigible Baroness Kitty used her telephone too—calling up a London friend, she had the audacity to say of the Duke: "As far as I'm concerned, anyone can have him any time!"

At the outset of the royal visit the Baroness did her utmost to lighten the melancholy of her guest, which, she thought, was deepened by the coming of Christmas. Kitty de Rothschild turned sentimental and decided to make it a happy holiday for the Duke away from his own home. She summoned decorators, entertainers and musicians from Paris, and in great secrecy had the principal dining room and one of the salons adorned in real Christmas style, complete with a glittering tree. But when the *heilige Abend* arrived the Duke sent word that he would be unable to attend. This made Baroness Kitty really sad, for apart from her other thoughtful preparations she had some presents for the Duke under the Christmas tree, and now she was pondering as to how to give them to him. Finally the beautiful sapphire studs made by Cartier for the occasion were placed on the Duke's breakfast tray on Christmas morning, with the Baroness' humblest and best wishes. The Duke responded instantly: he sent back an autographed photograph of himself.

After this fiasco perhaps Baroness Kitty adjudged the royal guest somewhat difficult, and probably she recalled the old Austrian saying, "*Zwei Tage ein Gast, am dritten zur Last.*" ("Fish and guests stink after three days.") But the Duke's stay at Enzesfeld was not for three days. He made the castle his headquarters for three months. According to the accounts of the contemporary press, he issued commands to everybody, shouted and exhibited a furious temper, and at times was incredibly sullen. He also appeared deeply depressed. But mainly he was bored. Once in a while he would go on a skiing excursion and order the police and railroad officials to stop the de luxe express trains at obscure stations for him. He asked—with satisfactory results, needless to say—the famous skiing instructor, Herr Delleharth, to teach him some of the more intricate tricks of the sport, half-price.

So there was some fast sliding, but still this was a stagnant life. Then the Duke suddenly made a discovery. He found that he could go and have his hair trimmed every day in the Hotel Bristol by an amusing barber called Leo, who entertained His Royal Highness with *gemütlich* local gossip. Having paid a few visits to this wizard of a barber, the Duke decided that his hair should be cut privately, and took a room for a couple of hours a day in the hotel. After this, Leo attended to him upstairs, but Windsor complained bitterly when he found out that Leo charged him the customary seven Austrian schillings for room service, over and above the regular barber shop tariff.

Going shopping also helped the Duke to pass the time which hung so heavily on his hands. He paid visits to some famous Viennese jewelers, and examined their wares minutely, but bought nothing. He did make some purchases, though: he bought some hunting knives and a few suitcases. However, a *grand seigneur* habitually carries no money on him, and so he asked that the bills be sent to the British Minister. These comparatively small bills remained unpaid for quite some time, until one of Windsor's equerries paid them out of his own pocket. There are some famous and excellent artisans and tradesmen in Vienna, and they had hoped that the wealthy Prince would make fabulous purchases in their city, so much in need in those critical times of a little hard cash. But these merchants were accustomed to the lighthearted Habsburg archdukes who, when in love, figuratively speaking threw money out of the window. When one shopkeeper related that after lengthy vacillation the Duke bought from him merely a flashlight valued at sixty cents, the comments were bitter. The well-known Austrian *gemütlichkeit* soured considerably. Like Baroness Kitty, the Viennese seem to have come to the conclusion that "anyone can have him any time."

But the Duke magnetized his host a little longer. Baron de Rothschild had been much attracted to Windsor. Particularly when the former Sovereign told him that he had decided to write a book in defense of the Jews. This lofty plan was immediately made public, and reporters succeeded in interviewing the former King and future author. They were most curious to find out if the Duke thought that the publication of such a book would be a really good idea at that crucial time. They received a ready answer: "To know what is the right thing to do, and not to do it, is cowardice!"

Baron de Rothschild was jubilant when he heard the Duke's reply; and he persuaded himself that this was not mere verbiage. For nothing would have pleased a Rothschild more than that his ancient race, once more under attack, should be upheld even by an ex-Defender of the Faith.

The plan progressed. In Enzesfeld's fine library the ex-King fingered folios and schemed. Methodically he began with fundamentals—he dreamed up the outward appearance of the book. The volume would be bound in royal blue morocco leather, and on the cover would appear the coat-of-arms of the Prince of Wales with the motto: "Ich Dien."

True there was no longer a Prince of Wales, but the motto remained, and it could still be put to some service. But alas! the proposed masterpiece died in embryo. No one really knew why the book was never written—some seemed to think that the Duke, who had never liked to concentrate on one particular matter for long, found other diversions.

His new avocation turned out to be daily visits to the British Legation. Formerly he had avoided his embassies altogether; but now in his exile the British Ministry represented home. He dropped in there for engrossing conversations with his former subjects, secretaries and the like, amusing them in turn with the cockney accent he affects. He seldom saw Sir Walford Selby, the Minister, who devoted his time to more pressing business. One day, however, he

collared Sir Walford. It was around noon. The Duke found the
Minister's company so interesting as to forget that it was lunchtime.
When the butler came to announce the second time that Lady
Selby and her daughter were waiting for Sir Walford in the dining
room, the Minister had to offer a hasty invitation. The Duke said
yes, he would be delighted to stay and eat with the family. When
they sat down at table, Windsor appeared stupefied. Lady Selby
turned to her royal guest: "Is there anything wrong, Sir?" she asked.
"Oh no!" said the Duke. "Only mayn't I ask you what those odd
little silver rings are for around your napkins? They look very curious,
and you know my inquisitive nature. I wish to know everything."
Lady Selby then explained that napkins are used at several meals,
and the rings serve to identify them. The Duke just could not believe
this. "Do you mean to tell me," he pressed Lady Selby, "that people
don't get a fresh napkin at each meal?"

When Marie Antoinette was told that her subjects were starving
because there was not enough bread to go round, she suggested that
they should eat cake. Even if the Duke of Windsor's napkin story
has not quite the same degree of inanity as the tale of Marie
Antoinette, it helps to show how little rulers know of the habits of
ordinary mortals. But some learn . . .

The long separation from Wallis totally exasperated the Duke
of Windsor. He was now short-tempered even with his equerries and
aides-de-camp, and they left him. He found a new and loyal adherent
in the person of Dudley Forwood, honorary secretary at the British
Legation, and the official intermediary between the Legation and
the Duke. He appointed Mr. Forwood to be his equerry.

Sometimes he spent a few hours in Vienna in the company of
Franz von Papen, the Nazi Ambassador, Princess Marie Fürstenberg,
Princess Elizabeth Hohenlohe, and a Mr. Wollie Seibel. (The last-
named appeared as Elliot Templeton in Somerset Maugham's book,
The Razor's Edge.) All this time Sir Walford prayed and hoped that
the Duke's stay in Austria would not last much longer—His Majesty's
envoy feared a possible attempt at assassination. Where there are
princes there are lunatics.

The Rothschilds were worried for quite other reasons. The upkeep
of Castle Enzesfeld had become exceedingly expensive since the Duke's
arrival. All the bills for Windsor and his entourage had been paid by
his hosts. When Lady Mendl had arranged with Baroness Kitty for
the stay at Enzesfeld, the Rothschilds had imagined that merely the

house would be lent, and that the Duke would pay for his own housekeeping. Instead, the bills never stopped pouring in, and the Rothschild fortune at that time was no longer what it had been. The press reported that early in March 1937, the hosts dropped a few hints about paying rent, or at least expenses, and the guest became apprehensive. But he went on living in the same fashion. At last the Rothschilds listened to some very knowledgeable legal advice, and as a result the township of Enzesfeld declared the Duke "Master of Castle Enzesfeld." The results immediately following this declaration were truly amazing—all the bills were now addressed to the "Master of Castle Enzesfeld." The Duke at once motored to Vienna and conferred with Sir Walford. He said that he was not prepared to stay any longer at the Rothschild castle. Sir Walford then telephoned to the Pension Appersbach, a nice little boarding-house on the shores of Lake St. Wolfgang. The Minister talked to the lady-owner of the place, explaining the situation, making reservations, and imploring her to make the Duke's stay comfortable but not too expensive. The proprietress agreed to charge only $10.00 per day for the whole party, and promised to install a bathroom next door to the Duke's bedroom.

It was out-of-season, anyhow, with wet, dreary weather for the three weeks' duration of the ducal residence; and the owner of Pension Appersbach was later justified in her kindness combined with foresight, because today the formerly obscure boardinghouse is a veritable shrine for romantic tourists. A former King's impatient, amorous sighs may still be echoing between those walls . . .

24

Marriage of the Century

*My childhood was not happy and my spring was not
decked with flowers, but now I shall enjoy a radiant
summer, and the most delightful of autumns. And
perhaps my happy marriage will provide you with
some personal consolation.*
                    —BALZAC, *announcing his marriage to a friend*

W<small>HILE</small> the Duke quarreled with his hosts, bargained with
a barber, and thought twice before making a sixty-cent purchase,
while he was consumed with longing for his betrothed, Mrs. Simpson
was spending her time and his money on preparing her trousseau.

Four dressmakers were hard at work—Mainbocher, an American;
Paquin, a Frenchman; Molyneux, an Englishman; and Schiaparelli,
an Italian. The colors were patriotic red, white and blue; but the
gem of the collection was Mainbocher's wedding gown of Wallis
blue—a new name but not a new shade. For "Wallis blue," so-called,
was simply the famous Windsor blue, the color of the ribbon worn by
Knights and Dames of the Garter. This wedding dress the Duchess
later sent to the Metropolitan Museum of New York.

The trousseau consisted of a mere forty-eight gowns. But just
before the wedding, Wallis could not resist ordering eighteen other
dresses. Of these six were for evening wear, eleven for daytime, and
one was a négligée.

One of the evening gowns was white with a full flared skirt; on
it crawled a bright red lobster that reached from the waist to the
knees. Another evening dress was also Wallis blue, printed with cute
little yellow butterflies. This motif was repeated on the lapels of a
blue tweed jacket. A simple day dress in black crepe was printed all
over with small, slow, white turtles. No one ever found out what, if
anything, was symbolized by all these creatures; but surely there
must have been some hidden significance. Perhaps the turtles had a
culinary meaning—the terrapin of Baltimore are famous.

Most glamorous of all was the négligée of blue and silver lamé, with long tight sleeves, cut very low in the back; for the future Duchess frowned at the mere hint of low front décolletage. Her collar bones were at that time still rather prominent.

Hats gave Wallis a headache. She never really liked hats and only because fashion rules even her, had she purchased even a few dozen at a time. For some time she pondered over the problem of a design. Finally she decided upon the Salvation Army bonnet style, perhaps to show that the Army's cause had always been near to her heart.

Antonio Magagnini was summoned from his hairdressing establishment in Paris to permanent-wave Mrs. Simpson's hair in a new way. This artist reputedly received $50 per trip plus expenses, and he had to make several trips, for soon after his first visit to Wallis women in Paris exhibited the latest Simpson coiffure! Antonio denied that he had given away the secret. But however it had happened, the secret had leaked out, and a new style was urgently needed. This brought on another headache. At last it dawned on Wallis that she could wear her hair in a knot at the back of her head, à la Salvation Army.

Mr. Mainbocher still sighs nostalgically when he talks about the Duchess' trousseau. It was, he says, the biggest job he ever did.

The Duke's immediate preparation for the marriage consisted of making certain requests to his family. They were:

1. That the wedding should receive public recognition.

2. That the Duke of Kent should act as best man.

3. That his wife should be recognized as a Royal Duchess, with the style of "Royal Highness," and addressed as "Madam" or "Ma'am."

4. That he himself should before long be permitted to return to England, and given a chance to make himself useful to the Empire.

None of these requests was granted.

Just before the ceremony at the hastily erected altar, the Duke was handed a telegram. He read it, and his face looked tragic. Then he crumpled the paper and thrust it into his pocket.

The marriage took place at the Château de Candé near Monts, which belonged to Charles Bedaux. Mr. Bedaux was then at the height of his career. Now, the world has half-forgotten him. He began life in the United States as a sandhog, and thereafter gained fame as the best-known and best-loathed efficiency expert in this country.

Mr. Bedaux was familiar with high personages; he had been very close to Herr von Ribbentrop, Otto Abetz, and other leading members of the Nazi hierarchy. But how the course of life changes!

Only seven years after the wedding he gave the Windsors, Charles Bedaux was dead. He took his own life in a jailhouse in Miami before he could be brought to trial on charges of treason and conspiracy with the Nazis.

But no ugly forebodings clouded the exciting day of the marriage, a day of brilliant sunshine. So that, contrary to rumor, Mrs. Simpson could not wear her brand-new tiara for the wedding. This noble ornament was suitable only for wear in the evening.

The mayor of the little town of Monts waxed his mustache, put on his frock coat and the tri-colored sash of the French Republic for the great occasion, and went out to the castle to solemnize the civil ceremony. It is not known if he insisted on seeing the documents that must be produced by other foreigners marrying in France. Such persons, if they have forgotten their birth certificates, are told to do their business at their native consulate. For the French lay greater stress on documentation than on the marriage itself.

Neither is it known if the Sovereign's permission for the marriage of a Royal Prince had been granted, as required by the Royal Marriages Act.

Out of the blue came a *presbyter vagans*, a wandering priest, the Reverend R. A. Jardine, to "officiate" at the nuptials. The good gentleman was so moved by his sense of an exalted mission that he paid not the least attention to a telegram which had been delivered to him the day before, forbidding him to celebrate the Windsors' wedding. This telegram had been sent by the Bishop of Durham, the ecclesiastical superior of the Reverend Mr. Jardine. The wire said: "You are without episcopal license or consent to unite the Duke of Windsor and Mrs. Simpson. Since your license has been revoked, under the circumstances you are unable to legally solemnize this marriage." The clergyman decided that a bird in the hand was worth two in the bush, and so he officiated even though this ceremony was regarded as of none effect by the Church of England.

But what agony the future may hold! Only six short years after the wedding the once-famous clergyman and his wife were arrested in Los Angeles, where they maintained a Lilliputian church, endearingly calling it the "Windsor Cathedral." They were charged by the immigration authorities with having overstayed their permit. When the Duke of Windsor, who was sojourning at Palm Beach at the time, was asked to help, he said that he could do nothing for the couple.

They made a handsome couple, the Windsors, on that June day, as they stood before the clergyman. The Reverend Mr. Jardine raised his voice: "Wilt thou love her, comfort her, honor her and keep her?" The Duke of Windsor cried in a shrill, almost hysterical, tone: "I will!" When he put on Wallis' finger the plain wedding ring, the gold of which had been mined in Wales, his hands trembled noticeably. No wonder! It was his first wedding. The bride, having had more experience, was calmer. Aunt Bessie, whose advice had helped the Duke on his way to happiness and Wallis to her heart's desire, lifted a tiny lace handkerchief to her eyes.

It would be interesting to know how the Duke obtained the Welsh gold for the wedding ring. Royal wedding rings are traditionally made from this gold, which is very rare. Queen Elizabeth was given hers by the people of Wales, but it is not very likely that the Welsh miners were responsible for sending the Duke his.

Yet the Duchess was not careless of the sufferings of the miners. After the marriage, she sent a doll to a charity drive which specialized in collecting toys for the children of the unemployed. Wallis specified that her gracious gift must be sent to the child of some jobless Welsh miner, expressing the wish that the little mother should call her new "child"—"Wallis." The New York *Times* reported this item under the headline: "Duchess Sends Doll for Jobless Welsh Miner's Child" and in the listing of items followed this one: "Duke Spends $300 a Day on Flowers for Wife."

On the wedding day itself, Cecil Beaton was the privileged photographer of the historic occasion; but even he, and even here, was not privileged enough to "shoot" the Duke's right profile. That was still forbidden. So Mr. Beaton, and the world, had to be satisfied with full face and left-side profile pictures.

At last the company trooped to the buffet to feast on hot chicken à la king, followed by French pastry and strawberries and cream. Of course there was plenty of champagne, and the wedding cake of six tiers was three feet high.

Soon after coffee and brandy the Duke of Windsor and his wife climbed into their limousine and started on their long honeymoon. Ahead of them went 226 pieces of luggage, including 183 steamer trunks. They motored as far as the Italian frontier, where they boarded a de luxe salon coach that was later in the evening hooked on to the Simplon-Orient Express. Mussolini, who was also the dictator of Italian railroads, is said generously to have lent his private coach to the Windsors.

The honeymooners visited first Venice, then Milan, and a few other picturesque Italian spots, at last coming to rest in Austria, at Castle Wasserleonburg near Arnoldstein. The Castle—which was *rebuilt* in 1570—was lent to them by the German Count Paul Muenster. And its ghost Anna (the "Lady Bluebeard," famed for having murdered eight husbands) behaved herself during the Windsors' visit.

The last part of the honeymoon was spent in Paris. But then Wallis was suddenly struck by homesickness. This was understandable—to return with great honors, almost a queen, to one's native country offers a supreme thrill. The new Duchess' name was on the lips of everybody in the United States. She had in fact become so famous that in Baltimore the East Biddle Street house where she lived as a girl had been turned into a museum.

The attendance at this museum in the beginning was quite large, admission charge being a dollar, and worth it. There were lifelike wax figures of King George V and Queen Mary with Wallis in the act of curtsying to Their Majesties. An enterprising New Jersey businessman negotiated to move the wax figures and the furnishings, including the tub in which Wallis had once bathed, to his own state. The important matter was brought before the aldermen of Baltimore. After due deliberation the city fathers declined to let the Wallis Warfield Museum go: in making their decision they were guided by the fact that it was the greatest tourist attraction Baltimore had had for many a year.

However, it was soon whispered that the only thing in the house that the Duchess of Windsor had actually used when she was still Bessie Warfield was an old stove on which she had occasionally made fudge. When someone confronted the curator with this story, she answered evasively: "The museum isn't a peep show. It is intended to preserve the girlhood home of Wallis as a popular shrine." After the old stove gossip got around, visitors became scarcer; and the admission fee was reduced to fifty cents. Finally, when the interest of the public waned altogether, the shrine business was given up. There were no takers, even in New Jersey.

In an effort to relieve the homesickness of the Duchess, Charles Bedaux after the honeymoon invited the Windsors to be his guests on an American tour. They readily accepted. The news of this impending visit soon reached the press, and provoked immediate public indignation—it was surely impossible that the former King of England would visit the United States as the guest of a man who had a good chance of being boycotted and even physically molested the moment the party landed!

A few of the Windsors' friends dropped respectful hints, but the Duke was not satisfied with their opinion and asked the then American Ambassador to France, William C. Bullitt, to give him the official view. Bullitt, who naturally wanted his country to reap the benefits of the world-famous couple's visit, made light of the matter and allegedly urged them not to change their plans. It remained for the British Ambassador in Paris, Sir Ronald Lindsay, to tell the Duke of Windsor that he felt deeply concerned over the effect upon public opinion if the Bedaux invitation were accepted. So Wallis sadly deferred the rediscovery of America to a later date.

It is difficult to understand the mental processes of the ducal pair. For upon abandoning the ill-conceived Bedaux plan, they made preparations for another, even more unfortunate visit. They accepted the invitation of a man hated far more widely than the efficiency expert. Windsor was already acquainted with this man, having been his guest before.

The headlines of the New York *Times* (October 23, 1937) concerning this trip were as usual conservative:

HITLER RECEIVES WINDSORS SIMPLY
Is Cordial but Gives Impression He Distinguishes
Between Past and Present Rulers.
Guests Early, Wait Hour

Before a portion of the article is quoted, it is necessary to report a rumor current in Germany at the time of the abdication. Those near the Fuehrer let it be known that when he first heard that the King would abdicate, Hitler was exceedingly gloomy. "I've lost a friend to my cause," he allegedly said. But a few minutes later he burst out in a Mephistophelean laugh and screamed: "I told you! The English are decadent!"

To return to the New York *Times* of October 23, 1937:

> The Duke and Duchess of Windsor received a rather puzzling reception today at Chancellor Hitler's mountain home here (Berchtesgaden). The Fuehrer was cordial but the former British King must have realized that his host evidently makes a distinction between abdicated royalty and reigning monarchs or dictators. For almost an hour after their arrival the Duke and Duchess remained at the foot of the mountain awaiting the scheduled hour of their appointment . . . The reward for

this rather drawn-out pilgrimage across South Germany was a two-hour conversation with Hitler . . . There can be no doubt that Hitler, like the German Foreign Office, regretted the abdication as a serious blow to German interests . . .

The Duke's decision to see for himself the Third Reich's industries and social institutions and his gestures and remarks during the last two weeks have demonstrated adequately that the abdication did rob Germany of a firm friend . . . The Duke is reported to have become very critical of English politics as he sees them and is reported as declaring that the British ministers of today and their possible successors are no match either for the German or Italian dictators.

The Duke of Windsor, of course, was not the only well-known Briton to be distinguished by the Fuehrer. Among others, his old friend Mr. Lloyd George had been invited to Berchtesgaden: he eagerly accepted. Mr. Winston Churchill had been invited twice; he neither declined nor accepted. And it is instructive to read his reasons for this policy:

I would gladly have met Hitler with the authority of Britain behind me. But as a private individual I should have placed myself and my country at a disadvantage. If I had agreed with the dictator-host, I should have misled him. If I had disagreed, he would have been offended, and I should have been accused of spoiling Anglo-German relations. Therefore I declined, or rather let lapse, both invitations. All those Englishmen who visited the German Fuehrer in these years were embarrassed or compromised. No one was more completely misled than Mr. Lloyd George, whose rapturous accounts of his conversations make odd reading today.

(*The Gathering Storm*, Book I)

In its October 12, 1937 issue, the New York *Times*, still following Windsor activities, reported that their real hosts were Dr. Ley and the Labor Front, naturally with the German Government behind them.

But on October 13, the *Times* surprisingly announced that the Duke and Duchess were Hitler's personal guests. Elsewhere, the newspaper told of a dinner party given in their honor by Joachim von Ribbentrop, at a fashionable restaurant. Hitler was unable to be present. But the twenty guests included Heinrich Himmler, Dr. Ley, Herr Hermann, Hitler's adjutant, and "other minor Foreign Office officials," as the *Times* put it. The story related that the former King clinked glasses with the former champagne salesman. On October 16

Listening to advice

He too was a King of England: the unlamented George IV.

that correct newspaper stated that the Duke "continues to give a modified Hitler salute."

Shortly before the Windsors paid their respects to Hitler, Ribbentrop appeared at a Court ceremony in London's Buckingham Palace. When the Nazi's turn came to salute the new King of England, Ribbentrop, approaching the Throne, thrust out his arm thrice—three greetings being the due of a Sovereign—in big, generous Nazi salutes, shouting three times "Heil Hitler!" But these cabalistic words, and even the threatening gestures, completely misfired. The King just looked through Ribbentrop, giving no sign of recognition whatever.

The coldness of the Sovereign was not at all surprising. Britain was preparing to defend itself from the promised onslaught of the Windsors' hosts. And shortly after their visit to Hitler, an object patently British came into prominence: Mr. Neville Chamberlain carried his umbrella back and forth to Germany, hoping against hope that he might dissuade the dictator from using the thing so patently Nazi: the devastating machinery of war.

On June 11, 1939, at a time when the Nazi armies were ready to march and plunder Europe and had in mind to attack England, the Windsors accepted an invitation to dine with the Nazi Ambassador to France, von Welczek. It was emphasized in the press that this dinner would be wholly informal and had no official character whatever. That can be easily believed. The Duke of Windsor could not hope to prevent the Nazis from carrying out their long-cherished plan. The die was cast . . .

Fraternizing with the Nazis was abruptly ended by the outbreak of war in September 1939. The Duke, a seasoned soldier, at once applied for a key job in the British Army, but there was no such thing available for him. The British detailed Major General the Duke of Windsor to light liaison duty. And since the war seemed to be slow in gathering momentum, and the Duke felt himself frustrated, the Windsors decided to go to their Antibes villa.

There, too, life soon became difficult. Things were beginning to be really uncomfortable. France was pulling in the belt; the Riviera, formerly so delightful, had become very gloomy, and the Duke's chef had been mobilized.

So the Windsors asked his old friend Winston Churchill, who had now become Prime Minister, to secure for him the Governor Generalship of Canada. Mr. Churchill again did his best. But this was such an important vantage point in the war against Hitler that even Churchill couldn't swing the job. It seemed that the Canadians were dead-set against the appointment, and the Duke's own family, including the King his brother, were not favorably disposed to it either. Churchill then compromised. He arranged for his royal friend to be named Governor of the Bahamas, one of the Empire's smallest and most remote possessions, a post as a rule given to a retired high-ranking British Civil Servant or an army officer in need of a well-deserved rest.

But first the Windsors had to make a wild dash across three countries to escape the invading armies. The Duke said that the Nazis wanted to capture him! Obviously, this was an absurd notion. Or did he forget that he was no longer the Prince of Wales nor the King of England? Now he was well-acquainted with the leaders of the new Germany; he was *persona grata*, who dined and wined with them. He was on visiting terms with Der Fuehrer. And it was admitted after the war: one of the top Nazis issued strict orders to the occupying troops not to touch anything that belonged to the Windsors. So on their return to France, the Duke and Duchess found all their possessions intact, packed with exquisite German care and stored with Nazi efficiency.

Longings are rarely fulfilled one hundred percent. But even if she was not going to her homeland, at least Wallis would be near it. So the fever of her homesickness lessened. At last she would leave that Europe which now looked so dismal, and would live with her Prince Charming in the Western Hemisphere. A fortnight after the devastating Nazi bombing of his native land, the preliminary to the intended invasion of Britain, had begun, the Duke of Windsor and his wife embarked in Portugal; and after a smooth, uneventful voyage reached the Bahamas on August 8, 1940.

25

Battle of the Bahamas

Antony . . . ceased to be a general, a consul, a triumvir, a citizen of Rome . . . and proved he was unfit to govern men, by suffering himself to be governed by a woman.
—Bolingbroke: *The Idea of a Patriot King*

At midsummer, 1940, the new Governor General of the Bahamas, His Royal Highness the Duke of Windsor, and his wife, arrived at Nassau aboard the American Export liner *Excalibur*.

The Bahamas, which consist of twenty-nine islands, 661 cays, 2,387 coral reefs and sandspits, are inhabited by 70,000 native Bahamians, plus a group of wealthy Britons who could not stand the foggy home climate, plus another group whom Britain could not stand. It was safely out of earshot of the bombs bursting in Europe.

Since July 10, 1940, there had already been some bombing of the mother country, apparently in preparation for the threatened invasion of England. The miracle of Dunkirk had passed into history, but the Blitz and the Battle of Britain were still on their way. The first days of September brought them, under a "bombers' moon." Then the flames of the ex-King's burning capital were visible for a hundred miles, and the Nazi fliers had only to point their bombers' noses toward the light and come in. Fortunately they did not bring about the quarter-million casualties for which the Government had prepared as a first instalment. They did provoke the defiance expressed in the story of the cockney who called his son into shelter with the words: "Get the 'ell inside and let that shrapnel fall down." They did ensure the resistance of such people as the fish-and-chip seller who was dug out of the ruins of his business, drew himself erect and spat into the wreckage shouting: "To 'ell with 'itler."

Sunlight was falling on the Bahamas when, at four o'clock of an unusually beautiful afternoon—usually the hour was marked by a downpour of tropical rain—the *Excalibur* was warped alongside the

Hamilton docks, and the smiling Duke and the happy Duchess, the inevitable dogs and the baggage, came down the gangplank. The baggage consisted of only fifty-seven pieces. Among them were trunks, suitcases, a sewing machine, a case each of champagne and gin, and two cases of old port. And, of course, the favorite Buick car. Most of the Windsors' belongings had been shipped previously, and more were to follow.

The Duchess of Windsor experienced the joy of being near to the land of her birth; still she apparently regarded the Bahamas appointment as a sort of banishment. Wisecracking Wallis is said to have remarked to friends about the distant post: "St. Helena—1940 style." But it was not really as bad as that. St. Helena must have been painful for an emperor who had lost his job. But Napoleon was alone—he had to endure exile without a wife by his side; while the Duke was comforted by the presence of Wallis. And she set out to make his home a happy one.

For immediately upon her arrival the Duchess busied herself with the interior decoration of Government House, summoning an old Baltimore friend, Mrs. Winthrop Curtis Bradley, to help her. While the work was going forward, the Windsors graciously accepted the offer of Sir Harry Oakes' villa to camp in.

First, Government House was painted inside and out, and wall-papered. Then the joint plan of the Duchess and Mrs. Bradley was carried out speedily but well in modernistic style, with occasional Regency touches; most of the furnishings having been sent from the United States.

There were low, glass-topped cocktail tables, long sofas, open cupboards displaying Sèvres china, some very smart bamboo furniture, and flowers everywhere. The Duchess' portrait by Brockhurst was hung over the living-room mantelpiece, and family photographs included one of Queen Mary, regal in crown, ermine-trimmed mantle, and Garter ribbon. This picture was rather a severe one, and did not bring out those soft maternal qualities which the Duke knew and loved best. "Can't we get a better picture of Mother, dear?" he once asked. "No," said the Duchess calmly, "that is the best one, dear."

Queen Mary's photo was placed on the Duke's desk. This desk, a very business-like affair, was in the Duke's den. To make him feel at home he kept on a side table two scarlet dispatch boxes displaying the words: "The King." But now that he was no longer practicing, so to speak, they were there only as ornaments.

At last the traveling Windsors felt that they had a home, "a place for everything and everything in its place." Even though the Duke had ceased to be an active soldier, his marshal's baton found its place on the table on the veranda. Windsor used the symbol of great military leaders, "the laurell'd captains," to point out places of interest to visitors, on a wall map of his domain.

His immediate domain, the grounds of Government House, was not extensive, but was very well kept by trustee convicts. At the gates there was a daily ceremony of the changing of the Guard. The outdoor swimming pool—which had been built during the ex-King's brief reign, so that one of the titles still displayed the crowned device "E.R. VIII"—was useful on particularly stifling days.

Government House in Nassau was probably never so cozy and stylish as when Wallis took matters in hand—to that utilitarian hand even inanimate objects seemed to respond. The exception to the rule was the front door, which had withstood the most devastating hurricanes. This venerable door simply refused to budge, no matter how the Duchess argued with it that it was an ugly thing and had to go. Finally she had the upper half of the eyesore covered with a black glass panel on which was printed in white: "Honi soit qui mal y pense." Just for ornamentation's sake.

There was still another stubborn thing to be dealt with: the highest church authority of the Bahamas, the Right Reverend A. H. Brown, Anglican Bishop of Nassau, had two years before their arrival shown his opinion of the Windsors by tearing down their picture from the wall of a local hotel. Later, he had apologized for his action, saying that he had acted on impulse.

Now he declined to attend the cocktail party arranged to meet the new Governor General and his wife, alleging a previous engagement. The Windsors then decided to enter the lion's den, and one Sunday morning drove in an open carriage to attend the service at the Cathedral. When it was over, the bishop appeared on the street, and the waiting Windsors offered him their compliments, just as ordinary people do when moved by a sermon. Flattery is an almost infallible weapon. Thus was peace declared between Church and State in the Bahamas.

The presence of the ex-King and his American-born wife, and their fabulous romance, fired the imagination of the islanders and of the tourists. Nassau experienced the greatest boom of its history. The hotels were filled; social entertainment was at its peak; and everyone tried to outdo everyone else in party giving. The Windsors frequented the ultra-chic Emerald Beach and Porcupine Clubs, together with their entourage—three equerries and their wives—and some new friends.

The most recent and closest friends of the Windsors in Nassau were the Axel Wenner-Grens. Mr. Wenner-Gren, a very wealthy Swede, had been on good terms with Field Marshal Goering before the war, but then he knew the top men in almost every country. The couple— Mrs. Wenner-Gren, now noted for her Swedish millionaire husband and for some beautiful jewels, hailed originally from Kansas City— had their magnificent yacht, the *Southern Cross*, moored in the harbor of Nassau. They entertained the Windsors on a lavish scale.

Mr. Wenner-Gren was also one of the few rich visitors to the islands who wanted to improve the lot of the Bahamian Negro. He had established a local foundation with a yearly budget of $25,000 for the social advancement of the colored population, and by his fish cannery and real-estate development provided steady employment for more than a thousand people.

It was sufficient for the Duke, who had always been interested in industrialists, to know that the Swedish Croesus was one, too, a manufacturer of Electrolux products. But Mr. Wenner-Gren had another manufacturing line—armaments. Though the Duke may have been in complete ignorance or chose to ask no questions on this score, the United States Government was not incurious; and eventually Mr. Wenner-Gren was placed temporarily on the State Department's black list. He had to leave the Bahamas. Following United States Government action, the Duke signed an expulsion warrant. The Governor of the Bahamas had his duty to perform, even when it concerned an intimate friend, one who had such a sumptuous yacht and had invested capital in this British colony. Luckily, by the time the Duke got around to signing the document, Mr. Wenner-Gren had already moved to Mexico.

While the Duke attended to official business, the Duchess carefully scrutinized her wardrobe. She discovered that it was inadequate for a tropical climate, and in her usual methodical manner set out to remedy such an unfortunate state of affairs. This was a sensible scheme—one should always try to keep up with the times even though condemned to vegetate on a remote island. After all, neither wars nor great distances should stop ladies of good taste from thinking of pretty clothes and impeccable elegance.

A visit to New York to refurbish her wardrobe was for the moment out of the question. So, being a practical woman, Wallis turned the tables and had the wardrobe come to her. It was easy for modistes and fitters and seamstresses to hop on the plane and come with their latest models to Nassau, there to sew a little. Mainbocher, the Duchess' favorite dressmaker, sent along pretty little Miss Genevieve, while Hattie Carnegie's envoy was Miss Rose, actually the star fitter. There were, of course, others. And the girls did not arrive alone— they brought with them plaster busts of the Duchess. It would have been unreasonable to rob Wallis of her valuable time, and so the dresses were tried on the bust in an upper room of Government House.

The modistes ate in their room as a rule. Once they were asked for cocktails, and Miss Rose was especially honored: she went on a day's cruise with the Duke and Duchess. Slowly, slowly, the wardrobe was put together. Just modest tropical nothings like silk shantung and voile and tulle dresses; linen, cotton and piqué suits; and net and organdie and chiffon gowns; and . . . In a few months a couple of efficient New York fitters and seamstresses can accomplish wonders.

In December 1940, the late President Roosevelt, cruising in Bahamian waters aboard the *Tuscaloosa*, received a passing visit from the Governor of the Bahamas. Since the Duke flew to the American cruiser in a fast Navy plane, the meeting was immediately linked by the press with the much-lamented death of Lord Lothian, which had occurred the day before. Lord Lothian had been the very able British Ambassador in Washington, and it was rumored that the Duke was going to succeed him.

It was no secret that Wallis would have liked to move to Washington and become the premier hostess in the capital. She often told friends that she wouldn't have minded settling there. When newshawks asked the Duke, after the Roosevelt visit, whether he was going to get the ambassadorship, he threw them a terse "No comment." In the end, the Earl of Halifax was appointed to succeed Lord Lothian.

But despite the Duke's work, the entertainments, the constant visits from the representative of famous dressmakers, golfing, swimming, playing double solitaire, the banjo and the bagpipe, the Windsors at last became a little bored in Nassau.

Back in the Duke's former capital, people had had everything to complain of but boredom. The experiences of Windsor's successor and of the Royal Family may be briefly reported in the words of *Time:*

> While the Duke of Windsor spent the war years in his Bahamas sinecure with the woman for whom he had abandoned the throne, the King held the fort in London, and endured like other Londoners. Like theirs, his home was bombed. His children, like theirs, were sent to the country; his relations, like theirs, died in the line of duty. He shared with his people the sweat and tears of war. A memorable wartime newsreel depicted on one side of the Channel a ranting, raving Hitler, surrounded by tanks and planes, and on the other side, all alone, the quiet figure of the steadfast King.
>
> Two nights a week George slipped into overalls, and stood at a bench in a nearby arms plant, turning out precision parts for R.A.F. guns . . .
>
> (*Time*, February 18, 1952)

On hearing of the bombardment of Buckingham Palace, the Duke sent his brother a proper message of sympathy. But though pitying other people's troubles, he could not forget those of the Duchess, who complained more and more frequently, not only of boredom, but also of the climate. Now this was one thing even the Duke could not change. He had already done his utmost to please his lady: the servants had been told to address her either as "Ma'am" or "Your Royal Highness," and everyone else had been asked not to say "Your Grace" to Wallis but to accord her the higher-sounding title. The Duke also arranged interesting trips, some of them aboard the *Southern Cross*, and after an absence of sixteen years visited Miami with the Wenner-Grens.

Of course the Bahamas post was not all play; the Windsors had their troubles. For instance, the *American Mercury* published an outspoken article on the Windsors by Miss Helen Worden. Miss Worden's article provoked a dignified rejoinder from the Duke, who pointed out that sallies of this sort were extremely dangerous in wartime. When Wallis and her husband alighted on her native American soil, he asked the *Mercury* to print a retraction, with special attention to two items: that the Duchess had no photo of Herr von Ribbentrop in her bedroom, and that she had not received new dresses from New York, in exchange for the Bahamian Government's care for United States sailors. "I give you my personal word," wrote the Duke, "that these statements are not true." The *Mercury* made some retraction.

Then, suddenly, all Nassau, and the Windsors with it, were electrified by the murder of Sir Harry Oakes, the self-made millionaire, in whose villa the Governor General and his wife had been living for a few months. The Duke was greatly shocked by the news of his death, and at once tried to help discover the murderer and bring him to book. He summoned the capable American policeman, Captain E. W. Melchen, who had been his bodyguard when he sojourned in Miami, to conduct the investigation.

Captain Melchen arrived in the next plane and, at the Duke's request, brought along with him a fingerprint expert, James O. Barker. After a consultation, they went to investigate the scene of the murder, Sir Harry's bedroom. They "managed" to find some fingerprints. Next morning the son-in-law of the millionaire, Alfred de Marigny, was arrested and charged with the murder.

It was apparently thought by some that the Governor General's intervention had been ill-advised. Certain persons closely connected with the De Marigny case assert that by bringing in the Miami policemen, the Duke set the course of the case in the beginning.

The Windsors went abroad for the duration of the trial, and returned only when De Marigny already had been acquitted. A score of Bahamians seemed to know the identity of the murderer, who was never brought to trial; and De Marigny still wonders today if the guilty party will ever be prosecuted. He addressed an interesting letter on the subject to Cholly Knickerbocker, who printed it in his column:

Dear Cholly:

A few days ago a man was arrested after having made a statement in a bar that he knew the name of the murderer of Sir Harry Oakes. I was interviewed by the Press about the incident. Unfortunately, as usual, comments were passed on my accent, my clothes, and my being broke. But nothing about my statement was printed.

I stated that neither the Government of the Bahamas nor the Oakes family have the slightest desire to have the party involved in the murder of Sir Harry Oakes made public.

Had they so desired, it would have been an easy matter at the time. Mr. Raymond Schindler, to whom I owe my life, endeavored to clear me by showing to the Nassau Police who was the party. An aide-de-camp of His Royal Highness, Edward Duke of Windsor, then Governor of the Bahamas, informed Schindler in the name of the Government that his action was an insult to the Crown.

He, Schindler, could not prove my obvious innocence by accusing the guilty party. The Crown had arrested me and my innocence had to be proven first before some one else could be accused.

Schindler returned to Nassau after my acquittal and subsequent deportation. He offered his services free of charge to the local authorities.

He wrote a letter to the Duke of Windsor stating that he felt certain
he could bring the guilty party to justice if he were allowed to do so.
HE RECEIVED A CURT NEGATIVE ANSWER.

Undaunted, Schindler returned to Nassau again. The Bahamian
Immigration informed him that he would be deported immediately if
he were to make the slightest attempt to investigate and re-open the
Oakes case.

Therefore, I doubt that seven years later, the same people should
make a sudden about-face. I would rather state that every effort will
be made to choke the issue and continue the venomous campaign
against me, and use me as a smokescreen to protect the large and in-
fluential interests who carry on their hands the blood of Sir Harry
Oakes.

This was a bitter and outspoken letter, serving no purpose whatever. The Duke was no longer Governor of the Bahamas. As it is, he
was never much interested in the machinery of justice, preferring to
spend his time in occupations which do not tax the mind as much as
does jurisprudence.

There was, for instance, a near-queen on a neighboring island,
Miss Jo Carstairs, a very rich lady, who leased Whale Cay from the
British Government. The Windsors paid a visit to Queen Jo on her
domain. She had taught the natives how to raise all the foods they
needed, and had turned Whale Cay into a model agricultural development. The Duke when he had inspected the island was very much
impressed. "Damn it!" he exclaimed. "Why can't all the islands look
like that? Something must be done."

Of course he had said something similar in Wales, and cynics were
quick to remark that he would have no more luck in his efforts to improve the lot of the Bahamian populace than he had had with the
Welsh miners. They were too right.

Nearly five years had passed. The holding of a colonial governorship is limited to a term of five years. But some time before the full
five years were up, the Governor of the Bahamas sent in his resignation. Poor Wallis was quite upset by the heat, despite the fine new
air conditioning in Government House.

The winds were blamed, the intolerable trade winds which were
stifling in Nassau. And of course the stagnant heat which rose from
the warm shoal waters of the Great Bahama Bank.

Apart from all this, it was spring, April 1945, and the important
dressmakers in New York and Paris were showing their collections.
The war had almost ended. The war of blood and sweat and tears.

26

La Vie Parisienne

*"Society women? Oh! some are charming. But as for
loving them, that is a serious matter."*
"Do you think so?"
*She gave him her hand, and abruptly vanished round
the corner of the Rue Spontini.*
　　　　　　　—ANATOLE FRANCE: *The Red Lily*

A pale complexion ill becomes a sailor.
　　　　　　　—OVID: *The Art of Love*

THE WINDSORS have always looked on the house at 85, Rue
de la Faisanderie, Paris, as if they were the owners; though in point
of fact it belongs to M. Paul Louis Weiller, one of the richest industrialists in France, from whom they "rent" it.

The Weiller family fortune comes from the *Gnôme et Rhône* auto-
motive engineering empire. Paul Louis did not need to work any
more, and so turned his attention to high society, with a preference for
retired royalty. He liked to amaze them by his extravagance. It was
pointed out to them, for instance, that the Rue de la Faisanderie
house was erected around a beautiful staircase from the Castle of St.
Cloud, a staircase which M. Weiller bought and put on the site of
Number 85.

Before he placed the mansion at the disposal of the Windsors, while
he himself lived there, M. Weiller gave lavish parties for the Duke
and Duchess; and knowing the liking of the Duke for the food prepared by the German restaurateur Horcher—who was also a favorite
of the Nazis—the considerate host arranged that the dinner should
be airmailed from Berlin, while the Duchess' best-liked gypsy musicians were flown to the Rue de la Faisanderie from Vienna.

In 1952, just as in every year before, the Windsors went back to this
Parisian heaven. But the Duke had not entirely recovered his spirits

since the passing of his brother; or there might have been some other, personal reason for his remaining at home while the Duchess did the town. Walter Winchell, who had been a foe of Nazis and Nazi sympathizers, as he later became a foe of communism, and who has his own good reasons for not approving of the ducal pair, resumed his reporting on them, and noted that the Duchess again, very unwisely, appeared at her favorite funny bistros, and that the Duke still went to bed at midnight while his wife danced on.

Apparently the dancing took place at home, too. And the Rue de la Faisanderie, a sleepy little street inhabited by the elite, all of a sudden experienced the horrors of insomnia. There was the elegant thoroughfare with its formerly peaceful nights turned into day by the Windsors, who were giving the noisiest parties in Paris. Probably not one resident in the street was a socialist or a Communist, but in June 1952 they became apprehensive—the Duchess was making more than merry just at a time when more Frenchmen than ever before were voting Communist.

Some of the oldest inhabitants even thought of barricading the entry to the street, in order to stop the modern *sansculottes* when they should begin their march. Of course, here imagination was traveling too fast; and anyhow the automobiles of the Windsors and their cronies, blocking the Rue de la Faisanderie, served as a sufficiently formidable barricade. Notable among the cars was a new station wagon, bearing on its door a bronze legend, well calculated to ensure the desired privacy: "The Duke of Windsor." The only other person who had her name written on the door of an automobile was Mrs. Anita Manville, the latest wife of Mr. Tommy Manville; but then Mrs. Manville went one better than the Duke of Windsor. While the Duke's name appeared in sober block letters, Anita had her signature copied onto her car door.

But about those all-night parties in the placid *quartier*. Many of the good Parisians became bitter. The masses of the have-nots, naturally; and the little group of haves because they felt that in this dangerous political-economic atmosphere, when the pendulum of the French nation might swing, at the slightest upset, to the extreme Left, the Windsors' behavior constituted a menace. The Parisians blamed the husband less than the wife—him they merely pitied.

Some members of the apprehensive elite were hoping that the Windsors would soon leave their sensitive city, and be on their way to the south of France, where they usually go after a stay in the capital. Formerly the ducal pair had a nice little place at Cap d'Antibes, the Château de la Croe, rented at an alleged $16,000 from Sir Pomeroy Burton, who in 1928 modernized it at a reported cost of $2-million. This sum does not seem so surprising when one learns that the Château is equipped with a swimming pool 250 feet long, and has one of the finest private harbors on the Riviera. However, in 1950, the Windsors, who never play too long at any one place, gave up de la Croe. Even the untaxed pound sterling bought less than before, hence economy was in order. Money was needed for other things, such as *modes*.

The Windsors first proposed to move on to Cap Ferrat, which remains more select, yet less expensive, than Cap d'Antibes; and with them the world proposed to move too—for according to Miss Elsa Maxwell, where the Duke and Duchess go, the world goes too.

It was known that the world at Cap Ferrat would include Lady Kenmare; Charles Munroe—who frequently plays golf with the Duke —and his wife Ann; Signor Gianni Agnelli, one of the big names in the auto industry—he is a Fiat magnate—and his perpetual fiancée, Pamela Churchill. Nearby, in the romantic setting of antique Eze, Mr. and Mrs. Sam Barlow entertained such friends as the clever composer, Signor Gian Carlo Menotti.

But this world of the Windsors had to be disappointed. In a flash, their plans were changed—they longed for the sea. So they chartered a fast yacht, the *Amazone*, 220 tons, in which they planned to tour the Italian coast. They would stop at Portofino and other picturesque Italian ports, proceeding in leisurely fashion to Venice and the Lido. In this activity another world of the Windsors came into focus. Mrs. Donahue immediately chartered a large yacht at Cannes, the Eric Loders rented a small but seaworthy craft, capable of keeping up with the Windsors, and even Prince Ibrahim, a cousin of exiled Farouk, navigated around them in his large sailing vessel.

For a moment it seemed to the world—that is to say, to the real, large world—that the ex-King of Egypt was also going to join his "cousin" of England's seagoing court. With Farouk in it, the tableau would certainly have been perfect, and he could have played his part in the rich little entourage—why, the fellow had saved up $50-million. But Miss Elsa Maxwell quickly stifled the wishful thinking of the outsiders. Farouk was neither liked nor wanted in this exclusive community. He was in bad repute, for despite his full coffers he refused to pay for some jewelry he had bought on credit, from the House of Winston in New York, while he still had a job.

Before embarking on the trip, the Duke celebrated the birthday of his wife in a becoming fashion, presenting her with two charming gifts. He bought her one house, and leased another for nine years. Obtaining this real estate was a complicated business. The Duchess had always wanted a house, which would be truly her own, in Paris, but she was very particular about the location, and wished it to be in that aristocratic quarter behind the *Chambre des Députés*. Finally she located an elegant and suitable *hôtel particulier*, Number 29 Rue Barbey-de-Jouet. But alas! the place belonged to the Government, and the Windsors were momentarily stymied. However, M. Weiller, their host for so many years, came to the rescue with alacrity. He presented to them the Minister of Education, M. André Marie, and after the Duchess' charm had won the Minister over, the objections to the sale were all set aside. The French Government even allowed the *hôtel* to go at the bargain price of 30-million francs (around $80,000). Although probably as much will have to be spent on renovation and in putting in a new plumbing system, for there is only one bathroom in the house.

But there are advantages: the place has a large courtyard, where many cars can be parked, so that they will not block up the street, as they unfortunately did in the Rue de la Faisanderie.

The gift of this town house was indeed a selfless act on the part of the Duke, for he always preferred to live in the country. But as ever he wanted to please his wife, and she in turn wanted to please him. So it was she who once more solved the problem, with her customary simplicity of approach, by suggesting that in order to satisfy the wishes of both, they should acquire two houses. After much diligent search, in 1952, they at last found an ideal country place. They did not have to travel far to this *bon repos*, or abandon their beloved path leading through the Bois de Boulogne to the beautiful countryside around Louveciennes. Near to this preferred locality, in the Valley de Chevreuse, at Marly-le-Roi, not quite twenty miles from Paris, they came upon an ancient and beautiful *moulin*, partly remodeled by the painter Driand.

Everybody who is anybody in the French *haut monde* week-ends in such a *moulin*. The fad for these old mills began with Alphonse Daudet, the author of *Lettres de Mon Moulin*. His example was followed by other artists, who often could not keep up with the cost, and were therefore forced to sell, or to lease to people with money.

The Duchess could look forward, after her summer cruise in the *Amazone*, to the exhilarating task of supervising the renovation of the two houses and their decoration. On the eve of their trip, the Windsors gave a dinner party on the terrace of a Riviera hotel. Among the guests were Eric Sawyer and Barry Dierks, the architects charged with the reconstruction of the Windsors' new homes. And then the ducal pair were off on their yacht trip.

At Portofino they were interviewed by the editor of an American pocket-size magazine. That publication tried hard to be informative, and to add to American culture by its clipped, two-sentence paragraphs; but by slanting the facts, it misinformed the nation. For one thing, it praised such plays, films, books, people, clothes, food, etc., as pleased its distaff editor. As this lady had her own Cinderella story, it is little wonder that she was a great champion of the Windsors, and seized every opportunity to justify their romance and mode of living.

Describing the interview, she assured her readers that the Windsors had much more important things on their minds than play. What they in fact had on their minds was work. For in the course of the conversation the Duchess revealed that, first, she will direct her energies to decorating their new homes. Then she added: "But after we are settled, we are not going to fold our arms."

And the story went on to say that Wallis was about to begin that autobiography which intimates thought had already been written and placed in a bank vault with instructions for its publication twenty-five years after the Duchess' death. This book will be a sort of companion to *A King's Story*, and will have the "blessing and approval of the Duke," as the lady editor put it.

She also told the world that there is still another book slowly forming in the royal author's mind. This will be an expert's account, not of kingship but of sportsmanship, by "one of the most daring and practiced of hunters" (who shot tigers in India with the help of ten thousand Nepalese, as he revealed in his memoirs).

Last but not least, the editor with one stroke of her powerful pen scratched out rumors about marital trouble between the Windsors. She learned from unimpeachable sources—the Duke and Duchess themselves—that the marriage was in great form. Once more the ability of this great lady reporter is seen. It is a rare and talented person indeed who can approach a married couple with the question: "Are you quarreling?"

From another source comes further news about the Duke as author. Now established as a master of the literary craft, H.R.H. has become quite critical about others not quite so able with the pen. When someone mentioned to him the new work of Gabriel-Louis Pringue, *Thirty Years of Dinners in the City*, the Duke wittily said: "Delicious indeed. But why didn't he write it with his fork?"

Having graciously received their American champion, the famous couple sailed in great spirits toward Elba. The weather was perfect, the boat, although not as palatial as the *Nahlin*, was most comfortable, there were a few hand-picked guests on board, and altogether this was a floating *Vie Parisienne*. Then suddenly—for tragedy often comes unforeseen and suddenly—a few hours out of Elba, where another monarch was once exiled, the self-exiled ex-King was struck down. And at once the wires of the news services all over the world were burning up with the news of the Duke's illness; for weeks there was speculation as to the cause of the attack. The trouble was variously put down to gastroenteritis, ulcers, lumbago, gout, gallstones, cirrhosis of the liver, etc. It was not once suggested that the origin of the illness might be psychosomatic.

The *Amazone* put in quickly at Montecatini, and in no time at all the famous English physician, Sir Daniel Davies, who attends upon the Royal Family, flew to examine the Duke. He had been sent posthaste by Queen Mary. No official bulletins were issued by Sir Daniel, but the Duke's friends felt easier when, after a brief professional visit, the English specialist turned his patient over to a local doctor, Professor Dante Pisani, and traveled back to England.

The trip was abandoned, the *Amazone* given up, and the Windsors hurried back to Paris. It was thought that the Duke might have to undergo an operation, and this was the reason for the return: he wanted a town which possessed an American hospital with the most modern surgical equipment.

Naturally the Windsors were photographed as they alighted from the train, but while the Duchess as usual wore a little smile, the Duke offered a truly sad spectacle. He was hardly able to walk, and was held up by his wife on one side, and by a detective on the other. He was ordered complete rest, while complete unrest awaited the Duchess: the chores of selecting her autumn wardrobe, and of supervising the work on the two houses.

Duke and Duchess watch coronation on TV in Paris

Then there were other chores. *Vogue*, together with Elizabeth Arden, *the* cosmetician, desired Wallis to be photographed in a new Paris gown. The Duchess decided on something simple from Dior's for the occasion, but Miss Arden was against this. She wanted Wallis to wear a gown from Dessés. Polemics ensued. But finally Dessés won, for Miss Arden was not in favor of Dior, and the Duchess would certainly not forego having her picture in *Vogue*—proof positive that she is still in the whirl.

The Duke, who has been accustomed all his life to do what he wanted, had to listen to his wife's advice. He could not even play golf! To add to his sufferings he, who was accustomed to eating and drinking the finest, had to observe a strict regimen. It got around that he was even forbidden caviar, and had been ordered to sip water. So it was not quite the same *Vie Parisienne* as the Windsors had formerly enjoyed.

Neither, for that matter, was it any longer quite the same for the ordinary Englishman, who could take less than $70 on his Paris spree, if any. This is a very small sum, certainly not enough to eat and also to sin on, and the saying that an Englishman goes to the Continent to sin is becoming dated.

But even though his former subjects are going broke, around the Duke of Windsor and his wife the stimulus of café society will not be lacking; particularly at Marly-le-Roi, where there is an excellent restaurant, the Castle of Shadows, owned by a Russian and run by the daughter of an English Duke. So there will be neighbors and hosts, and possibly a trickle of interesting guests, with the promise of that "morbid curiosity" the Duke declares he dislikes so much.

Some English visitors to Paris commented on the French custom of granting indiscriminate political asylum, when they heard that Sir Oswald Mosley, the would-be English Fuehrer, was also firmly entrenched in the French countryside in 1952, and also gave all-night parties in his magnificent place at Dorsay, not far from Marly-le-Roi.

But the most significant thing about the acquisition of their French properties by the Windsors was the tacit admission that they had now abandoned all thought of living in England.

Wallis does not allow this to trouble her. Worrying is left to the press, which at this time was deep in the discussion of the coronation of Queen Elizabeth II. In its anxiety to keep American democracy completely *au fait* with the etiquette of British Monarchy, the New York *Journal-American* informed its readers:

> If the Windsors lived in Britain he would be in the tiny knot of
> royalties. His wife would be relatively far down in the list of precedence
> ...It is believed here in London that the Duke will not live in England
> unless his wife is elevated to rank equal with him.

This is quite consistent with a report in the London press that the
Duke had let it be known that until his wife was accepted by the
Royal Family, he would not return to England. This may mean a
long wait—a very long wait.

So England is out, even as a temporary residence. The Duchess
just could not go around there as she does in the United States or in
France. For one thing, the London shops do not afford, to a lady of
her proclivities, the same scope as do those of Paris or New York. For
another, all the Windsor glamour would bewilder, to put it mildly,
a nation which is wondering whether to wash with the soap or eat it.
"It's all because of that woman," commented one bitter Briton,
quite forgetting the word "Fate." He added that the Duchess shows
her charitable side only to jewelers and dressmakers.

But if the Windsor legend is not much appreciated in Great
Britain, the same cannot be said of international society, where, after
all, the Windsors are happiest. Some time ago the Romeo and Juliet
division of the New York *Daily News* carried a touching note:

> "Divorce for the Duke and Duchess is absolutely unthinkable," said
> a French countess who knows the Windsors well. "They have been
> through so much for each other, and have made such terrific sacrifices
> that they could never dream of leaving each other."

This comment was provoked by those recurring divorce rumors
about the interesting couple which time has long since disproved.
And the obtaining of their French homes has served to show how
firmly cemented is the union of the Duke and the Duchess.

United States admirers of the ducal pair wondered uneasily if Paris,
rather than the Waldorf Tower, would be in the future their principal
stopover. The Windsors, however, make it their business to rediscover
America each year, there to enjoy the sovereignty denied them elsewhere. For as Cholly Knickerbocker, the famous syndicated columnist,
so happily expresses it: "The Duke and Duchess of Windsor rule the
clique of American millionaires."

And all of a sudden, the clique of American millionaires received
a further ray of hope from Miss Elsa Maxwell who came to their

rescue with a sensational statement—she said in her October 18, 1952 *Journal-American* column that the Duchess changed her mind about the Paris house: the Windsors are not going to buy it after all. Far too expensive. This bit of news to the careful readers of "Elsa's Log" seemed rather inconsistent; for in her previous reports Miss Maxwell assured them that the house had already been paid for, architects, masons and plumbers were busy rebuilding it, and that the Duchess had already started decorating it. Obviously, Miss Maxwell's latest manifesto on the subject had to be checked, and a person very close to her and to the Windsors had to be interrogated. When it was put to this nobleman that according to the "Log" the Paris deal fell through, he commented with a wink: "That's what Elsa says." And after a while he added: "She can only say what she is told. Besides, there was too much publicity about that Paris house, purchase price and everything. Now and then even the Windsors realize that what people don't know doesn't hurt them."

27

A King's Ransom

*The art of getting rich consists not in industry, much
less in saving, but in a better order, in timeliness, in
being at the right spot.*
—EMERSON: *The Conduct of Life*

We often buy money very much too dear.
—THACKERAY: *Barry Lyndon*

IN THESE times, when practically the whole world has to fret
about finances, one may find vicarious pleasure in contemplating the
fortunes of two people who have had few money troubles.

Until recently—for on May 22, 1952, the New York *Daily Mirror*
carried a headline: "Windsor Off to Beg Queen 'Be Generous.' "

The Queen, of course, was Elizabeth II of England. During her
father's lifetime, Windsor enjoyed an income of around $70,000 given
him by his brother; but with the death of George VI, this allowance
was in danger and might be cut off. For six months after a Sovereign's
demise a new Civil List is presented to Parliament, where a special
commission goes over the figures of the Royal expenditure very
carefully.

Reported the *Daily Mirror*, under the "begging" headline:

> It has been rumored in Palace circles that King George's Royal
> Codicil, which assured Windor's life-time stipend, cannot be found.
> The Duke was said to have appealed to the Earl of Clarendon, Lord
> Chancellor, to intercede with the Queen, and also to his mother,
> Queen Mary. Both were quoted as being reluctant to interfere "with
> the wishes of the new monarch."

The wishes of the Queen are not the only factors in the case. For
though successive Monarchs fall heirs to immense wealth in the form
of such things as, say the royal palaces, the Crown jewels, and the

great art collection housed in Windsor Castle, yet these cannot be regarded as their absolute personal property. They are a trust, to be enjoyed and then handed down even as they were received. And they are not sources of income.

Some idea of the wealth accruing to the Crown can be gained from figures published at the time of the accession of Edward VIII in the year 1936. At that time the royal residences—Buckingham Palace, Windsor Castle, Sandringham, Balmoral, St. James' Palace, and Fort Belvedere—were valued at £5-million. The Crown jewels were worth £700,000, and the pictures at Windsor £1-million. Beside this, the royal library was valued at £400,000, and the stamp collection of George V at £450,000. The superb service of gold plate used at Buckingham Palace banquets, with places for a thousand people, would be worth £2-million on the open market.

Then of course there are various items of royal freehold property, which belong to the Sovereign personally. They include the New Gallery Theatre, Her Majesty's Theatre, the Holborn and the Criterion restaurants, and the Carlton Hotel. Besides this list, there are such investments at Carlton House Terrace, the south side of Piccadilly Circus, Regent Street; and properties in such London boroughs as Finchley, Hampstead, and Dalston. Moreover, a fraction of every penny dropped in the slots of the public lavatories in London parks goes to the Queen.

Nor are the royal holdings confined to London: throughout Great Britain certain greenhouses, vineyards, swimming pools, even pubs and resort hotels belong to Her Majesty. The Crown Lands, excluding the Duchies of Lancaster and Cornwall, total a half-million acres.

All these English possessions are looked after by a Mr. Osmund Somers Cleverly, the Permanent Commissioner of Crown Lands, who works for Her Majesty in an old-fashioned office near the London Zoo. But overseas investments may receive the personal super-intendence of Queen Elizabeth herself. She owns, for instance, a nice little slice of New York: there is a twenty-two-story building right opposite the Public Library on 42nd Street, Number 501 Fifth Avenue, of which "the most high and mighty princess" is landlady.

So the income of an English Sovereign, and of members of the Royal Family generally, is derived from his or her private fortune, as well as from the Civil List.

The reigning Monarch of England is the quasi-sacred being who embodies and carries on the tradition which is the lifeblood of the country. But he, or she, is also a salaried official. This state of affairs dates from the reign of America's old "friend" George III. Before George's time the King "lived of his own," that is, from the income he, as an independent owner, derived from his own lands. George III was willing to hand over the revenue from these Crown Lands to Parliament in exchange for a fixed income: the Civil List. And every Monarch since has, upon accession, placed these revenues at the disposal of the House of Commons, requesting that the House vote upon the Civil List. This falls into two parts, one providing for the official expenses of the Crown, the other for the personal income of the various members of the Royal Family.

Therefore, when the new Civil List was debated in August 1952, the Duke of Windsor must have been looking anxiously toward Buckingham Palace as well as toward Her Majesty's Palace of Westminster (to give the Houses of Parliament their proper title).

However, to judge by recent reports, his anxiety cannot have been of long continuance. As the Duke has bought one house in France at a reported cost of 30-million francs and leased another for nine years, it seems safe to conclude that his income is secured. No doubt this is due to the filial piety of Queen Elizabeth II, who is willing to continue her father's generosity from her devotion to his memory.

The Duke's happy position in respect of finance contrasts sharply with that of another member of the Royal Family: Princess Marina Duchess of Kent. In 1942, the Duke of Kent was killed in a flying accident during a journey undertaken in fulfilment of his wartime duties. The income of £35,000 which he had enjoyed during life ceased with his death, and his widow and family were left to depend, not on what they received by right, but on what was given them by the kindness of King George VI. This prompted one Conservative Member of Parliament, Mr. Astor, to ask, during the 1952 discussion of the Civil List, that Her Royal Highness should be granted two-thirds of her late husband's income during her widowhood. Mr. Astor was moved by the spirit of chivalry, no doubt; but he fully justified his plea by pointing out that the Duchess of Kent took a full share in the public life of the country, and everyone knew of the great work she had done.

This debate followed upon Queen Elizabeth II's formal surrender, to the House of Commons, of the revenues of the Crown Lands. The Crown usually receives back about half the value of what is thus given up, for the Commons are always reluctant to part with money.

There was, for instance, loud and not always kind discussion of the sum to be paid to Prince Albert: Queen Victoria asked for £50,000 and he was given £30,000. Victoria herself, at a later time in her reign, came under fire: a pamphlet was published with the title: "What Does She Do With It All?"

And certain criticisms were made in the debate following upon Her Majesty's, Elizabeth II's, message to her faithful Commons of 1952:

> The demise of the Crown renders it necessary that renewed provision shall be made for the Civil List. Her Majesty places unreservedly at the disposal of the House of Commons those hereditary revenues which were so placed by her predecessor and has commanded that the papers necessary for full consideration of the subject shall be laid before the House . . .
> Her Majesty recommends consideration of these several matters to her faithful Commons and relies on their attachment to her person and Family to adopt such measures as may be suitable for the occasion.

Queen Elizabeth did not mention any figures; but she asked that provision should be made for His Royal Highness, the Duke of Edinburgh; for Princess Margaret, in the event of her marrying, for any future wife of the Duke of Cornwall, and for any royal children other than the Duke of Cornwall. (The Duchy of Cornwall, that valuable—and exceedingly beautiful and romantic—county, brings in about £90,000, about $250,000 a year, but this does not mean that the Duke of Cornwall receives $250,000 a year.)

Queen Elizabeth II has also asked the Commons to consider that the Duke of Cornwall's future wife must be provided for. But in the years that must pass before any marriage can take place, and during the Duke's minority, the revenues of the Duchy will, as to the greater part, be applied "in relief of the charge for Her Majesty's Civil List." And again, if these revenues become vested in the Queen—which would happen only if Prince Charles were to die—the whole income of the Duchy will be so applied.

This proposed use of a part, or the whole, accruing income "in relief of the Civil List" means, in plain language, that Queen Elizabeth is asking the Commons for less money than she might otherwise request; in other words, she is following the example of her father and grandfather, and attempting to lighten the taxpayer's burden.

In England, the thrifty habits of the Royal Family are matter of common knowledge. During the great depression of 1929 and onward,

King George V and Queen Mary went over their accounts, and then handed back to the nation quite a nice little sum. George VI too was exceedingly careful with the country's money. Similarly, it is reported that the Duke of Edinburgh wishes to close Sandringham House, the Royal Family's country home during the winter and at Christmas.

The Duke of Edinburgh, however, is not the only one to have considered closing royal homes. Certain Socialist Members of Parliament criticized not only the sums to be paid to the Royal Family, but also their maintenance of such places as Buckingham Palace, Balmoral and Holyrood. One of these Socialists, Mr. Emrys Hughes, argued that there would be a huge public opinion in London in favor of making "Buck House" into flats. He was promptly answered by his fellow-Socialist, Mr. Gaitskell:

> I think there would be far more people absolutely horrified. One has only to go and see the people standing outside Buckingham Palace.

And as he also pointed out, the popularity of the Royal Family is one of England's great assets.

The Civil List was eventually granted in a total sum of £475,000 ($1,235,000), which includes a "contingencies provision," i.e., a sum put aside for a rainy day. And from this total of £475,000, Her Majesty must pay: Salaries of H.M. Household and Retired Allowances; Expenses of H.M. Household; Royal Bounty, Alms and Special Services—as well as the expenses of the Privy Purse.

The difficult business of dealing with the Queen's accounts is in the capable hands of Sir Ulick Alexander, Keeper of the Privy Purse since 1936.

Besides the items listed above, the Civil List also provided £70,000 a year for the late Queen Mary and a similar sum for the Queen Mother Elizabeth. Princess Margaret receives £6,000 a year. This is not too much, but probably this tightening of the purse strings was meant to act as a gentle persuader, for the moment she marries the sum will be increased to £15,000 ($42,000). The Duke of Gloucester presumably continues to get £35,000 ($98,000)—as he did during the reign of his brother, the late George VI—and the Princess Royal £6,000 ($16,800).

As the London press pointed out when the question of royal incomes first came under review, there was no mention of the Duke of Windsor in Her Majesty's message to the House of Commons. It is true that from the "contingencies provision" some £25,000 ($70,000) is available, but from this sum come the unavoidable expenses of other members of the Royal Family for whom no other provision has been made. This Parliamentary phraseology covers quite a number of people, so the Duke's $70,000 cannot come from this source.

Besides members of the Royal Family, some one hundred eighty other persons receive pensions from the Civil List. In 1951 they received a total of £32,671 (nearly $92,000)—a very modest sum, when one considers that, first, many pensioners get less than £100 a year, and second, that these pensions are granted to persons who have made distinguished contributions to science, art and literature. So that the Civil List pensions represent a gesture, on the part of the Sovereign and the Lords and Commons in council assembled, in recognition of learning and the graces of life. For this reason the discussion of Civil List pensions is always interesting to the Commons, and in 1952 they willingly agreed to raise the ceiling on them, from £2,500 ($7,000) to £5,000 ($14,000). However, it is not likely that even the publication of *A King's Story* will secure the placing of its author's name on the list of pensioners.

Eventually the Civil List of 1952 was carried after a number of Socialist "amendments" had been heavily defeated. This was what might have been expected: when in 1937 the sum of £410,000 was voted to George VI certain Labor M.P.'s opposed the grant, arguing that His Majesty must learn to economize. But their opposition was unsuccessful, perhaps because a majority of the faithful Commons felt that the Royal Family had nothing to learn on that score.

In any case, a time soon came when everybody had to cut down spending, whether they liked it or not; there was very little to buy except rations, War Bonds and Savings Certificates. And four years after the war, King George was still receiving, for his various expenses, precisely the sum he had been granted in 1937, twelve years earlier: £410,000. Prices had skyrocketed, but not the royal income.

In 1945 a change of Government took place. A Labor Government dispossessed Churchill, and the Members of Parliament who had once been so anxious for the King to economize, began their own reign by voting themselves an increase in salary.

In spite of this, a spirit of economy persisted in high places. But when it became known that Princess Elizabeth might have an austerity wedding, with the Guards attending in khaki battle-dress instead of scarlet, there was public protest. It was remarked that recently the Brigade of Guards had been employed, in full-dress uniform, to make the movie "An Ideal Husband." Why should not Princess Elizabeth have at least as much splendor as Sir Alexander Korda or Mr. Arthur Rank? The King acceded to the public wish, and the nation's daughter had a splendid wedding. It is probable that the film made of this occasion paid for any expense connected with the Guards' uniform several times over.

But whatever the social and economic success of the wedding, the need for economy went on; and when Mr. Churchill returned to office in 1951, he showed his awareness of the nation's danger by cutting his own and his fellow-Ministers' salaries—indeed, one Cabinet Minister gave up his salary altogether.

But the press did not then, or ever, report the Duke of Windsor as giving up part of the money he receives from Great Britain. As he does not live in his native England, but in foreign countries, he is not required to pay British income tax; and as his income is not derived from the United States, he presumably does not pay American income tax. At present rates, he would, were he a private person, pay in England some 90 percent of his income in taxes: for nobody in England today, outside of the Royal Family, is permitted to have more than $16,000 a year.

As a member of the Royal Family, the Duke would in fact not pay income tax. Though even if he did, this would not go far to rescue his country from the bankruptcy which now threatens it; a threat which drew from Mr. Churchill, in the summer of 1952, the grave warning:

> England is standing on a treacherous trapdoor . . . In all history there has never been a community so large, so complex, so sure of its way of life, poised at such a dizzy eminence and on so precarious a foundation.

There have been quite a few versions of the fortune and income of the former King of England and his wife. Calculations of their money have been appearing in the press ever since the abdication. One newspaper had it that Windsor inherited $4-million from Queen Victoria, another newspaper said that this inheritance only came to $2-million. The wills of British royalty are never probated, so the private fortune of the Duke of Windsor, inherited from his grandfather, grandmother, great-grandmother, and now from his mother, will perhaps never be known in detail to the general public. It is certain, however, that these Monarchs and their consorts were very wealthy, and that the apple of their eye has not been disinherited.

The Duke's father left money to all the members of his family except his eldest son. For Edward, said George V, would receive the largest allowance from the Civil List, and also the revenues of the Duchy of Cornwall. Of course, upon abdicating, Edward gave up all rights in the Civil List, forfeiting also any claim upon the Duchy of Cornwall, which is an appanage of the Crown, and therefore was vested in George VI immediately upon Edward's abdication.

The bargaining in 1936 must have been quite sharp. This is how *Time* reported one phase of the financial "negotiations" of Edward VIII and Baldwin:

> ... In the cursing, mind-changing rage of the Sovereign, books were flung as well as epithets of embarrassing virility ... Much of the dispute was about money, and at least once His Majesty took back a verbal proffer of abdication when he found that he would not receive for life the $500,000 annual revenue of the Duchy of Cornwall. * In the evening he expressed regret that he had abdicated earlier that day ...
>
> (December 20, 1938)

Mr. Churchill told Baldwin that a former King of England must have a sufficient income abroad in order to uphold the dignity of the Crown and country; at least, so ran the reports. Mr. Baldwin thereupon went to work, sounding out the Cabinet and the House of Commons on a proposal to give the Duke of Windsor an allowance sanctioned by Parliament. He was strongly discouraged. So he sought an audience with George VI, and suggested an allowance out of the family income. Yet in his book the Duke attacks Mr. Baldwin.

Time later reported (May 24, 1937) that a marriage settlement gave the Duke and Duchess of Windsor $500,000 from the private funds of the Royal Family, and in addition an annual income of $100,000 each. In the United States this was believed until February 20, 1938, when the nearly infallible New York *Times* wrote on the matter of the Windsors' finances:

> Although they often complain about money, the Windsors are quite well off. They received a lump sum of about £900,000 in consideration of the transfer to King George of Sandringham and Balmoral, which their father had left to the Duke in his will. The Duke receives an annuity of £25,000, so his total income is about £56,000 a year.

*This was the value of the income from the Duchy at 1936 rates of exchange.

Janet Flanner, an exceedingly careful reporter, whose statements are never refuted, ten years ago estimated the Duke's private fortune —which had nothing to do with this annual income from the Royal Family—at £1-million, that is $5-million as the pound stood then. The Duke is said to have settled on the Duchess before his marriage some £300,000, but upon reviewing the sorry state of his finances, Wallis allegedly tore up this settlement in exchange for a new one of £100,000. It was about this time that the Duke was reported to have said: "I don't wish Wallis to have an end like that of Lady Hamilton."

The "sorry state" of the Duke's affairs may have been due to the fact that he began his reign with generous gifts, and had even mortgaged his future income. Shortly after the abdication *Time* noted that the bills contracted by the former King were being rapidly settled by the Government.

Of course interest in the Windsors' private affairs did not end either in 1937, or with the *Mirror's* account on the Duke's financial pilgrimage in 1952. Shortly after the purchase of the Duchess' new home was made known to the wide circle of Windsor-lovers by Elsa Maxwell, a story was circulated to the effect that the furnishing of this house would not make any very great hole in the ducal coffers. Jimmy Donahue's mother, Mrs. Jessie Donahue, has hoped for an opportunity to manifest her gratitude. When she heard of the new house, ran the story, she begged to be allowed to decorate Her Grace's bedroom at her own expense. Her generous example fired others: Mrs. Margaret Thompson Schulze Biddle, the mining heiress who makes her home in Paris, promptly made a like offer. So, if the tale were true, it seemed that the Windsors would be saved the ordinary couples' worry about purchasing furniture on the instalment plan.

Within a couple of days, however, the story was denied. Mrs. Biddle had given Wallis a picture, and from this one small gift had sprouted the legend of Mrs. Donahue and Mrs. Biddle each arriving with, so to speak, her own moving van.

The denial pointed out that, quite apart from any other consideration, the Duchess is herself a gifted interior decorator, with much practice; so that she would wish to do her own furnishing and decorating. She can afford to.

Apart from the French acquisitions, the Duke has some landed property—a ranch in Calgary, Canada (managed since 1951 by the Canadian Pacific). Some time ago oil was struck on the adjoining properties. The Socony Vacuum Company of the United States had already made oil tests on the Windsor ranch, but until now no liquid gold has gushed up from the ground. But it is reported that Socony Vacuum will continue drilling because there is a possibility of finding oil here, so near to other gushing wells. A lucky strike would make the Windsors tremendously wealthy. At any rate, they are not going to lose much by trying. In most cases the expenses of drilling for oil are partly footed by the Government. And no doubt the Duchess bears in mind that she could buy many beautiful jewels with even a tiny trickle of oil.

The 4,300-acre ranch doesn't serve any apparent purpose anyhow. When the Duke of Windsor, as Prince of Wales, bought the place, he was going to breed the finest livestock on a grandiose scale; but in the spring (when as a rule domestic animals give birth) of 1950, there were only eight new Windsor calves.

The Duchess visited the beautiful Calgary ranch twice in ten years, but she was not at first favorably impressed with the twelve-room ranch house. The last time the Windsors were there, in April 1950, she commented that she found the house looking better than she had expected. To other people, with less exacting tastes, it appears very charming.

Coming to the United States end of finances, it is presumed that here the Duke pays income tax on certain items. Reputedly he received $1-million for his memoirs. According to the Margaret Mitchell Act, very justly an author cannot be taxed like an ordinary wage earner. Writing is not ordinary work, an author may carry the seeds of a masterpiece in his brain for three years, eventually sitting down and writing it in a few months. Mrs. Mitchell in fact took ten years to write *Gone with the Wind*.

So this humane Margaret Mitchell Act allows the author of a book three years to spread his taxes on his major opus. The Duke accordingly takes care to mention in his autobiography that it took him three years of hard work to produce his book.

If the Duke paid his taxes after this reputed $1-million had accrued, as presumably he did, the money should have dwindled down to around $180,000. However, it may be that in his case the capital gain tax was applied, in which case he only paid capital gain tax, a much smaller sum, as a one-book man.

The original manuscript of the first part of the memoirs, which appeared in *Life* magazine, was generously offered by the Duke to the United Hospital Fund. Obviously this charitable organization just would not know what to do with the manuscript—to donate it to the library of one of the eighty-nine hospitals in New York City would serve but little purpose. Firstly, eager convalescent fingers would mark the historic pages beyond recognition in a matter of days; and secondly, there are many corrections and deletions on them which were put there by a royal hand, true, but which tend to slow up reading.

So the Duke stipulated that, after being exhibited at the august Knoedler Galleries, the manuscript must be bound in leather and auctioned off for the benefit of the United Hospital Fund. His liberal gesture was widely discussed, but apparently the auction has not yet taken place. In case the manuscript, complete with illuminations, ever comes under the hammer, it might fetch somewhat less than a Gutenberg Bible.

The Duke has always had a high regard for American business methods, and for a number of years he has been on friendly terms with financiers and important businessmen in this country. It is possible that these people, knowing the Duke's admiration for Big Business and for their own money-making ability, have given him pointers to judicious investments. It is not known if he has stocks and bonds or what they are, but it is reasonable to suppose that the commercial and industrial magnates who hobnob with the ducal pair would help the poor dears with a hint or two on how to turn an honest "buck." Making money is no crime. More power to him. As the saying is, money goes to money . . .

Of course, the Windsors are bound to cut down on spending somewhere, and this means that they are obliged to restrain their generous impulses where they would perhaps prefer to let them expand. In the town of Baltimore, for instance, a priest whose position enables him to speak with authority, remarked that during their visits there the wealthy Duke and his wife did not give a cent to charity. This leads one to ask how often their name is mentioned in connection with any charity or welfare organization. True, the Duke (as recounted elsewhere) once gave $100 to the Salvation Army, and thanks to a photographer the memorable occasion was recorded for posterity. And he and the Duchess were also photographed with Mrs. George F. Baker, studying plans for a benefit performance of *Darkness at Noon*. The proceeds of this performance were eventually given to refugees from Communist-dominated countries: but of course the money did not come out of the Windsors' pockets.

If ever the Windsors' pockets should empty, the Duchess might go to work. "Should Wives Work?" is hardly a debatable topic any longer, the working wife is so prominent a figure in the social landscape. About two years ago reports went round that Wallis was trying for a job the second time—she tried the first time, it will be remembered, in 1928.

On January 5, 1950 the London *News Review* ran a story that the Duchess of Windsor intended to collaborate with an important French couturier. Tired of being boycotted by the Royal Family and by the Court, she apparently felt that she might as well go into business. She later denied the accusation, but the British press insisted that the talks between her and a certain French dressmaking house were continuing.

Now no matter how ethereal the language of the French couturiers, theirs is an acutely keen business sense. Quite naturally they want to capture the vast American market. They sell their models for, say $1,500 each to the American couturiers, who bring these creations here, have them copied, and manufacture them in considerable quantities, to sell for, say $27.50.

The American modistes don't mind putting the money on the line for the superb handmade French gowns. But they hate the stiff United States customs duties on imported fineries. And they deplore the delay while the models are being appraised, and carefully evaluated, on this side of the ocean.

N'importe comment—the shrewd French dressmakers who approached the Duchess must have had an inkling that she enjoys the privileges of the Port of New York; that The Best-Dressed Woman in the World goes through customs without customs going through her, and that consequently the Duchess would be a most valuable asset in a billion-dollar business. Of course the wise Duchess of Windsor would never permit herself to be a tool in the hands of the cunning French dressmakers. And most probably this is the reason why the important job did not materialize.

There is a truly human touch about the Windsors' arrivals in the United States: it is a polite, civilized and benign point in State Department protocol that very highly placed persons may come in here as easily as the ordinary man stops at the corner bar for a drink.

Who said immigration authorities were slow? They work like magic! Of course, this country expects some reciprocity.

When some American at the Windsor level, for instance, arrives in England, passport officials and the customs people smile, salute and bow low. But how many American citizens rank with the Windsors? Only four names come to mind: those of ex-Presidents Hoover and Truman, Mrs. Coolidge and Mrs. Eleanor Roosevelt.

Mr. Hoover, who knows the inside of British courtrooms, would know better than to take more than a few cans of sardines and fruit juices with him. As for the ladies, the names of Mesdames Coolidge and Roosevelt have never appeared on the select list of The Ten Best-Dressed Women. As a matter of fact, Mrs. Roosevelt has been listed as one of the Ten Worst-Dressed Women in the World. It is not likely that these two serious-minded ladies would stand on their privileges at the English port of entry, and tease that sadly divested country by importing, say, the latest in lingerie.

British customs officials are very strict, particularly since all this nonsensical austerity started, and a Virginia ham has just as much difficulty in slipping past the inspectors' Argus eyes as a diamond engagement ring. That pretty little princess merely of the movies, Jean Simmons, found this out to her great dismay when she returned to her native England from Hollywood, proudly wearing the betrothal token of Stewart Granger on her finger. British customs insisted on her paying the duty on this modest bauble, a sort of necessary luxury, although she only came over for a brief visit to see her mama.

When O'Dwyer was Mayor of New York, just after World War II, he was visited by his sister from Ireland. On her return to the auld sod, this lady carried with her no fewer than one thousand pairs of nylon stockings. This proved to be a miscarriage—they were confiscated by the Irish Customs, who also heartlessly imposed a heavy fine.

The Duchess of Windsor would never be subjected to such awkwardness and unnecessary expense: she enjoys the full immunity. If the U. S. Customs look at her jewels or clothes it is only in sincere admiration.

So it is plain that she is well placed to bestow a double boon by a single act, or by entering into partnership with a couturier she would both help him to earn his living, and assist American women to make the best of themselves.

However, nothing more has been heard of this scheme, so presumably it fell through. But though the Duchess has not got her job, there need be no fear that the Windsors will ever experience privation. The Duchess will never have to use butter on her face instead of cold cream; neither will the Duke be forced to exchange his fragrant Havana for a ten-cent cigar . . .

Conquering heroes in ancient Rome were satisfied with a laurel wreath, a bust, a chariot, six horses, an earthenware pot complete with frankincense and myrrh to burn in it, a bull for sacrifice, and a new toga. Around $3,000 all told in today's money.

But times change. Prices go up. The modern conqueror of "the woman I love" had to hold out for more than peanuts. Probably no one except the Windsors and their financial advisers know the exact amount. One of the bankers of the Royal Family is the very private and exclusive banking house of Coutts in London. It would be more difficult to get a word from Coutts as to the Windsors' finances than to slip into Fort Knox and make that gold talk.

Of course there is one question which even Coutts may not be able to answer. Even the Windsors can't take it with them. So, who will inherit their fortune? Perhaps the poor for whom the Duke, when Prince of Wales, was said to have cared quite a bit . . .

There have been kings and queens famous for their patronage of learning and for their charity. Henry VI founded Eton as a place of learning for poor scholars who could not pay for their own schooling, a use to which it has in part reverted. The eleventh-century St. Margaret, Princess of Hungary and Queen of Scotland, received the poor in her castle courtyard, and with her own hands washed and bandaged their sores.

Now it is not suggested that the Duke and the Duchess of Windsor should proceed to the Bowery, there to delouse the unfortunates. *Autres temps, autres moeurs.* The straightforward fraternizing of rich and poor, as characteristic of the Middle Ages as darker things, does not suit this age: the Foundation has, in the field of humanitarian endeavor, to a certain extent taken the place of the monastery. Perhaps a Windsor Foundation will perpetuate—and palliate—the memory of the Greatest Love Match of the Century.

28

Gems and Gowns

*A modest woman, dressed out in all her finery, is the
most tremendous object of the whole creation.*
—OLIVER GOLDSMITH: *She Stoops to Conquer*

THE cost of maintaining the role of The Best-Dressed Woman
in the World cannot be negligible. The Duchess of Windsor buys
about one hundred dresses each year, and this alone must represent
an expenditure of around $100,000. For while some of the gowns
may cost a mere $400, some others set her back over $2,000.

This figure of $100,000 does not include furs, hats, shoes, lingerie,
gloves, stockings, girdles or other accessories, necessary luxuries; and
obviously no jewelry.

In the last year or so, the Duchess bought very little jewelry.
Members of the firm of Cartier have been heard to express regret
about this; and when asked if the Duchess still borrows jewels for an
important soirée as she has done in the past, their sad sigh is
unanimous and resounding: "We wish she would! Our trade knows
no better manner of advertising."

The Duchess of Windsor does not need to buy or borrow any
more jewelry. Ever since she met the Prince of Wales, some two
decades ago, one of her principal hobbies has been collecting baubles.
Appropriately enough, a favorite piece is a beautiful pin representing
the Prince of Wales' feathers: the famous badge of three ostrich
plumes which has been the insignia of so many princes. (The plumes
were originally displayed by King John of Bohemia; then they were
adopted by the Black Prince, who wore them at the Battle of Crécy;
and he left a will ordering that the plumes, with the motto, Peace,
Jousts, and Tournaments, be placed on his tomb.) In this pin, upon
pliant stalks of precious metal, diamonds of the purest water are set
in so realistic a representation of frond-like, gracefully curling plumes,
that feathers seem to have become jewels, gaining luster while keeping
airy lightness. The three plumes are banded together by a miniature

Prince of Wales crown. This wonderful jewel, a remembrance of things past, was made for the Duchess by Van Cleef and Arpels, Paris branch. She wears it as casually as the girls of New York wear their costume jewelry, on the right lapel of the suit.

Probably the most valuable piece in her possession is the diamond known to naughty newshawks and their readers as "Dookess's Big Ice." This stone is a little less than one-half the weight of the famed Koh-i-noor, "the Mountain of Light," adorning the State Crown of the Queen of England. The Koh-i-noor weighs 106 1/6 carats, the "Big Ice" some fifty carats only, but in its perfect color, clarity and cut it may truly be called a royal gem.

The Duchess rarely wears this stone. Back in the days of World War II, the Windsors, while on a visit to the United States from the Bahamas, were invited by the president of one of the largest automobile companies to see a film upon the firm's war effort. The Duchess' immense diamond sparkled brilliantly in the darkened room. Next morning the New York papers reported this bright news alongside melancholy war bulletins in a silly, chiding, even intolerant fashion, and ever since Her Grace has been very circumspect in exhibiting her solitaire.

Sapphires are among the Duchess' favorite colored stones. Naturally, for they match her eyes, and she has the most valuable Kashmir stones, beautifully cut and set, of a delicate cornflower blue, which under changing lights may fluctuate from ultramarine through indigo to violet, varying like the color of their wearer's eyes. Her set of rubies is worthy of the gorgeous East whence they come: for the best rubies are found in Burma and Ceylon, and obviously only the best are good enough for the Duchess.

Aquamarines also find a place in Wallis' jewel box. And she simply cannot resist emeralds, which are her birthstone—June—according to the ancient calendar. Modern almanacs have complicated the matter by assigning to this month pearls and moonstones; but the Duchess solves the problem with her usual aplomb: she has sets of all three.

In short, Wallis has an assemblage of jewelry for every day of the week, so that her gems may be perfectly matched with her gowns. Fashion demands accord of dress and adornment; and it is of course attention to such minute detail which has won for the Duchess her title of "The Best-Dressed Woman in the World" for ten years in succession.

Unfortunately superstition has deprived her of one stone. The playful, varying, rainbow tint of opals would seem especially suited to express the "complex, elusive" personality (to use the Duke's words) of the Duchess of Windsor; but they are said to bring bad luck, and she had therefore to banish them from her collection.

Formerly she disliked pearls: "I am not the pearl type," she told friends; and indeed the dreamlike beauty of "the dew of the Sea" might seem not wholly suited to her quality of decisiveness. But there are pearls and pearls: the most unusual though not the costliest are, strange as it may seem, those which lack the rondure, or the pear shape, of the perfect pearl. The so-called baroque pearls are not the most valuable yet the Duchess' three-row necklace of perfectly matched, oblong baroque pearls is probably worth not less than $25,000. She has also single string necklaces of cultured baroque pearls bought at Hattie Carnegie's. She often wears her pearls with a tweed or woolen suit; materials which form an excellent background for another favored ornament (with, of course, matching pearl earrings), a pair of medallions. Their rich, gem-circled color of purest gold finely contrasts with the quiet beauty of the necklace. These medallions account for another $6,000 or $7,000 of Wallis' pin money; and as one must save on something, the simple woolen suit is priced at the nonprohibitive sum of $600. A good investment, for it may last a season.

But the diamond, the queen of gems, is the best investment. So it must not be supposed that the "Big Ice" and the glittering plumes already described represent the Duchess' total subscription to De Beers. At a benefit at New York's Metropolitan Opera in 1952 Wallis appeared, rich as one of her own rubies, in an eye-filling dress of scarlet-red; and the socialites in the Diamond Circle were further electrified by the splendor of her Van Cleef and Arpels diamond tiara, a work of such subtlety and skill that, like the reversible Burberry coat, it can be worn in two ways: as a tiara and as a necklace. One of her several other famous tiaras was made by Cartier of pearls and diamonds.

Wallis Windsor does not need brilliant color to make her the cynosure of all eyes. In the spring of 1951, Dior created for her a ball dress of dull white satin; true, it was "embroidered as it were a mede." With such a robe elegance does not permit ostentation in jewelry; and so the Duchess wore, with this fairy garment—whose crystal broideries glittered like winter frost in sunlight—only earrings and a stiff diamond choker. Its subtle simplicity of line could not disguise the value—about $60,000.

The Duchess of Windsor has complete matching sets of jewels— emerald, topaz, onyx, turquoise, aquamarine. She never wears the same set twice in succession, but there are some jewels she never takes off: these are her charm bracelets, given to her by the Duke, with dangling bijoux carrying such legends as "To my Darling," "I will always love you," "My sweetheart," and so on. Little can be said about her rings, for most of the time she wears short gloves. But since her hands are not her best feature—and being a clever woman she knows this—presumably she does not wish to draw attention to them by the wearing of many rings.

While the Duchess is in New York the major part of the most valuable jewels are kept in the vaults at Cartier's, but some of them are always readily accessible in the Waldorf-Astoria's safe-deposit boxes.

Lately Wallis has become interested in old snuffboxes. The new hobby was encouraged by her young friend, Jimmy Donahue, who had quite a collection of eighteenth-century snuffboxes. The Duchess first admired, then acquired, some of the precious works of art of English and French goldsmiths; several of them extremely rare and of historic interest and artistic value, though their monetary worth is not great. One of these boxes, superbly chased and engraved, is said to have belonged to George IV: the hallmarks show that King's head and a figure of Britannia. This precious object was formerly in the possession of Terence Philip, a friend of the Windsors, who shortly before his death sold it to Mrs. Donahue, Jimmy's mother, for $2,000. And there are others equally attractive, one of them initialed by Edmé Pierre Balzac, the great French goldsmith. What use the Duchess has for this bric-a-brac, except as a feast for the eyes, is not clear; Dunhill's, the fashionable but traditionally minded tobacconists who still grate the stuff, have no record of either the Duke or the Duchess as customers for snuff.

The Windsors often visit the outstanding New York jewelers, the Duke browsing around at Cartier's—buying very little, and inexpensive knicknacks at that—and the Duchess spending quite some time at Harry Winston's fabulous "House of Winston," or at Van Cleef and Arpels, her favorite jewelers. The association with the latter firm, which may be called a sort of trade friendship, goes back a long time. When later, in the nineteen-forties, Wallis was criticized by the press for her continual buying of gems, her advisers became alarmed, and warned her that this was not the way to win the American public. So she let it be known, through friends, that her jewels were only borrowed, lent to her by Van Cleef and Arpels. This, the firm declared, was true in fact; adding that they would be happy to lend her a complete set of jewels to match every one of her new ensembles, not only because they were grateful for her recognition, but also because they, like Cartier, could not imagine a better business policy. It was also mentioned that the Duchess had recently spent with them $285,000.

Perhaps believing that the public was satisfied that her jewels were only lent, the Duchess showed a selection in 1944, at a newspaper dinner. But the New York *Evening Sun*, in its September 2, 1944 issue refused to accept this established fact, and ran an account with the following headlines: "Windsor's Lady Likes Jewels and Has Plenty." There was a description of "some of the Duchess' jewels," the writer remarking that her sapphires and rubies were the light of the party; adding that she wore them because, being about to enter a nursing home for an appendectomy, she could not know when such another occasion might occur.

Next to the art of Van Cleef and Arpels, and of Cartier's, Wallis likes that of Messrs. Schlumberger. This small but important firm is famed for its creation of Cellini-like pieces. But they are grieved to have to admit that the Duchess has never favored them with a purchase. On a dozen or so occasions she has paid a late afternoon visit to the shop, shown a hearty interest in the jewels, and, singling out one piece, or a whole set, has asked that it should be sent to her Waldorf-Astoria Tower home. Naturally her royal wish was complied with: the baubles were sent, along with a silent prayer that they would be bought. Invariably they were returned the next day. But they had served their purpose. Customers of Schlumberger's would call and ask if the piece they had seen the Duchess wearing was the firm's work; and if so, was a similar piece available? It was.

The Duchess makes her really serious jewel purchases in Paris; on this the New York firms are agreed. There are several good reasons for this. First, of course, the exchange rate must be considered: precious objects cost less in francs (made in France) than in dollars; then the European jewelry-designing and hand-tooling art is on a much higher level than that of America; and thirdly, the Paris press is not as clever as that of New York in finding out such details. Moreover, a few years ago the finest jewelers of London and Paris got together and made a firm decision to stop lending their jewels to ladies, no matter how newsworthy. The practice had to be abandoned, because in Europe the flaunted baubles did not sell as easily as they do in America.

Some of the most beautiful jewels of the Duchess of Windsor formerly belonged to Queen Alexandra. The Duke inherited a part of these (while still King), purchased others from a London firm, who had had them for sale for a long time, and bought some for very advantageous prices in a Rue de Lafayette antique store in Paris. But these gems looked old-fashioned, and had to be reset; the work being done, most expertly, by the Paris branch of Cartier. After the abdication the press made various comments on these royal jewels, and *Time* magazine explained (in its February 15, 1937 issue) that the King's bill with Cartier—left behind for the Government to ponder over—came to $600,000, and that of this sum a substantial portion went to pay for the resetting of Queen Alexandra's precious stones for Mrs. Simpson.

A decade after her hasty exit in 1936, the Duchess returned with her husband to the "precious stone set in the silver sea." But her sojourn was once again an unhappy one. As they have no English home, the Windsors accepted the invitation of a friend; and shortly after their arrival at the borrowed house, the Duke visited London to dine with the King, his brother. The Duchess remained at home, dining with a feeling of perfect security in the land of law and order. Unfortunately this feeling was not wholly justified, for a pussyfoot thief had the audacity and skill to climb up to her bedroom and steal her jewelry. In the first excitement the loot was valued at a quarter-million dollars; this figure was later amended to $80,000, and at long last was correctly stated as only $25,000.

When later the Windsors came to America, ship reporters in New York harbor asked the Duke, during an interview, whether the Duchess had brought with her "the rest of her jewels." The Duke replied that there were not many of them left. Yet cool connoisseurs, experts in the precious stone business, who appraise ladies solely by their jewels, declared in 1950 that if she were ever up against it, the Duchess could pawn her collection without the least trouble for $1,500,000.

Formerly America boasted of two competing queens of diamonds, the late Miss Mabel Boll, and Miss Peggy Hopkins Joyce; but they have long been eclipsed by the Duchess of Windsor. To begin with, neither of them ever owned a gold bath—the Duchess, at one time in her Cap d'Antibes villa actually had a 22-carat gold bathtub. There again a thief was unable to resist temptation—the New York *Times* reported in its April 23, 1938, issue that "a burglar recently hacked a sizeable chunk out of the Duchess' gold bathtub."

Wallis weighs consistently around one hundred pounds, and she is the envy of all other ladies of her generation who cannot keep a slim silhouette. She keeps her figure by almost constant dieting and attention to the advice of her friend, Mr. Gayelord Hauser, the nutrition faddist. Of course, the daily massage helps, too. She has a perfect size 10 Tanagra figure, a little over five feet tall, with a 34″ bust, 25″ waist, 34″ hips measurements. Early in 1952 her light-brown hair was dyed a modified Titian red by her New York coiffeur, Monsieur Roger Vergne. This latter gentleman dresses the Duchess' hair (always parted in the middle) every evening at her apartment.

M. Vergne is a short, very distinguished looking, gray-haired man. It was natural therefore that when one evening, in 1951, he excitedly paced the corridor in front of the Duchess' room in a nursing home, the passersby should take him for some grieving royal relative. But he was merely there to dress the Duchess' hair for next morning's operation. Wallis could never bear the thought that anybody should see her except at her best.

But it is often left to another woman to appraise and describe realistically the looks of one of her own sex. Therefore, some lines from Miss Helen Worden's article on the Duchess (*American Mercury*, June 1944) may be quoted here:

> The Duchess gives the impression of terrific neatness, not a hair out of place, not a line awry. Her nose never shines. Her slip never shows. She looks like a period room done by a furniture house, a room in which nobody lives comfortably. Figuratively speaking, there are no ashes on her rugs, no papers lying around, no blinds askew. To give a real picture of the Duchess, I must describe her clothes. In them—it sounds harsh, but it is true—a large part of her personality resides. And she spares no effort to put it there. She has lost none of her flair for style. It has become her prime passion. She is proud to be called the best dressed woman in the world. It is a profession with her. She enjoys setting the style. She has launched many fashions. The vogue for high-necked evening gowns for example, may be traced directly to her—she wears them because of her flat-chested and boyish figure.

This may be quite an incisive, brief word-portrait, but the last sentence in it is inaccurate: nowadays the Duchess loves strapless evening dresses, and there is no longer evidence of a flat chest. She favors big-flared short skirts for the evening, for she likes to show her very shapely ankles. These dresses are usually of tulle in two different tones, with one part of the dress superbly embroidered. In the evening she often wears pretty sandals made by Italian or Spanish shoemakers; the inevitable gloves (lately also long ones reaching above her elbow); and a tiny purse for a compact and a lip rouge. Although she wears glasses at home for reading, she never carries these when going out. Now and then she sports a beautiful, tremendous ostrich fan, but this is only for special occasions, for big balls.

As to her collection of furs, that too is awe-inspiring—she owns full-length sable, ermine, mink and Russian broadtail coats and capes also short ermine, mink and broadtail jackets; countless neckpieces and other sundry fur pieces. She is very much attached to a unique suit of broadtail, made for her in 1950 by Maximilian, the famous New York furrier. This suit is of an easy cut, with a collar copied from a Chinese coolie's jacket, and with two small slanting pockets. Wallis wears this fur suit under a mink coat. In the season of 1951-52, she made only one purchase at Maximilian's, a blond otter coat, but she is said to have regretted her decision, because toward the end of the winter otter was no longer exclusive or expensive.

One is puzzled to know why she should buy so many furs, for she is not often exposed to severe weather: when she ventures abroad in New York the trip is usually short, a few minutes' drive to a restaurant or a party, and takes place in one of her special-bodied Cadillacs. She has two of these automobiles, one in New York, and the other in Paris, both made for her by General Motors Company from designs that follow the graceful lines of a Rolls-Royce town car. She employs an English chauffeur.

Her hats are always off-the-face, often halo-like, worn as incidental little things; they are practically invisible. "The less hat the better," says the Duchess. But this does not refer to numbers—she has been known to order forty-five at a time from the New York milliner, Florelle, and thirty-four at Mr. John's (at $100 per hat). These little nothings always sit snugly back on her head. As has been said before, she adores short doeskin gloves, which she very rarely takes off in public. (A notable exception to the rule was when she threw a glove to the Captain of the Black Dragoons at the Paris horse show in 1951.) Her shoes—she has rows of them—are the long-vamped pump type. She likes the handbags made by the American, Louis Coblentz. In 1951, she bought fifteen of these Coblentz bags in Paris to bring back to the United States. On being told that they are also on sale in every department store in America, she commented that the American copies are never as good as the French originals. Mr. Coblentz, the creator and manufacturer of the bags, was pained to see this in the gossip columns, for Wallis' comments on fashion are very influential.

Although she much prefers the dressmakers in Paris, the Duchess does patronize a few American houses. Her principal designer in New York is Mainbocher. She also goes sometimes to a showing at Hattie Carnegie's. Not long ago out of fifty Carnegie dresses paraded before her by mannequins, she picked 13 in about as many minutes. These particular gowns started at $450 and up. This was only a portion of the Duchess' purchases during that season (spring 1951): she also bought 15 suits designed by Mr. Castillo at Elizabeth Arden's, a few originals at Sophie Gimbel's Custom Shop, and presumably some things at Mainbocher's, for this designer is always first on the list. As the reader already knows, the Duchess donated her Mainbocher wedding dress to a fashion museum in New York. The favorite Paris dressmakers, where she buys far more extensively than in New York include Balenciaga, Jacques Fath, Dior, Balmain, Dessés, and Grès.

While in New York, she seldom goes to fashion shows, public or private; her appearance at the Carnegie showing was quite unusual. As a rule, the dressmakers send their new creations to the Duchess, and she selects at home. In Paris she does go to the showings of the fashion giants; but neither in New York nor in Paris does she go for the fittings. This important session always takes place at the Duchess' house, whether in Paris, New York, or Palm Beach. Fortunately, most dressmakers have on hand a plaster torso of the Duchess' figure, and some of the fittings can be done in their workshop.

When some of the more important corrections must be attended to on the Duchess' person, the saleslady who assisted her in buying the clothes from a particular *maison*, accompanied by a fitter, brings them over. All designers are agreed that no one knows more about gowns and their details than the Duchess, and that while she is being fitted, Wallis offers valuable suggestions. But she and the two other ladies do not long remain alone—the Duke often joins them, and sitting in on these fashion conferences, he also gives advice as to the raising or lowering of a hemline, doing away with a frill here or there, making a sleeve shorter or longer. After the representatives of the dressmaker have finished their job, the Duke, with great courtesy, helps with tying up their parcels. And when the girls throw away some string, he picks it up and puts it in his pocket. "I save strings," he says with a little smile, "one never knows when one may need them."

Obviously all the Duchess' lingerie is handmade, mostly in Paris. However, even in New York she is always on the lookout for that little out-of-the-way lingerie shop which produces the ultimate in underthings. Once she heard about such a unique place, on West 57th Street. She telephoned the proprietress, a recently arrived French-woman, asking her to bring her collection to the Waldorf-Astoria. The Frenchwoman politely refused. A lady who was in the shop when this telephone conversation took place, was aghast. "I should think you would find it a great honor to serve the Duchess," she said. The proprietress replied that it was an honor she could not afford.

Her firm attitude was typical of Paris, where the wizards of fashion are much concerned with finances; and where people do not scrape before royalty. But she may also have been conditioned by rumors in the highest Parisian lingerie circles; years ago the Duchess ordered some beautiful linen sheets at the famous Maison Porthault, and specified that they should be embroidered with the unicorn and the rampant lion. The owner of this luxurious shop, Mme. Madeleine Porthault, has often been confronted with odd demands by elegant women, like spraying sheets with flowers, appliqueing butterflies, and scalloping ornate monograms, but never before had she been asked to embroider a royal coat of arms on bedding. However, the unusual order was carried out with the customary excellence of this great firm. But for some reason or other the Duchess refused to accept the sheets, and presumably they are still in the possession of the Maison Porthault. Perhaps someone told Wallis that coats of arms are somewhat eccentric on sheets.

Some other tradespeople behave in the same irritating way as the Parisian lady. For instance, a very well-known New York furrier said that he would rather not sell to the Duchess because he is not pre-pared to give special prices. For Wallis, just like every woman, wel-comes bargains. Some time back she went to Bronzini's, the New York haberdashers, and admired a man's weekend case. She asked the clerk for its price, and when she heard it emitted a little "Oh!" Later the same day, her secretary rang up the shop and asked for the name of the manufacturer of the weekend case. This information was supplied. She then telephoned the manufacturer, mentioned her name, and ordered one of the cases to be sent to her directly—of course, at the wholesale price.

In connection with fashion, the Duchess was recently quite annoyed with two American magazines. One was *Time*, sister magazine of *Life* which ran *A King's Story* in its serial form. *Time*, in the Duchess' eye, committed two almost unpardonable mistakes—they printed her picture (in the June 4, 1951 issue) next to that of Mrs. Henry Ford II, both wearing the same Mainbocher suit! And the Duchess disliked this other item in that magazine (September 25, 1950), because of the direct quotes:

> "I love shopping for something simple at Dior's," confessed the perennially best-dressed Duchess of Windsor. "It's like looking for a needle in a haystack. But you know, I'm not particularly interested in clothes. I'm far more interested in housekeeping."

She has said to friends that such publicity is not helpful to her, because it contains an undertone, and that *Time* especially ought to be more delicate in the accounts about her. Likewise, she was very much put out by her favorite magazine, *The New Yorker*, when this latter periodical in a January 1952 issue, referred to her in its editorial (commenting on her title, "The Best-Dressed Woman in the World") as "the old duchess." She was certain that this ugly remark got into the magazine because Mr. Harold Ross, the editor, with whom she was acquainted, was no longer alive, and she had no other champion on *The New Yorker*.

Sometimes, in other press organs, the Duchess is severely criticized in connection with her hobbies, jewels and dressing. Once there were rather serious repercussions in England. That was when the Duke was the Governor General of the Bahamas. In the House of Commons an M.P. interpellated His Majesty's Secretary for the Colonies—"Is the Secretary aware of the bitter comment being made in the United States regarding the visit of the Governor of the Bahamas, the Duke of Windsor, and his wife? And more especially with regard to the ostentatious display of jewelry and finery at a period when the people of this country are strictly rationed, and if so, will he make representations to the Prime Minister [*who was then the Right Hon. Winston*

Churchill] to have this gentleman and his wife recalled from this Government post?"

The Secretary for the Colonies was not present to explain the Government's attitude on the matter, and in his absence, the Under Secretary, Mr. G. H. Hall, replied in an eloquent sentence: "No, sir, the Colonial Secretary's attention has not been called to the matter referred to." The M.P. with the embarrassing question sat back on his bench; whether with a frustrated expression or not is not recorded; neither is data available showing if the matter was further pursued in the Commons, or no.

The Duke of Windsor, however, denied the implied accusation at once. Back at his post in Nassau, he issued the following terse statement from Government House:

1. Only four writers made unfavorable comment about the Duke and the Duchess on their recent trip in the United States.

2. A "private survey" (sic.) showed more than 80 per cent of the United States press favorable. (*To the Windsors.*)

3. The unfriendly writers emphasized the quantity of luggage needed for the Windsor trip, ignoring that it was for the entire party and not for the Duke and Duchess alone.

4. The Duchess went shopping in New York at only one store, and that one operated by the Red Cross.

The Governor General's official communication—duly recorded in the world's press through the facilities of the wire services—must have made the troublesome M.P. change his mind; he must have regretted his hastiness in allowing himself to be influenced by those four hostile writers before he had ascertained the precise facts from the best source—the Duke of Windsor. It was regrettable also that this M.P. heeded newspaper accounts telling the world that the Duchess of Windsor made her purchases in Miami and Palm Beach, the day she set foot on her native soil, before proceeding to New York. Perhaps he had an informant, an expert, who enlightened him as to the American way of life: with the opening of the winter season, New York's best dresses migrate to Florida. That is exactly where the Duchess bought a few—twenty or thirty—gowns, the day she landed from the Bahamas, before proceeding to New York. True, she did not go to the shops—the shops came to her. That is to say, there was a special showing arranged for her at the hotel, with mannequins parading in the latest creations.

It is quite understandable, from the above, why the Duchess avoids British soil; she does not wish to expose herself to unjustifiable criticism of her private life. The scarcity of such materials as silk and nylon and the finest woolens in England and some other parts of the Empire may also deter her; also, in England, there is the little matter of 100 percent luxury tax on jewelry. Then, the present plight of the English, who are forced to get along on one shilling five pence (14 cents) worth of meat a week per person, might cause chagrin to a woman whose dieting is voluntary; it is best to steer clear of misery in order to restrain one's compassion.

So the Duchess spends her life in America and France. Before the Duke's 1952 birthday present of real estates, she gave orders to French real-estate dealers to find a suitable villa for her; not as large as her Cap d'Antibes house (which had thirty rooms in it) but not too small, either. One of her specifications being that the new villa must contain sufficient space to accommodate her twelve servants. A year or so ago the Windsors almost bought the perfect place in France. It was situated in Louvecienne, just beyond the Bois de Boulogne, and it was originally built for Mme. Du Barry. But so much publicity appeared in connection with this contemplated purchase that the Windsors finally gave up the idea. Although certain features of the place were well-nigh irresistible: dignified seclusion, servants' quarters to house a regiment, a good golf course nearby, a gem of a circularly shaped library. It is an interesting coincidence that the Duchess of Windsor bears a strong facial resemblance to Louis XV's lady. Du Barry made a fateful journey to England in order to sell her fabulous jewels. Upon her return to Paris, she lost her most fabulous gem— her head.

With so large a wardrobe and so many possessions the twelve servants seem to be direly needed. According to Miss Elsa Maxwell, the columnist, the Duchess some time ago remarked that she has to have the servant situation well in hand because "I have married a bell-ringer." But the evidence available shows that the Duchess also is addicted to ringing the bell and issuing commands. Her former French staff complained that, on returning at daybreak from night clubs, she would press all the bells, summoning the sleepy servants; who in consequence left her service. Nowadays, in France or any-where else, it is not easy to replace a competent staff, a few of whom must at all times look after the Duchess' valuable effects. The respon-

sibilities of a wardrobe mistress in the Duchess of Windsor's employment must indeed be great.

Once a personal maid of Wallis' was asked what the secret of her
famous mistress was; what were the factors accounting for her allure
and fascination. The maid replied, "Her Highness is a most orderly,
downright pedantic person. There is no man who doesn't appreciate
a lady's fastidiousness." On the other hand, a friend of the Duchess
was positive that Wallis' secret is her gift of concentrating completely
on the particular person she talks to at a time, making him think that
he is the only person in the whole world and no one else exists. Her
conversation, her quick repartee, her wit, were also put down by
friends as tremendous assets, apart from her great flair for gastronomy,
the last-named proverbially attractive to men. Wallis' conversation
is breezy, a leading sort of "bavardage," setting the pace, tossing a
subject up in the air and letting someone catch it. She maintains
that, for a hostess, the most exciting realm in conversation is politics;
but since her husband is a member of the British Royal Family, although they both possess decidedly strong views on politics, their
position excludes them from that field. She said in an article which has
appeared under her by-line (*Vogue*, November 15, 1949) that "I
myself never made a point of building dinners around celebrities of
the hour."

According to everyone who ever knew her, Wallis' talk and wit
leave nothing to be desired. And according to the Duke of Windsor,
she is sparkling and exceedingly well-informed. These accomplishments plus her impeccable looks and her desire to please the inner
man are sufficient explanation of any woman's ascendancy over any
man. Her famous *bon mot* when playing bridge, "My King doesn't
take tricks—he just abdicates," is repeated in the press every now
and then, and justly so.

However, every now and then the Duchess loses her good humor.
In 1950, when London's *News Review* reported that she was looking
for a job, and that very serious talks on the subject had been going on
between the Duchess and a Paris dressmaker, she was furious. Wallis
at once denied the story; nevertheless *News Review* went on insisting
that there was some basis for it, and that the Duchess saw no reason
why she should not go into business. If she did, the public knows
nothing about it. Of course, The Best-Dressed Woman in the World
would have all the authority in the matter of fashion; and this in spite

of certain much too severe French critics who hold it against her that she fancies too much jewelry, eccentric trimmings, oversize buttons, incessant pockets, and those short little gloves. Other faultfinders censure her because she has allowed dressing and modes to become an obsession. They cite J. C. Fluegel, the British psychologist, and other experts, who maintain that extreme preoccupation with clothes may be a defense against doubt of one's physical attractiveness, and an overwhelming desire to be perfectly groomed is a definite sign of nervous anxiety. That one should have a sense of humor about clothes, as about everything else. There was no smile on the Duchess' face when Dimitri, the well-known color photographer, respectfully told her that she had a small spot on her dress as a result of sitting on the parapet of the swimming pool at Government House, in Nassau. The Duchess immediately excused herself, ran upstairs and reappeared shortly in a new gown.

Even before the outbreak of the recent jewel robbery wave in New York's elegant East Side, the Duchess was well-protected. When the Duke was Governor General of the Bahamas, the Waldorf was teeming with plain-clothes men. Today a single New York City detective from the nearest police station guards the Windsors officially; this man is changed every eight hours, and fortunately has nothing to do. It is worthy of note here that at the end of her first visit to New York from the Bahamas, she called in the detectives who had been assigned to guard the Windsors' suite at the Waldorf. She turned to them with a benign smile, "I have a little memento for you." And with that she gave each of the eleven detectives a picture post card of the hotel, signed by the Duke and herself.

There are some who say that all this stress on glamour is bewildering. But even dissenters must agree that the Duchess of Windsor has a fetching and youthful appearance. One of these people, an American lady who had not seen Wallis since China days, said that she found her completely well gowned, completely gracious, completely composed, completely complete.

Indeed, the cost of maintaining such perfection cannot be negligible. The $25,000 annuity (apart from the Duke's $70,000 per year) which was reportedly settled on the Duchess of Windsor back in England in 1937, can help but little in the yearly budget of The Best-Dressed Woman in the World.

29

Is She a Duchess?

A duchess is never more than thirty to a bourgeois.
—STENDHAL

AUTHORITIES on titles are still disagreeing as to whether there is a Duchess of Windsor or not. There is, for instance, the Heralds' College, or College of Arms, in England, a royal corporation which ever since 1483 has been looking after trees. Family trees, that is. The College fixes orders of precedence, keeps track of genealogies, tells interested parties how to begin their letter to the Sovereign ("Madam") and how to conclude it ("I remain, with the profoundest veneration, Your Most Excellent Majesty's faithful subject and dutiful servant"), and sends them their family's coat of arms, executed minutely. (For a fee, of course.)

The hereditary head of this College is always the Duke of Norfolk, the Earl Marshal of England, who doesn't keep office hours, but pays a call now and then to make sure that the noble clerks, called Heralds, and *their* clerks, keep their noses to the grindstone.

Immediately under the Duke of Norfolk comes the proudly named Garter Principal King of Arms, with his fellow-"monarchs," Clarenceux King of Arms South of Trent, Norroy King of Arms North of Trent; the heralds Windsor, Chester, Richmond, Somerset, York and Lancaster; and the pursuivants Rouge Croix, Bluemantle, Rouge Dragon and Portcullis.

The College has its busiest time at a coronation, when it sets up a Court of Claims to decide who shall do service at the country's greatest ceremony. As early as September 1952, the Earl Marshal had to acquire a coronation headquarters. There was a search for a suitably large house, and at last one was found: one of the mansions in Belgrave Square, London, which NATO had recently evacuated. It had been requisitioned at the beginning of the War. When the news that the Court of Claims had found a home was brought to the Earl Marshal, he said in amazement: "Belgrave Square? What's the number?" He was told that it was Number 14. "It used to be my town house," reminisced Norfolk, adding: "Well, not quite mine. I leased it from Westminster. That is, the Duke of Westminster."

If someone is knighted or ennobled, the Heralds at once go into a huddle and determine the new knight's or nobleman's place in the royal procession. Even if there is no royal procession actually in progress, there will certainly be one in the future, and provision for the newcomer's exact position in the ranks must be in the files.

This official and august body, after the Duke of Windsor married Wallis Warfield Spencer Simpson, refused to record any precedence for her "on the advice of the King" (*George VI*, New York *Times* December 17, 1937). Steadfastly the Heralds declined to place her in a group or category, or accord her a place in the royal procession.

It is certain that the name of the Duchess of Windsor does not appear in a booklet which circulates in the Royal Household, and which is entitled: "Confidential—Precedence at Court." Immediately a decision is taken in matters affecting the Household there appears a new edition of this booklet with the change duly recorded. Thus when Queen Elizabeth II was proclaimed she made it known that the Duke of Edinburgh was to rank immediately after her, and this was done long before the *London Gazette* officially announced the Duke's position in the Order of Precedence, in October 1952.

English laws are seldom changed. The statutes are old, and they could still hang people for about one hundred offenses, for, say, stealing a horse or a loaf of bread. But of course these antiquated statutes are dormant or altogether in abeyance.

Not so the Order of Precedence. "Who's Who" in the royal pageant was established by Henry VIII, and nowadays it is practically the same as it was then.

Precedence is tradition working with extreme efficiency. It is a serious business. An earl would not be beheaded were he to get a step ahead of a duke; but murderous looks would soon put him in his place, and chances are the press lords would make hash of the poor fellow in next morning's newspapers.

So the highest authority on this solemn matter of precedence, the Heralds' College, just can't see a Duchess of Windsor at all.

Lesser authorities, like Burke's Peerage, reason that the Duke of Windsor is the twenty-ninth duke, taking into consideration the date of the creation of the dukedom. According to English custom, a duke's wife becomes a duchess through marriage; therefore, the Duchess of Windsor is the twenty-ninth duchess of the realm, and in the procession would walk after the twenty-eighth duchess. Since there is no thirtieth duchess, the Duchess of Windsor would be last in the group of duchesses.

But here comes a difficulty. After the abdication the Duke of Windsor was given the title His Royal Highness, to tell the world that he is of royal blood; but the style was withheld from the Duchess. Consequently His Royal Highness, the Duke of Windsor, although excluded from the succession to the throne by his Act of Abdication, would be ninth in the royal procession. He would walk so far in front that his wife, the Duchess, wouldn't even be able to see him.

Because the Duchess of Windsor is left unplaced so far as the Order of Precedence is concerned, it is perhaps fortunate that until recently there have been few occasions for full-fledged honest-to-goodness pomp. But then came two royal funerals, and the coronation. Before these, the wedding of Her Royal Highness, Princess Elizabeth, to His Royal Highness the Duke of Edinburgh, took place. The Windsors were not present at this ceremony, either. But an American lady reporter who had known Philip in his raw youth was invited to the wedding. She told the present writer that the day before the marriage some one *very high* in court circles said to her, "For Heaven's sake, don't bring up to any member of the Royal Family the names of certain people who will be absent!" The reader may guess the identity of the highly placed person who uttered these words, to whom, and about whom.

There is one Social Register in the United States, but in England there are two—Burke's Peerage and Debrett's Peerage. Burke also publishes a work known as Burke's Landed Gentry. Back in 1836 this included four hundred families, and registered a vow never to include more. Today it lists five thousand families—half of whom have no land! Originally those who qualified for the Landed Gentry owned 5,000 acres. Today to qualify for inclusion, one must own 500 acres —or none. The formerly landed gentry have been forced to sell their lands to pay taxes and the confiscatory death duties.

The Windsors are in both Debrett's and Burke's. But volumes such as these, if not official, may be mistaken sometimes. Any other work on society and rank, for instance Who's Who, or the various encyclopedias, may be misleading too, on occasions. The real Bible of the aristocracy can only be found in Continental Europe.

This is the *Almanach de Gotha*, a venerable book, which is reliable on nobility, genealogy and precedence. The *Almanach* does not list the Duchess of Windsor. Hitler interfered with its 1944 production, but he did not arrange for the insertion of any note recording the marriage of his former admirers, the Duke and Duchess of Windsor.

On the other hand, the Duke of Windsor is in the book. In this most recent, 1944 edition, he is naturally listed as a member of the Royal Family of England. The *Almanach* starts the Royal Family with King George VI, then reigning, his Queen and their two daughters. Then comes the Duke of Gloucester, his Duchess and their children. Next comes the widow of the late Duke of Kent and her children. And finally the Duke of Windsor. This entry omits all mention of his former titles and honors, while all the titles and honors of the other members of the Royal Family are duly listed. The omission suggests that the *Almanach* decided to interpret the word "abdication" according to Roman Law—"A sovereign divesting himself of *all* his powers and titles."

Being an exceedingly pedantic work, with the memory of an elephant, the *Almanach* remembers the many royal persons who bartered their crowns for loved ones. The book recalls proud kings and princes, full of resignation and humility, who chose privacy and obscurity as light penance for entering into a *mésalliance*.

To quote just one example, there was once a Habsburg archduke who married a commoner, and his mile-long names immediately shrank to the short John Orth.

But to continue studying the *Almanach* on the Windsors: to judge by the listing of the Royal Family, the Duke is still a bachelor; even if only by omission. But a footnote immediately after his entry provokes the hope that the Duchess may still be mentioned elsewhere. This note says: "For further information, see Part III of this volume." In this part of the work the nonreigning princely and ducal houses are listed in detail, together with all wives and relations. There is no family named under the single, lonely word "Windsor."

However, an asterisk next to "Windsor" on this page indicates that one must turn to yet another part of the book to find the explanation for the mark. Hope is born anew.

But the *Almanach's* asterisk merely indicates a dukedom which has been created by the Sovereign, and bestowed on a *single* member of the family, *with no other member entitled to use the rank*. And here must end the search in this particular work of reference. To sum up, the

Almanach conveys the idea that there is no such person as the Duchess of Windsor; it even fails to point out that the Duke of Windsor is married; and that he is married to the former Mrs. Wallis Warfield Spencer Simpson. The silence of the Bible of nobility is much too loud a silence.

Since the few remaining dynasties in Europe accept and use the *Almanach de Gotha* as an authoritative textbook, chances are that the Duchess would have no place allotted to her in the pageantry of any Monarchy. And since the United States does not recognize titles of nobility, in its Order of Precedence (for, believe it or not, the United States has one too) she would not figure either, except perhaps as a distinguished visitor walking after the Secretary of the Smithsonian Institution, who happens to be the last in the President's official march.

The attitude of the journalists also makes the Duchess' rank seem less imposing. One of the columnists, Dorothy Kilgallen, plainly shows her feelings by such remarks as these:

> The Duchess of Windsor, Jimmy Donahue and Russell Nype made a gay, gay trio at the Polonaise Restaurant the other night. Gadzooks, but the Duchess is living these days!

But not everybody takes this ironic view of the Duchess' social activities. When the Duke and Duchess went holidaying on their chartered yacht *Amazone* in the summer of 1952, Cholly Knickerbocker wrote that:

> The D. and D. don't bother to mix much with the French or the British. They're always in the thick of an American swarm. In fact, by now—they have almost become American royalty.
> (New York *Journal-American*, July 22, 1952)

With her position among her own friends, and in the society of her own country so well assured, the Duchess of Windsor is above the need to worry about American or British rules of precedence, or the fact that the British and French do not mix with her. Being almost American royalty, and as such standing on the highest rung of café society, she can set her own standards, instead of having to conform with those of a European duchess. After all, those standards are very exacting, and must be considered unsuited to the free-and-easy atmosphere of the New York smart set.

For a duchess, at least until the present era, had certain rules to go by. There were the very important negative aspects of her station: a duchess might be well-known, even famous, but she must not be ostentatious. Certainly she was not a night club queen. She might be noted for her entertaining, she might lead a *salon*, but she was known for something other than the giving of rowdy all-night parties. A *real* duchess, according to the popular conception as the standards of her class, was not a person who devoted her whole time and energy to pleasure-seeking, and who shone only by her jewels.

On the positive side, it was the first duty of a duchess to be the mother of the heir—this certainly called for her to perform the task of imbuing her family with a sense of their responsibility to society.

But even before and during the fulfilment of this most important task, a duchess had onerous duties. She was the mistress of a great country house, charged with its upkeep and the supervision of its inhabitants and guests. She presided, with tact and charm, at house parties and balls. She was on friendly terms with the local people, and saw to it that the ducal name headed any subscription list; she helped friends down on their luck. Indeed, she might be as famed for her charities, public or private, as that Duchess of York who kept the aging Beau Brummell alive, or the Baroness Burdett-Coutts, or the Duchesse de Talleyrand, who were known to support so many people less fortunate than themselves, as also was Lady Carnarvon, widow of the Egyptologist.

Such a lady, often a patroness of the arts and of literature, when in town would spend her evenings at the glittering balls and in the *salons* of her equals. In the country she would begin the day with a visit to the home farm, and of course she would accompany her husband to the annual County Cattle Show. Here she would hand out the prizes, with a smile and a gracious pat for a winning bull.

All this, however, presupposes (at least in England) a certain background which in the case of the Windsors simply does not exist. The ducal title of Windsor is not a territorial title: it does not carry with it possession of land, or of an ancestral home. Windsor Castle is not the private property of the Sovereign, it belongs to the Crown: hence the Duke of Windsor could not retain it as his territorial home. As for Sandringham and Balmoral, these formerly the property of Edward VIII, were sold by him, when he became Duke of Windsor, to the new King, George VI.

Apparently the Duke has owned landed property in the United States, for on August 27, 1952, the columnist, Danton Walker, reported that the Duke was "disposing of his very considerable real-estate holdings in the U. S." But he has never sought, either in the United States or elsewhere, a dwelling place and estate such as in England are considered suitable to the dignity of a royal duke and his consort. By living in the Waldorf, and being entertained and entertaining at restaurants, the Windsors show that they are up-to-date, in tune with the general trend of a labor-saving age.

Of course, the purchase of a new home in France may mark a change in the ducal design for living. For the *Journal-American* recently reported that:

> Friends say that the Duke of Windsor is tired of the steady diet of golf and globe-trotting.

As has been pointed out, the Duke does own a ranch at Calgary. But it is not to be expected that so much beauty and charm as are represented by Wallis Windsor should be buried in the wilds of Canada. And a lady who is the acknowledged leader of a brilliant and polished society in cosmopolitan New York will hardly succumb to the bucolic attractions of a State Fair. So it is not surprising that the Windsors are never seen in pictures of the sort familiar to readers of the London *Sphere* or the *Tatler*, which depict titled persons, including members of the Royal Family, in the company of cows and sheep.

But the Duchess may definitely be considered a patron of the arts, at least such as come under the influence of the Muses Thalia and Terpsichore. As "Prince" Mike Romanoff, the famous California restaurateur and stanch defender of his title against all criticism, once said sadly: "I don't know if I ought to go on keeping up the relationship with my cousins, the Windsors. The Duchess has gone artistic."

"Prince" Mike was surely a little too ready to condemn. For the Windsors' artistic inclinations do not carry them to the intellectual heavens. Perhaps this is due to modesty. The Duchess may feel that the light and sparkling conversation for which she is famed would not be agreeable to such mental heavyweights as Professor Einstein, Bertrand Russell or Henry Steele Commager. No doubt she, and the Duke, admire the work of such writers as George Macaulay Trevelyan and Arnold Toynbee, the historians, or Thomas Mann, the novelist; but they do not seek the company of these people. As for art, they

own an oil painting; but it is not the work of so noted and able an
artist as, say, Augustus John, the grand old man of English portraitists.
The Windsors, indeed, are more familiar with the work of Mr. John
the milliner, than with that of Augustus John.

After all, the Duchess is her own best work of art. And this calls
for constant effort on her part. One cannot be in two places at
once; and the hours that are passed at, say, Mainbocher's or Carnegie's, leave little time for Wildenstein's or Carnegie Hall. Dance
music is not often heard at concerts. And as a self-portrait of a successful woman, the Duchess certainly outshines all the pictures of the
famed gallery; nor is she justly to be censured because her tastes, or
the Duke's, are not those of, say mad Maximilian of Bavaria, who
made his castle of Hohenschwangau a nursery of the arts and sciences.

When King, the Duke was officially associated with church life
and church dignitaries both in England and in Scotland. But this is
one of the interests which seem to have been crowded out of his life.
Certainly neither he nor the Duchess include on their visit list such
clerics as, say, the Episcopal Bishop of New York, Dr. Manning, or
a man well-known for his trenchant comments on the modern religious
scene, Canon Iddings Bell.

But what, it may be asked, can an exiled Monarch do? Although
the list of "ex's" lengthens from year to year—it now includes,
besides Edward of England, the former Kings Zog of Albania, Peter
of Yugoslavia, Humbert of Italy, Leopold of the Belgians and
Farouk of Egypt—no one, not even in America, the land of how-to-
do-it books, has yet written a treatise on "How to Be an Ex-King."
The Windsors do but "fleet the time carelessly, as they did in the
golden world."

Most true. Yet other former Monarchs have not found it necessary to fleet the time in quite such evanescent pastimes nor with quite
so much gilded exhibitionism. Upon the collapse of the Central
Powers in 1918, the former Emperor of Austria-Hungary retired to a
private station, and led an exemplary family life, not (as might be
thought) in luxury, but in great poverty. The former Empress Zita
might in happier days have patronized the foremost jeweler and
dressmaker in Vienna, that city of luxurious living; but after the loss
of her husband's crown, she was never heard to complain, even when
she had but one black dress to her name, and had to feed her many
children in a Sixth Avenue cafeteria.

After the end of World War I, no fewer than twenty-five ruling princes of the German Empire gave up their thrones, and retired into private life, where they lived without scandal or display. There were people, many of them, whose names had come down in history.

The Duke is a figure who will go down in history, albeit not a very fine one; the Duchess will be at his side as The Girl Who Wrote Home: "Having wonderful time."

But the Windsors, being "almost" royalty in the United States, where there is no Royal Family to cold-shoulder them, are of course unique. And the Duchess of Windsor has so many advantages and high honors that she will probably always lead the procession in kingless lands, such as that realm of Cockaigne which is international society. Being Number One Best-Dressed Woman in the World is no laughing matter. And take her jewels, figuratively speaking. They overprice those of an old-style maharanee.

Then of course there are other titles to fame and honor, far dearer to the feminine heart than anything which can be thought up by the College of Heralds. For instance, the late Ambassador James W. Gerard, in his amusing book *My First Eighty-Three Years in America*, mentions the Duchess, principal title—*femme fatale*.

Ambassador Gerard declared that he would like to write a volume on the fatal women of the last fifty years, because he is convinced such a book would outsell all others. "Just to name a few of the fatal women," he wrote, "consider Wallis Warfield, for whom King Edward VIII gave up the throne of Britain; Magda Lupescu, Carol of Rumania's love; the women in Hitler's life; and the incredible woman of the Mayerling tragedy."

This was undiplomatic language, except for the fact that Mr. Gerard, so accustomed to protocol, very correctly placed the Duchess at the head of his list. Besides, the word "fatal" when applied to a woman is reckoned better than royal rank. There are few women in the world who wouldn't want to be *femmes fatales*. It is a far more interesting title than queen.

A mother's instinct is keen; and as though realizing that her daughter would one day be almost a queen and in need of such data, Mrs. Warfield, shortly before she died, undertook some genealogical research. At the end of several months' diligent work, she was able to exhibit the family tree—without the aid of the Heralds' College— in all its splendor, and assert that through the female line the Mon- tagues—her maiden name—were descended from the knight Drogo de Monteceau, a noble warrior who had helped William the Conqueror invade England in 1066. Relationship with the Dukes of Manchester and the Earls of Sandwich was also claimed.

Mrs. Warfield looked up her husband's family too. She found that he was descended from another knight, Pagan de Warfield, to whom the Conqueror gave a manor called Warfield Walks, right in the Forest of Windsor.

The number of noble families in England who can trace their ancestry even to the reign of King John, in the thirteenth century, is steadily decreasing. In fact, only three English families can go back with their pedigrees in the male line from pre-Conquest times—the families of Berkeley, Arden and Swinton. Mrs. Warfield must have known this, so she modestly traced her descent from the time of the Conqueror. Almost nine hundred years had passed since William's D-Day, and during this time there had been fires and floods, wars and pestilences in England. This makes it very difficult to establish a venerable pedigree; especially as the registration of births only began in 1538! But perhaps it was easier in peaceful Baltimore . . .

In answer to a recent inquiry, the College of Arms refused to comment on the American branch of Montagues, who may have been descendants of Drogo de Monteceau. And with all due respect to the Montagues and the Warfields, it may be pointed out that there are forty-three Montagues and twelve Warfields listed in the Manhattan telephone directory alone.

The writer once called one of the Montagues and put to him the simple question: "Are you descended from Drogo de Monteceau?"

"You must have the wrong number," said Mr. Montague, and hung up.

A telephonic attempt was also made to engage one of the Warfields in genealogical conversation; but his answers were so ignoble that they are not worthy of being recorded for the benefit of posterity.

The science of genealogy has exercised a fascination over great minds. Thackeray treated it in his own funny way: he introduced his readers to Sir Alured Mogyns Smyth de Mogyns, who was born Alfred Smith Muggins, but who traced his descent to Hogyn Mogyn of the Hundred Beeves.

A former Lord Chief Justice of England, Lord Crewe, handled the same subject in a more realistic manner. In the year 1626, he handed down a decision in the course of which he said: "There is an end of name and dignities and whatsoever is terrene."

30

The Firm of Windsor

*Without departing from her dignity, which she knew
well how to preserve, she acquired a popularity
beyond what any of her predecessors could attain.*
—HUME: on Elizabeth I in his *History of England*

*The man that's resolute and just,
Firm to his principles and trust,
Nor hopes nor fears can blind.*
—WALSH

WE are not a family—we are a firm," once remarked King
George VI. This sounds like a mere witticism, but actually it was a
wise, business-like observation. The Royal Family is the Firm of
Windsor, an efficiently working, closely knit corporation, carrying
on the craft of kingship as the family business of England.

The chairman of the board, the head of the firm today, is a handsome, dignified young woman, Elizabeth II, who has at her side a
young man, a real man, the Duke of Edinburgh. When the time
comes for the Queen to go, when she resigns her office as British
Monarchs usually do, by breathing her last, their son will take over
the management.

There were other royal firms before the Windsors in England, but
of the Saxon, Norman and Plantagenet dynasties nothing remains. It
should not be a disquieting thought that both the Firm of Tudor and
the Firm of Stuart ended with the reign of a queen: legitimacy, the
continuity of the family business through direct descendants, plays a
decisive part—neither Elizabeth Tudor nor Anne Stuart had a direct
heir, although Anne did her best (all her children predeceased her).

England's business affairs were often prosperous when the management was in a woman's hands; when the country was, so to speak,
a matriarchy. And since the king business is in constant evolution

307

today the English seem to have the paragon of Monarchs, who, although still a young woman, knows everything the head of such a firm should know. She perhaps profits by the wise example of Caroline, wife of George II, who treated friends with as much discretion as if they might one day be enemies; and enemies with as much courtesy as if they might one day be friends. And, sieving out the good from the bad in the reign of Victoria, Elizabeth already shows all the firmness and dignity of her great-great-grandmother, with none of Victoria's capriciousness and prejudices.

Powers and functions of the head of the Firm of Windsor are limited, but not as limited as is generally believed; and worth-while members had an active share in the management of the Empire. Their method was not unlike that of the executives of a vast American business concern—they worked by suggestion, by influence, by mediation. As in an American office, when something goes wrong and the executive vice-president wants to smooth things over, the Prime Minister contacts the head of the firm. If the matter on hand is of grave importance, there may be a conference. At such a conference, the head of the firm presides, the grievances are bared, the Sovereign listens, weighs matters, offers advice, and tries to arrange a fusion between the warring parties. The advice is always considered, and never peremptory.

Thus in 1931, when the Great Depression had brought about a crisis in the economic life of England, King George V played a decisive part in the formation of a National (coalition) Government under Ramsay MacDonald. The Prime Minister, in a state of abject fright, declared that "all was up"; it was left to the King to encourage him, to urge him to lead the country through the crisis, thus ensuring that MacDonald would continue in office, and that the necessary measures would be taken to re-establish world confidence in Great Britain.

Years later, when Britain faced an external crisis in her relations with India, George VI played his decisive part: he commanded Lord Louis Mountbatten to accept, from a Labor government, the post of Viceroy of India, when the Viceroy's unenviable task would be to arrange the transfer of power from Britons to Indians.

English royalty's task is truly prodigious, and demands certain virtues. The earlier heads of the Firm of Windsor—Victoria, Edward VII, George V and his son George VI—were all methodical, hardworking, and honest. They were supposed to be figureheads, and it was even thought that they were stupid people. They were not.

Gifted with strong native intelligence, their mental gifts developed with experience; and they had, besides brains, an immense interest in the affairs of the Empire. Every one of them helped to mold many Parliamentary measures. As Mr. Attlee once expressed it:

> The monarch, being continuously in touch with public affairs, acquires great experience. A party leader who becomes prime minister has, as a rule, been out of office for some years . . . Where the monarch has good judgment, as had King George VI, this experience is a great advantage, and he would be an unwise prime minister who did not avail himself of it.

Yet George VI, like his good predecessors, adhered strictly to the constitutional system which had put him into business; and like the rest of the conscientious "hereditary presidents," probably never had a day entirely free. These monarchs, excepting Edward VIII, earned their salaries by very hard work.

In 1947 the Firm of Windsor acquired a new member. In comparison with British royalty, Philip Mountbatten was a rather obscure princeling. He was an exiled prince from Athens (without a drop of Greek blood in him), without a fortune, but well-connected: his uncle, Earl Mountbatten of Burma, is the most able of Queen Victoria's descendants, and is *persona grata* with the rest of the Firm of Windsor.

But apart from this, Philip has his own personal endowments. He is good-looking, well-born and well-bred, and there is nothing of the prig in him. Besides, he is brave (during the Second World War he fought just like any other Englishman of his age, often in the thick of it, in Burma and elsewhere), and the English lay great stress on personal courage. "What is his war record?" is asked in business, when people apply for a job, seek a girl's hand in marriage, try for a loan, or when a man is about to be sentenced. This is not because the English are a bellicose nation, but because during a crisis, an emergency, the true character comes out; and Britons therefore assess a man by the way he behaves in adversity.

Philip eventually went ashore to perform higher duties, that is, to become the husband of the most important woman in the world, when he quickly showed that he had many peacetime gifts. Above all, he has proved that he has that certain gravity, an earnestness of mind, indispensable in the husband of the Queen (according to Prince Consort Albert); yet besides the seriousness he has a sense of humor, and it is known that he said to the Queen, when she was still Princess

Elizabeth: "Get on with you, you old sausage!" When this homespun humor got around the English took him to their hearts. The remark was so husbandly, so domestic, and people in England always look to the Royal Family in domestic matters. The Prince at once seemed like one of them.

He, too, shows democratic feeling, like another prince now gone. But Philip has not thrown away his dignity. His level head has not been turned, nor has he been mesmerized by any so-called "smart set." He knows that familiarity breeds contempt.

The English like to have a royal hero, and Philip seems to answer the need admirably. He can be discussed endlessly, for every English family makes the Firm one of its chief topics of conversation, talking about it as though they are relatives. The frocks, the friends, the joys and sorrows of the Royal Family are minutely discussed by the people. There is only one party in England where the Firm of Windsor is concerned—people may be Socialists, Tories or Liberals, of any political party or none, but all factions are united around *the* Family. And this is another great advantage of legitimism. Figuratively speaking, it is a relay race, and one that goes on. Unless the unprecedented happens, and one of the runners drops out, unwilling to sacrifice "pleasure" to usefulness . . .

Philip's influence on the Queen is obvious: it may be seen from a series of photographs. As a Princess, the newly married Elizabeth seems to have had only a slight interest in clothes, or in dressing for appearance's sake. She perhaps did not know or care enough about such things, and allowed her modistes to advise her. A study of the photos taken at various times since her marriage, shows that Philip's advice was accepted, with the result that she blossomed out. Only a man who takes a very great interest in a wife who loves him can bring this about. Gradually Elizabeth's silhouette changed. For instance, there was published a couple of years ago a certain picture of her on horseback taking the salute during the Trooping of the Colour; it was a majestic picture, but she was too rounded. The next Trooping of the Colour took place after her accession—and her uniformed figure was slim to perfection.

The pleasant tasks of the Sovereign's husband are interspersed between many of much more serious import: opening hospitals, making speeches, presiding at banquets, inspecting military and naval units, visiting coal mines, to mention a few. And keeping faith with a trusting people.

For the rest of his life, Philip will carry the burden that is the lot of the second most important member of the Firm of Windsor. Fortunately, he does it with a smile, with masculine grace, and with a certain wisdom of that wise man who said that serious things must be taken lightly, and small things must be taken seriously.

Elizabeth's husband has before him the good example of the Prince Consort Albert. What the impish Lord Melbourne, Victoria's Prime Minister, said to the newly wed Queen when she proudly remarked that Albert never looked at another woman: "No, that sort of thing is apt to come later," never came to pass. There is much less reason for supposing that it will come to pass in this case. Victoria was not a beauty.

Thackeray once churlishly remarked: "The Queen has no business to be a woman." The author of *Vanity Fair* was rather harsh in his judgment, though many people echoed his words in that middle period of Victoria's reign, when she retired into selfish widowhood (and in consequence a wave of Republicanism swept the country). Living as she did in a well-ordered age, Victoria could afford to treat herself as "a poor, lone widow," isolating herself in a luxury of grief in Windsor, Osborne or Balmoral.

Earlier Queens Regnant did not have it so good. The twelfth-century Matilda, daughter of Henry I and first female Sovereign of England, had to fight for the Throne; but because she had no idea how to get on with the Londoners, whose city has always decided the fates of Sovereigns, she lost her crown to her cousin Stephen.

No better fortune attended the next Queen Regnant, misguided Mary I, "Bloody" Mary, the daughter of Henry VIII and Catherine of Aragon. When she came to the Throne in 1553, the country had for twenty years been suffering the pangs of violent revolution. Its economic life had been ruined by the plundering of the monasteries and the guilds; and the major part of the national wealth had been sucked into the maw of the monstrous nobles, old and new. On Mary's accession, a wave of popular rejoicing swept the miserable people. But the Queen, whose mother's unfortunate experience, and whose "bastard" youth had conditioned her, tried to re-establish the Catholic religion, and the ensuing persecutions helped to establish Protestantism. And so Mary could not accomplish the restoration of the national well-being. Her advisers were men not fit to be trusted, their only thought being their own aggrandizement at no matter whose expense. After five years' reign she died, abandoned even by her husband, Philip of Spain.

Elizabeth I was much better equipped to reign: she was strong in mind and character, statesman, diplomat, politician, all molded into one. And she knew how to play along with the nobles. That they steadily impoverished England; that they left the sailors who had fought the Spanish Armada to die of starvation in the street; that Government was by a spy system backed by the torture chamber: all this seems to have mattered little to Elizabeth provided she could keep her grip upon the nation and the scepter. She was a woman of brilliant intellect, and the most lasting glory of her reign—the Elizabethan drama and poetry—became a world literature.

Elizabeth could be base and cruel as her policy dictated. But she was every inch a queen, brave in the face of the gravest danger. When there was a threat of foreign invasion she rode to Tilbury and told the troops that she would rather perish in battle than survive the ruin of her people. "I know I have the body of a weak and feeble woman, but I have the heart of a king, and of a King of England too." By the most astute diplomacy she gave the nation thirty years of peace. And when once Parliament confronted her and asked why she was not yet married, she held up her finger with the coronation ring on it. "Good people, I am! I am married to England."

Mary II (1662-1694) has been wittily described as "the only feminine King in English history." This, because the Crown of England having been offered to her during the life of her father, James II, she refused to accept it for herself alone; and it was therefore settled upon herself and her husband jointly. Besides, William flatly refused to be known simply as the Queen's consort. The "royal tandem" turned out to be more than a form: William did the ruling, while the "King-Queen" sat at home at Hampton Court, sewing a fine seam.

The "tandem" was succeeded by Mary's sister, Anne. The good-hearted Queen inherited all her father's sincerity and inflexibility. She was not very intelligent; and she was in the hands of a favorite—but that favorite's husband, the Duke of Marlborough, was the greatest of generals, and a brilliant diplomat into the bargain.

However, Marlborough was only one of the "architects of our magnitude and renown" in the later seventeenth century. It was the Silver Age of English literature, counting such giants as Swift, Defoe, Pope, Steele and Addison, with Dryden's "towering crest" above all;

Isaac Newton was the age's Einstein; Christopher Wren was filling London with splendid neoclassical buildings; Hogarth, that reporter of the age with his brush, was the forerunner of Gainsborough, Reynolds and Raeburn. And it seemed that England was destined to be mistress of the North American continent.

But when, in 1837, Victoria Regina ascended the throne, only Canada remained. There were compensations: even though England did not become mistress of all North America, she was the acknowledged mistress of the seas, the "Dread Nought."

Under Victoria, the small island became the dominant power of the world; besides her naval, her military power, the trade, the literature and religion of Great Britain, were so to shape the thought and events of the time, that the nineteenth century is known as "the English Century." To this result, Victoria herself contributed in no small part.

For one thing, this head of the Firm was a woman of considerable intelligence as well as of strong character. Consciously she might in all sincerity say that women ought not to govern; she might denounce "this mad, wicked nonsense of women's rights," as a natural result of her happy marriage. In fact, she delighted in governing; nor was her delight in authority entirely unconscious: released from her mother's dominance, the girl of eighteen took to command like a duck to water.

But this was not the mere intoxication of power. From the first few days of her reign she showed an acute sense of her responsibilities; and sixty years later the same firm will was at work, triumphing over increasing blindness, over the mischance of war, and still preserving the rights of the Crown against the encroachments of ministers less able than demagogic.

Not that Victoria was ignorant of the limitations of her Sovereign power. When she read a book listing the formidable powers accruing in theory to the Crown of Great Britain, her sense of humor provoked her to say: "Oh, the wicked man, to write such a story!" For according to the author, she could make every subject a peer or peeress; she could disband the army; she could declare war; she could pardon all offenders, and dismiss most of the government employees. But as a constitutional Monarch, who ruled by the advice of her Ministers, Victoria naturally regarded this as "a story."

For, despite these clear-cut definitions, the rights of a constitutional Monarch are curiously elastic. Theoretically they are many; in practice they are very few. The Monarch must be consulted by the Prime Minister; she may encourage one course of action or discourage another. It is plain that the interpretation, and the exercise of the Sovereign's rights, will vary greatly with the circumstances of the times, with the character of the Ministers and also with the character of the Monarch. Let alone the immediate damage he may do to the country, a weak or foolish Sovereign will disable the Crown, and pass on to his heir a diminished inheritance. An able Monarch, a strong Monarch, will preserve or even augment the power of the Crown.

Having duties far more formidable than her powers, the present head of the Firm, Queen Elizabeth, must every day read and sign hundreds of papers. She is the fountain of honor, conferring titles and decorations, appointing the judges and magistrates who act in her name. She must familiarize herself with the bills about to become law by the addition of her signature. Being Supreme Head of the Church of England and the Church of Scotland, she is an Anglican in the one country and a Presbyterian in the other, and must attend to church appointments. As guardian of infants and lunatics she might have a busy time, but the Lord Chancellor takes this particular job partly off her hands.

Elizabeth II pays the utmost attention to any business laid before her: she is evidently determined that nobody shall put anything over on her, because she is a woman, and young. Besides, she has had the advantage of training in kingcraft by her father; she was not only brought up *in* the business, but she was brought up *to* the business. Fortunately she inherits her strong ancestors' physique as well as her parents' inflexible devotion to the affairs of the Firm of Windsor, that is, the affairs of the Commonwealth. This is so well-known that Parliament, after scrutinizing the royal program for Coronation Year, expressed the hope that "Her Majesty's strong sense of duty shall not be allowed to injure Her Majesty's excellent hereditary health." Frail George VI, who was never really meant to reign, and whom "Fate" forced to become the head of the Firm, helped to kill himself by overwork; but the average age of English Monarchs from George I on, has been better than seventy.

Certainly the Queen needed all her strength during her Coronation Year. The coronation service with its long hours, followed by her broadcast to the Commonwealth, state banquets, investitures, garden parties, had taken up much of her time. There had been formal visits to the City of London—whose Lord Mayor and Aldermen *are* a privileged body—and to Windsor, and the long visits to Scotland, Ireland and Wales had not been mere pleasure junkets.

Perhaps it is her well-known strength of mind that has provoked the suggestion that, under certain circumstances, Queen Elizabeth II might employ the royal right of veto. The Government of Great Britain is theoretically carried on by the Sovereign in Council, so that, even after acceptance by Lords and Commons, no measure becomes law until it has received the assent of the Monarch. More than two hundred years have passed since Queen Anne last withheld the royal assent. All her successors since have bowed, with however ill a grace on some occasions, to what was presumably the will of the people expressed through Parliament.

But though the royal signature has never yet been withheld, through such a length of years that "the memory of living man runneth not to the contrary," yet the power of refusal remains *theoretically* with the Sovereign: so that, *theoretically* instead of the expected "*La reine la veult*," the startled Commons might hear instead "*La reine s'avisera*." Of course, there is hardly a chance that this would ever happen. It would mean that Parliament would have to think better of the matter, even if this involved "going to the country," the English term for holding a general election.

To force a general election takes great courage. But the Firm does not lack examples of feminine bravery. During the twelfth century the Windsors' remote ancestors, the Guelphs (or Welfs—wolves) were lords of Weinsberg in Wurtemberg, and here in 1140 Welf VI was defeated by Conrad III, King of Germany. Willing to soften the hardships of defeat, Conrad proposed to hold only the men, and gallantly told the women that they might leave with whatever they could carry on their backs. But how great was his surprise, when they marched through the gates, each bearing on her back a father, a husband, a brother or a son, who thus escaped the conquerors! From this legend, it is said, the fortress above the town of Weinsberg has received the name of Weibertreu—true wives. Of course at the time that this happened the Guelphs had no notion that their descendants would be Kings of England, a distant country.

One would expect to find common traits running through the characters of these Kings of England. But such was not the case, though some kings in their moral and physical traits seem to revert back to their predecessors. There are, for instance, striking resemblances between the Duke of Windsor and George IV. Despite his early education and environment, Windsor ignored the fine example set him by his father and struck a personal note of his own (*notre volonté c'est le destin*), forgetting that his subjects demanded of their Sovereign physical bravery, royal magnificence, but above all, good judgment. Some of the kings before Edward VIII had power, some had popularity, some had talent, some had industry and principle, but nothing counted so much as judgment, that is to say, the ability to make the right decision at the right moment. This was the most important of all the kingly virtues, and the lack of it could unseat the most amiable of Sovereigns.

It was a part of that good judgment to uphold the dignity of the Monarchy, but Edward VIII was negligent in this respect:

> The King himself forfeited that peculiar respect and admiration which the public is always ready to entertain for the monarch . . . He insisted, in spite of Ministerial advice, on marrying the woman of his choice; he was careless about his ceremonial duties, and roused suspicions that he might play a personal and partisan part in public affairs.

Such was the comment recently made by the *New Statesman and Nation*, which also remarked that "the short reign of Edward VIII destroyed much of the magic, the glamour of monarchy."

The spurious "glamour" which surrounds the Windsors in the United States has no place in England, not even in Madame Tussaud's famous waxworks. There the Royal Family appear as a group in a conspicuous place. Only two figures are missing. Those who are sufficiently curious may find the Windsors tucked away in a quiet corridor nearby.

For the former head of the Firm of Windsor is now doing *his* business elsewhere. Other members of the Firm are hard at work in the traditional way. Accompanied by her sixteen-year-old son, the Duchess of Kent goes to Singapore, no longer a bastion of England only, but of the world's freedom. Meanwhile the House of Commons thoughtfully reminds the younger members of the Firm that the carefree sociability of many teen-agers is not for them; they must soon be taking their part in the exacting "royal show."

The Princess Royal, Windsor's only sister, like many another mother, knew years of anxiety during World War II: her elder son was a prisoner in German hands. She was then, as she is now, most active in the work of the Red Cross. In 1953 she visited Trinidad, not on a mere pleasure cruise, but as a busy envoy of the Firm of Windsor.

The Queen Mother has recently bought a castle in a romantically remote part of Scotland. Journeying north to visit it, she took with her two favorite dogs. The Queen Mother of England and Scotland, a noblewoman of doubly royal descent—of bluer blood even than the husband who raised her to a throne—might not unjustly allow herself a certain humorous latitude in naming her canine pets. But there are no Disraelis and Bismarcks among the Queen Mother's dogs; instead, they bear the simple, domestic and doggy names of Honey and Tony.

The Queen Mother's purchase of a castle, at a fraction of the price that would be asked for any halfway decent *moulin*, has led to criticism. The Royal Family, it was said, already owns several homes. (The Queen Mother herself spent her childhood in one of the most romantic of Scottish castles—Glamis, where Macbeth slew the gracious Duncan. It is the most famous of all Britain's fifty haunted castles, where the haunters and the haunted divide the house between them.) But such comments are unjustified. It is no part of Queen Elizabeth's plan to retire, as to a Scottish Escorial, there to live a weeping hermit. On the contrary, having shown her duty in her daughter's coronation, she visits Southern Rhodesia to open the Rhodes Centenary Exhibition.

The Duke of Windsor does his business, no longer the Firm's business, rather differently. An hour or so with one or other of those American businessmen he admires, following tips on the market, looking over the quotations in stocks and bonds, and he has nothing more to do or trouble about for the day—or the next month or so; until another empty hour obtrudes itself in the almost ceaseless round of "pleasure," like a hole in time waiting to be plugged by something, anything.

> If all the year were playing holidays,
> To sport would be as tedious as to work,

acidly observed Shakespeare. And how bitterly Windsor must feel the truth of these words! On the last page of *A King's Story* he speaks of his having been obsessed by a desire to share in the chosen life in the "real world."

What is this "real world"? Presumably, for the Duke, not the world of unremitting attention to duty; of continual consideration of plans involving the welfare of millions, of exactitude in even minute details; the world of unfailing kindness, of rapturous attention to cathedrals and cornerstones, to cockneys and Cabinet Ministers and the county bore. No, the "real" world into which the Duke has entered by his "own" free will is international café society, that glittering, gilded bubble floating above the stormy seas of history. It is the world in which the cause of communism is helped, however unintentionally, by arrogant display, by festivals costing thousands or tens of thousands of dollars—such as, for instance, that party held, in a Venice where the meatless gondoliers struggle with their heavy poles, upon the pretext of reviving international show and splendor in the threatened remnant of a truncated Europe. A world in which business magnates who ignore the claims of social justice and wise teachings buy their toys of *hôtels* and yachts, of diamond necklaces and costly gowns, while the workers go home to their cramped and cabbage-smelling rooms to read *l'Humanité;* and in which champagne and caviar are more plentiful, sometimes, than the aforementioned cabbages in the workers' dwellings. It is in short that Land of Cockaigne, the luster of whose girandoles has too often paled before the fierce glare of the light that beats upon a scaffold, the music of whose pavane and polka have died into the noise of the Carmagnole and the Red Flag. It is that least real of worlds portrayed in Poe's *The Masque of the Red Death.*

The Duke might have remained in a real world; that uncomfortable one in which his former subjects saw it through, and his brother and sister-in-law saw it through with their people. When the Battle of Britain was going on and Buckingham Palace was bombed—nine times in all—some of the royal entourage suggested that the Princesses should go to Canada. The Queen's reply was simple but eloquent:

> The King will not leave London. My daughters could not go without me. And I shall not leave the King.

The head of the Firm whose wife spoke thus was not a mere ceremonial figurehead. Had custom permitted, the King would certainly have been at the scene of action in June 1944.

While the fight was still raging, two ordinary women one night met the Queen in London—the housekeeper in a business building decided to go with a friend to Buckingham Palace shelter. There the two women sat on suitcases, waiting for the all-clear to sound. Presently in came Their Majesties. They had been intending to leave for Windsor, but had been delayed, and had been caught by the raid. The Queen noted the uncomfortable perches of her subjects. "Haven't you anything better to sit on?" she asked. "No, Ma'am," they said. Her Majesty turned to the King. "Go and find these people some chairs immediately." Obedient as any suburban husband, His Majesty went off, to return presently with two ancient and battered-looking chairs. He was sorry, he said, that he had not been able to find anything nicer for the ladies.

At this time the Duke of Windsor was in the Bahamas, toiling at his golf. The Duchess, anxious not to play while her husband worked, struggled with the problems of her wardrobe and at the redecoration of one remote royal residence, the Government House in Nassau, not notably in danger of being blown off its base. It must be supposed that their hearts were wrung with distress as they read of others in the Firm less fortunate than themselves; it is impossible to suppose otherwise. What wonder, then, that once the all-clear sounded, they returned to England, to see for themselves, to condole with the family over the past, perhaps even to bind up a few wounds.

They came back, in short, to inspect the damage.

It is a long time ago, now. The war itself, which filled the world's horizon, has become a set of records. But it will be a longer time still before Wallis Windsor repeats her experiment. The Duke, it is true, returns from time to time, moving like a tragic shadow amid the scenes of his former splendor.

As to the Duchess, she may have sighed to be in England when summer was there, but she stayed in her own petty world of international society, which in spite of the Duke's claim, is not the real world. Reality is not to be found in that small luxury-loving group, but in the great society, the family of nations, of which the Duke's niece was recently crowned and anointed Queen.

It must be remembered that the coronation is, in a sense, the marriage of England, when the country is united to a new Monarch. It is a living page of history: every item in the ceremonial has its roots far back in time. For instance, the Queen walked up the Abbey aisle under a canopy upheld by four Barons of the Cinque Ports.

The Cinque Ports are the little towns dotted along the south coast of England, Hastings, Romney, Hythe, Dover and Sandwich (with Winchelsea and Rye as later additions to the original five). These are the ports that once held the keys of England and guarded the narrow seas. When the Barons' turn came to be heard, they laid before Bernard Marmaduke Fitzalan Howard, Duke of Norfolk, presiding over the Court of Claims, their claim to carry the Queen's canopy; they were granted their ancient privilege.

And what was true of this one item in the service was true of the innumerable others: each one had a meaning, and the sum total was the whole of England's past speaking to England's present.

But above all the coronation was a religious service. In the words of the Dean of Westminster:

> The very heart of the whole ceremony is not the crowning but the anointing, when by her hallowing with the Holy Oil, the Queen is "anointed, blessed and consecrated Queen over the peoples whom the Lord God hath given her to rule and govern."

Consistently with this idea of religious dedication, the Queen was given the sacred Scriptures, with the reminder that these are "the lively Oracles of God"; and she received the Holy Communion.

But as the Dean pointed out, the Coronation Service implied the dedication, not only of the Monarch, but of all her people:

> The Queen must be fortified by the knowledge that we, her loyal subjects, are one with her in heart and will . . . The inward meaning of the Coronation may be summed up in the words of Scripture: "Bear ye one another's burdens, and so fulfill the law of Christ."

That, and not the provision of a sufficiency of souvenirs—coronation statuettes, mugs, plates and ashtrays—was the principal part played by her loyal and rejoicing subjects on the day that Queen Elizabeth II was crowned.

The intended coronation of Edward VIII brought forth a rich supply of such souvenirs. Not so long ago a certain businessman unearthed, and unloaded on to the American market, a cargo of ashtrays bearing the portrait of Edward VIII, Rex, Imperator. This astute fellow is reported to have netted a pretty tidy sum from the sentimentalists. (Or from people careful of the carpet.)

But what can be the state of mind of the man whose "best" profile is now buried under ashes?

The Duke of Windsor is now fifty-nine: he has arrived at that time of middle age when a man begins to weigh up his life and all that he has done with it, and to ask himself whether he has done anything worthy, if not of others' remembrance, at least of his own.

What can he remember? That having come to the Throne the most beloved of all Princes, the darling of a nation that would have followed him through hell-fire, or whom he might have conducted to "broad and sunlit uplands," he threw away that love; that he escaped the heavy tasks, threw away the tiresome restraints of kingship, to gain—what?

The long, long trail that winds from New York to Palm Beach to Paris and the Côte d'Azur, through the travail of the cocktail party and the unending treadmill of the social round, is one trodden under a superincumbent weight of weariness that, as experience goes to show, only becomes heavier as time goes on. "I called for madder music and stronger wine." It is a recognized, though not a sovereign, specific for the martyrs of boredom as well as the victims of passion. And when the specific can no longer be employed—when the wine is by doctors' orders changed into water and the madder music serves only to exasperate the neighbors—what then?

"Remember your position and who you are!" These words of fatherly caution must echo and re-echo in the Duke's mind with an oracular note of doom; with an irony worthy of the author of *Macbeth*. He forgot who he was, he abandoned his position, and the poor shadow of a king he has become now struts the high stage of publicity upon the way to dusty death. Meanwhile, the royal line stretches out before his mental gaze: George VI . . . Elizabeth . . . (with Charles to come) . . . All too like the spirit of George V: candid, dutiful, hard-working—and beloved.

The sensations of the Duchess of Windsor as she, too, arrives at the age of self-assessment, cannot be pleasant. She has been very near to a crown

> Within whose circle is Elysium,
> With all that poets feign of joy and bliss.

How much more bitter it is *almost* to have attained than never to have been anywhere near the prize! The coronation of Elizabeth must have brought to the Duchess' mind thoughts of the might-have-been. "It could have been *my* royal show." Press discussions of her absence at the coronation were merely academic. The mere sight of the Crown upon a brow "fresher than May" would have surely seared

her eyeballs. With all her sympathy for young women because,
"poor dears, they have all their mistakes before them," the Duchess
of Windsor, even were she *Her Royal Highness* the Duchess of Windsor,
could not hope to patronize a Sovereign whose mistakes will certainly
not include throwing her Crown over the windmill.

But the Bard condensed the matter of this book into a few lines:

> His rash fierce blaze of riot cannot last,
> For violent fires soon burn out themselves;
> Small showers last long, but sudden storms are short;
> He tires betimes that spurs too fast betimes;
> With eager feeding food doth choke the feeder:
> Light vanity, insatiate cormorant,
> Consuming means, soon preys upon itself.

Over against this nothing, remains this one solid thing:

> This royal throne of kings, this sceptr'd isle,
> This earth of majesty, this seat of Mars,
> This other Eden, demi-paradise,
> This fortress built by Nature for herself
> Against infection and the hand of war,
> This happy breed of men, this little world,
> This precious stone set in the silver sea,
> Which serves it in the office of a wall
> Or as a moat defensive to a house,
> Against the envy of less happier lands,
> This blessed plot, this earth, this realm, this England . . .
> England, bound in with the triumphant sea!

INDEX

323